PENGUIN CLASSICS

BRAVE MEN

ERNIE PYLE (1900–1945) was a Pulitzer Prize–winning war correspondent. He worked as managing editor of *The Washington Daily News* and later became a roving journalist for Scripps-Howard Alliance. After many years following the fighting in Europe, he traveled to the South Pacific, where a sniper's bullet took his life.

DAVID CHRISINGER is the author of *The Soldier's Truth: Ernie Pyle and the Story of World War II* and several other books. He directs the Harris Writing Workshop at the University of Chicago's Harris School of Public Policy and leads memoir-writing workshops for military veterans and their families through The War Horse, an award-winning nonprofit newsroom named in honor of Ernie Pyle that aims to improve our understanding of the true costs of military service. He lives in Chicago.

D0878810

ERNIE PYLE

Brave Men

Introduction by
DAVID CHRISINGER

PENGUIN BOOKS

PENGUIN BOOKS

An imprint of Penguin Random House LLC
penguinrandomhouse.com

First published in the United States of America by Henry Holt and Company 1944
Published with an introduction by David Chrisinger in Penguin Books 2023

Published by arrangement with the Ernie Pyle Legacy Foundation

LIBRARY OF CONGRESS CATALOGING-IN-PUBLICATION DATA
Names: Pyle, Ernie, 1900–1945, author. |
Chrisinger, David, 1986– writer of introduction.
Title: Brave men / Ernie Pyle ; introduction by David Chrisinger.
Description: [New York] : Penguin Books, 2023. |
Includes bibliographical references and index.
Identifiers: LCCN 2022042310 (print) | LCCN 2022042311 (ebook) |
ISBN 9780143137177 (trade paperback) | ISBN 9780593511169 (ebook)
Subjects: LCSH: World War, 1939–1945—Personal narratives, American. |
Pyle, Ernie, 1900–1945. | World War, 1939–1945—Campaigns—Italy. |
World War, 1939–1945—Campaigns—France.
Classification: LCC D811.5 .P88 2023 (print) | LCC D811.5 (ebook) | DDC
940.54/21/092273 [B]—dc23/eng/20220920
LC record available at https://lccn.loc.gov/2022042310
LC ebook record available at https://lccn.loc.gov/2022042311

Printed in the United States of America
1st Printing

Set in Sabon LT Pro

In solemn salute to those thousands of our comrades—
great, brave men that they were—
for whom there will be no homecoming, ever.

I heard of a high British officer who went over the battlefield just after the action was over. American boys were still lying dead in their foxholes, their rifles still grasped in firing position in their dead hands. And the veteran English soldier remarked time and again, in a sort of hushed eulogy spoken only to himself, "Brave men. Brave men!"

—from the author's *Here Is Your War*

Contents

x

Introduction

I saw that he was a worried man. It is the worry of a man who has been universally credited with having written the truth. He tried to tell me that you couldn't really tell it in words. Not war, you couldn't.

—Arthur Miller, 1944[1]

"Aren't you Ernie Pyle?" the young man asked.[2] The red cross on his shoulder told Pyle the man was a medic; the insignia on his collar showed he was an officer. Pyle looked up with his graying eyes from a champagne cocktail in the street-level bar of the Hôtel Scribe, a storied establishment across from Opéra National de Paris, which had, until a couple of days prior, served as the regal headquarters for dozens of Nazi propagandists.

Even though Pyle never courted fame, in the late summer of 1944 he *was* famous, perhaps the most famous, most loved, and most trusted of any American war correspondent before or since. At the peak of its popularity, Pyle's column ran in more than two hundred daily newspapers and four hundred weeklies. Two collections of his best columns, *Here Is Your War*, which covered the North African campaign, and this one you're reading now, which details Pyle's journey from Sicily through central Italy and France, were bestsellers. *Time* magazine put his grinning face on its iconic cover. While he continued reporting from France, Hollywood was producing a movie, *The Story of G.I. Joe*, based on his columns, and in the weeks leading up to D-Day, Pyle was awarded the Pulitzer Prize for distinguished war correspondence during the year 1943.

"Yes, I am," Pyle replied. This sort of thing happened wherever he went. There was no such thing as anonymity for the shy farmer's son from Indiana.

"I just want to thank you," the medic said earnestly. "You've done some great things for us in your column. I read it whenever I can."

"You won't be reading it much longer," Pyle replied, looking back down at his drink, his smile turning more serious as he gently rotates his glass on the tabletop. "I'm going back to the States in a couple of days."

"Are you?" The medic looked relieved. "By God, I'm glad," he said. "You've seen enough of it."

Several days later, in a column that would be read by more than twelve million of his adoring readers back home,[3] Pyle broke the news. "I'm leaving for one reason only," he began, "because I have just got to stop."[4]

"I've been immersed in it too long," he continued. "My spirit is wobbly and my mind is confused. The hurt has finally become too great."

He didn't end things there, though. As with many of the columns he wrote to deliver hard truths, Pyle sprinkled in enough reassurance to keep the overall tone of his final dispatch from the European theater more optimistic than it might otherwise have been.

"It may be that a few months of peace will restore some vim to my spirit," he wrote, "and I can go war-horsing off to the Pacific."

In 1940, after years of living on the road with his wife, Geraldine, as a roving correspondent in Depression-era America, Pyle discovered what would become his professional and spiritual home for the rest of his life: the Second World War in Europe. A series of columns he wrote that year on the destruction wrought by German bombing raids over London alerted one of his bosses to his potential as a foreign correspondent. Two years later, as America prepared its young army to plunge into another world war, and as Pyle's personal life plunged to traumatic depths, his bosses at the Scripps-Howard Newspaper Alliance gave Pyle the green light to head overseas for about six months while Geraldine sought care at a sanitarium in a last-ditch effort to get her manic depression under better control. If Pyle's six-days-per-week column were to take off, great. If not, they all agreed, at least he could rest easier knowing he'd done his bit before coming home to manage the care of his wife.

From the spring of 1942 to the late summer of 1944, Pyle would write more than seven hundred thousand words about "our boys" waging war in North Africa, Sicily, mainland Italy, and France. By living among the troops as an embedded reporter, Pyle gained what he called a "worm's-eye view" of the war that many take for granted all these decades later. Before Pyle, there was no way for readers in the United States to reach any sort of understanding about frontline fighting and the day-to-day realities of life at war from someone who had experienced it firsthand. This book draws from the best of Pyle's prodigious output and includes a great deal of new material Pyle contributed after he decided to leave the war but before the book was published that fall. "It is a deeply human portrait of the American soldiers in action," Pyle's fellow newspaperman Joseph F. Dineen wrote of *Brave Men* for *The Boston Globe* soon after it was published. "Ernie gives a picture of them in action by writing of ordinary things— what they eat; how they sleep and where; what they talk about; how they react to hunger, dirt, fatigue and danger on a fighting front. He writes as though he were one of them, as in fact he was, and he brings the war very close."[5] Another contemporary reviewer summed up the impact of Pyle's book this way: "No one in this war has been able to do as much as he did to transform the blood and sweat of battle into printer's ink. Or brought the war with such intimacy into more distant homes."[6]

I personally cherish *Brave Men* for three main reasons: Pyle's descriptions of scenes he witnessed; his simple, unassuming style; and his ability to recognize the humanity in everyone he meets. There are so many scenes contained in this book from which I could choose to illustrate this first point; however, the one that immediately comes to mind is the final column in his series on D-day, titled "A Long Thin Line of Personal Anguish." Pyle wrote of what he observed as he strolled along the blood-soaked beaches of Normandy, lost in a silence all his own the day after the invasion. "It extends in a thin little line, just like a high-water mark, for miles along the beach," he wrote about the detritus of the battle. "Here in a jumbled row for mile on mile are soldiers' packs. Here are socks and shoe polish, sewing kits, diaries, Bibles and hand grenades. Here are the latest letters from home. . . . Here are toothbrushes and razors, and snapshots of families back home staring up at you from the sand. Here are pocketbooks, metal mirrors, extra trousers and bloody, abandoned shoes."

These depictions give the overwhelming impression of honest, stunned confusion. Through his eyes, we too are dazed witnesses to the gambles and losses on a scale that nobody back home could comprehend without a narrative that forced some meaning out of the chaos. By allowing the objects he saw in the sand not only to set the scene, but also to tell an eloquent story of loss, Pyle showed his readers the true cost of the fighting without resorting to explicit descriptions of blood and mangled bodies.

"I picked up a pocket Bible with a soldier's name in it, and put it in my jacket," Pyle continued. "I carried it half a mile or so and then put it back down on the beach. I don't know why I picked it up, or why I put it back down." This eye for detail, what is essentially the eye of a poet, is on full display throughout *Brave Men* and is a master class in how embedded witnesses can convey the truth about an experience that cannot be fully understood unless it is lived.

In addition to showing the truth more than he preached it, Pyle could string short words together to create the effect of casual, artless, sincere ease. Take, for example, this brief excerpt from the end of what may be Pyle's most beloved and well-known column, "The Death of Captain Waskow":

Another man came; I think he was an officer. It was hard to tell officers from men in the half light, for all were bearded and grimy dirty. The man looked down into the dead captain's face, and then he spoke directly to him, as though he were alive. He said: "I'm sorry, old man." Then a soldier came and stood beside the officer, and bent over, and he too spoke to his dead captain, not in a whisper but awfully tenderly, and he said: "I sure am sorry, sir."

Then the first man squatted down, and he reached down and took the dead hand, and he sat there for a full five minutes, holding the dead hand in his own and looking intently into the dead face, and he never uttered a sound all the time he sat there. And finally he put the hand down, and then reached up and gently straightened the points of the captain's shirt collar, and then he sort of rearranged the tattered edges of his uniform around the wound. And then he got up and walked away down the road in the moonlight, all alone.

Eight sentences. A grand total of 193 words. But only 94 unique words. The most learned language he uses is probably the verb "uttered," and even that word was no doubt well understood by most of his readers at the time. There's also no passive voice, no long noun phrases, no late predicates or detached subjects, and there isn't a single nominalization—all those clumsy writing crutches so many lesser writers unintentionally use that gum up their prose and raise doubts in the readers' minds about the sincerity and authenticity of the storytelling. As a writer (and teacher of writing) myself, I can attest that it takes great skill to deliver monosyllables in such a natural, pleasing, and objective rhythm. And Pyle was very clever, even if he didn't always believe that himself.[7]

Perhaps the most important thing I've learned from Pyle has to do with the main attribute that seems to have separated him from the rest of his ilk: his deep empathy for humanity, rooted in his experiences battling mental health issues—his wife's and his own, which I explore in great detail in *The Soldier's Truth*, a biography of Pyle during the war. In so much of the heady and imposing commentary that other more "seasoned" war correspondents used, there's a clear disconnect between the world of abstract politics and campaigns on the one hand, and the world of flesh-and-blood people living their lives as best they can on the other. Some countries invaded other countries that had to "take up arms." Cities were then destroyed. Ships were sunk. Ground was lost and gained. That was the war of menacing arrows showing lines of advance in the morning papers. But Pyle knew that wasn't the *true* war. The *true* war, for Pyle, was a war of apathy, disconnection, and misunderstanding—a war that could be won only if the "folks back home" could understand, if they could really *see* what their sons and sweethearts were suffering through, if they could put a name and a hometown and a personal history on the nameless, faceless divisions of young men slaughtering other young men in the name of freedom. There was a cost to that freedom, Pyle knew all too well, but unless the truth about that cost was made clear, he feared, America would never have what it took to cultivate peace in whatever world was left when the war ended.

If swashbuckling tales of heroic deeds in combat couldn't humanize the American GI, perhaps what could were stories of soldiers like the kid down the block who shipped off the week after graduation, the kid you watched grow up, the kid who'd likely rather be anywhere else but on the front lines in some distant battle. That kid, the one who answered his call to serve anyway, that was the kid Pyle knew better than anyone. And he knew, because he saw firsthand, a war can't be won without kids like that.

Why reprint *Brave Men*? Why now? The truth is that even though he's been dead for nearly eight decades, Pyle had so much to say about the world we find ourselves living in today. The horrors of Pyle's time are different from our own, of course, but not as different as we might like to believe. As I write these words, a great power in Europe spent years systematically flooding the media ecosystem with disinformation before invading a weaker power, simply because its leader convinced himself he must—because he asserted some unimpeachable claim to historical greatness spawned in a climate of mistrust, heightened fear, and despair. Meanwhile, thousands of men, women, and children are dying, many crushed under the rubble of bombed-out apartment buildings, some left ignominiously at the bottom of mass graves with their hands tied behind their backs. It's the kind of obscenity the world hasn't seen in Europe in decades, and it's a reminder that the stories we tell ourselves matter, and that perhaps the only effective means by which to defeat the untruth is to tell a better story—something Pyle understood, even if he never articulated it exactly that way.

All this leads me to wonder what Pyle would write, if he were with us today, about Russia, Ukraine, and the state of our world. We can never know for sure, but maybe I can offer some clues by taking a closer look at the final chapter of *Brave Men*. Not long after his conversation with the medic in the street-level bar of the Hôtel Scribe, Pyle was granted permission to return home to his wife in New Mexico. Before he left Europe for the last time, however, he spent a few days at American general Omar Bradley's headquarters, on the grounds of the Château de Vouilly, a castle built by the Normans in the tenth century, around the time of the fateful Battle of Hastings.

It's easy for me to imagine Pyle seated at a dark green folding table, pitched in the shade under an apple tree out past the château's ancient moat. I can see him pecking at the keys on his typewriter with the broken carriage return. The smoke from a cigarette dangling from his bottom lip quickly dissipates in the farm-fresh breeze. "It could well be that the European war will be over and done by the time you read this book," he wrote. "Or it might not. But the end is inevitable, and it cannot be put off for long. The German is beaten and he knows it."

But how did it come about? How were the Allies able to rally together to defeat the Nazis? How were average folks from humble beginnings able to endure so much for so long? Again, I picture him at his table, a pencil in his hand. He's scribbling out dead-end sentences, or maybe swapping out a clause here and there. I see him stop to breathe in the breeze, the smell of mistletoe in his nose. He tucks the pencil behind his ear, takes a swig of something strong in the cup beside his typewriter, and pokes out his thoughts.

There was the fact that the Axis powers had been weakened from those earlier battles Pyle had seen for himself. He started there. Then there were our brave men, of course, but there was also "Russia, and England, and the passage of time, and the gift of nature's materials." We did not prevail, he continued to type, "because destiny created us better than all other peoples." It was, in turn, Pyle's sincerest hope that the hundreds of thousands of words he wrote during the war would lead Americans to show more gratitude than pride, for "the dead men would not want us to gloat." Instead, he concluded, "All we can do is fumble and try once more—try out of the memory of our anguish—and be as tolerant of each other as we can."

DAVID CHRISINGER

NOTES

1. Arthur Miller, *Situation Normal* (New York: Reynal & Hitchock, 1944).
2. Sgt. Mack Morriss, "GIs Glad War-Weary Ernie Pyle Finally Has Come Home for a Rest," *YANK: The Army Weekly*, October 22, 1944.
3. Lee Miller letter to Ernie Pyle, August 11, 1944, "A United Features ad in E&P says you have 322 papers and 12 1/2 million circulation."
4. "Farewell to Europe," September 5, 1944, David Nichols, ed., *Ernie's War: The Best of Ernie Pyle's World War II Dispatches* (New York: Random House, 1986), 357–59.
5. Joseph F. Dineen, "GI's Like Ernie Pyle: So Do Fathers, Mothers, Sisters, Brothers, Cousins, Uncles, Aunts," *Boston Globe*, December 7, 1944.
6. "Brave Men—John Mason Brown (essay date 1946)," Jennifer Gariepy, ed., *Twentieth-Century Literary Criticism*, vol. 75, (Detroit, MI: Gale Cengage, 1998).
7. In 2011, a senior political columnist named John Avlon reported that "The Death of Captain Waskow" was the "top American column in history," according to a survey he distributed to columnists who belong to the National Society of Newspaper Columnists, columnists.com/2011/06/top-ten-american-columns-in-history.

Suggestions for Further Reading

OTHER BOOKS BY ERNIE PYLE

Home Country (New York: William Sloane Associates, Inc., 1947)

Pyle once said the writing he did while crisscrossing America from 1935 to 1940 was the best writing he ever did. Published after his death, *Home Country* collects the best of his best.

Here Is Your War: Story of G.I. Joe (New York: Henry Holt & Company, 1943)

After reading this collection of Pyle's best columns from the North African campaign, Eleanor Roosevelt said: "He has told a story of our Army as it is, of its life, day by day. It will give a vivid picture to anyone who has never been near a front. In the future, it will be one of the books to which historians will turn to explain the kind of men who fought this war."

Ernie Pyle in England (New York: Robert M. McBride & Company, 1941)

A collection of Pyle's reporting during the tail end of the Battle of Britain, when German bombers attempted to blast the British into submission. His vivid descriptions of the bombings, the damage they did, and the effects the war was having on the stiff-upper-lip Limeys make this a classic piece of human-focused wartime reporting.

At Home with Ernie Pyle, edited by Owen V. Johnson (Bloomington: Indiana University Press, 2016)

A celebration of Pyle's Indiana roots, collecting his writings about his home state and its denizens.

Ernie's War: The Best of Ernie Pyle's World War II Dispatches, edited by David Nichols (New York: Random House, 1986)

Come for the foreword written by the legendary journalist and oral historian Studs Terkel, and stay for some of the best reporting from World War II. Drawn from Pyle's complete body of work, from the London Blitz to the Battle of Okinawa, this collection also includes a fifty-page biography of Pyle written by the editor.

BIOGRAPHIES AND BOOKS ABOUT ERNIE PYLE

A Death in San Pietro: The Untold Story of Ernie Pyle, John Huston, and the Fight for Purple Heart Valley by Tim Brady (Boston: Da Capo Press, 2013)

If Pyle's dispatch "The Death of Captain Waskow" left you wanting more, this book tells the full story through the lens of two incredible storytellers—not only Pyle but also John Huston, who filmed a documentary about the battle that cost Waskow and 80 percent of his company their lives and limbs.

Ernie Pyle's War: America's Eyewitness to World War II by James Tobin (New York: Free Press, 1997)

A biography based on dozens of interviews with the people who knew Pyle best, along with never-before-seen archival material.

An Ernie Pyle Album: Indiana to Ie Shima by Lee G. Miller (New York: William Sloane Associates, Inc., 1946)

More a family photo album than a biography, compiled by Pyle's longtime friend and editor. It includes more than a hundred personal photos, from Pyle's childhood until his death on Ie Shima at the end of the war, providing a captivating glimpse into the famous newspaperman's life.

The Story of Ernie Pyle by Lee G. Miller (New York: Viking Press, 1950)

The first biography of Pyle, which includes information drawn from Pyle's private correspondence.

ONLINE RESOURCES

The Media School at Indiana University: sites.mediaschool.indiana
  .edu/erniepyle

Dedicated to the Hoosier legend himself, Indiana University's journalism school website is the home for information and history about Pyle, including a photo gallery and scans of his most influential wartime columns.

The Ernie Pyle World War II Museum: erniepyle.org

In July 1976, Pyle's childhood home was moved to downtown Dana, Indiana, and in 1995, a museum was built out of two Quonset huts. It includes fabulous exhibits, a theater, a research center, and a gift shop, and the museum's web page includes photo galleries, artifacts, and scans of some of his columns.

The Albuquerque and Bernalillo County Public Library: abqlibrary.org
  /whowaserniepyle

For all things Pyle in the American Southwest, the public library system in Albuquerque is your go-to resource. It includes dozens of links to Pyle's books, articles, and other material, including a video on the brief history of Pyle and his adopted hometown.

Brave Men

SICILY

JUNE–SEPTEMBER, 1943

ONE

INVASION PRELUDE

In June, 1943, when our military and naval forces began fitting the war correspondents into the great Sicilian invasion patchwork, most of us were given the choice of the type of assignment we wanted—assault forces, invasion fleet, African Base Headquarters, or whatever. Since I had never had the opportunity in Africa to serve with the Navy, I chose the invasion fleet. My request was approved. From then on it was simply a question of waiting for the call. Correspondents were dribbled out of sight a few at a time in order not to give a tipoff to the enemy by sudden mass exodus.

Under the most grim warnings against repeating what we knew or even talking about it among ourselves we'd been given a general fill-in on the invasion plans. Some of the correspondents disappeared on their assignments as much as three weeks before the invasion, while others didn't get the call until the last minute.

I was somewhat surreptitiously whisked away by air about ten days ahead of time. We weren't, of course, permitted to cable our offices where we were going or even that we were going at all. Our bosses, I hope, had the good sense to assume we were just loafing on the job—not dead or kidnaped by Arabs.

After a long plane hop and a couple of dusty rides in jeeps, I arrived at bomb-shattered Bizerte in Tunisia. When I reported to Naval Headquarters I was immediately assigned to a ship. She was lying at anchor out in the harbor—one of many scores—and they said I could go aboard right away. I had lived with the Army so long I actually felt like a soldier; yet it was wonderful to get with the Navy for a change, to sink into the blessedness of a world that was orderly and civilized by comparison with that animal-like existence in the field.

Our vessel was neither a troop transport nor a warship but she was mighty important. In fact, she was a headquarters ship. She was not huge, just big enough so we could feel self-respecting about our part in the invasion, yet small enough to be intimate. I came to be part of the ship's family by the time we actually set sail. I was thankful for the delay because it gave me time to get acquainted and get the feel of warfare at sea.

We did actually carry some troops. Every soldier spent the first few hours on board in exactly the same way. He took a wonderful shower bath, drank water with ice in it, sat at a table and ate food with real silverware, arranged his personal gear along the bulkheads, drank coffee, sat in a real chair, read current magazines, saw a movie after supper, and finally got into a bed with a real mattress.

It was too much for most of us and we all kept blubbering our appreciation until finally I'm sure the Navy must have become sick of our juvenile delight over things that used to be common to all men. They even had ice cream and Coca-Cola aboard. That seemed nothing short of miraculous.

We weren't told what day we were to sail, but it was obvious it wasn't going to be immediately for there was still too much going and coming, too much hustle and bustle about the port. The activity of invasion preparation was so seething, those last few weeks, that in practically every port in North Africa the harbor lights blazed, contemptuous of danger, throughout the night. There simply wasn't time to be cautious. The ship loading had to go on, so they let the harbor lights burn.

Our vessel was so crowded it took three sittings in officers' mess to feed the men. Every bunk had two officers assigned to it; one slept while the other worked. The bunk assigned to me was in one of the big lower bunkrooms. It was terrifically hot down there, so the captain of the ship—a serious, thoughtful veteran naval aviator—had a cot with a mattress on it put up for me on deck and there I slept with the soft fresh breezes of the Mediterranean night wafting over me. Mine was the best spot on the ship, even better than the captain's.

In slight compensation for this lavish hospitality, I agreed to lend a professional touch to the ship's daily mimeographed news-paper by editing and arranging the news dispatches our wireless picked up from all over the world during the night. This little chore involved getting up at 3 a.m., working about two hours, then sit-ting around chinning and drinking coffee with the radio opera-tors until too late to go back to sleep. As a sailor I didn't have much rest but, as we say in the newspaper business, you meet a lot of interesting radio operators.

In the week aboard ship before we set out on the invasion, I nat-urally was not permitted to send any columns. I spent the days reading and gabbing with the sailors. Every now and then I would run in to take a shower bath, like a child playing with a new toy.

I got to know a great many of the sailors personally and almost all of them by nodding acquaintance. I found them to be just peo-ple, and nice people like the soldiers. They were fundamentally friendly. They all wanted to get home. They were willing to do ev-erything they could to win the war. But I did sense one rather sub-tle difference between sailors and soldiers, although many of the former will probably resent it: the sailors weren't hardened and toughened as much as the soldiers. It's understandable.

The front-line soldier I knew lived for months like an animal, and was a veteran in the cruel, fierce world of death. Everything was abnormal and unstable in his life. He was filthy dirty, ate if and when, slept on hard ground without cover. His clothes were greasy and he lived in a constant haze of dust, pestered by flies and heat, moving constantly, deprived of all the things that once meant stability—things such as walls, chairs, floors, windows, fau-cets, shelves, Coca-Colas, and the little matter of knowing that he would go to bed at night in the same place he had left in the morning.

The front-line soldier has to harden his inside as well as his outside or he would crack under the strain. These sailors weren't sissies—either by tradition or by temperament—but they weren't as rough and tough as the Tunisian soldiers—at least the gang I had been with.

A ship is a home, and the security of home had kept the sail-ors more like themselves. They didn't cuss as much or as foully as soldiers. They didn't bust loose as riotously when they hit town.

They weren't as all-round hard in outlook. They had not drifted as far from normal life as the soldiers—for they had world news every morning in mimeographed sheets, radios, movies nearly every night, ice cream. Their clothes, their beds were clean. They had walked through the same doors, up the same steps every day for months. They had slept every night in the same spot.

Of course, when sailors die, death for them is just as horrible—and sometimes they die in greater masses than soldiers—but until the enemy comes over the horizon a sailor doesn't have to fight. A front-line soldier has to fight everything all the time. It makes a difference in a man's character.

I could see a subtle change come over the soldiers aboard that invasion ship. They were no longer the rough-and-tumble warriors I had known on the battlefield. Instead, they were quiet, almost meek; I figured they were awed by their sojourn back in the American way. There was no quarreling aboard between soldiers and sailors, as you might expect—not even any sarcasm or words of the traditional contempt for each other.

One night I was talking with a bunch of sailors on the fantail and they spoke thoughts you could never imagine coming from sailors' mouths. One of them said, "Believe me, after seeing these soldiers aboard, my hat's off to the Army, the poor bastards. They really take it and they don't complain about anything. Why, it's pitiful to see how grateful they are just to have a hard deck to sleep on."

And another one said, "Any little thing we do for them they appreciate. We've got more than they have and, boy, I'd go three miles out of my way to share something with a soldier."

A third said, "Yes, they live like dogs and they're the ones that have to take those beaches, too. A few of us will get killed, but a hell of a lot of them will."

And a fourth said, "Since hearing some of their stories, I've been down on my knees every night thanking God I was smart enough to enlist in the Navy. And they're so decent about everything. They don't even seem to resent all the things we have that they don't."

The sailors were dead serious. It brought a lump to my throat to hear them. Everyone by now knows how I feel about the infantry. I'm a rabid one-man movement bent on tracking down and stamping out everybody in the world who doesn't fully appreciate the common front-line soldier.

Our ship had been in African waters many months but the Sicilian invasion was the first violent action for most of its crew. Only three or four men, who'd been torpedoed in the Pacific, had ever before had any close association with the probability of sudden death. So I know the sailors went into that action just as soldiers go into the first battle—outwardly calm but inside frightened and sick with worry. It's the lull in the last couple of days before starting that hits so hard. In the preparation period fate seems far away, and once in action a man is too busy to be afraid. It's just those last couple of days when there is time to think too much.

One of the nights before we sailed I sat in the darkness on the forward deck helping half a dozen sailors eat a can of stolen pineapple. Some of the men of the group were hardened and mature. Others were almost children. They all talked seriously and their gravity was touching. The older ones tried to rationalize how the law of averages made it unlikely that our ship out of all the hundreds involved would be hit. They spoke of the inferiority of the Italian fleet and argued pro and con over whether Germany had some hidden Luftwaffe up her sleeve that she might whisk out to destroy us. Younger ones spoke but little. They talked to me of their plans and hopes for going to college or getting married after the war, always winding up with the phrase "If I get through this fracas alive."

As we sat there on the hard deck—squatting like Indians in a circle around our pineapple can—it all struck me as somehow pathetic. Even the dizziest of us knew that before long many of us stood an excellent chance of being in this world no more. I don't believe one of us was afraid of the physical part of dying. That isn't the way it is. The emotion is rather one of almost desperate reluctance to give up the future. I suppose that's splitting hairs and that it really all comes under the heading of fear. Yet somehow there is a difference.

These gravely-yearned-for futures of men going into battle include so many things—things such as seeing the "old lady" again, of going to college, of staying in the Navy for a career, of holding on your knee just once your own kid whom you've never seen, of again becoming champion salesman of your territory, of driving a coal truck around the streets of Kansas City once more and, yes, even of just sitting in the sun once more on the south side of a house in New Mexico. When we huddled around together on the dark decks, it was these little hopes and ambitions that made up the sum total of our worry at leaving, rather than any visualization of physical agony to come.

Our deck and the shelf-like deck above us were dotted with small knots of men talking. I deliberately listened around for a while. Each group were talking in some way about their chances of survival. A dozen times I overheard this same remark: "Well, I don't worry about it because I look at it this way. If your number's up then it's up, and if it isn't you'll come through no matter what."

Every single person who expressed himself that way was a liar and knew it, but, hell, a guy has to say something. I heard oldsters offering to make bets at even money that we wouldn't get hit at all and two to one we wouldn't get hit seriously. Those were the offers but I don't think any bets actually were made. Somehow it seemed sacrilegious to bet on our own lives.

Once I heard somebody in the darkness start cussing and give this answer to some sailor critic who was proclaiming how he'd run things: "Well, I figure that captain up there in the cabin has got a little more in his noggin than you have or he wouldn't be captain, so I'll put my money on him."

And another sailor voice chimed in with "Hell, yes, that captain has slept through more watches than you and I have spent time in the Navy."

And so it went on one of the last nights of safety. I never heard anybody say anything patriotic, the way the storybooks have people talking. There was philosophizing but it was simple and undramatic. I'm sure no man would have stayed ashore if he'd been given the chance. There was something bigger in him than the awful dread that would have made him want to stay safe on land. With me that something probably was an irresistible egoism in seeing myself part of an historic naval movement. With others I think it was just the application of plain, unspoken, even unrecognized, patriotism.

For the best part of a week our ship had been lying far out in the harbor, tied to a buoy. Several times a day "General Quarters" would sound and the crew would dash to battle stations, but always it was only an enemy photo plane, or perhaps even one of our own planes. Then we moved in to a pier. That very night the raiders came and our ship got her baptism of fire—she lost her virginity, as the sailors put it. I had got out of bed at 3 a.m. as usual to stumble sleepily up to the radio shack to go over the news reports which the wireless had picked up. There were several radio operators on watch and we were sitting around drinking coffee while we worked. Then all of a sudden around four o'clock General Quarters sounded. It was still pitch-dark. The whole ship came to life with a scurry and rattling, sailors dashing to stations before you'd have thought they could get their shoes on.

Shooting had already started around the harbor, so we knew this time it was real. I kept on working, and the radio operators did too, or rather we tried to work. So many people were going in and out of the radio shack that we were in darkness half the time, since the lights automatically went off when the door opened.

Then the biggest guns on our ship let loose. They made such a horrifying noise that every time they went off we thought we'd been hit by a bomb. Dust and debris came drifting down from the overhead to smear up everything. Nearby bombs shook us up, too.

One by one the electric light bulbs were shattered by the blasts. The thick steel bulkheads of the cabin shook and rattled as though they were tin. The entire vessel shivered under each blast. The harbor was lousy with ships and every one was shooting. The raiders were dropping flares from all over the sky and the searchlights on the warships were fanning the heavens. Shrapnel rained down on the decks, making a terrific clatter.

The fight went on for an hour and a half. When it was over and everything was added up we found four planes had been shot down. Our casualties aboard were negligible—three men had been wounded—and the ship had suffered no damage except small holes from near-misses. Best of all, we were credited with shooting down one of the planes.

This particular raid was only one of scores of thousands that have been conducted in this war. Standing alone it wouldn't even be worth describing. I'm mentioning it to show you what a taste of the genuine thing can do for a bunch of young Americans. As I have remarked, our kids on the ship had never before been in action. The majority of them were strictly wartime sailors, still half civilian in character. They'd never been shot at and had never shot one of their own guns except in practice. Because of this they had been very sober, a little unsure and more than a little worried about the invasion ordeal that lay so near ahead of them. And then, all within an hour and a half, they became veterans. Their zeal went up like one of those skyrocketing graph-lines when business is good. Boys who had been all butterfingers were loading shells like machinery after fifteen minutes, when it became real. Boys who previously had gone through their routine lifelessly had yelled with bitter seriousness, "Dammit, can't you pass those shells faster?"

The gunnery officer, making his official report to the captain, did it in these gleefully robust words: "Sir, we got the son of a bitch."

One of my friends aboard ship was Norman Somberg, aerographer third class, of 1448 Northwest 62nd Street, Miami. We had been talking together the day before and he told me how he'd studied journalism for two years at the University of Georgia, and how he wanted to get into it after the war. I noticed he always added, "If I live through it."

Just at dawn, as the raid ended, he came running up to me full of steam and yelled, "Did you see that plane go down smoking! Boy, if I could get off the train at Miami right now with the folks and my girl there to meet me I couldn't be any happier than I was when I saw we'd got that guy."

It was worth a month's pay to be on that ship after the raid. All day long the sailors went gabble, gabble, gabble, each telling the other how he did it, what he saw, what he thought. After that shooting, a great part of their reluctance to start for the unknown vanished, their guns had become their pals, the enemy became real and the war came alive for them, and they didn't fear it so much any more. That crew of sailors had just gone through what hundreds of thousands of other soldiers and sailors already had experienced—the conversion from peaceful people into fighters. There's nothing especially remarkable about it but it was a moving experience to see it happen.

When I first went aboard I was struck with the odd bleakness of the bulkheads. All paint had been chipped off. I thought it was a new and very unbecoming type of interior decoration. Shortly, however, I realized that this strange effect was merely part of the Navy procedure of stripping for action. Inside our ship there were many other precautions. All excess rags and blankets had been taken ashore or stowed away and locked up. The bunk mattresses were set on edge against the bulkheads to act as absorbent cushions against torpedo or shell fragments.

The Navy's traditional white hats were to be left below for the duration of the action. The entire crew had to be fully dressed in shoes, shirts, and pants—no working in shorts or undershirts because of the danger of burns. No white clothing was allowed to show on deck. Steel helmets, painted battleship gray, were worn during engagements. Men who stood night watches were awakened forty-five minutes early, instead of the usual few minutes, and ordered to be on deck half an hour before going on watch. It takes that long for the eyes to become accustomed to the darkness.

Before we sailed, all souvenir firearms were turned in and the ammunition thrown overboard. There was one locked room full of German and Italian rifles and revolvers which the sailors had got from front-line soldiers. Failure to throw away ammunition was a court-martial offense. The officers didn't want stray bullets whizzing around in case of fire.

Food supplies were taken from their regular hampers and stored all about the ship so that our entire supply couldn't be destroyed by one hit. All movie film was taken ashore. No flashlights, not even hooded ones, were allowed on deck. Doors opening on deck had switches just the reverse of refrigerators—when the door was opened the lights inside went out. All linoleum had been removed from the decks, all curtains taken down.

Because of weight limitations on the plane which had brought me to the ship, I had left my Army gas mask behind. Before departure, the Navy issued me a Navy mask, along with all the sailors. I was also presented with one of those bright yellow Mae West life preservers like the ones aviators wear.

Throughout the invasion period the entire crew was on one of two statuses—either General Quarters or Condition Two. "General Quarters" is the Navy term for full alert and means that everybody is on full duty until the crisis ends. It may be twenty minutes or it may be forty-eight hours. Condition Two is half alert, four hours on, four hours off, but the off hours are spent right at the battle station. It merely gives the men a little chance to relax.

A mimeographed set of instructions and warnings was distributed about the ship before sailing. It ended as follows: "This operation will be a completely offensive one. The ship will be at General Quarters or Condition Two throughout the operation. It may extend over a long period of time. Opportunities for rest will not come very often. You can be sure that you will have something to talk about when this is over. This ship must do her stuff."

The night before we sailed the crew listened as usual to the German propaganda radio program which featured Midge, the American girl turned Nazi, who was trying to scare them, disillusion them and depress them. As usual they laughed with amusement and scorn at her childishly treasonable talk.

In a vague and indirect way, I suppose, the privilege of listening to your enemy trying to undermine you—the very night before you go out to face him—expresses what we are fighting for.

TWO

THE ARMADA SAILS

The story of our vast water-borne invasion from the time it left Africa until it disgorged upon the shores of Sicily is a story of the American Navy. The process of transporting the immense invasion force and protecting it on the way was one of the most thrilling jobs in this war.

Our headquarters ships lay in the harbor for a week, waiting while all the other ships got loaded. Finally, we knew, without even being told, that the big moment had come, for all that day slower troop-carrying barges had filed past us in an unbroken line heading out to sea. Around four o'clock in the afternoon the harbor was empty and our ship slipped away from the pier. A magnificent sun was far down the arc of the sky but it was still bright and the weather warm. We steamed out past the bomb-shattered city, past scores of ships sunk in the earlier battle for North Africa, past sailors and soldiers on land who weren't going along and who waved good-bye to us. We waved back with a feeling of superiority which we all felt inside without expressing it; we were part of something historic, practically men of destiny.

Our vessel slid along at half speed, making almost no sound. Everybody except the men on duty was on deck for a last look at African soil. The mouth of the harbor was very narrow. Just as we were approaching the neck a voice came over the ship's loudspeaker:

"Port side, attention!"

All the sailors snapped upright and I with them, facing shore-ward. There on the flat roof of the bomb-shattered Custom House at the harbor mouth stood a rigid guard of honor—British tars and American bluejackets—with our two flags flying over them.

The bugler played, the officers stood at salute. When the notes died out, there was not a sound. No one spoke. We slid past, off on our mission into the unknown. They do dramatic things like that in the movies, but this one was genuine—a ceremony wholly true, old in tradition, and so real that I could not help feeling deeply proud.

We sailed on past the stone breakwater with the waves beating against it and out onto the dark blue of the Mediterranean. The wind was freshening and far away mist began to form on the watery horizon. Suddenly we were aware of a scene that will shake me every time I think of it the rest of my life. It was our invasion fleet, formed there far out at sea, waiting for us.

There is no way of conveying the enormous size of that fleet. On the horizon it resembled a distant city. It covered half the skyline, and the dull-colored camouflaged ships stood indistinctly against the curve of the dark water, like a solid formation of uncountable structures blending together. Even to be part of it was frightening. I hope no American ever has to see its counterpart sailing against us.

We caught up with the fleet and through the remaining hours of daylight it worked slowly forward. Our ship and the other command ships raced around herding their broods into proper formation, signaling by flag and signal light, shooing and instructing and ordering until the ship-strewn sea began to be patterned by small clusters of vessels taking their proper courses.

We stood at the rails and wondered how much the Germans knew of us. Surely this immense force could not be concealed; reconnaissance planes couldn't possibly miss us. Axis agents on the shore had simply to look through binoculars to see the start of the greatest armada ever assembled up to that moment in the whole history of the world. Allied planes flew in formation far above us. Almost out of sight, great graceful cruisers and wicked destroyers raced on our perimeter to protect us. Just at dusk a whole squadron of vicious little PT boats, their engines roaring in one giant combination like a force of heavy bombers, crossed our bow and headed for Sicily. Our guard was out, our die was cast. Now there was no turning back. We moved on into the enveloping night that might have a morning for us, or might not. But nobody, truly nobody, was afraid now, for we were on our way.

———

Once headed for Sicily, our whole ship's crew was kept on Condition Two—all battle stations manned with half crews while the other half rested. Nobody slept much.

The ship was packed to the gunwales. We were carrying extra Army and Navy staffs and our small ship had about 150 people above normal capacity. Sittings went up to four in the officers' mess and the poor colored boys who waited tables were at it nearly every waking hour. All bunks had at least two occupants and many officers slept on the deck. A man couldn't move without stepping on somebody.

Lieutenant Commander Fritz Gleim, a big Regular Navy man with a dry good humor, remarked one morning at breakfast, "Everybody is certainly polite on this ship. They always say 'Excuse me' when they step on you. I've got so I sleep right ahead while being walked on, so now they shake me till I wake up so they can say 'Excuse me.'"

Since anything white was forbidden on deck during the operation, several sailors dyed their hats blue. It was a fine idea except that they turned out a sort of sickly purple. It was also the rule that everybody had to wear a steel helmet during General Quarters. Somehow I had it in my head that Navy people never wore life belts but I was very wrong. Everybody wore them constantly in the battle zone. From the moment we left, getting caught without a life belt meant breaking one of the ship's strictest rules. Almost everybody wore the kind which is about four inches wide and straps around the waist, like a belt. It is rubberized, lies flat, and has two little cartridges of compressed gas—exactly the same things you use in soda-water siphons at home. When pressed, they go off and fill the life belt with air.

I chose for my own life jacket one of the aviation, Mae West type. I took that kind because it holds a man's head up if he's unconscious and I knew that at the first sign of danger I'd immediately become unconscious. Furthermore, I figured there would be safety in numbers, so I also took one of the regular life belts. I was so damned buoyant that if I'd ever jumped into the water I would have bounced right back out again.

A mass of two thousand ships can't move without a few accidents. I have no idea what the total was for the fleet as a whole, but for our section it was very small. About half a dozen assault craft had engine breakdowns and either had to be towed or else straggled along behind and came in late—that was all. Allied planes flew over us in formation several times a day. We couldn't see them most of the time but I understand we had an air convoy the whole trip.

The ship's officers were told the whole invasion plan just after we sailed. Also, Charles Corte, Acme photographer, who was the only other correspondent aboard, and I were given a detailed picture of what lay ahead. The first morning out the sailors were called on deck and told where we were going. I stood with them as they got the news, and I couldn't see any change in their expressions, but later I could sense in them a new enthusiasm, just from knowing.

That news, incidentally, was the occasion for settling up any number of bets. Apparently the boys had been wagering for days among themselves on where we would invade. You'd be surprised at the bad guesses. Many had thought it would be Italy proper, some Greece, some France, and one poor benighted chap even thought we were going to Norway.

One man on the ship had a hobby of betting. He was George Razevich, aerologist's mate first class, of 1100 Douglas Avenue, Racine, Wisconsin. George was a former bartender and beer salesman. He would bet on anything. And if he couldn't get takers he'd bet on the other side. Before this trip, George had been making bets on where the ship would go, but he practically always guessed wrong. He was more than $100 in the hole. But what he lost by his bad sense of direction he made up with dice. He was $1,000 ahead on craps. George didn't make any invasion bets because he said anybody with any sense knew where we were going without being told. His last bet that I heard of was $10 that the ship would be back in the United States within two months. (It wasn't.)

Every evening after supper the sailors not on duty would gather on the fantail—which seems to be equivalent to the quarter-deck—and talk in jovial groups. We carried two jeeps on the deck to be used by Army commanders when we landed. The vehicles had signs on them forbidding anyone to sit in them, but nobody paid a bit of attention to the signs. Once under way, in fact, there didn't seem to be the slightest tenseness or worry. Even the grimness was gone.

The fleet of two thousand ships was many, many times the size of the great Spanish Armada. At least half of it was British. The planning was done together, British and Americans, and the figures were lumped together, but in the actual operation we sailed in separate fleets, landed in separate areas. The two thousand figure also included convoys that were at sea en route from England and America. They arrived with reinforcements a few days later. But either section of the invasion, American or British, was a gigantic achievement in itself. And the whole plan was originated, organized and put into effect in the five short months following the Casablanca conference. The bulk of our own invasion fleet came into existence after November of 1942.

The United States Navy had the whole job of embarking, transporting, projecting and landing American invasion troops in Sicily, then helping to fight the shore battle with their warships and afterward keeping the tremendously vital supplies and reinforcements flowing in steadily. After being with them throughout that operation I must say my respect for the Navy is great. The personnel for the great task had to be built as quickly as the fleet itself. We did not rob the Pacific of anything. We created from whole cloth. There were a thousand officers staffing the new-type invasion ships and fewer than twenty of them were Regular Navy men. The rest were all erstwhile civilians trained into sea dogs almost overnight. The bulk of the assault craft came across the ocean under their own power. They were flat-bottomed and not ideal for deep-water sailing. Their skippers were all youngsters of scant experience. Some of them arrived with hardly any equipment at all. As one Navy man said, this heterogeneous fleet was navigated across the Atlantic "mainly by spitting into the wind."

The American invading force was brought from Africa to Sicily in three immense fleets sailing separately. Each of the three was in turn broken down into smaller fleets. It was utterly impossible to sail them all as one fleet. That would have been like trying to herd all the sheep in the world with one dog. The ships sailed from North Africa, out of every port, right down to the smallest ones. It was all worked out like a railroad schedule.

Each of the three big United States fleets had a command ship carrying an admiral in charge of that fleet, and an Army general in command of the troops being transported. Each command ship had been specially fitted out for the purpose, with extra space for "war rooms." There, surrounded by huge maps, officers toiled at desks and scores of radio operators maintained communications. It was through these command ships that the various land battles were directed in the early stages of the invasion, before communication centers could be set up ashore.

Our three fleets were not identical. One came directly from America, stopping in Africa only long enough for the troops to stretch their legs, then moving right on again. The big transport fleets were much easier to maneuver, but once they arrived their difficulties began. Everything had to be unloaded into the lighter craft which the big ships carried on their decks, then taken ashore. That meant a long process of unloading. When assault troops are being attacked by land, and waiting ships are catching it from the air, believe me the speed of unloading is mighty important.

In addition to the big transports and our hundreds of ocean-going landing craft, our fleet consisted of seagoing tugs, mine sweepers, subchasers, submarines, destroyers, cruisers, mine layers, repair ships and self-propelled barges mounting big guns. We had practically everything that floats. Nobody can ever know until after the war what planning the Sicilian invasion entailed, just what a staggering task it all was. In Washington, huge staffs worked on it until the last minute, then moved bag and baggage over to Africa. Thousands of civilians worked day and night for months. For months, over and over, troops and ships practiced landings. A million things had to be thought of and provided. That it all could be done in five months is a human miracle.

"And yet," one high naval officer said as we talked about the invasion details on the way over, "the public will be disappointed when they learn where we landed. They expect us to invade Italy, France, Greece, Norway—and all of them at once. People just can't realize that we must take one step at a time, and this step we are taking now took nearly half a year to prepare."

Our first day at sea was like a peacetime Mediterranean cruise. The weather was something you read about in travel folders, gently warm and sunny, and the sea as smooth as velvet. But all the same, we kept at a sharp alert, for at any moment we could be attacked by a submarine, surface ship or airplane. And yet, any kind of attack—even the idea that anybody would want to attack anybody else—was so utterly out of keeping with the benignity of the sea that it was hard to take the possibility of danger seriously.

I had thought I might be afraid at sea, sailing in a great fleet that by its very presence was justification for attack, and yet I found it impossible to be afraid. I couldn't help but think of a paragraph of one of Joseph Conrad's sea stories which I had read just a few days before. It was in a story called "The Tale," written about the last war, and it perfectly expressed our feeling about the changeless sea:

"What at first used to amaze the Commanding Officer was the unchanged face of the waters, with its familiar expression, neither more friendly nor more hostile. On fine days the sun strikes sparks upon the blue; here and there a peaceful smudge of smoke hangs in the distance, and it is impossible to believe that the familiar clear horizon traces the limit of one great circular ambush. . . . One envies the soldiers at the end of the day, wiping the sweat and blood from their faces, counting the dead fallen to their hands, looking at the devastated fields, the torn earth that seems to suffer and bleed with them. One does, really. The final brutality of it—the taste of primitive passion—the ferocious frankness of the blow struck with one's hand—the direct call and the straight response. Well, the sea gave you nothing of that, and seemed to pretend that there was nothing the matter with the world."

And that's how it was with us; it had never occurred to me before that this might be the way in enemy waters during wartime.

The daytime was serene, but dusk brought a change. Not a feeling of fear at all but somehow an acute sense of the drama of that moment on the face of a sea that has known so major a share of the world's great warfare. In the faint light of the dusk forms became indistinguishable. Ships nearby were only heavier spots against the heavy background of the night. Now we thought we saw something and now there was nothing. The gigantic armada on all sides of us was invisible, present only in our knowledge.

Then a rolling little subchaser out of nowhere took on a dim shape alongside us and with its motors held itself steady about thirty yards away. We could not see the speaker but a megaphoned voice came loud across the water telling us of a motor breakdown in one of the troop-carrying barges farther back.

We megaphoned advice back to him. His response returned to us; out in the darkness the voice was youthful. I could picture a youngster of a skipper out there with his blown hair and his life jacket and binoculars, rolling to the sea in the Mediterranean dusk. Some young man who shortly before had perhaps been unaware of any sea at all—the bookkeeper in your bank, maybe—and then there he was, a strange new man in command of a ship, suddenly a person with acute responsibilities, carrying out with great intentness his special, small part of the enormous aggregate that is our war on all the lands and seas of the globe.

In his unnatural presence there in the heaving darkness of the Mediterranean, I realized vividly how everybody in America had changed, how every life had suddenly stopped and as suddenly begun again on a different course. Everything in this world had stopped except war and we were all men of a new profession out in a strange night caring for each other.

That's the way I felt as I heard this kid, this pleasant kid, shouting across the dark water. The words were odd, nautical ones with a disciplined deliberation that carried the very strength of the sea itself, the strong, mature words of a captain on his own ship, saying, "Aye, aye, sir. If there is any change I will use my own judgment and report to you again at dawn. Good night, sir."

Then darkness enveloped the whole American armada. Not a pinpoint of light showed from those hundreds of ships as they surged on through the night toward their destiny, carrying across the ageless and indifferent sea tens of thousands of young men, fighting for . . . for . . . well, at least for each other.

THREE

D-DAY:—SICILY

We had a couple of bad moments as we went to invade Sicily. At the time they both looked disastrous for us, but they turned out to have such happy endings that it seemed as though Fate had deliberately plucked us from doom.

The cause of the first near-tragedy was the weather on the morning of the day on which we were to attack Sicily. The night before, it had turned miserable. Dawn came up gray and misty, and the sea began to kick up. Even our fairly big ships were rolling and plunging and the little flat-bottomed landing craft were tossing around like corks. As the day wore on it grew progressively worse. At noon the sea was rough even to professional sailors. In midafternoon it was breaking clean over our decks. By dusk it was mountainous. The wind howled at forty miles an hour. We could barely stand on deck, and our far-spread convoy was a wallowing, convulsive thing.

In the early afternoon the high command aboard our various ships had begun to wrinkle their brows. They were perplexed, vexed and worried. Damn it, here the Mediterranean had been like a millpond for a solid month, and now this storm had to come up out of nowhere! Conceivably it could turn our whole venture into a disaster that would cost thousands of lives and prolong the war for months. These high seas and winds could cause many serious hazards:

1. The majority of our soldiers would hit the beach weak and indifferent from seasickness, two-thirds of their fighting power destroyed.

2. Our slowest barges, barely creeping along against the high waves, might miss the last rendezvous and arrive too late with their precious armored equipment.

3. High waves would make it next to impossible to launch the assault craft from the big transports. Boats would be smashed, lives lost, and the attack seriously weakened.

There was a time when it seemed that to avoid complete failure the landings would have to be postponed twenty-four hours. In that case, we would have had to turn around and cruise for an extra day, thus increasing the chance of being discovered and heavily attacked by the enemy.

I asked our commanders about it. They said, "God knows."

Certainly they would have liked to change the plans, but by then it was impossible. We'd have to go through with it. (Later I learned that the Supreme High Command did actually consider postponement.)

Many ships in the fleet carried barrage balloons against an air attack. The quick snap of a ship's deck when she dropped into a trough would tear the high-flying balloon loose from its cable. The freed silver bag would soar up and up until finally in the thin, high air it would burst and disappear from view. One by one we watched the balloons break loose during the afternoon. Scores of them dotted the sky above our convoy. That night, when the last light of day failed, only three balloons were left in the entire fleet.

The little subchasers and the infantry-carrying assault craft would disappear completely into the wave-troughs as we watched them. The next moment they would be carried so high they seemed to leap clear out of the water. By afternoon, many of the sailors on our vessel were sick. We sent a destroyer through the fleet to find out how all the ships were getting along. It came back with the appalling news that thirty per cent of all the soldiers were deathly seasick. An Army officer had been washed overboard from one craft but had been picked up by another about four ships behind.

During the worst of the blow we hoped and prayed that the weather would moderate by dusk. It didn't. The officers tried to make jokes about it at suppertime. One said, "Think of hitting the beach tonight, seasick as hell, with your stomach upside down, and straight off you come face to face with an Italian with a big garlic breath!"

At ten o'clock I lay down with my clothes on. There wasn't anything I could do and the rolling sea was beginning to take nibbles at my stomach, too. Never in my life had I been so depressed. I lay there and let the curse of a too-vivid imagination picture a violent and complete catastrophe for America's war effort—before another sun rose. As I finally fell asleep the wind was still howling and the ship was pounding and falling through space.

The next thing I knew a booming voice over the ship's loudspeaker was saying: "Stand by for gunfire. We may have to shoot out some searchlights."

I jumped up, startled. The engines were stopped. There seemed to be no wind. The entire ship was motionless and quiet as a grave. I grabbed my helmet, ran out onto the deck, and stared over the rail. We were anchored, and we could see the dark shapes of the Sicilian hills not far away. The water lapped with a gentle, caressing sound against the sides of the ship. We had arrived. The storm was gone. I looked down and the surface of the Mediterranean was slick and smooth as a table top. Already assault boats were skimming past us toward the shore. Not a breath of air stirred. The miracle had happened.

The other bad moment came on the heels of the storm. As long as that ship of ours sails the high seas, I'm sure the story of the searchlights will linger on in her wardroom and forecastle like a legend. It is the story of a few minutes in which the fate of the ship hung upon the whim of the enemy. For some reason which we probably shall never know the command to obliterate us was never given.

Our ship was about three and a half miles from shore—which in the world of big guns is practically hanging in the cannon muzzle. Two or three smaller ships were in closer, but the bulk of our fleet stood far out to sea behind us. Our admiral had the reputation of always getting up close where he could have a hand in the shooting and he certainly ran true to form throughout the invasion.

We'd been stopped only a minute when big searchlights blinked on from the shore and began to search the waters. Apparently the watchers on the coast had heard some sounds at sea. The lights swept back and forth across the dark water and after a few exploratory sweeps one of them centered dead upon us and stopped. Then, as we held our breaths, the searchlights one by one brought their beams down upon our ship. They had found their mark.

All five of them, stretching out over a shore line of several miles, pinioned us in their white shafts as we sat there as naked as babies. I would have been glad to bawl like one if it would have helped, for this searchlight business meant the enemy had us on the block. Not only were we discovered, we were caught in a funnel from which there was no escaping.

We couldn't possibly move fast enough to run out of those beams. We were within simple and easy gunning distance. We were a sitting duck. We were stuck on the end of five merciless poles of light, and we were utterly helpless.

"When that fifth searchlight stopped on us all my children became orphans," one of the officers said later.

Another one said, "The straw that broke my back was when the anchor went down. The chain made so much noise you could have heard it in Rome."

A third one said, "The fellow standing next to me was breathing so hard I couldn't hear the anchor go down. Then I realized there wasn't anybody standing next to me."

We got all set to shoot at the lights, but then we waited. We had three alternatives—to start shooting and thus draw return fire; to up anchor and run for it; or to sit quiet like a mouse and wait in terror. We did the last. Our admiral decided there was some possibility they couldn't see us through the slight haze although he was at a loss to explain why all five lights stopped on the ship if they couldn't see it.

I don't know how long the five lights were on us. It seemed like hours, it may have been five minutes. At any rate, at the end of some unbelievably long time one of them suddenly blinked out. Then one by one, erratically, the others went out too. The last one held us a long time as though playing with us. Then it too went out and we were once again in the blessed darkness. Not a shot had been fired.

———

Assault boats had been speeding past us all the time and a few minutes later they hit the beach. The searchlights flashed on again but from then on they were busy fanning the beach itself. From close range, it didn't take our attacking troops long to shoot the lights out.

I'm not certain but that some of them weren't just turned out and left off for good. We never did find out for sure why the Italian big guns didn't let us have it. Several of us inquired around when we got to land after daylight. We never found the searchlight men themselves, but from other Italian soldiers and citizens of the town we learned that the people ashore were so damned scared by whatever was about to attack them from out there on the water that they were afraid to start anything.

I guess I'm always going to have to love the Italians who were behind those searchlights and guns that night. Thanks to them, St. Peter will have to wait a spell before he hears the searchlight yarn.

Just before daylight I lay down for a few minutes' nap, knowing the predawn lull wouldn't last long once the sun came up. Sure enough, just as the first faint light was beginning to show, bedlam broke loose for miles around us. The air was suddenly filled with sound and danger and tension, and the gray-lighted sky became measled with countless dark puffs of ack-ack.

Enemy planes had appeared to dive-bomb our ships. They got a hot reception from our thousands of guns, and a still hotter one from our own planes, which had anticipated them and were waiting.

A scene of terrific action then emerged from the veil of night. Our small assault craft were all up and down the beach, unloading and dashing off again. Ships of many sizes moved toward the shore, and others moved back from it. Still other ships, so many they were uncountable, spread out over the water as far as the eye could see. The biggest ones lay far off, waiting their turn to come in. They made a solid wall on the horizon behind us. Between that wall and the shore line the sea writhed with shipping. Through this hodgepodge, and running out at right angles to the beach like a beeline highway through a forest, was a single solid line of shorebound barges, carrying tanks. They chugged along in Indian file, about fifty yards apart—slowly, yet with such calm relentlessness that I felt it would take a power greater than any I knew to divert them.

The attacking airplanes left, but then Italian guns opened up on the hills back of the beach. At first the shells dropped on the beach, making yellow clouds of dust as they exploded. Then they started for the ships. They never did hit any of us, but they came so close it made our heads swim. They tried one target after another, and one of the targets happened to be our ship.

The moment the shooting began we got quickly under way—not to run off, but to be in motion and consequently harder to hit. One shell struck the water fifty yards behind us and threw up a geyser of spray. It made a terrific flat quacking sound as it burst, exactly like a mortar shell exploding on land. Our ship wasn't supposed to do much firing, but that was too much for the admiral. He ordered our guns into action. And for the next ten minutes we sounded like Edgewood Arsenal blowing up.

A few preliminary shots gave us our range, and then we started pouring shells into the town and into the gun positions in the hills. The whole vessel shook with every salvo, and scorched wadding came raining down on the deck.

While shooting, we traveled at full speed—parallel to the shore and about a mile out. For the first time I found out how such a thing is done. Two destroyers and ourselves were doing the shelling, while all the other ships in close to land were scurrying around to make themselves hard to hit, turning in tight circles, leaving half-moon wakes behind them. The sea looked actually funny with all those semicircular white wakes splattered over it and everything twisting around in such deliberate confusion.

We sailed at top speed for about three miles, firing several times a minute. For some reason I was as thrilled with our unusual speed as with the noise of the steel we were pouring out. By watching closely I could follow our shells almost as far as the shore, and then see the gray smoke puffs after they hit.

At the end of each run we turned so quickly that the ship heeled far over. Then we would start right back. The two destroyers did the same, and we would meet them about halfway. It was just like three teams of horses plowing a cornfield—back and forth, back and forth—the plows taking alternate rows. The constant shifting put us closest to shore on one run, and farthest away a couple of runs later. At times we were right up on the edge of pale-green water, too shallow to go any closer.

During all this action I stood on a big steel ammunition box marked "Keep Off," guns on three sides of me and a smokestack at my back. It was as safe as any place else, it kept me out of the way, and it gave me a fine view of everything.

Finally the Italian fire dwindled off. Then the two destroyers went in as close to shore as they could get and resumed their methodical runs back and forth. Only this time they weren't firing. They were belching terrific clouds of black smoke out of their stacks. The smoke wouldn't seem to settle, and they had to make four runs before the beach was completely hidden. Then under this covering screen our tank-carrying barges and more infantry boats made for the shore.

Before long we could see the tanks let go at the town. They had to fire only a couple of salvos before the town surrendered. That was the end of the beach fighting in our sector of the American front. Our biggest job was over.

In invasion parlance, the day a force strikes a new country is called D-day, and the time it hits the beach is H-hour. In the Third Infantry Division for which I was a very biased rooter, H-hour had been set for 2:45 a.m., July 10.

That was when the first mass assault on the beach was to begin. Actually the paratroopers and Rangers were there several hours before. The other two large American forces, which traveled from North Africa in separate units, hit the beaches far down to our right about the same time we did. We could tell when they landed by the shooting during the first hour or so of the assault.

Out on our ship it seemed to me that all hell was breaking loose ashore, but later when I looked back on it, actually knowing what had happened, it didn't seem so very dramatic. Most of our special section of coast was fairly easy to take, and our naval guns didn't send any fireworks ashore until after daylight. The assault troops did all the preliminary work with rifles, grenades and machine guns. From our ship we could hear the bop, hop, hop of the machine guns, first short bursts, then long ones.

I don't know whether I heard any Italian ones or not. In Tunisia we could always tell the German machine guns because they fired so much faster than ours, but that night all the shooting seemed to be of one tempo, one quality. Now and then we could see a red tracer bullet arcing through the darkness. I remember one that must have ricocheted from a rock, for suddenly it turned and went straight up a long way into the sky. Once in a while there was the quick flash of a hand grenade. There wasn't even any aerial combat during the night and only a few flares shot up from the beach.

In actuality, our portion of the assault was far less spectacular than the practice landings I'd seen our troops make back in Algeria.

A more dramatic show was in the sector to our right, some twelve or fifteen miles down the beach. There the First Infantry Division was having stiff opposition and its naval escort stood off miles from shore and threw steel at the enemy artillery in the hills. On beyond, the Forty-fifth had rough seas and bad beaches.

This was the first time I'd ever seen big-gun tracer shells used at night and it was fascinating. From where we sat it was like watching a tennis game played with red balls, except that all the balls went in one direction. A golden flash would appear way off in the darkness. Out of the flash would come a tiny red dot. That was the big shell. Almost instantly, it covered the first quarter of the total distance. Then uncannily it would drop to a much slower speed, as though it had put on a brake. There didn't seem to be any tapering down between the high and low speeds. The shell went from high to low instantly, and instead of starting to arc downward as it hit the slower speed, it amazingly kept on in an almost flat trajectory as though it were on wheels being propelled along a level road. Finally, after a flight so long it seemed unbelievable that the thing could still be in the air, it would disappear in a little flash as it hit something on the shore. Long afterward the sound of the heavy explosion came rolling across the water.

When daylight came we looked from the boat deck across the water at the city of Licata. We could see the American flag flying from the top of a sort of fort on a hill directly behind the city.

Although the city itself had not yet surrendered, some Rangers had climbed up there and hoisted the flag.

Our Navy can't be given too much credit for putting the troops ashore the way they did. You can't realize how nearly impossible it is to arrive in the dead of night at exactly the right spot with a convoy, feel your way in through the darkness, pick out the designated pinpoint on an utterly strange shore line, and then put a ship safely ashore right there. In our sector every ship hit every beach just right. They tell me it was the first time in history that such a thing had ever been accomplished. The finest tribute to the Navy's marksmanship came from one soldier who later told Major General Lucian Truscott, Third Division commander:

"Sir, I took my little black dog with me in my arms and I sure was scared standing in that assault boat. Finally we hit the beach and as we piled out into the water we were worse scared than ever. Then we waded ashore and looked around and there right ahead of me was a white house just where you said it would be and after that I wasn't scared."

Since I was a correspondent duly accredited to the Navy, I had intended to concentrate on the sea-borne aspect of the invasion and had not planned to go ashore at all for several days. After the way things went, however, I couldn't resist the chance to see what it was like on land. I hopped an assault barge and went ashore there on the south coast about six hours after our first assault troops had landed.

They had found nobody at all. The thing apparently was a complete surprise. Our troops had been trained to such a point that instead of being pleased with no opposition they were thoroughly annoyed.

I stopped to chat with the crew of a big howitzer which had just been dug in and camouflaged. The gun crew was digging foxholes. The ground was hard and it was very tough digging. Our soldiers were mad at the Italians. "We didn't even get to fire a shot," one of them said in real disgust.

Another one said, "They're gangplank soldiers"—whatever that means.

I talked with one Ranger who had been through Dieppe, El Guettar and other tough battles, and he said Sicily was by far the easiest of all. He added that it left him jumpy and nervous to get trained to razor edge and then have the job fizzle out. The poor guy, he was sore about it!

That Ranger was Sergeant Murel White, a friendly blond fellow of medium size, from Middlesboro, Kentucky. He had been overseas a year and a half. Back home he had a wife and a five-year-old daughter. He used to run his uncle's bar in Middlesboro and he said when the war was over he was going to drink the bar dry, and then just settle down behind it for the rest of his life.

Sergeant White and his commanding officer were in the first wave to hit the shore. A machine-gun pillbox was shooting at them and they made uphill for it, about a quarter mile away. They used hand grenades. "Three of them got away," White said, "but the other three went to Heaven."

Our sector, on the western end of the invasion, covered the territory each side of the city of Licata—about fourteen miles of beach front. When I landed the beach was already thoroughly organized, and it was really an incredible scene—incredible in that we'd done so much in just a few hours. It looked actually as though we'd been working there for months. Shortly after dawn, our shore troops and Navy gunboats had knocked out the last of the enemy artillery on the hillsides. From then on that first day was just a normal one of unloading ships on the beach, as fast as possible. The only interruptions were a half dozen or so lightning like dive bombings.

Each separate invading fleet operated entirely independently from the others. Ours carried infantry and had hundreds of ships; the bulk of it was made up of scores of new-type landing craft carrying men, trucks, tanks, supplies of all kinds.

Every ship in our fleet, except the gunboats, was flat-bottomed and capable of landing on the beach. The ships lay like a blanket over the water, extending as far out in the Mediterranean as the eye could see. The beach wasn't big enough to handle them all at once, so they'd come in at signals from the command ship, unload, and steam back out to the convoy for a second load.

Small craft, carrying about two hundred soldiers, could unload in a few minutes, but the bigger ones with tanks and trucks and heavy guns took much longer. It was not a specially good beach for our purposes, for it sloped off too gradually, making the boats ground fifty yards or more from shore. Most of the men had to jump into waist-deep water and wade in. The water was cold, but a high wind dried them out in less than half an hour, all but their shoes which kept squishing inside for the rest of the day. As far as I know, not a man was lost by drowning in our sector of the operation.

The beach itself had been immediately organized into a great metropolitan like dock extending for miles. Hundreds of soldiers wearing black and yellow arm bands with the letters SP—Shore Patrol—directed traffic off the incoming boats. Big white banners about five feet square, with colored symbols on them, were used to designate the spots where they should land. On the shore, painted wooden markers were immediately set up directing various units to appointed rendezvous areas. There were almost no traffic jams or road blocking. Engineers had hit the beach right behind the assault troops. They laid down hundreds of yards of burlap and placed chicken wire on top of it, making a firm roadbed up and down the beach.

Our organization on shore took form so quickly it left me gasping. By midafternoon the countryside extending far inland was packed with troops and vehicles of every description. On one hillside there were enough tanks to fight a big battle. Jeeps were dashing everywhere. Phone wires were laid on the ground and command posts set up in orchards and old buildings. Medical units worked under trees or in abandoned stone sheds.

The fields were stacked with thousands of boxes of ammunition. Field kitchens were being set up and before long hot food would replace the K rations the soldiers had carried on with throughout that first day.

The Americans worked grimly and with great speed. I saw a few officers who appeared rather excited, but mostly it was a calm, determined, efficient horde of men who descended on that strange land. The amazed Sicilians just stood and stared in wonder at the swift precision of it all.

The enemy defenses throughout our special sector were almost childish. They didn't bother to mess up their harbor or to blow out the two river bridges which would have cut our forces in half. They had only a few mines on the beaches and practically no barbed wire. We'd come prepared to fight our way through a solid wall of mines, machine guns, artillery, barbed wire and liquid fire, and we even expected to hit some fiendish new devices. Yet there was almost nothing to it. It was like stepping into the ring to meet Joe Louis and finding Caspar Milquetoast waiting there.

The Italians didn't even leave many booby traps for us. I almost stepped into one walking through a field, but obviously it had been dropped rather than planted. Down at the docks we found whole boxes of them. They hadn't even been opened.

The road blocks outside town were laughable. They consisted merely of light wooden frameworks, about the size of a kitchen table, with barbed wire wrapped around them. These sections were laid across the road and all we had to do was pick them up and lay them aside. They wouldn't have stopped a cow, let alone a tank.

Since the invading soldiers of our section didn't have much battle to talk about, they looked around to see what this new country had to offer, and the most commented-upon discovery among the soldiers that first day was something totally unexpected. It wasn't signorinas, or vino, or Mount Etna. It was the fact that they found fields of ripe tomatoes! And did they eat them! I heard at least two dozen men speak of it during the day, as though they'd located gold. Others said they came upon some watermelons too, but I couldn't find any.

I hitched a ride into the city of Licata with Major Charles Monnier, of Dixon, Illinois, Sergeant Earl Glass, of Colfax, Illinois, and Sergeant Jaspare Taormina of 94 Starr Street, Brooklyn—engineers all.

Taormina did the driving and the other two held tommy guns at the ready, looking for snipers. Taormina himself was so busy looking for snipers that he ran right into a shell hole in the middle of the street and almost upset our jeep. He was of Sicilian descent. Indeed, his father had been born in a town just twenty miles west of Licata and for all the sergeant knew his grandmother was still living there. He could speak good Italian, so he did the talking to the local people on the streets. They told him they were sick of being browbeaten and starved by the Germans, who had lots of wheat locked in granaries in Licata. The natives hoped we would unlock the buildings and give them some of it.

Licata is a city of about thirty-five thousand souls. A small river runs through the town, which has a wide main street and a nice small harbor. The buildings are of local stone, dull gray and very old—but substantial. The city hadn't been bombed. The only damage came from a few shells we had thrown into it from the ships just after daylight. The corners were knocked off a few buildings and some good-sized holes were gouged in the streets, but on the whole, Licata had got off pretty nicely.

The local people said the reason their army put up such a poor show in our sector was that the soldiers didn't want to fight. It was obvious they didn't, but at that stage of the game we had little contact with other American forces and we thought the Italians might have lain down there in order to fight harder somewhere else.

Before the sun was two hours high our troops had built prisoner-of-war camps, out of barbed wire, on the rolling hillsides, and all day long groups of soldiers and civilians were marched up the roads and into the camps. At the first camp I came to, about two hundred Italian soldiers and the same number of civilians were sitting around on the ground inside the wire. There were only two Germans, both officers. They sat apart in one corner, disdainful of the Italians. One had his pants off and his legs were covered with Mercurochrome where he had been scratched. Some civilians had even brought their goats into the cages with them.

After being investigated, the harmless captives were turned loose. The Italian prisoners seemed anything but downhearted. They munched on biscuits, talked cheerfully to anyone who would listen to them, and asked their American guards for matches. As usual, the area immediately became full of stories about prisoners who'd lived twenty years in Brooklyn and who came up grinning, asking how things were in dear old Flatbush. They seemed relieved and friendly, like people who had just been liberated rather than conquered.

Civilians on the roads and in the towns smiled and waved. Kids saluted. Many gave their version of the V sign by holding up both arms. Over and over they told us they didn't want to fight. Our soldiers weren't very responsive to the Sicilians' greetings. They were too busy getting equipment ashore, rounding up the real enemies and establishing a foothold, to indulge in any

hand-waving monkey business. After all we were still at war and
these people, though absurd and pathetic, were enemies and caused
us the misery of coming a long way to whip them.

On the whole the natives seemed a pretty third-rate lot. They
were poorly dressed and looked as if they always had been. Few
of their faces had much expression, and they kept getting in the
way of traffic, just like the Arabs. By nightfall most of our invading soldiers summed up their impressions of their newly acquired
soil and its inhabitants by saying, "Hell, this is just as bad as
Africa."

When we got our first look at Sicily we were all disappointed. I
for one had always romanticized it in my mind as a lush, green,
picturesque island. I guess I must have been thinking of the Isle
of Capri. Instead, the south coast of Sicily seemed to us a drab,
light-brown country, and there weren't many trees. The fields of
grain had been harvested and they were dry and naked and dusty.
The villages were pale gray and indistinguishable at a distance
from the rest of the country. Water was extremely scarce. On the
hillsides a half mile or so back of the beach grass fires—started
by the shells of our gunboats—burned smokily.

It was cooler than North Africa; in fact, the weather would have
been delightful had it not been for the violent wind that rose in
the afternoon and blew so fiercely we could hardly talk in the
open. That wind, whipping our barges about in the shallow
water, delayed us more than the Italian soldiers did.

At the end of that first day of our invasion of Sicily we Americans looked about us with awe and unbelief and not a little alarm.
It had all been so easy that we had the jumpy, insecure feeling of
something dreadfully wrong somewhere. We had expected a terrific slaughter on the beaches and there was none. Instead of thousands of casualties along the fourteen-mile front of our special
sector, the total was astonishingly small.

By sunset the Army had taken everything we had hoped to get
during the first five days. Even by midafternoon the country for
miles inland was so saturated with American troops and vehicles
it looked like Tunisia after months of our habitation, instead of
a hostile land just attacked that morning. And the Navy's job of

bringing the vast invading force to Sicily was three days ahead of its schedule of unloading ships.

Convoys had started back to Africa for new loads before the first day was over. Our own invading fleet had escaped without losses other than normal, mechanical breakdowns. It was wonderful and yet it was also illogical. Even if the Italians did want to quit, why did the Germans let them? What had happened? What did the enemy have up its sleeve? Nobody was under any illusion that the battle of Sicily was over. Strong counterattacks were probably inevitable. Also, German dive bombings had begun at the rate of two per hour, but everyone felt that whatever happened we had a head start that was all in our favor.

FOUR

THE NAVY STANDS BY

I went back to the ship and stayed aboard almost a week before going ashore more or less permanently. It was my hope to do a complete picture of the Navy's part in such actions as this, and the Navy's part didn't end the moment it got the assault troops ashore. In the days that followed the landings our headquarters vessel patrolled back and forth between the American sectors, kept an eye on the shore in case help was needed, directed the fire of other ships, mothered new convoys by wireless, issued orders and advice throughout the area, and from time to time scurried in swift circles when planes appeared in the sky. For despite the enemy's obvious air weakness, he did manage to sneak over a few planes several times a day. On D-day Plus 1, General Quarters was sounded fifteen times on our ship. Nobody got any rest the clock around. The sailors worked like Trojans.

Whenever I think of our soldiers and sailors in camps back home, I am apt to visualize—and no doubt wrongly—a draftee who is going through his training like a man, but still reluctantly and without intense interest. If I'm right about that, once he goes into action that attitude will vanish, because he'll be working— working to stay alive and not because somebody tells him to work. When General Quarters was sounded our sailors didn't get to their stations in the manner of school kids going in when the bell rings. They got there by charging over things and knocking things down. I saw them arrive at gun stations wearing nothing but their drawers. I saw officers upset their dinner and be out of the wardroom by the time the second "beep!" of the alarm signal sounded. I always froze wherever I was for about five minutes, to keep from getting bowled over in the rush.

And the boys on the guns—you could hardly recognize them.

Shooting at planes wasn't a duty for them; it was a completely absorbing thing. I doubt if they ever watched a ball game or gave a girl the eye with the complete intentness which they used to follow a distant plane in the sky. A gun has one blessing in addition to the one of protecting a man: it occupies him.

Having no vital part to play in moments of extreme danger is one of the worst curses of being a correspondent. Busy people aren't often afraid.

Bombs fell in our vicinity for several days. The raiders went mostly for the beaches, where the barges were unloading. The number of narrow escapes we had must have been very discouraging to the Axis fliers. The Axis radio said our beaches were littered with the wrecked and burned-out hulks of our landing ships. Actually, in our fourteen-mile area they hit very few. But we had our tense moments.

The enemy fliers were brave, I had to admit that. They would come right in through the thickest hail of fire I had ever seen thrown into the sky. Dozens of our ships had escapes that were uncanny. Once two bombs hit the water just a good stone's throw from the stern of our vessel. And late one afternoon a lone Italian—I really believe he must have gone mad, for what he did was desperate and senseless—dove right down into the midst of a hundred ships. He had no bombs, and was only strafing. He went over our fantail so low we could almost have caught him in a net.

Everything in the vicinity cut loose on him at once. It was like throwing a bucketful of rice against a spot on the wall. He was simply smothered with steel. Yet somehow he pulled out and up to about a thousand feet. He charged at our barrage balloons like an insane bee and shot two of them down afire. And then at last the bullets we had put into him took effect. He burst all aflame and fell in wide circles until he hit the water. No parachute ever came out.

Air raids at night were far more nerve-racking than the daylight ones. The enemy couldn't be seen, he could only be heard. The ghostly flares were visible, though, and the sickening bomb flashes that accompanied the heavy thunder rolling across the water.

With us it was always a game of hide and seek. Sometimes we would sit on the water as quiet as a mouse. No one spoke loudly. The engines were silent. We could hear the small waves lapping at the sides of our ship. At other times we would start so suddenly that the ship would almost jump out from under us. We would run at full speed and make terrifically sharp turns and churn up an alarmingly bright wake in the phosphorescent water. But we always escaped.

And then after the third day, all of a sudden there was never an enemy plane again. They quit us cold. If they still fought, they fought some other place than our front.

Our first few days aboard ship after the landings were punctuated by many things besides air raids: Wounded soldiers were sometimes brought from shore for our doctors to treat before the hospital ships arrived. Generals came to confer on our ship. Equally exciting, once we had fresh tomatoes and watermelon at the same meal. We took little trips up and down the coast. Repair parties back from the beaches brought souvenir Fascist banners, and stories of how poor the Sicilians were and how glad they were that the war was over for them. The weather remained perfect.

Our waters and beaches were forever changing. I think it was at daylight on the third morning when we awoke to find the Mediterranean absolutely devoid of ships, except for a few scattered naval vessels. The vast convoys that brought us over had unloaded to the last one and slipped out during the night. For a few hours the water was empty, the shore seemed lifeless, and all the airplanes had disappeared. It was hard to believe that we were really at war.

And then after lunch we looked out again, and the sea was once more veritably crawling with new ships—hundreds of them, big and little. Every one was coated at the top with a brown layer like icing on a cake. When we drew closer, the icing turned out to be decks crammed solid with Army vehicles and khaki-clad men.

We kept pouring men and machines into Sicily as though it were a giant hopper. The schedule had all been worked out ahead of time: On D-day Plus 3, Such-and-such Division would arrive. A few hours later another convoy bringing tanks would appear. Ships unloaded and started right back for new cargoes. The whole thing went so fast that I heard of at least one instance in which the Army couldn't pour its men and equipment into the African embarkation ports as fast as the returning ships arrived.

The Navy sent salvage parties of Seabees ashore right behind the assault troops and began reclaiming the Sicilian harbors and fixing up beaches for unloading. We ran some ships up to the shore, we emptied others at ports, and we would unload big freighters by lightering their cargoes in hundreds of assault barges and amphibious trucks. Great ships filled with tanks sometimes beached and unloaded in the fantastic time of half an hour. Big freighters anchored a mile from shore were emptied into hordes of swarming, clamoring small boats, in a matter of eighteen hours. The same unloading job with all modern facilities at a New York pier would take four days. The number of vehicles that had to be landed to take care of this was almost beyond conception.

The Army worked so smoothly that material never piled up on the beaches but got immediately on its way to the front. We had stevedoring regiments made up of New York professional stevedores. We had naval captains who in civil life ran worldwide ship-salvaging concerns and made enormous salaries. Convoys arrived, discharged, and slipped away for another load. Men worked like slaves on the beaches. Bosses shouted and rushed as no construction boss ever did in peacetime. Speed, speed, speed!

I walked gingerly on big steel pontoon piers, and I couldn't tell a naval lieutenant commander in coveralls from an Army sergeant in a sun helmet. Sometimes it seemed as if half the men of America were there, all working madly together. Suddenly I realized what all this was. It was America's long-awaited power of production finally rolling into the far places where it had to go to end the war. It sounds trite when it is put into words, but the might of material can overwhelm everything before it. We saw that in the last days of Tunisia. We saw it again there in Sicily.

The point was that we on the scene knew for sure that we could substitute machines for lives and that if we could plague and smother the enemy with an unbearable weight of machinery in the months to follow, hundreds of thousands of our young men whose expectancy of survival would otherwise have been small could someday walk again through their own front doors.

Fewer than a third of the sailors on our ship were Regular Navy. And most of that third hadn't been in many years. The crew was chiefly composed of young landlubbers who became sailors only because of the war and who were longing to get back to civil life. Here are a few sketches of some of the men who made the wheels go round:

Joe Raymer, electrician's mate first class, of 51 South Burgess Avenue, Columbus, Ohio, was a married man with a daughter four years old. Joe had been in the Navy from 1924 to 1928, so he knew his way around ships. Of medium height, he was a pleasant fellow with a little silver in his hair and a cigar in his mouth. I don't know why, but sailors smoking cigars have always seemed incongruous to me. Before the war Joe was a traveling salesman, and that's what he intended to go back to. He worked for the Pillsbury flour people—had the central-southern Ohio territory. He was a hot shot and no fooling. The year before he went back to the Navy he sold more pancake flour than anybody else in America, and won himself a $500 bonus.

Warren Ream, of Paradise, California, had worked for several years in the advertising departments of big Los Angeles stores—Bullock's, Barker Brothers, Robinson's. He arrived overseas just in time for the invasion. Ream was a storekeeper third class, but that doesn't necessarily mean he kept store. In fact he did a little bit of everything from sweeping up to passing shells. Actually he thought he wasn't supposed to be aboard ship at all, but he was glad he didn't miss it. His Navy life was a great contrast to his personal past. He was the kind of fellow who might well have been made miserable by the rough life of the Navy. But we were standing at the rail one day and he said, "I wonder what's happened to the old Navy we used to read about. I remember hearing of skippers who could cuss for forty-five minutes without repeating themselves. But from what I've seen, skippers today can't cuss any better than I can. I'm disappointed."

Harvey Heredeen was a warrant officer, which means he ate in the wardroom and was called "mister." But a man's a man by any other name, and Mr. Heredeen looked exactly what he was—a regular old-time chief petty officer. He had had orders to return to the States just before we sailed, but you wouldn't get an old-timer to miss a show like that. He got permission to postpone the homeward trip until after we had made the invasion. Mr. Heredeen had retired from the Navy in 1935 after seventeen years of it, twelve of them in submarines. He had met a Memphis schoolteacher, married her, and settled down there in a job at the Linde Air Products Company, making oxygen. He went back to the Navy in 1941 when he was forty-five years old. After the invasion he had orders to go back to America and serve as an instructor at a submarine school. His nickname was "Spike," and his home was at 1200 Tanglewood Street, Memphis. Back home he used to be a deacon in the London Avenue Christian Church. He begged me not to make any wisecracks about his cussing and tobacco-chewing when I wrote him up. Okay, deacon.

Joe Talbot was an aviation ordnanceman first class, and since there was no aviation aboard our ship he was a round peg in a square hole. Of course that wasn't his fault. What he actually did was a little bit of everything when things were normal. During battle, he was the head of a crew down in a magazine of big shells and upon orders passed more ammunition up to the gun batteries above. Joe was a black-haired, straight-shouldered Southerner from Columbus, Georgia. In civil life he was a photographer on the Columbus *Ledger-Inquirer*; the last big story he photographed was Eddie Rickenbacker's crash near Atlanta. Joe had been married four years. His wife worked at Woolworth's store in Columbus. This was Joe's second time in the Navy. He had served from 1931 to 1935, and went back again in 1941, but he had no intention of making it a career. His one great postwar ambition—he said he was going to do it in the first six months after he got out—was to buy a cabin cruiser big enough for four, get another couple, and cruise down the Chattahoochee River to the Gulf of Mexico, then up the Suwannee, making color photos of the whole trip.

Tom Temple, or rather Thomas Nicholas Temple, was a seaman second class. His father deliberately put in the middle name so the initials would make TNT. Tom, aged nineteen, was tall and thin, very grave and analytical. He talked so slowly I thought sometimes he was going to stop altogether. After the war he hoped to go to Harvard and then get into the publishing business. Tom told me his mother was a high-school teacher at Far Rockaway, Long Island, and that she wrote on the side. She used to write for the magazine *Story* under the name Jean Temple. Tom's father was wounded in the last war, and since then has been in the big veterans' hospital at Albuquerque, only a short distance from my home. Tom said that when he first went into the Navy the sailors' profanity shocked him, but before long it rolled off his back like water off a duck. He was very sincere and thoughtful and one of my favorites aboard ship.

Joe Ederer was a lieutenant commander and chief engineer of the ship. He was also my part-time host while I was aboard, since I did all my writing in his cabin. Furthermore, I ate his candy, smoked his cigarettes, used his paper, and would have read his mail if I could have found it. Commander Ederer had been at sea for more than a quarter of a century. He came from the Merchant Service, and he indulged in constant pleasant feuds with his Regular Navy friends. His home was at 2724 Northeast 35th Place, Portland, Oregon. His wife was used to waiting, so perhaps his absence was not as hard on her as it is on many wives. They had a fifteen-year-old boy upon whom the chief engineer doted. There were two pictures of his family on his shelves.

Ederer was one of the few officers who were genuine salts. He was not exactly a Colin Glencannon, but they had many things in common. Ederer spent many years on the Orient run and had a personal hatred for the Japs. He had been with our ship ever since she was commissioned in 1941, and he hoped the invasion would soon be over so he could get to the Pacific. Like all sailors he wanted someday to get five acres, preferably in the Oregon woods, build a cabin and have a creek running past his door. If he ever does he will probably go nuts.

Dick Minogue, bosun's mate first class, had been in the Navy six years and intended to stay. He came from White Bear Lake, Minnesota, and aboard ship they called him "Minny." It is men like Minogue who form the backbone of the present-day Navy. He was young and intelligent, yet strong and salty enough for any job. He definitely had the sea about him, but it was modern sea. He wore his bosun's pipe from a cord around his neck, and a white hat cocked far down over one eye. He said the worst moment he ever had in the Navy was while piping a British admiral over the side. Dick had a chew of tobacco in his mouth, and right in the middle of his refrain the whistle got full of tobacco juice and went gurgly.

Arch Fulton, of 493 East 129th Street, Cleveland, Ohio, was an electrician's mate second class. Before the war he worked as a lineman for the Cleveland Illuminating Company. Fulton was married and had two children. He was thirty-seven—much older than most of the crew. He was born a Scotsman, and went to America at seventeen. His parents were still living at Kilmarnock, Scotland. He had a brother, a sergeant major in the British Army, and a sister who was a British WREN. Arch had a short pompadour which slanted forward and gave him the look of standing with his back to the wind. He had a dry Scottish humor, and he took the Navy in his stride. Back in Cleveland he used to read my columns, so you can see he was a smart man.

We had eleven Negro boys aboard, all in the stewards' department. They waited table in the officers' mess, and ran the wardroom pantry where hot coffee was on tap twenty-four hours a day. They were all quiet, nice boys and a credit to the ship. Three of them were exceedingly tall and three were exceedingly short. They all had music in their souls. Sometimes I had to laugh—when the wardroom radio happened to be playing a hot tune during meals I'd notice them grinning to themselves and dancing ever so slightly as they went about their serving.

One of these boys was George Edward Mallory, of Orange, Virginia. He was thirty-two, and before the war he worked as an unloader at a chain grocery store in his home town. He had been in the Navy for a year and was operated on for appendicitis after arriving in the Mediterranean. He used to get seasick but it didn't bother him any more. He was tall, quiet, and serious. He had never waited table before but he had become an expert.

Another was Fred Moore, who was little and meek. Fred had a tiny mustache and a perpetually startled look on his good-natured face. He was very quiet and shy. His home was at 1910 Tenth Avenue, South Birmingham, Alabama. He was just twenty-one and had been in the Navy only a few months. He liked it fine, and thought he might stay in after the war. Before joining up he did common labor at Army camps and fruit farms. Fred had a gift. He was a wizard at baking delicate and beautiful pastries. He made all the pastry desserts for the officers' mess. He had never done any cooking before joining the Navy, except to fry a few hamburgers at a short-order joint. He couldn't explain his knack for pastry baking. It was just like somebody who can play the piano beautifully without ever taking lessons. The whole ship paid tribute to his streak of special genius. Fred said he had never been seasick nor very homesick, but during some of our close shaves in action he said he sure was scared.

In wartime it is an axiom that the closer you get to the front the less you know about what is going on. During the invasion of Sicily we would often say to each other that we wished we were back in New York so we could find out how we were doing. During the first two days, we in our sector had no word at all about the two American sectors to our right. Even though we were within sight and sound of their gunfire we knew nothing about how they were faring. The people in America knew, but we didn't. Aboard ship, we were somewhat better off than the troops on land, because we did get some news by radio. But many of the troops inland didn't know about the bombing of Rome, for instance, till nearly a week later.

The ship's news came mostly from BBC in London, the German radio in Berlin, and our little daily newspaper assembled from worldwide short-wave broadcasts picked up during the night. Our skipper, Commander Rufus Young, felt that a lack of news was bad for morale, so he did all he could to let the ship's crew know what was going on. He was the one who asked me to edit the daily mimeographed paper, and he also took one radio operator off his regular watch and gave him his own time just to sit and sample various air channels for news.

This operator was Frank Donohue, radioman second class, of 139–49 87th Avenue, Jamaica, Long Island. He had started in as a child with the Commercial Cable Company and had been a radio operator for eighteen years, though he was still a young man. He was working for Press Wireless when he joined the Navy in 1942. Donohue had so much experience taking down news dispatches that he had a good news sense. He took as much pride in our little paper as I did, and it got so he would sort out the stories by subjects before waking me at 3 a.m. Then while I assembled and rewrote the stuff he would bring us cups of coffee and cut the stencils for the mimeograph. We did our work in a big steel-walled room where about thirty radio operators were taking down code messages by typewriter, so it did seem sort of like a newspaper office. Throughout the invasion period we missed getting out our paper only one day. That was on the morning of our landings.

It was always daylight when we finished, and I would stop on the bridge to talk for a little while with the men of the early-morning watch. Getting up at three every day and not getting any sleep in the daytime almost got me down before it was over, but there was considerable satisfaction in feeling that I was not entirely useless aboard ship. Off Sicily, as everywhere else in the world, dawn is the most perfect part of the day, if you've got the nerve to get up and see it.

Every night throughout our invasion, we listened to the Berlin broadcasts and to the special propaganda program directed at American troops. A purported American, Midge (nicknamed Olga by the boys), worked hard at her job. She tried to tell them that their sweethearts would marry somebody else while they were overseas fighting a phony war for the "Jewish" Roosevelt, and that there would be no jobs for them when they got home. The boys listened to her partly to get mad, partly because the program always had excellent music, and partly to get a laugh. The biggest laugh the boys had had since joining the Navy was the night the traitorous Olga was complaining about something horrible President Roosevelt had done. She said it made her almost ashamed to be an American!

Olga had a come-hither voice, and she spoke straight American. Every night I'd hear the boys conjecturing about what she looked like. Some thought she was probably an old hag with a fat face and peroxide hair, but the majority liked to visualize her as looking as gorgeous as she sounded. The most frequently expressed opinion heard aboard ship was that if they ever got to Berlin they'd like first to sock Olga on the chin—and then make love to her.

One member of our regular ship's crew didn't make the invasion trip with us. She was the ship's dog. Her master was a Regular Navy man, a chief petty officer of many years' service. He was tattooed, windburned, a bachelor, and quietly profane. His officers said he was an excellent worker.

It seems that several months before the invasion some sailors from our ship had picked up a German shepherd puppy. She belonged to the whole crew, but the puppy took to our friend and he took to her, and by common consent she became recognized as his. The puppy grew into a beautiful dog, smart, alert and sweet. But when hot weather came along she got the mange. Our friend doctored it with everything he could find, and other sailors helped him with the doctoring, but still the mange got worse. They finally clipped her hair close, so they could get medicine on her skin more thoroughly, but nothing did any good.

When they hit the last port before leaving Africa, my friend went ashore and searched the country for a French or American Army veterinary, but couldn't find any. The sailors had given up all hope of curing her. Something had to be done. The others left it up to our friend. Whatever he chose to do would have their approval. He told me later that he couldn't just put her ashore, for she had grown up aboard ship and wouldn't know how to take care of herself on land.

So our friend solved it in his own way, the morning after I came aboard. He didn't ask anybody to help him or tell anybody what he was going to do. He just tied a weight around her neck and let her down into the water. That was her end—in the tradition of the sea.

I heard about it a few hours later, and stopped by the rail to tell our friend I was sorry. He couldn't talk about it. He just said, "Let's go below and have a cup of coffee."

A few hours after that, I noticed that he had started having something else. In midafternoon I saw one of the ship's officers talking to him very seriously. It didn't look too good. Drinking aboard ship just doesn't go. The next day our friend was called before the mast and given a light suspension of privileges. At lunch the boys were kidding him about it and he said, well, hell, he wasn't sore about it, for obviously they had to do something to him.

That evening I happened to be sitting with the officer who had sentenced our friend, and just to make conversation I mentioned that it was sad about the dog being gone.

The officer sat up and said, "What!"

I said yes, the dog was gone.

He said, "My God!" And then, "He's one of the best men on

the ship, and I knew something was wrong, but I tried for half an hour to get it out of him and he wouldn't tell me."

The officer sat there looking as though he were sick, and again he said, "So that was it! My God!"

By the end of the first week after the Sicilian invasion there was almost no indication of warfare along our beach front. Every night the German radio told us we were getting bombed, but actually a stultifying peace had settled over us. Hour by hour we could feel the ship slide back into her normal ways. The watches were dropped down to Condition Three, which is almost the peacetime regime. The ship's laundry reopened for the first time in weeks. Movies were borrowed and shown after supper. The wearing of white hats became optional once more. The men went swimming over the side, and fished with rod and reel from the forecastle head. The captain had time on his hands and played gin rummy with me when I was worn out with writing. Finally liberty parties were let ashore for sightseeing. I knew then that the war, for our ship's family in that special phase, was over.

So I shouldered my barracks bags and trundled myself ashore in Sicily for good. Those few weeks with the Navy had been grand, and I hated to part from the friends I had made. Too, that taste of civilized living had been a strange delight, and yet in a perverse way I looked forward to going back to the old soldier's routine of sleeping on the ground, not washing before breakfast, and fighting off fleas.

Man is a funny creature.

FIVE

MEDICS AND CASUALTIES

Behind me is a distinguished and unbroken record for being sick in every country I ever visited. Since Sicily was new terrain for me I figured I might as well get sick right away and get it over with. So on my fifth day ashore they threw me into an ambulance and off we went hunting for a hospital.

We were looking for a certain clearing station, and we couldn't find it because it was moving forward while we were moving back, and we passed on different roads. The result was that the determined ambulance boys drove nearly halfway across Sicily before they finally gave up and started back. We drove a total of seventy-five agonizing miles over dusty gravel roads, and then found the hospital all set up and ready for business within four miles of where we had started from in the first place.

The clearing station was a small tent hospital of the Forty-fifth Division, a sort of flag stop for wounded on the way back from the lines. The first regular hospital was about fifteen miles to the rear. The average patient stayed in the clearing station only a few hours at most. But once the doctors got a squint at me they beamed, rubbed their rubber gloves, and cried out, "Ah! Here is the medical freak we have been waiting for. We'll just keep this guy and play with him awhile."

So they put me to bed on a cot, gave me paregoric and bismuth, aspirin and codeine, soup and tomato juice, and finally wound up with morphine and a handful of sulfaguanidine. The only thing I can say on behalf of my treatment is that I became well and hearty again.

My family physician in this case was Captain Joe Doran, of Iowa City, Iowa. Captain Doran, a young and enthusiastic doctor, was different from most front-line doctors in that his main interest lay in treating sick soldiers rather than wounded ones. Captain Doran liked to get at the seat of a man's ills. To further this interest he had set up a nice little laboratory in one of the tents, complete with microscope and glass tubes. He was always taking specimens from his patients and then peering at his test tubes, like Dr. Arrowsmith.

Captain Doran's germ quest upon me was somewhat agitated by the fact that on the evening of my arrival he received a letter saying he had become a father for the second time, about six weeks previously. He was so overjoyed he gave me an extra shot of morphine and I was asleep before I could say "Congratulations!"

The doctors kept me in what is known as a semicomatose condition for about twenty-four hours, and then they began to get puzzled. At first they thought I had dysentery, but the little laboratory showed no dysentery. Then they thought I had malaria, so they called in a couple of Italian malaria experts from down the highway. They chatted in English, punched my finger, took blood specimens, and reported back later that I had no malaria. By that time I was getting better anyhow, so they decided that what I had was a nonconforming and at the moment fairly common illness which they called "battlefield fever." A man with this ailment aches all over and has a high temperature. The doctors thought it was caused by a combination of too much dust, bad eating, not enough sleep, exhaustion, and the unconscious nerve tension that comes to everybody in a front-line area. A man doesn't die of battlefield fever, but he thinks he's going to.

They put me in a corner of a tent, and in my section at various times there were three officers with similar fevers. Their illnesses were even briefer than mine; they all graduated before I did.

One of my classmates was a redheaded and bespectacled lieutenant named Rahe Chamberlin, from Clarksville, Ohio. After going into the Army, Chamberlin bought a half interest in a grocery store back home. Whenever they brought us fruit juice in cans he would take a good gander to see if it was a product his partner was selling back in the States.

Another fellow sufferer was Lieutenant Richard Van Syckle, of Sewaren, New Jersey. He used to be in the automobile business at

Perth Amboy. He was married to Clare Raftery, a delicious former Powers model, and he carried magazine-cover pictures of her in his map case.

The third was Major Ellzey Brown of Okmulgee, Oklahoma, who used to be president and general sales manager of the Cleveland Tractor Company. He was a tough outdoor man, and he was so thoroughly disgusted at getting sick that it made him even sicker. He celebrated his forty-fourth birthday just before entering the hospital. Major Brown distinguished himself in our midst by paying a flat hundred dollars to the station's chaplain for a fourteen-dollar air mattress. His own gear was all lost in the original Sicily landings and, as he said, money meant nothing over there anyhow, so why not pay a hundred dollars for something that would help a little?

All my life I have enjoyed being in hospitals (as soon as the original moaning-and-groaning stage is past), and my stay at this front-line army clearing station was no exception. On the third day I was scared to death for fear I was well enough to leave. But the doctor looked thoughtful and said he wanted me to stay another day. I would have kissed him if he had been a nurse instead of a man with a mustache and a stethoscope.

That was the only trouble with the hospital—it didn't have any nurses. In fact we lacked a number of the usual hospital touches. We were hidden, inevitably, in an olive grove, and our floors were merely the earth. The toilet was a ditch with canvas around it. And if we washed we did so in our own steel helmets. There were no such things as hospital pajamas or bathrobes. I arrived in my Army coveralls and left in my coveralls, and I never once had them off all the time I was there.

Every morning a chaplain came around with a big boxful of cigarettes, tooth powder and stuff. During the day they kept the sides of our tent rolled up, and it was pleasant enough lying there with nothing to do. But at night the tent had to be tightly closed for the blackout, and it became deadly stuffy. And all night long the litter-bearers would be coming and going with new wounded. In the dim glow of our single lantern the scene was eerie, and sleep was almost impossible. So the last couple of nights we moved our cots outdoors and slept under the wide starry skies of Sicily, and attendants brought our medicine out there in the dark. German bombers came over but we just stayed put.

The doctor had me on a liquid diet at first, but I gradually talked him into advancing me to a soft diet and finally to a regular one. The progression from liquid to soft to regular diet was one of the great experiences of my life, for believe it or not, all three diets were exactly the same thing—soup and canned tomato juice.

When I accused the doctor of duping me he grinned and said, "Well, it comes under the heading of keeping the patient happy by pretending to humor his whims."

Happy! I was hungry! But I survived, and actually I have never been treated better anywhere than by those doctors and men of the Forty-fifth Division.

During the time I lay at the clearing station with my own slight aches and pains, hundreds of wounded soldiers passed through on their way back to hospitals in the rear. I was in one of five small tents in which they were deposited on litters while waiting for ambulances. I lay right among them for four days and nights. It couldn't help being a moving and depressing experience, and yet there was something good about it too.

It was flabbergasting to me to lie there and hear wounded soldiers cuss and beg to be sent right back into the fight. Of course not all of them did that; it depended on the severity of their wounds and on their individual personalities, just as it would in peacetime. But at least a third of the less severely wounded men asked if they couldn't return to duty immediately.

The two main impressions I got from all the wounded men were (1) their grand spirit and (2) the thoughtful and attentive attitude of the doctors and wardboys toward them. Pitiful as wounded men are, it is easy to become hardened and cross with so many passing through your hands. A person could eventually get to look upon them all as just so many nuisances who came deliberately to cause more work. Yet the wardboys treated their wounded as though they were members of their own family. I paid particular attention to this matter as I lay there, and no wounded man ever made a request that a wardboy didn't go jumping to fulfill. This was especially true of the wardmasters, who were responsible for whole tents. There were three—all from Oklahoma—that impressed me greatly.

One was Corporal Herman Whitt, of Enid. Before the war he was a salesman for a biscuit company. He had married a beautiful Indian girl back home. Corporal Whitt was tall, nice-looking, and talked very slowly and softly. He said he felt better about the war, doing this job—caring for the wounded—than if he had to be up front killing people himself.

Our night wardmaster was Corporal Woodrow Cox of Milo. He too was tall, more than six feet; he had been a ranch hand back home, and his voice was almost like a musical instrument. He talked with that snaillike Oklahoma drawl that is so soothing in times of excitement.

The third was Corporal Rodney Benton, of 8030 West Fifth Street, Oklahoma City. It was easy to see the difference between city and country in those boys. Rodney was all git-up-and-git. He talked faster and moved faster than the others. But all three had the same deep conscientiousness about their work and the same compassionate feeling for the wounded. Rodney was one of twins, and his identical brother Robert was a corporal in the division's other clearing station. They were twenty-three years old. Both had had two years of premedical work at the University of Oklahoma and they intended to be doctors. They were in their glory at our clearing stations; in fact they almost drove the doctors nuts asking questions all the time.

The Forty-fifth Division was originally made up largely of men from Oklahoma and West Texas. I didn't realize how different certain parts of our country are from others until I saw those men set off in a frame, as it were, in a strange, faraway place. The men of Oklahoma are drawling and soft-spoken. They are not smart alecks. Something of the purity of the soil seems to be in them. Even their cussing is simpler and more profound than the torrential obscenities of Eastern city men. An Oklahoman of the plains is straight and direct. He is slow to criticize and hard to anger, but once he is convinced of the wrong of something, brother, watch out.

Those wounded Oklahomans were madder about the war than anybody I had seen on that side of the ocean. They weren't so mad before they went into action, but by then the Germans across the hill were all "sonsabitches."

And those men of the Forty-fifth, the newest division over there, had already fought so well they had drawn the high praise of the commanding general of the corps of which the division was a part.

It was those quiet men from the farms, ranches and small towns of Oklahoma who poured through my tent with their wounds. I lay there and listened for what each one would say first.

One fellow, seeing a friend, called out, "I think I'm gonna make her." Meaning he was going to pull through.

A second asked, "Have they got beds in the hospital? Lord, how I want to go to bed."

A third complained, "I'm hungry, but I can't eat anything. I keep getting sick at my stomach."

Another, as he winced from the deep probing for a buried piece of shrapnel in his leg, said, "Go ahead, you're the doc. I can stand it."

A fifth remarked jocularly, "I'll have to write the old lady tonight and tell her she missed out on that ten thousand dollars again."

The youngster who was put down beside me said, "Hi, pop, how you getting along? I call you pop because you're gray-headed. You don't mind, do you?"

I told him I didn't care what he called me. He was friendly, but you could tell from his forward attitude that he was not from Oklahoma. When I asked him, it turned out he came from New Jersey.

One big blond infantryman had slight flesh wounds in the face and the back of his neck. He had a patch on his upper lip which prevented him from moving it, and made him talk in a grave, straight-faced manner that was comical. I've never seen anybody so mad in my life. He went from one doctor to another trying to get somebody to sign his card returning him to duty. The doctors explained patiently that if he returned to the front his wounds would become infected and he would be a burden to his company instead of a help. They tried to entice him by telling him there would be nurses back in the hospital. But in his peaceful Oklahoma drawl he retorted, "To hell with the nurses, I want to get back to fightin'."

Dying men were brought into our tent, men whose death rattle silenced the conversation and made all of us thoughtful. When a man was almost gone, the surgeons would put a piece of gauze over his face. He could breathe through it but we couldn't see his face well.

Twice within five minutes chaplains came running. One of those occasions haunted me for hours. The wounded man was still semiconscious. The chaplain knelt down beside him and two wardboys squatted nearby. The chaplain said, "John, I'm going to say a prayer for you."

Somehow this stark announcement hit me like a hammer. He didn't say, "I'm going to pray for you to get well," he just said he was going to say a prayer, and it was obvious to me that he meant the final prayer. It was as though he had said, "Brother, you may not know it, but your goose is cooked." Anyhow, he voiced the prayer, and the weak, gasping man tried vainly to repeat the words after him. When he had finished, the chaplain added, "John, you're doing fine, you're doing fine." Then he rose and dashed off on some other call, and the wardboys went about their duties.

The dying man was left utterly alone, just lying there on his litter on the ground, lying in an aisle, because the tent was full. Of course it couldn't be otherwise, but the aloneness of that man as he went through the last few minutes of his life was what tormented me. I felt like going over and at least holding his hand while he died, but it would have been out of order and I didn't do it. I wish now I had.

Probably it isn't clear to most people just how the Army's setup for the care of the sick and wounded works on a battlefront. Let's take the medical structure for a whole division. A division runs roughly fifteen thousand men. And almost a thousand of that number are medical men. To begin right at the front, three enlisted medical-aid men go along with every company. They give what first aid they can on the battlefield. Then litter-bearers carry the wounded back to a battalion aid station. Sometimes a wounded man is taken back right away. But at other times he may be pinned down by enemy fire so that the aid men can't get to him, and he will have to lie out there for hours before help comes. Right there is the biggest difficulty and the weakest feature of the Army's medical setup.

Once a soldier is removed from the battlefield his treatment is superb. The battalion aid station is the first of many stops as he is worked to the rear, and ultimately to a hospital. An aid station is merely where the battalion surgeon and his assistant happen to be. It isn't a tent or anything like that—it's just the surgeon's medical chest and a few stretchers under a tree. Each station is staffed by two doctors and thirty-six enlisted men. Frequently it is under fire.

At an aid station a wounded man gets what is immediately necessary, depending on the severity of his wounds. The idea all along the way is to do as little actual surgical work as possible, but at each stop merely to keep a man in good enough condition to stand the trip on back to the hospital, where there are full facilities for any kind of work. For instance, if a soldier's stomach is ripped open the doctors perform an emergency operation right at the front but leave further operating to be done at a hospital. If another man has had his leg shattered by shrapnel, they bind it up in a metal rack, but the operating and setting aren't done till he gets back to the hospital. They use morphine and blood plasma copiously at the forward stations to keep sinking men going. The main underlying motive of all front-line stations is to get patients evacuated quickly and keep the decks clear so they will always have room for any sudden catastrophic run of battle casualties.

From the battalion aid station the wounded are taken by ambulance, jeep, truck or any other means back to a collecting station. The station is a few tents run by five doctors and a hundred enlisted men, anywhere from a quarter of a mile to several miles behind the lines. There is one collecting station for each regiment, making three to a division.

Here are facilities for doing many things the aid station can't do. If the need is urgent, the medics redress wounds and give the men more morphine. Also, they perform quite a lot of operations. Then the men are sent by ambulance back to the clearing station. Some divisions have two clearing stations. Ordinarily, only one works at a time while the other takes a few hours' rest. The second then leapfrogs ahead of the first, sets up its tents and begins receiving patients. In emergencies, both clearing stations work at once, temporarily abandoning their rest-and-leapfrog routine.

All these various crews—the company aid men, the battalion aid station, the collecting station, and the clearing station—are part of the division. They move with it, work when it fights, and rest when it rests.

The clearing station I lay in was really a small hospital. It consisted of five doctors, one dentist, one chaplain, and sixty enlisted men. It was contained in six big tents and a few little ones for the fluoroscope room, the office, and so forth. Everybody slept outdoors on the ground, including the commanding officer. The mess was outdoors under a tree. The station could knock down, move, and set up again in an incredibly short time. They were as proficient as a circus. Once, during a rapid advance, my station moved three times in one day.

Behind the clearing stations the real hospitals begin, the first ones usually forty miles or more to the rear of the fighting. These hospitals are separate units; they belong to no division, but take patients from everywhere.

The farther back they are, the bigger they get, and, in Sicily, patients were evacuated from the hospitals right onto hospital ships and taken back to still bigger hospitals in Africa.

Army ambulances carry four stretchers each, or nine sitting wounded. When they reached our clearing station, they backed up to the surgical tent and unloaded. The men lay there on their stretchers on the floor of the tent while the aid men, in order to handle the worst cases first, looked at their medical tags to see how severe the wounds were. Those who didn't need immediate further attention were carried right on through to the ward tents to wait for the next ambulance going back to a hospital.

Those who had graver wounds were carried into the operating room. Two big army trunks sat upended there on the dirt floor. The trunks contained all kinds of surgical supplies in drawers. On top of each trunk was fastened a steel rod which curved up at each end. The wounded man was carried in his litter and set on these two trunks. The curved rods kept him from sliding off. Thus his litter formed his operating table.

A portable surgical lamp stood in a tripod over the wounded man. A little motor and generator outside the tent furnished power, but usually the doctors just used flashlights. One or two surgeons in coveralls or ordinary uniform bent over the man and removed his dressings. Medical-aid men crowded around behind, using steel forceps to hand the doctors compresses or bandages from a sterile cabinet. Other aid men gave the patient another shot of morphine or injected blood plasma or offered him a drink of water through a rubber tube they put in his mouth.

Just outside the surgical tent was a small trench filled with bloody shirt sleeves and pant legs the surgeons had snipped off wounded men in order to get at the wounds more quickly. The surgeons redressed the wounds, and sprinkled on sulfanilamide powder. Sometimes they poked for buried shrapnel, or recompressed broken arteries to stop the flow of blood.

They didn't give general anesthesia there. Occasionally they gave a local, but usually the wounded man was so doped up with morphine by the time he reached the station that he didn't feel much of anything. The surgeons believed in using lots of morphine. It spares a man so much pain and consequently relieves the general shock to his system.

On my third day at the clearing station, when I was beginning to feel better, I spent most of my time around the operating table. As they undressed each new wound I held firmly to a lamp bracket above my head, for I was still weak and I didn't want to disgrace myself by suddenly keeling over at the sight of a bad wound. Many of the wounds *were* hard to look at, and yet Lieutenant Michael de Giorgio said he had never seen a human body so badly smashed up in Sicily as he had in traffic accidents back in New York, where he used to practice.

One soldier had caught a machine-gun bullet right alongside his nose. It had made a small clean hole and gone clear through his cheek, leaving—as it came out—a larger hole just beneath his ear. It gave me the willies to look at it, yet the doctors said it wasn't serious at all and would heal with no bad effects.

The man with the most nerve was one who had two big holes in his back. I could have put my whole hand in either one of them. As the surgeons worked on him he lay on his stomach and talked a blue streak. "I killed five of the sonsabitches with a hand grenade just before they got me," he said. "What made me so damn mad was that I was just out of reach of my rifle and couldn't crawl over to it, or I'da got five more of them. Jeez, I'm hungry! I ain't had nothing to eat since yesterday morning."

But most of the wounded said nothing at all when brought in— either because they saw no acquaintances to talk to or because they were too weak from their wounds or too dopey from morphine. Of the hundreds that passed through while I was there I heard only one man groan with pain.

Another thing that struck me, as the wounded came through in a ceaseless stream on their stretchers, was how dirt and exhaustion reduce human faces to such a common denominator. Everybody they carried in looked alike. The only break in the procession of identically tired and dirty men would be when an extreme blond was carried in. His light hair would seem like a flower in a row of weeds.

Every day at the front produces its quota of freak wounds and hairbreadth escapes. Almost any wounded man has missed death by a matter of inches. Sometimes a bullet can go clear through a man and not hurt him much, while at other times an infinitesimal fragment of a shell can pick out one tiny vital spot and kill him. Bullets and fragments do crazy things. Our surgeons picked out more than two hundred pieces of shrapnel from one man. There was hardly a square inch of him, from head to toe, that wasn't touched. Yet none of them made a vital hit, and the soldier lived.

I remember one soldier who had a hole in the front of his leg just below the hip. It was about the size of a half dollar. It didn't look bad at all, yet beneath that little wound the leg bone was shattered and arteries were severed, and the surgeons were working hard to get the arteries closed so he wouldn't bleed to death.

Another had caught a small shell fragment in the wrist. It had entered at a shallow angle and gone clear up the arm to the elbow, and remained buried there. The skin wasn't even broken at the elbow, but right over the spot where the fragment stopped was a blister as big as a pigeon's egg. The blister had been raised by the terrific heat of that tiny piece of metal.

That's one thing most people don't realize—that fragments from bursting shells are white-hot. During the air raid just before our ship left Africa, a heavy bomb had burst about a hundred yards away. Among the many fragments that hit our ship was one about half as big as a tennis ball. It first struck a bronze water pipe along the ship's rail, then tore through a steel bulkhead into the radio room, wounded a sailor in the shoulder, turned at right angles and went through a radio set, and finally shot through one more steel bulkhead before it stopped.

When we picked up the fragment it had a quarter-inch plate of solid bronze on one side of it. The fragment's intense heat had simply welded on a sheet of bronze as it went through the water pipe at the rail. It was as solid as though it had been done on purpose.

There in northern Sicily it was all hill fighting, as it had been in northern Tunisia, only worse. Getting the wounded out was often a problem. We had one wounded man who had been lowered by ropes over a sheer 75-foot cliff. He said he wasn't so concerned about his wounds, but the thought that maybe the rope would break gave him the worst scare of his life.

German medical facilities were apparently as good as ours. Captured medical supply dumps showed that they were well-stocked with the finest stuff. We knew that their system for collecting their wounded and burying their dead was efficient, for it was only after the most sudden and rapid advances on our part that we found their dead unburied.

We also captured several big Italian medical dumps. Our doctors found our surgical instruments far superior to the Italians', but both the Germans and the Italians had bandages and compresses that were better than ours.

There were many kinds of human beings among the wounded in our clearing-station tent during the time I spent there.

We had a couple of slightly wounded Puerto Ricans, one of whom still carried his guitar and sat up on his stretcher and strummed lightly on it. There were full-blooded Indians, and Negroes, and New York Italians, and plain American ranch hands, and Spanish Americans from down Mexico way. There were local Sicilians who had been hit by trucks. There was a captured Italian soldier who said his own officers had shot him in the face for refusing to attack. There were two American aviators who had been fished out of the sea. There were some of our own medics who had been wounded as they worked under shellfire.

There was even one German soldier, who had been shot apparently while trying to escape to Italy in a small boat. He was young, thin, scared to death, and objected furiously to being given a shot of morphine. He seemed to think we were torturing him. When he finally discovered he was being treated exactly like everybody else, his amazement grew. I could see bewilderment and gratitude in his face when the wardboys brought him water and then food. And when at last the chaplain, making his morning rounds, gave him cigarettes, candy, tooth powder and soap, the same as all the rest, he sat up grinning and played with them as though he were a child on Christmas morning. It took him five minutes to find out how to get the cellophane wrapper off his pack of cigarettes, and our whole tent stopped to watch in amusement.

Some of the wounded were sick at the stomach. One tough-looking New York Italian, faint with malaria, tried to crawl outside the tent to be sick but passed out cold on the way. He was lying there on the ground in his drawers, yellow as death, when we noticed him. He was carried back, and ten minutes later was all over his sudden attack and as chipper as anybody.

Other men were as hungry as bears. Still others couldn't eat a bite. One fellow, with his shattered arm sticking up at right angles in its metal rack, gobbled chicken-noodle soup which a wardboy fed him while the doctor punched and probed at his other arm to insert the big needle that feeds blood plasma.

That front-line clearing station was made up of doctors and men who were ordinary, normal people back home. The station commandant was Captain Carl Carrico of 2408 Reba Drive, Houston, Texas. His wife and eight-year-old boy were in Houston. He was a slow, friendly man, speckled all over with big red freckles. He took his turn at surgery along with the others, usually wearing coveralls. The other surgeons were Captain Carson Oglesbee, of Muskogee, Oklahoma, Captain Leander Powers, of Savannah, Georgia, Captain William Dugan, of Hamburg, New York, and Lieutenant Michael de Giorgio, New York. The station's medical doctor was Captain Joe Doran, of Iowa City, and the dentist was Captain Leonard Cheek, of Ada, Oklahoma.

These men lived a rough-and-tumble life. They slept on the ground, worked ghastly hours, were sometimes under fire, and handled a flow of wounded that would sicken and dishearten a person less immune to it. Time and again as I lay in my tent I heard wounded soldiers discussing among themselves the wonderful treatment they had had at the hands of the medics. They'll get little glory back home when it's all over, but they had some recompense right there in the gratitude of the men they treated.

SIX

THE ENGINEERS' WAR

During the latter days of the Sicilian campaign, I spent all my time with the combat engineers of two different divisions. The engineers were in it up to their ears. Scores of times during the Sicilian fighting I heard everybody from generals to privates remark that "This is certainly an engineers' war." And indeed it was. Every foot of our advance upon the gradually withdrawing enemy was measured by the speed with which our engineers could open the highways, clear the mines, and bypass the blown bridges.

Northeastern Sicily, where the mountains are close together and the valleys are steep and narrow, was ideal country for withdrawing, and the Germans made full use of it. They blew almost every bridge they crossed. In the American area alone they destroyed nearly 160 bridges. They mined the bypasses around the bridges, they mined the beaches, they even mined orchards and groves of trees that would be logical bivouacs for our troops.

All this didn't fatally delay us, but it did give the Germans time for considerable escaping. The average blown bridge was fairly easy to bypass and we'd have the mines cleared and a rough trail gouged out by a bulldozer within a couple of hours; but now and then they'd pick a lulu of a spot which would take anywhere up to twenty-four hours to get around. And in reading of the work of these engineers you must understand that a 24-hour job over there would take many days in normal construction practice. The mine detector and the bulldozer were the two magic instruments of our engineering. As one sergeant said, "This has been a bulldozer campaign."

In Sicily, our Army would have been as helpless without the bulldozer as it would have been without the jeep. The bridges in Sicily were blown much more completely than they were in Tunisia. Back there they'd just drop one span with explosives. But in Sicily they'd blow down the whole damned bridge, from abutment to abutment. They used as high as a thousand pounds of explosives to a bridge, and on one long, seven-span bridge they blew all seven spans. It was really senseless, and the pure waste of the thing outraged our engineers. Knocking down one or two spans would have delayed us just as much as destroying all of them.

The bridges of Sicily were graceful and beautiful old arches of stone or of brick-faced rubble fill, and shattering them so completely was something like chopping down a shade tree or defacing a church. They'll all have to be rebuilt after the war and it's going to take a lot more money to replace all those hundreds of spans than was really necessary. But I suppose the Germans and Italians figured dear old Uncle Sam would pay for it all, anyhow, so they might as well have their fun.

Frequently the Germans, by blowing up a road carved out of the side of a sheer cliff, caused us more trouble than by bridge-blowing. In those instances, it was often impossible to bypass at all, so traffic had to be held up until an emergency bridge could be thrown across the gap.

Once in a while we would come to a bridge that hadn't been blown. Usually that was because the river bed was so flat, and bypassing so easy, it wasn't worth wasting explosives. Driving across an occasional whole bridge used to make me feel queer, almost immoral. There was even one whole bridge the Germans didn't count on our having. They had it all prepared for blowing and left one man behind to set off the charge at the last moment. But he never got it done. Our advance patrols spotted him and shot him dead.

The Germans were also more prodigal with mines in Sicily than they had been in Tunisia. Engineers of the Forty-fifth Division found one mine field, covering six acres, containing eight hundred mines. Our losses from mines were fairly heavy, especially among officers. They scouted ahead to survey demolitions, and ran into mines before the detecting parties got there.

The enemy hit two high spots in their demolition and mine-planting. One was when they dropped a fifty-yard strip of cliff-ledge coast road, overhanging the sea—with no possible way of bypassing. The other was when they planted mines along the road that crosses the lava beds in the foothills north of Mount Etna. The metal in the lava threw our mine detectors helter-skelter, and we had a terrible time finding the mines.

Sicily was known to be short of water in summertime, so our invasion forces brought enough water with them to last five days. In the case of the Forty-fifth Division, this amounted to 155,000 gallons, transported both in tanks and in individual five-gallon cans. There were three ships with tanks of 10,000 gallons each. On the transports there were 125,000 gallons, all in five-gallon cans. That meant that this one division brought with it from Africa 25,000 cans of water. And other divisions did the same.

Actually we didn't have as much trouble finding water as we'd expected, and we needn't have brought so much with us, but you never know. Napoleon said an army marches on its stomach, but I think you could almost say an army marches on its water. Without water you're sunk. (As an old punster, how in the hell can you sink without water?)

Throughout the Sicilian campaign, the Forty-fifth Division used about 50,000 gallons of water a day, or two gallons per man. Just as a comparison, the daily water consumption in Las Vegas, New Mexico, a city of 12,000, is a million gallons a day, or almost a hundred gallons a person. Although the difference seems fantastic, still our troops used more than absolutely necessary, for an army can exist and fight on one gallon a day per man.

It fell to the engineers to provide water for the Army. Engineer officers scouted the country right behind the retiring enemy, looking for watering places. They always kept three water points set up constantly for each division—one for each of the three regiments— and usually a couple of extra ones. When a water point was found, the engineers wheeled in their portable purifying unit. This consisted of a motorized pump, a sand filter, a chlorinating machine, and a collapsible 3,000-gallon canvas tank which stood about shoulder-high when put up. Purified water was pumped into this canvas tank. Then all day and all night vehicles of the regiment from miles around lined up and filled their cans, tanks, and radiators.

Painted signs saying "Water Point," with an arrow pointing the direction, were staked along the roads for miles around.

The sources of our water in Sicily were mainly wells, mountain springs, little streams, shell craters, and irrigation ditches. The engineers of the Forty-fifth Division found one shell crater that contained a broken water main, and the seepage into this crater provided water for days. They also discovered that some of Sicily's dry river beds had underground streams flowing beneath them, and by drilling down a few feet they could pump up all they needed.

Another time they put pumps into a tiny little irrigation ditch only four inches deep and a foot wide. You wouldn't have thought it would furnish enough water for a mule, yet it kept flowing and carried them safely through.

In their municipal water system the Sicilians used everything from modern twenty-inch cast-iron pipe down to primitive earthen aqueducts still surviving from Roman days. But our engineers made it a practice not to tap the local water supplies. We made a good many friends that way, for the Sicilians said the Germans used no such delicacy. In fact we leaned over the other way, and furnished water to scores of thousands of Sicilians whose supply had been shattered by bombing.

It didn't make much difference what condition the water was in when we found it, for it was pumped through the filter machine and this took out the sediment. Then purifying substances were shot in as it passed through the pumps. The chlorine we injected came in powder form in one-gallon cans. We generally used one part of chlorine to a million parts of water. The Forty-fifth's engineers had brought with them enough chlorine to last six months. In addition to chlorine, alum and soda ash were injected into the water. After a while we didn't even notice the odd taste.

The Forty-fifth also brought along six complete water-purifying units and also a unit for distilling drinking water out of sea water. The latter never had to be used.

When he marches or goes into battle, an infantryman usually carries two canteens instead of one, but there in the hot summer it wasn't unusual at all to see a soldier carrying six canteens tied to the end of a leather strap like a bunch of grapes—half his canteens being captured Italian ones covered with gray felt for keeping the water cool.

And, I might add out of the side of my mouth, if a person had got real nosey he might have discovered that a couple of those canteens, instead of holding our beautiful pure water, were bearing a strange red fluid known colloquially as "vino," to be used, no doubt, for rubbing on fleabites.

I lived for a while on the Sicilian front with the 120th Engineers Battalion, attached to the Forty-fifth Division. The bulk of the 120th hailed from my adopted state of New Mexico. They were part of the old New Mexico outfit, most of which was lost on Bataan. It was good to get back to those slow-talking, wise and easy people of the desert, and good to speak of places like Las Cruces, Socorro, and Santa Rosa. It was good to find somebody who lived within sight of my own picket fence on the mesa.

The 120th was made up of Spanish Americans, Indians, straight New Mexicans, and a smattering of men from the East. It was commanded by Lieutenant Colonel Lewis Frantz, who was superintendent of the Las Vegas (New Mexico) Light and Power Company before entering service. Colonel Frantz had then been in the Army for three years and had not been home during all that time. The Forty-fifth Division spent nearly two and a half years in training, and everybody almost went nuts thinking they'd never get overseas.

The strangest case of self-consciousness along that line that I'd run into was Captain Waldo Lowe of Las Cruces. He had had a chance to go home on furlough the previous Christmas, but didn't because he was ashamed to be seen at home after spending two years in the Army and still not getting out of the United States. Then after he had leaped the overseas hurdle and felt qualified, to go home he couldn't get there, of course.

The executive officer of the unit was Major Jerry Hines, for many years athletic director of the New Mexico Aggies. Major Hines was expecting a football player in his family about mid-September. He said he hoped to get home in time to see him graduated from college.

Two of my Albuquerque home-towners were Captain James Bezemek, 2003 North 4th Street, whose father was county treasurer there, and Captain Richard Strong, 113 Harvard Street.

Captain Strong was company commander when I saw him, but shortly after was promoted to the battalion staff. He and his two sergeants had one of the narrowest escapes in the battalion when their jeep (which they'd abandoned for a magnificent ditch about two seconds before) got a direct hit from an "88" and blew all to pieces. The sergeants were Martin Quintana, who used to be a machinist for the Santa Fe at Albuquerque, and John W. Trujillo, of Socorro.

A few days later, a similar narrow escape happened to Captain Ben Billups, of Alamogordo, when his brand-new amphibious jeep which he'd had just one day was hit and burned up. I would have been with him if I hadn't got sick and gone to the hospital that morning.

It's a smart guy who knows just when to get sick.

The unit's losses from mines and shellfire were moderately heavy. Colonel Frantz estimated that half their work had been done under at least spasmodic shellfire, and at one time his engineers were eight and a half miles out ahead of the infantry.

The colonel himself was a big, drawling, typical Southwesterner whose stamina amazed everybody, for he was no spring chicken. During the critical periods he would be on the go till 4 a.m., snatch a couple of hours' sleep on the ground, and be off again at seven.

In action, the officers just flopped down on the hard rocky ground like everybody else, but when they went into reserve they fixed up bedrolls on smooth places under trees, with blankets and mosquito nets. In fact a few of the battalion officers sported the luxury of white silk sheets. They found a torn parachute and, for the price of some canned food, got a Sicilian woman to cut it up and sew it into sheets for them.

A large percentage of the battalion spoke Spanish, and occasionally I heard some of the officers talking Spanish among themselves, just to keep in practice, I suppose. That New Mexico bunch missed more than anything, I believe, the Spanish dishes they were accustomed to back home. Their folks occasionally sent them cans of chili and peppers, and then they had a minor feast. Captain Pete Erwin, of Las Vegas and Santa Fe, had a quart of chicos—New Mexico dried corn—which he was saving for Christmas dinner.

You may seldom have seen it mentioned, but a map is as common a piece of equipment among front-line officers as a steel helmet. A combat officer would be absolutely useless without his map.

It is the job of the engineers to handle the maps for each division. Just as soon as a division advances to the edge of the territory covered by its maps, the map officer has to dig into his portable warehouse and fish out thousands of new maps. The immensity of the map program would amaze you. When they went to Sicily, the Forty-fifth Division brought along eighty-three tons of Sicilian maps! I forgot to ask how many individual maps that was, but it would surely run close to half a million.

The Forty-fifth's maps were far superior to any we'd been using and here's the reason: Formerly our maps were essentially based on old Italian maps. Then for months ahead of the invasion our reconnaissance planes flew over Sicily taking photographs. These photos were immediately flown across the Atlantic to Washington. There, if anything new was discovered in the photographs, it was superimposed on the maps.

They kept this process of correction open right up to the last minute. The Forty-fifth sailed from America only a short time before we invaded Sicily, and in the last week the Map Section in Washington printed, placed in waterproofed cases, and delivered to the boats those eighty-three tons of maps, hot off the presses.

The 120th Engineers went back into antiquity to solve one of their jobs. They were scouting for a bypass around a blown bridge when they stumbled onto a Roman stone road, centuries old. It had been long unused and was nearly covered with sand grass. They cleaned up the old highway, and used it for a mile and a half. If it hadn't been for this antique road, it would have taken 400 men 12 hours to build a bypass. By using it, the job was done in 4 hours by 150 men.

The engineers were very careful throughout the campaign about tearing up native property. They used much extra labor and time to avoid damaging orchards, buildings or vineyards. Sometimes they'd build a road clear around an orchard rather than through it. Consideration like this helped make us many friends.

I met a bulldozer driver who operated his huge, clumsy machine with such utter skill that it was like watching a magician do card tricks. The driver was Joseph Compagnone, of 14 Middle Street, Newton, Massachusetts. He was an Italian who had emigrated to America about seven years before, when he was sixteen years old. He was all American when I met him. A brother of his in the Italian Army had been captured by the British in Egypt. His mother and sisters lived near Naples, and he hoped to see them before the war was over. I asked Joe if he had a funny feeling about fighting his own people and he said, "No, I guess we've got to fight somebody and it might as well be them as anybody else."

Compagnone had been a "cat" driver ever since he started working. I sat and watched him for two hours one afternoon while he ate away a rocky bank overhanging a blown road, and worked the stone into the huge hole until the road was ready for traffic again. He was so astonishingly adept at manipulating the big machine that groups of soldiers and officers gathered at the crater's edge to admire and comment.

Joe had one close shave. He was bulldozing a bypass around a blown bridge when the blade of his machine hit a mine. The explosion blew him off and stunned him, but he was not wounded. The driverless dozer continued to run and drove itself over a fifty-foot cliff, turning a somersault as it fell. It landed right side up with the engine still going.

Our troops along the coast occasionally got a chance to bathe in the Mediterranean. (As an incidental statistic, during the campaign the engineers cleared mines off a total of seven miles of beaches just so the soldiers could get down to the water to swim.) Up in the mountains I saw hundreds of soldiers, stark-naked, bathing in Sicilian horse troughs or out of their steel helmets. The American soldier has a fundamental complex about bodily cleanliness which is considered all nonsense by us philosophers of the Great Unwashed, which includes Arabs, Sicilians and me.

When the Forty-fifth Division went into reserve along the north coast of Sicily after several weeks of hard fighting, I moved on with the Third Division, which took up the ax and drove the enemy on to Messina.

It was on my very first day with the Third that we hit the most difficult and spectacular engineering job of the Sicilian campaign. You may remember Point Calava from the newspaper maps. It is a great stub of rock that sticks out into the sea, forming a high ridge running back into the interior. The coast highway is tunneled through this big rock, and on either side of the tunnel the road sticks out like a shelf on the sheer rock wall. Our engineers figured the Germans would blow the tunnel entrance to seal it up. But they didn't. They had an even better idea. They picked out a spot about fifty feet beyond the tunnel mouth and blew a hole 150 feet long in the road shelf. They blew it so deeply and thoroughly that a stone dropped into it would never have stopped rolling until it bounced into the sea a couple of hundred feet below.

We were beautifully bottlenecked. We couldn't bypass around the rock, for it dropped sheer into the sea. We couldn't bypass over the mountain; that would have taken weeks. We couldn't fill the hole, for the fill would keep sliding off into the water.

All the engineers could do was bridge it, and that was a hell of a job. But bridge it they did, and in only twenty-four hours.

When the first engineer officers went up to inspect the tunnel, I went with them. We had to leave the jeep at a blown bridge and walk the last four miles uphill. We went with an infantry battalion that was following the retreating Germans.

When we got there we found the tunnel floor mined. But each spot where they'd dug into the hard rock floor left its telltale mark, so it was no job for the engineers to uncover and unscrew the detonators of scores of mines. Then we went on through to the vast hole beyond, and the engineering officers began making their calculations.

As they did so, the regiment of infantry crawled across the chasm, one man at a time. A man could just barely make it on foot by holding on to the rock juttings and practically crawling. Then another regiment, with only what weapons and provisions they could carry on their backs, went up over the ridge and took out after the evacuating enemy. Before another twenty-four hours, the two regiments would be twenty miles ahead of us and in contact with the enemy, so getting that hole bridged and supplies and supporting guns to them was indeed a matter of life and death.

It was around 2 p.m. when we got there and in two hours the little platform of highway at the crater mouth resembled a littered street in front of a burning building. Air hoses covered the ground, serpentined over each other. Three big air compressors were parked side by side, their engines cutting off and on in that erratically deliberate manner of air compressors, and jackhammers clattered their nerve-shattering din.

Bulldozers came to clear off the stone-blocked highway at the crater edge. Trucks, with long trailers bearing railroad irons and huge timbers, came and unloaded. Steel cable was brought up, and kegs of spikes, and all kinds of crowbars and sledges.

The thousands of vehicles of the division were halted some ten miles back in order to keep the highway clear for the engineers. One platoon of men at a time worked in the hole. There was no use throwing in the whole company, for there was room for only so many.

At suppertime, hot rations were brought up by truck. The Third Division engineers went on K ration at noon but morning and evening hot food was got up to them, regardless of the difficulty. For men working the way those boys were, the hot food was a military necessity. By dusk the work was in full swing and half the men were stripped to the waist.

The night air of the Mediterranean was tropical. The moon came out at twilight and extended our light for a little while. The moon was still new and pale, and transient, high-flying clouds brushed it and scattered shadows down on us. Then its frail light went out, and the blinding nightlong darkness settled over the grim abyss. But the work never slowed nor halted throughout the night.

The other men of the Third Division didn't just sit and twiddle their thumbs while all this was going on. The infantry continued to get across on foot and follow after the Germans. Some supplies and guns were sent around the road block by boat, and even some of the engineers themselves continued on ahead by boat. They had discovered other craters blown in the road several miles ahead. These were smaller ones that could be filled in by a bulldozer except that they couldn't get a bulldozer across that vast hole they were trying to bridge. So the engineers commandeered two little Sicilian fishing boats about twice the size of rowboats. They lashed them together, nailed planking across them, and ran the bulldozer onto this improvised barge. They tied an amphibious jeep in front of it, and went chugging around Point Calava at about one mile an hour.

As we looked down at them laboring along so slowly, Lieutenant

Colonel Leonard Bingham, commanding officer of the Third Division's 10th Engineers, grinned and said, "There goes the engineers' homemade Navy."

During the night the real Navy had carried forward supplies and guns in armed landing craft. These were the cause of a funny incident around midnight. Our engineers had drilled and laid blasting charges to blow off part of the rock wall that overhung the Point Calava crater.

When all was ready, everybody went back in the tunnel to get out of the way. When the blast went off, the whole mountain shook and we quivered too—with positive belief that the tunnel was coming down. The noise there in the silent night was shocking.

Now just as this happened, a small fleet of naval craft was passing in the darkness, just offshore. The sudden blast alarmed them. They apparently thought they were being fired upon from the shore. For just as our men were returning to their work at the crater edge, there came ringing up from the dark water below, so clear it sounded like an execution order, the resounding naval command, "Prepare to return fire."

Boy, you should have seen our men scatter! They hit the ground and scampered back into the tunnel as though Stukas were diving on them. We don't know to this day exactly what happened out there, but we do know the Navy never did fire.

Around 10:30 Major General Lucian Truscott, commanding the Third Division, came up to see how the work was coming along. Bridging that hole was his main interest in life right then. He couldn't help any, of course, but somehow he couldn't bear to leave. He stood around and talked to officers, and after a while he went off a few feet to one side and sat down on the ground and lit a cigarette.

A moment later, a passing soldier saw the glow and leaned over and said, "Hey, gimme a light, will you?" The general did and the soldier never knew he had been ordering the general around.

General Truscott, like many men of great action, had the ability to refresh himself by tiny catnaps of five or ten minutes. So instead of going back to his command post and going to bed, he stretched out there against some rocks and dozed off. One of the working engineers came past, dragging some air hose. It got tangled up in the general's feet. The tired soldier was annoyed, and he said crossly to the dark, anonymous figure on the ground, "If you're not working, get the hell out of the way."

The general got up and moved farther back without saying a word.

The men worked on and on, and every one of the company officers stayed throughout the night just to be there to make decisions when difficulties arose. But I got so sleepy I couldn't stand it, and I caught a commuting truck back to the company camp and turned in. An hour before daylight I heard them rout out a platoon that had been resting. They ate breakfast noisily, loaded into trucks, and were off just at dawn. A little later three truckloads of tired men pulled into camp, gobbled some breakfast, and fell into their blankets on the ground. The feverish attack on that vital highway obstruction had not lagged a moment during the whole night.

It wasn't long after dawn when I returned to the crater. At first glance it didn't look as though much had been accomplished, but an engineer's eye would have seen that the groundwork was all laid. They had drilled and blasted two holes far down the jagged slope. These were to hold the heavy uprights so they wouldn't slide downhill when weight was applied. The far side of the crater had been blasted out and leveled off so it formed a road across about one-third of the hole. Small ledges had been jackhammered at each end of the crater and timbers bolted into them, forming abutments of the bridge that was to come. Steel hooks had been embedded deep in the rock to hold wire cables. At the tunnel mouth lay great timbers, two feet square, and other big lengths of timber bolted together to make them long enough to span the hole.

At about 10 a.m. the huge uprights were slid down the bank, caught by a group of men clinging to the steep slope below, and their ends worked into the blasted holes. Then the uprights were brought into place by men on the banks, pulling on ropes tied to the timbers. Similar heavy beams were slowly and cautiously worked out from the bank until their tops rested on the uprights.

A half-naked soldier, doing practically a wire-walking act, edged out over the timber and with an air-driven bit bored a long hole down through two timbers. Then he hammered a steel rod into it, tying them together. Others added more bracing, nailing the parts together with huge spikes driven in by sledge hammers. Then the engineers slung steel cable from one end of the crater to the other, wrapped it around the upright stanchions and drew it tight with a winch mounted on a truck.

Now came a Chinese coolie scene as shirtless, sweating soldiers—twenty men to each of the long, spliced timbers—carried and slid their burdens out across the chasm, resting them on the two wooden spans just erected. They sagged in the middle, but still the cable beneath took most of the strain. They laid ten of the big timbers across and the bridge began to take shape. Big stringers were bolted down, heavy flooring was carried on and nailed to the stringers. Men built up the approaches with stones. The bridge was almost ready.

Around 11 a.m., jeeps had begun to line up at the far end of the tunnel. They carried reconnaissance platoons, machine gunners and boxes of ammunition. They'd been given No. 1 priority to cross the bridge. Major General Truscott arrived again and sat on a log talking with the engineering officers, waiting patiently. Around dusk of the day before, the engineers had told me they'd have jeeps across the crater by noon of the next day. It didn't seem possible at the time, but they knew whereof they spoke. But even they would have had to admit it was pure coincidence that the first jeep rolled cautiously across the bridge at high noon, to the very second.

In that first jeep were General Truscott and his driver, facing a 200-foot tumble into the sea if the bridge gave way. The engineers had insisted they send a test jeep across first. But when he saw it was ready, the general just got in and went. It wasn't done dramatically but it was a dramatic thing. It showed that the Old Man had complete faith in his engineers. I heard soldiers speak of it appreciatively for an hour.

Jeeps snaked across the rickety bridge behind the general while the engineers kept stations beneath the bridge to watch and measure the sag under each load. The bridge squeaked and bent as the jeeps crept over. But it held, and nothing else mattered. When the vital spearhead of the division got across, traffic was halted again and the engineers were given three hours to strengthen the bridge for heavier traffic. A third heavy upright inserted in the middle of the span would do the trick.

That, too, was a terrific job, but at exactly 4 p.m. the first 34-ton truck rolled across. They kept putting over heavier and heavier loads until before dark a giant bulldozer was sent across, and after that everything could follow.

The tired men began to pack their tools into trucks. Engineer officers who hadn't slept for thirty-six hours went back to their olive orchard to clean up. They had built a jerry bridge, a comical bridge, a proud bridge, but above all the kind of bridge that wins wars. And they had built it in one night and half a day. The general was mighty pleased.

I don't know what it is that impels some men, either in peace or in wartime, to extend themselves beyond all expectation, or what holds other men back to do just as little as possible. In any group of soldiers you'll find both kinds. The work of combat engineers usually comes in spurts, and it is so vital when it does come that the percentage of fast workers is probably higher than in most other branches. I've never seen men work any harder than the engineers I was with. On the Point Calava road crater job there were two men I couldn't take my eyes off. They worked like demons. Both were corporals and had little to gain by their extraordinary labors, except maybe some slight future promotion. And I doubt that's what drove them. Such men must be impelled by the natures they're born with—by pride in their job, by that mystic spark which forces some men to give all they've got, all the time.

Those two men were Gordon Uttech, of Merrill, Wisconsin, and Alvin Tolliver, of Alamosa, Colorado. Both were air-compressor operators and rock drillers. Uttech worked all night, and when the night shift was relieved for breakfast, he refused to go. He worked on throughout the day without sleep and in the final hours of the job he went down under the frail bridge to check the sag and strain, as heavier and heavier vehicles passed over it.

Tolliver, too, worked without ceasing, never resting, never even stopping to wipe off the sweat that made his stripped body look as though it were coated with olive oil. I never saw him stop once throughout the day. He seemed to work without instruction from anybody, knowing what jobs to do and doing them alone. He wrastled the great chattering jackhammers into the rock. He spread and rewound his air hose. He changed drills. He regulated his compressor. He drove eye-hooks into the rock, chopped down big planks to fit the rocky ledge he'd created. Always he worked as though the outcome of the war depended on him alone.

I couldn't help being proud of those men, who gave more than was asked.

Lieutenant Colonel Leonard Bingham, commander of the 10th Engineers, who bridged the Point Calava crater, was a Regular Army man and therefore his home was wherever he was, but his wife lived in St. Paul, at 1480 Fairmount Avenue, so he called that home. We usually picture Regular Army officers as cut in a harsh and rigid cast, but that has not been my experience. I've found them to be as human as anybody else and the closer I got to the front the finer they seemed to be. Colonel Bingham, for instance, was the kind of man who was so liked and respected by his subordinates that they took me aside to ask that I give him credit. He worked all night along with the rest, and he never got cross or raised his voice.

The commander of the company was Lieutenant Edwin Swift, of Rocky Ford, Colorado. In civil life he was a geophysicist, and just before the war he spent two years in Venezuela with Standard Oil. He hadn't discovered oil in Sicily, but some German-blown holes he filled were almost deep enough to hit oil.

Lieutenant Robert Springmeyer was from Provo, Utah. He was an engineer by profession and a recent father. When he got the parental news, he somehow managed to buy a box of cigars, but he ran out of recipients when the box was about half gone. So thereafter, when a hard day's work was done, he would go back to base, shave, take a helmet bath, put on clean clothes, sit down against a tree and light a big gift cigar in his own honor.

Lieutenant Gilmore Reid came from 846 North Hamilton, Indianapolis. His dad ran the Purity Cone & Chip Company, which made potato chips. Young Reid was an artist and also a railroad hobbyist. He studied railroads with the same verve that some people show in collecting stamps. He once did a painting of a freight train at a small midwestern station, and when he got word over-

seas that it had been printed in color in a railroad magazine he
felt he'd practically reached the zenith of his heart's desire.

The backbone of any Army company is the first sergeant. The
10th Engineers had a beaut. His name was, of all things, Adelard
Levesque. He pronounced it "Levek" but the soldiers called him
"Pop." He was forty-two years old, but didn't begin to look it.
Of all the thousands of men I've met in the Army, he comes the
nearest to being the fictional version of the tough, competent,
old-line first sergeant. Levesque was in the last war as a mere
boy. He fought in France and stayed on with the Army of Occupation in Germany until 1921. He wasn't a Regular Army man.
Between wars he spent twenty years out in the big world, raising
a family, making a living, and seeing and doing things. He had
been a West Coast iron worker and practically anything else you
can mention. He had four sons in the Army and, if I remember
correctly, one daughter in the Navy.

The sergeant called Marysville, California, his home. He was
a ruggedly handsome fellow with a black mustache and clothes
that were always neat, even when dirty. His energy never ran down.
He talked loud, and continuously; he cussed fluently, and he ordered everybody around, including officers.

At first my mouth hung open in amazement but gradually I
began to catch the spirit of Levesque. He wasn't smart-alecky or
fresh. He was just a natural-born center of any stage, a leader,
and one of those gifted, practical men who could do anything
under the sun, and usually did it better than the next fellow. To
top it all off he spoke perfect French and was picking up Italian
like a snowball. One of his commanders told me, "He talks too
much and too big, but he can back up every word he says. I sure
hope we never lose him."

I asked the enlisted men about him, since they were the ones
his tongue fell on most heavily. One man said, "Hell, I don't know
what this company would do without him. Sure he talks all the
time, but we don't pay any attention. Listen at him beatin' his
gums now. He musta got out on the wrong side of the bed this
morning."

Actually, the sergeant wasn't so ferocious. He was widely informed, and his grammar was excellent. He could discuss politics

as well as bulldozers and was alert to every little thing that went
on. One day on a mountain road he stopped our jeep and asked
the driver some questions. As he walked back to his own jeep,
he turned and ordered my driver, "Go get those maps. Send a
bulldozer back up here. Bring five gallons of gas, and get your
spare tire fixed. Goddammit, why don't you take care of your
vehicle?"

"Spare tire?" the driver asked.

"Yes, goddammit," the sergeant roared. "It's flat."

He had discovered it merely by the slight pressure of his hand
as he leaned against it while talking to us. Everything he did was
like that.

During the last half hour of work on the Point Calava bridge,
I saw as fine a drama as ever I paid $8.80 a seat for in New York:
The bridge was almost finished. The climax of twenty-four hours
of frenzied work had come. The job was done. Only one man
could do the final touches of bracing and balancing. That man
was sitting on the end of a beam far out over the chasm, a hammer in his hand, his legs wrapped around the beam as though he
were riding a bronco.

The squirrel out there on the beam was, of course, Sergeant
Levesque. He wore his steel helmet and his pack harness. He
never took it off, no matter what the weather or what he was doing.
His face was dirty and grave and sweating. He was in complete
charge of all he surveyed. On the opposite bank of the 5 crater,
two huge soldier audiences stood watching that noisily profane
craftsman play out his role.

Their preoccupation was a tribute to his skill. I've never seen
a more intent audience. It included all ranks, from privates to
generals.

"Gimme some slack. Gimme some slack, goddammit," the sergeant yelled to the winch man on the bank. "That's enough—hold
it. Throw me a sledge. Where the hell's a spike, goddammit? Hasn't
anybody got a spike?

"How does that look from the bank now, Colonel? She about
level? Okay, slack away. Watch that air hose. Let her clear down.
Hey, you under there, watch yourself, goddammit."

Sergeant Levesque drove the final spike deeply with his sledge.
He looked around at his work and found it finished.

With an air of completion, he clambered to his feet and walked the narrow beam back to safety. You could almost sense the curtain going down, and I know everybody in the crowd had to stifle an impulse to cheer.

If somebody writes another *What Price Glory?* after this war I know who should play the leading role. Who? Why, Sergeant Levesque, goddammit, who do you suppose?

SEVEN

CAMPAIGNING

At one time in central Sicily we correspondents were camped in a peach orchard behind the country home of an Italian baron. Apparently the baron had skedaddled, as royalty has been known to do, before the fighting started. Anyhow, the baron had built himself a big stone house that was pink and palatial, with a marvelous view over miles of rolling country. It had the usual royal peacocks strutting around but not a bath in the place. The dining-room ceiling was hand-painted and the staircase gigantic, yet the royal family used porcelain washbowls and old-fashioned thundermugs. It was the perfect shabby rococo domicile of what H. R. Knickerbocker calls the "wretched aristocracy of Europe."

While the baron lived in this comparative luxury his employees lived in sheds and even caves in the big rocky hill just back of the house. They looked like gypsies.

German and Italian troops had been occupying the place before we came. When we arrived, the interior of the castle was a wreck. I've never seen such a complete shambles. Every room was knee-deep in debris. The enemy had thoroughly looted the place before fleeing. And servants gave us the shameful news that most of the looting and destruction was done by Italian soldiers rather than German. They'd gone through the house shelf by shelf, drawer by drawer. Expensive dishes were thrown on the tile floor, antique vases shattered, women's clothes dumped in jumbled heaps, pictures torn down, medicine cabinets dashed against walls, dressers broken up, wine bottles dropped on the floor, their contents turning the trash heap into a gooey mass as it dried.

It was truly the work of beasts. We tiptoed into the place gingerly, suspecting booby traps, but finally decided it had not been fixed up. Then some of us rummaged around the debris to see if anything left was worth taking as souvenirs. As far as I have observed, Americans have been good about not looting. Usually they take only what is left from the Germans' and Italians' destruction or what the inhabitants voluntarily give them. All I could salvage was a few pieces of lace I found on the baroness's sewing-room floor.

Then we decided the dining room was the least messy place in the building, so we set to with grass brooms and shovels and water and cleaned it up. Thus it became our press room. The Signal Corps ran wires from a portable generator to give us light so we could work by night.

One day while I was writing in there and all the other correspondents were away, a stray soldier peered in at me after having wandered with astonishment through the jumbled house.

He asked, "What is this place?"

I told him it was the former home of an Italian baron. His next question was so typically American I had to laugh despite a little shame at the average soldier's bad grammar and lack of learning.

He said, "What is these barons, anyway? Is they something like lords in England?"

To avoid a technical discussion, I told him that for all practical purposes they were somewhat along the same line. He went away apparently satisfied.

Our orchard bivouac behind the castle was fine except for one thing. That was the barnyard collection that surrounded us. About an hour before dawn we were always awakened by the most startling orchestra of weird and ghoulish noises ever put together. Guinea hens cackled, ducks quacked, calves bawled, babies cried, men shouted, peacocks jabbered and turkeys gobbled. And to cap it all a lone donkey at just the right dramatic moment in this hideous cacophony would let loose a long sardonic heehaw that turned our exasperation into outraged laughter.

The baron's servants were a poor-looking lot, yet they seemed nice enough. Their kids hung around our camp all day, very quiet and meek. They looked at us so hungrily we couldn't resist giving them cans of food. We tried to teach them to say *grazie* (thanks, in Italian) but with no success.

One day some of us correspondents were doing our washing when one of the Sicilian women came up and took it away from us and washed it herself.

When she finished we asked her, "How much?"

She said, "Nothing at all." We said, well, then, we'd give her some food. She said she didn't expect any food, that she was just doing it for us free. We gave her some food anyway.

Stories like that were countless. The Army engineers told me how the Sicilians would come up where they were working, grab shovels and start digging and refuse to take anything for it. Whatever else you can say about them the Sicilians don't seem lazy. One soldier summed it up when he said, "After living nine months with Arabs the sight of somebody working voluntarily is almost too much for me."

I ran across Bob Hope and his crew. In fact for a couple of days we did the highlights and shadows of one bombed Sicilian city in such hilarious conjunction that it looked as though I were becoming a member of the troupe.

There were certain dissenters to the policy of sending American entertainers overseas to help brighten the lives of our soldiers. Now and then I heard some officer say, "After all, we're over here to fight, not to be entertained. Don't they know there's a war on?" But it was my experience that the most confirmed users of such phrases were usually a good many miles behind the lines. I was all for giving the troops a little touch of America through those movie stars, and I can testify that the boys enjoyed and appreciated it.

Bob Hope was one of the best that ever went to Africa. He had the right touch with soldiers. He could handle himself as well in a hospital full of suffering men as before a rough audience of ten thousand war-coarsened ones. When Hope went into a hospital he was likely to go up to a poor guy swathed in bandages, and instead of spreading out the old sympathy he would shake hands and say something such as, "Did you see my show this evening, or were you already sick?"

At his regular show, Hope carefully explained the draft status of his troupe, so that the soldiers wouldn't think they were draft dodgers. He said that his singer, Jack Pepper, had been classified 5-X, or "too fat to fight." Hope himself was in class 4-Z, meaning "Coward." And their guitar player, Tony Romano, was Double S Double F, meaning "Single man with children." Sure, it got a laugh.

The Hope troupe, which included lovely Frances Langford as the fourth member, really found out about war. Every time they'd stop in a city, there'd be a raid there that night. Actually it got to look as though the Germans were deliberately after them. I was in two different cities with them during raids, and I will testify that they were horrifying things.

The troupe had the distinction, while in Sicily, of playing closer to the front lines than any other entertainers, and playing to the biggest audiences. One afternoon they did their outdoor show for nineteen thousand men. Everywhere they went, both in public and in private, the Hope gang was popular—mainly because, clear down (or up) to Frances, they were regular and natural.

Let this be taken as legal testimony in verification: no matter what narrow-escape story Bob tells about Sicily, it's true.

Strange though it seems now, it used to be the fashion to sneer at the engineers, but that day has passed. The engineering forces with the Army are trained and organized to a high degree, and engineering morale is proud and high. In Sicily even the infantry took off its hat to them—for not infrequently the engineers were actually out ahead of the troops.

Each infantry division had a battalion of engineers which was an integral part of that division and worked and suffered with it. The battalion consisted of four companies totaling around eight hundred men. Sometimes all the companies were working in separate places with various infantry regiments. At other times, in mountainous country, when the whole division was strung out in a single line twenty miles or more long, the engineer companies kept leapfrogging each other, letting one company go into 24-hour reserve for a much-needed rest about every three days.

Behind the division engineers were the corps engineers. They were under control of the Second Army Corps and could be shifted anywhere at the corps' command. Corps engineers followed up the division engineers, strengthening and smoothing the necessarily makeshift work of the division engineers.

Captain Ben Billups of Alamogordo, New Mexico, put it this way: "Our job is to clear the way for our division of roughly two thousand vehicles to move ahead just as quickly as possible. We are interested only in the division. If we were to build a temporary span across a blown bridge, and that span were to collapse one second after the last division truck had crossed, we would have done the theoretically perfect job. For we would have cleared the division, yet not wasted a minute of time doing more than we needed to do when we passed. It is the corps engineers job to create a more permanent bridge for the supply convoys that will be following for days and weeks afterward."

Often there was jealousy and contempt between groups of similar types working under division and corps. But in the engineers it was a sort of mutual-esteem society. Each respected and was proud of the other. The corps engineers were so good they constantly tripped on the heels of the division engineers, and a few times, with the division engineers one hundred per cent occupied with an especially difficult demolition, they even pushed ahead and tackled fresh demolitions themselves.

Particularly at first, all the officers of the engineers' battalion were graduate engineers in civil life, but with the Army expanding so rapidly and professional experience running so thin, some young officers assigned to the engineers had just come out of officers school and had little or no engineering experience. Of the enlisted men only a handful in each company ever had had any construction experience. The rest were just run of the mine—one-time clerks, butchers, cowpunchers. That little handful of experienced enlisted men carried the load and they were as vital as anything in the Army.

Practically every man in an engineering company had to double in half a dozen brasses. One day he'd be running a mine detector, next day he'd be a stonemason, next day a carpenter, and the day after a plain pick-and-shovel man. But unlike the common laborer at home, he was picking and shoveling under fire about half the time.

In the Table of Organization the duties of the engineers are manifold. But in the specialized warfare in Sicily many of their official duties just didn't exist and their main work was concentrated into four vital categories: road building and bridge bypassing; clearing mine fields; finding and purifying water for the whole division; and providing the division with maps. The last two don't sound spectacular but, believe me, they're *important*.

The awarding of bravery medals is a rather dry and formal thing and I had never bothered to cover any such festivities. One night, however, I learned that three old friends of mine were in a group to be decorated, so I went down to have supper with them and see the show.

My three friends were Lieutenant Colonel Harry Goslee, 3008 Neil Avenue, Columbus, Ohio, Major John Hurley, 66 Rockaway Avenue, San Francisco, California, and Major Mitchell Mabardy, of Assonet, Massachusetts. Goslee was headquarters commandant of one of the outfits, and Hurley and Mabardy were provost marshals in charge of military police. (Major Hurley was later killed in Italy.)

They were camped under big beech trees on the Sicilian hillside just back of the battlefront. I went down about 5:30 and found my friends sitting on folding chairs under a tree outside their tent, looking through field glasses at some fighting far ahead.

Any soldier will agree that one of the outstanding traits of war is those incongruous interludes of quiet that pop up now and then in the midst of the worst horror. That evening was one of them. Our troops were in a bitter fight for the town of Troina, standing up like a great rock pinnacle on a hilltop a few miles ahead. That afternoon our High Command had called for an all-out air and artillery bombardment of the city. When it came it was terrific. Planes by the score roared over and dropped their deadly loads, and as they left our artillery put down the most devastating barrage we'd ever used against a single point, even outdoing any shooting we did in Tunisia. Up there in Troina a complete holocaust took place. Through our glasses the old city seemed to fly apart. Great clouds of dust and black smoke rose into the sky until the whole horizon was leaded and fogged. Our biggest bombs exploded with such roars that we felt the concussion clear back where we were, and our artillery in a great semicircle crashed and roared like some gigantic inhuman beast that had broken loose and was out to destroy the world.

Germans by the hundreds were dying up there at the end of our binocular vision, and all over the mountainous horizon the world seemed to be ending. And yet we sat there in easy chairs under a tree—sipping cool drinks, relaxed and peaceful at the end of the day's work. Sitting there looking at it as though we were spectators at a play. It just didn't seem possible that it could be true. After a while we walked up to the officers' mess in a big tent under a tree and ate captured German steak which tasted very good indeed.

Then after supper the six men and three officers who were to receive awards lined up outside the tent. They were nine legitimate heroes all right. I know, for I was in the vicinity when they did their deed:

It was the night before my birthday and the German bombers kept us awake all night with their flares and their bombings, and for a while it looked as though I might never get to be forty-three years old. What happened in this special case was that one of our generator motors caught fire during the night and it had to happen at a very inopportune moment. When the next wave of bombers came over, the Germans naturally used the fire as a target.

The three officers and six MPs dashed to the fire to put it out. They stuck right at their work as the Germans dived on them. They stayed while the bombs blasted around them and shrapnel flew. I was sleeping about a quarter of a mile away, and the last stick of bombs almost seemed to blow me out of the bedroll—so you can visualize what those men went through. The nine of them were awarded the Silver Star.

They lined up in a row with Colonel Goslee at the end. The commanding general came out of his tent. Colonel Goslee called the nine to attention. They stood like ramrods while the citations were read off. There was no audience except myself and two Army Signal Corps photographers taking pictures of the ceremony.

Besides the three officers, the six who received medals were Sergeant Edward Gough, 2252 East 72nd Street, Brooklyn, New York, Sergeant Charles Mitchell, 3246 Third Avenue, Brooklyn,

New York, Sergeant Homer Moore, of Nicholls, Georgia, Sergeant Earl Sechrist, of Windsor, Pennsylvania, Pfc. Barney Swint, of Douglasville, Texas, and Pfc. Harold Tripp, of Worthington, Minnesota.

I believe those men went through more torture receiving the awards than they did in earning them, they were all so tense and scared. It was either comical or pathetic, whichever way it happened to strike you. Colonel Goslee stared rigidly ahead in a thunderstruck manner. His left hand hung relaxed, but I noticed his right fist was clamped so tightly his fingers were turning blue. The men were like uncomfortable stone statues. As the general approached, each man's Adam's apple went up and down two or three times in a throat so constricted I thought he was going to choke.

The moment the last man was congratulated, the general left and the whole group broke up in relief. As a spectacle it was sort of dull, but to each man it was one of those little pinnacles of triumph that will stand out until the day he dies. You often hear soldiers say, "I don't want any medals. I just want to see the Statue of Liberty again." But just the same you don't hear of anybody forgetting to come around, all nervous and shined up fit to kill, on the evening he is to be decorated.

My friends and I went back to the tent where one of them lived and sat there talking about old times and how good it was to get together again. One officer had a bottle of champagne he had been saving for some occasion and since this seemed to be at least a good imitation of an occasion he got it out and we passed it around, the half dozen of us drinking it warm and out of the bottle. My palate has never been educated up to champagne and I'd just as soon have had a good swig of Bevo—but an event is an event.

We sat out under the trees and a chill wind came up and somebody brought me a jacket to slip on. It had lieutenant colonel's leaves on the shoulders and I suppose I could have been arrested for impersonating an officer, but I was in a nice position, having the head military policeman of the area sitting next to me, so I just flaunted my colonel's leaves and hoped some stranger would come by to salute me.

Our host, Lieutenant Colonel Goslee, called himself a professional reserve officer as he had been on active duty for ten years.

He was with us back in the first days at Oran, then got shunted off to another job and missed the fighting in Tunisia. But that summer he got switched back onto the main track again and he'd been making hay fast while the bombs fell.

Back home he had a wife, and a daughter of fifteen who kept writing him, the lovely child, asking if he'd seen me. He also had a Dalmatian dog named Colonel who volunteered—or was volunteered—in the Dogs for Defense Army and was then serving somewhere in Virginia. Colonel Goslee's home flew two service stars in the front window—one for the man and one for the dog.

Dusk came on and we moved inside the tent so we could light our cigarettes. Our conversation drifted back to other days—Oran in November and bitter cold Tebessa in January and the sadness of our retreat from Sbeitla and the chill sweeping winds of Gafsa and later in the spring the beauties of Béja and the final wonderful feeling of victory at Ferryville.

And we talked of how tired we had all gradually become, and nobody seemed like a hero who'd just been decorated for bravery. We talked of the miles we'd covered and the moves we'd made in the previous nine months, of countries we'd seen and how the whole war machine, though it grew dirtier and tireder month after month, also grew mature and smooth and more capable.

In that long time all of us overseas had met thousands of different soldiers and officers. Yet those of us who became friends right at the very beginning in Africa or even back in England seemed to share a bond as though we were members of a fraternity or a little family, and getting back together again was comfortable and old-shoelike. We talked of people no longer with us— such people as Lieutenant General Lloyd Fredendall and Major Ed Adkins, both on duty back in Memphis then. Ed, in his job as headquarters commandant, used to be a focal point of the little sitting-around group in Tunisia, just as Colonel Goslee was in the same job there in Sicily.

Ed Adkins was a favorite and his name came up frequently in our conversation. He was crazy to get back to the States and we knew he was happy there, and yet we laughed and prophesied that when he read about us—read how we were still going on and on, still moving every few days, still listening now and then for the uneven groan of the German night bombers, still fighting dust, darkness, and weariness and once in a while sitting around talking after supper, on cots in a blacked-out tent—when he read about it, and visualized us, he would be so homesick for the front that he'd probably cry.

They tell me all the soldiers who have been through the mill and have returned to America are like that. They get an itch for the old miserable life—a disgusting, illogical yearning to be back again in the place they hated. I'm sure it's true, but I know a lot of soldiers who would like a chance to put that theory to the test.

Outside of the occasional peaks of bitter fighting and heavy casualties that highlight military operations, I believe the outstanding trait in any campaign is the terrible weariness that gradually comes over everybody. Soldiers become exhausted in mind and in soul as well as physically. They acquire a weariness that is mixed up with boredom and lack of all gaiety. To sum it all up: A man just gets damned sick of it all.

The infantry reaches a stage of exhaustion that is incomprehensible to folks back home. The men in the First Division, for instance, were in the lines twenty-eight days—walking and fighting all that time, day and night.

After a few days of such activity, soldiers pass the point of known human weariness. From then on they go into a sort of secondwind daze. They keep going largely because the other fellow does and because they can't really do anything else.

Have you ever in your life worked so hard and so long that you didn't remember how many days it was since you ate last or didn't recognize your friends when you saw them? I never have either, but in the First Division, during that long, hard fight around Troina, a company runner one day came slogging up to a certain captain and said excitedly, "I've got to find Captain Blank right away. Important message."

The captain said, "But I am Captain Blank. Don't you recognize me?"

And the runner said, "I've got to find Captain Blank right away." And he went dashing off. They had to run to catch him.

Men in battle reach that stage and still go on and on. As for the rest of the Army—supply troops, truck drivers, hospital men, engineers—they too become exhausted, but not so inhumanly. With them and with us correspondents it's the ceaselessness, the endlessness of everything that finally worms its way through us and gradually starts to devour us.

It's the perpetual, choking dust, the muscle-racking hard ground, the snatched food sitting ill on the stomach, the heat and the flies and dirty feet and the constant roar of engines and the perpetual moving and the never settling down and the go, go, go, night and day, and on through the night again. Eventually it all works itself into an emotional tapestry of one dull, dead pattern—yesterday is tomorrow and Troina is Randazzo and when will we ever stop and, God, I'm so tired.

I noticed this feeling had begun to overtake the war correspondents themselves. It is true we didn't fight on and on like the infantry, that we were usually under fire only briefly and that, indeed, we lived better than the average soldier. Yet our lives were strangely consuming in that we did live primitively and at the same time had to delve into ourselves and do creative writing.

That statement may lay me open to wisecracks, but however it may seem to you, writing is an exhausting and tearing thing. Most of the correspondents actually worked like slaves. Especially was this true of the press-association men. A great part of the time they went from dawn till midnight or 2 a.m. I'm sure they turned in as much toil in a week as any newspaperman at home does in two weeks. We traveled continuously, moved camp every few days, ate out, slept out, wrote wherever we could and just never caught up on sleep, rest, cleanliness, or anything else normal.

The result was that all of us who had been with the thing for more than a year finally grew befogged. We were grimy, mentally as well as physically. We'd drained our emotions until they cringed from being called out from hiding. We looked at bravery and death and battlefield waste and new countries almost as blind men, seeing only faintly and not really wanting to see at all. Suddenly the old-timers among the correspondents began talking for the first time about wanting to go home for a while. They wanted a change, something to freshen their outlook.

They felt they had lost their perspective by being too close for too long.

I am not writing this to make heroes of the correspondents, because only a few look upon themselves in any dramatic light whatever. I am writing it merely to let you know that correspondents, too, can get sick of war—and deadly tired.

EIGHT

SICILY CONQUERED

The north coast of Sicily is a strange contrast to the south. On the south coast the towns were much filthier and the people seemed to be of a lower class. Coming from the south to the north there was a freshness about the country and the people. The macadam road that follows the sea all the way from Palermo to Messina is a scenic one. I heard a dozen soldiers say, "If you could only travel this road in peacetime it would be a nice vacation, wouldn't it?"

The interior roads through the mountains are few, mostly gravel and quite rough. All through the campaign we had to use mules to get supplies up to our troops in the mountains, and three times during the battle men went without food and water for as long as sixty hours. How they kept going is beyond me, but I've reached the point where nothing the infantry does startles me any more.

The Third Division had more than five hundred mules at the end of the campaign. They brought thirty burros with them from Africa but discovered the burros couldn't keep up with the infantry so they had to abandon them for the stronger Sicilian mules. Most of the mules were pretty poor and we lost lots of them both by artillery fire and by plain exhaustion. Toward the end of the campaign the division got so it hauled mules in 2½-ton trucks, right up to the foot of the mountains, so the poor beasts could start all fresh on their pack journey.

The American doughboy's fundamental honesty shows up sometimes in comical ways. All through the campaign the various Army headquarters were flooded with Sicilians bearing penciled notes written on everything from toilet paper to the backs of envelopes saying, "I owe you for one mule taken for the U. S. Army on Aug. 2. Signed, Private John Smith."

Actually the appropriating of captured enemy equipment (including mules) for military use is legitimate and no restitution needed to be made, but the doughboys—in their simplicity—never thought of that.

Captured supply dumps were impounded by the Army for re-issue later but our soldiers often got in to help themselves before the Army took over officially. For example, at one time practically every soldier I saw was carrying a packet of German bread—thin, brittle stuff that resembled what we call Ry-Krisp at home. The soldiers seemed to like it or maybe it was just the novelty of the thing.

The Germans, as usual, were well-equipped and we were soon sporting lots of their doodads. Many of the officers' outdoor field messes were furnished with brand-new German folding tables and the diners sat on individual, unpainted German stools. Also I saw quite a few officers sleeping in German steel cots with German mosquito-net framework above them.

Speaking of mosquitoes, by the end of August the heat and the lack of sanitation began to take their toll. Diarrhea was common, there was a run of the same queer fever I had had, and a good many men came down with malaria. In fact, in the last weeks of the campaign, the correspondents themselves dropped off like flies with malaria. Usually they went to the Army hospital for a few days until the attack passed, and then returned to work.

Our soldiers were careless about their eating and drinking but I couldn't blame them. One of the most touching sights was to see a column of sweat-soaked soldiers, hot and tired, march into a village and stop for rest. In a moment the natives were out by the hundreds carrying water in glass pitchers, in earthen jugs, in pans, in anything—filling the men's empty canteens. It was dangerous to drink the water, but when a man's really thirsty he isn't too particular.

Most of the time I approached native food and drink pretty much like a persnickety peacetime tourist who avoids all fresh vegetables and is very cagey about drinking water, but despite my caution I came down with the fever. A couple of days after getting back to normal I was hit with the "GIs," or Army diarrhea.

Half our camp had it at the same time. We all took sulfaguanidine but still mine hung on. Then I moved into the field again with the troops, feeling like death, and getting weaker by the moment.

One day we drove into a mountain village where the Americans hadn't been before and the natives showered us with grapes, figs, wine, hazelnuts and peaches, and I finally said, "Oh, the hell with it," and started eating everything in sight. Within two days I felt fine again.

On the whole our troops found Sicily perhaps a little better than North Africa. Certainly the people were just as friendly, if not more so. If only there were a little more modernity and sanitation in Sicily I think a good many of us would have mildly liked the place. The whole thing seemed kind of ridiculous, when I sat down and thought about it. Those people were our enemies. They declared war on us. We went clear over there and fought them and when we had won they looked upon us as their friends.

If anything, their attitude was more that of a liberated people than was the case in French North Africa, and they seemed to look to us more eagerly for relief from their hunger. In several of the smaller mountain towns our troops were greeted by signs saying "Welcome," in English, pasted on the walls of buildings, and American flags were fluttering from windows.

Of course there were some Sicilians who treated us as enemies. There was some small sabotage, such as cutting our phone wires, but on the whole the Sicilians certainly were more for us than the French and the Arabs of Africa had been. Actually most of us felt friendlier toward the Sicilians than we had toward the French. And in comparison with the Arabs—well, there just wasn't any comparison.

Sicily is really a beautiful country. Up in the north it is all mountainous, and all but the most rugged of the mountains are covered with fields or orchards. Many of the hillsides are terraced to prevent erosion. By August everything was dry and burned up, as we so often see our own Midwest in dry summers. They said it was the driest summer in years.

Our ceaseless convoys chewed up the gravel roads, and the dust became suffocating, but in springtime Sicily must look like the Garden of Eden. The land is wonderfully fertile. Sicilians would not have to be poor and starving if they were capable of organizing and using their land to its fullest.

Driving over the island, I had a feeling of far greater antiquity than I got even from looking at the Roman ruins in North Africa. Everything is very old and if only it were clean as well it would be old in a nice, gentle way. Towns sit right smack on the top of needle-point mountain peaks. They were built that way in the old days for protection. Today a motorcar can't even get up to many of them.

In the mountain towns the streets are too narrow for vehicles, the passageways are dirty, and the goat and burro are common.

In the very remotest and most ancient town, we found that half the people had relatives in America, and there was always somebody popping up from behind every bush or around every corner who had lived for twelve years in Buffalo or thirty years in Chicago.

Farming is still done in Biblical style. The grain-threshing season was on then, and how do you suppose they did it? Simply by tying three mules together and running them around in a small circle all day long while a fellow with a wooden pitchfork kept throwing grain under their hoofs.

We had hit Sicily in the middle of the fruit and vegetable season. The troops went for those fresh tomatoes like sourdoughs going for gold in the Klondike. Tomatoes and watermelons too. I've never seen so many watermelons in my life, even if I did miss out on them that first day on the beach. They were mostly small round ones, and did they taste good to an old watermelon devourer like myself! Also we ate fresh peaches, grapes, figs and even mulberries.

At first when we hit a new town the people in their gratitude gave away their fruit to the troops. But it didn't take them long to learn, and soon they were holding out for trades of rations or other Army stuff. The people didn't want money. When we asked them to work for us they said they would but that we must pay them in merchandise, not money. The most sought-after thing was shoes. Most of the people were going around in sandals made of old auto tires. I believe you could have bought half the island of Sicily with two dozen pairs of GI shoes.

As the Sicilian campaign drew to an end and we went into our rest bivouac, rumors by the score popped up out of thin air and swept like a forest fire through the troops.

No. 1 rumor in every outfit, of course, was that ships already were waiting to take them back to the States. That one was so old I don't think half the men will believe it's true when the war ends and they actually do start back.

Other rumors had them staying in Sicily as occupation troops, going to England, going to China, and—ugly thought—going right on as the spearhead of the next invasion. Some people worry about rumors such as these, which are constantly sweeping our armies, but personally I think they are harmless. When the Army doesn't have women, furloughs, ice cream, beer or clean clothes, it certainly has to have something to look forward to, even if only a faint hope for some kind of change that lies buried in an illogical rumor.

In fact, I don't know how we would endure war without its rumors.

A few days after the Sicilian campaign had actually ended I went back to Palermo to get in touch with what we jokingly called "civilization." The Army had commandeered several hotels, and I was put up in a dungeonlike cell that overlooked an alley inhabited by a melee of Sicilians who screamed constantly and never cleaned up anything. They apparently had the concession for raising and furnishing the hotel with mosquitoes, for these came floating up like smoke from that alley. I tried mosquito netting over my bed, and just before climbing in for my first repose off the ground in five weeks, I decided I had better inspect the lovely white sheets.

My haul was three bedbugs and a baby scorpion. Civilization, she is wonderful.

In the field, most of us had mosquito nets. The mosquitoes weren't really so bad in the country but there were just enough to keep us worried about malaria. We strung up nets over our bedrolls in scores of fashions—all the way from tying them to tree branches to hanging them over Italian aluminum tent poles stuck in the ground.

The climate was ideal for our Sicilian campaign. The days were hot, but nothing approaching the summer heat of Kansas or Washington, DC. Down on the coast the nights were just right for sleeping with one blanket. Up in the mountains, it actually got cold at night. There wasn't a drop of rain. Every hour, the Army engineers thanked Allah for the dryness, because rains would have washed out their bypasses around the blown bridges and made the movement of our vehicles almost impossible.

Because of the climate, nobody used tents any longer for sleeping. We just threw our blankets down on the ground and slept in the open. Until you sleep under the open skies, you never realize how many shooting stars there are in the heavens.

And one night, there was a frightening red glow in the east that lasted only a couple of seconds. It colored the whole eastern heavens. It was neither flares nor gunfire, so it must have been Mount Etna, boiling and snarling.

In the Sicilian villages we passed through, the local people would take little embroidered cushions out of their parlors and give them to our soldiers to sit on while resting. It was funny to march with a sweaty infantry company, and see grimy doughboys with pink and white lacy cushions tucked under their harness among grenades, shovels and canteens.

The hazelnut and almond season reached its peak just as the campaign ended. Practically every camp had a hundred-pound sack of almonds lying on the ground where the soldiers could just sit and crack the nuts on rocks and gorge as though it were Christmas. The local people gave us hazelnuts as we passed through the towns. I saw one company in which nearly every man took off his steel helmet and filled it full of hazelnuts, and then marched on down the road with the heavily laden hat held in the crook of his arm.

Hazelnuts, red wine, hardtack and thou. Or what am I thinking of?

ITALY

DECEMBER, 1943–APRIL, 1944

NINE

ARTILLERYMEN

In November, after a two months' leave back home in the States, I headed again for the Mediterranean theater. All during the long trip over, I had a vague feeling that something bad was going to happen. It wasn't exactly a premonition, and I didn't really worry about it. Yet a slight fear was there. So when at last we came over Algiers, after eight thousand miles of probably the most perfect long trip I ever had, I thought to myself, "Well, we crack up when we land here, I suppose. It's our last chance for anything to happen."

I was pretty tense when we skimmed down the runway. It seemed as if the pilot would never get the wheels on the ground. But finally they did touch, light as a feather; we ran smooth and straight. And nothing happened at all.

The airport was thronged with British, American and French travelers in uniform, hundreds of them. As we were waiting for a jeep to come for us, a British captain I'd known months before came up and asked if he could ride into town with us. Soon after, Dick Hottelot from London came past and said a startled hello. Next came Fred Clayton of the Red Cross, just landed from Italy. A young naval lieutenant I'd known in Morocco and an officer I'd never seen before yelled across the crowd, "Welcome home!"

Then I knew that the old fraternity of war had enmeshed me once more.

Algiers had changed since I left it nearly three months before. The blackout had been lifted in favor of a dimout. Everybody felt far from the war. The barrage balloons still flew over the harbor, but they were fewer. The streets were packed with soldiers of three nationalities.

There were even some American civilian women where before

there had been none. There were more WACs, too. Soldiers were always saluting us correspondents, so there must have been new troops in town. Great rows of boxed engines lined the roads, supply dumps filled the fields, and the road in from the airport was rougher from much convoying.

It looked as if North Africa from the Atlantic to Cairo had become a war depot of unprecedented proportions.

Everybody was friendly and terribly anxious to know how things were at home. "Can you get enough to eat?" they asked. "Can you still have any fun? Have things changed much? Can you go up to a bar and buy a drink? Is there any traffic in the cities? Can you still get a glass of milk? Can you buy eggs? Are prices terribly high?"

A dozen soldiers told me their families had intimated that they were probably better off in Africa for food than the folks were at home. Some even wondered whether they should go home if they got a chance.

The Army mess where I used to eat during infrequent visits to Algiers was staffed at one time by soldier-waiters. Later we had French girls, but upon my return the waiters were Italian prisoners. They were the best of all; they were most attentive, and grinned all the time, apparently because they were so happy in their jobs. They didn't speak English, and very few of us spoke Italian, so a neat system of dining-table communication had been devised.

At every place was a little typed menu, with each dish numbered. With it was a tiny slip of paper with numbers running up to about fifteen. We simply took a pencil and circled the numbers of whatever we wanted and handed the slip to the waiter.

Pretty soon he came back with exactly what we ordered, no matter how illogical our appetite might be. They simply never made a mistake that way. I think we ought to try it at home.

Private George McCoy used to do a daily buttonhole broadcast for WEAF on the steps of the Astor Hotel in New York. The program was called "The Real McCoy." On the staff of *Stars and Stripes* he was doing the same thing—buttonholing soldiers on the streets and having them talk into the microphone. He called his program "The Sidewalks of North Africa."

On my way home in September, George buttonholed me, got

me up to his studio and made a record for broadcasting to the soldiers. I don't know what I said, because it was the second time in my life I'd ever done such a thing, and I was so scared I can't remember, but anyhow I got through it and the recording was later broadcast to the troops over there.

I ran into Private McCoy again and he was all aflutter. Seems he'd read in a clipping from the States how I'd turned down an offer of $1,500 for one broadcast. So he had been running around all over Algiers telling people what a wonderful person I was because I turned down $1,500 at home but did one for nothing over there.

It was nice of George, but the truth is I'm just plain silly.

Transient correspondents at Algiers stayed in six rooms set aside for them at the Aletti Hotel. A newcomer just went from room to room until he found either an empty bed or some floor space for his bedroll, and moved in. The first night I stayed with John Daly of CBS. The second night I slept on a balcony in the new sleeping bag That Girl bought me as a farewell gift. And then I shared a room with Red Mueller of NBC, who was about to start home for the first time in twenty months.

My battle friend, Chris Cunningham of the United Press, was still there after nearly two years at war. His plans for a return home were canceled at the last minute. There too were Hal Boyle and Boots Norgaard of AP, Don Coe of UP, and Graham Hovey of INS, all old pals of the winter in Tunisia, and all of them getting tireder and tireder of war.

On the second day back in Algiers I went up to Allied Headquarters to give General Eisenhower a copy of my book. In the outer lobby I had to show my credentials to a soldier behind the desk. After the soldier had made out my entry pass he said, "I'm almost from your home town."

"Where's that?" I asked.

"Montezuma, Indiana," he said.

The soldier was Luther C. Manwaring, a quiet, gentlemanly young man of twenty-five, who hadn't been home in nearly two years. He was from a family quite well known in our part of Indiana, because there were triplets in the home. Luther's younger brother was Jack Manwaring, the only boy of that trio. He served on Guadalcanal and was still somewhere in the Southwest Pacific. I had been in Montezuma about a month before, so I was able to tell Private Manwaring that our respective home towns were still there and thriving and hardly missing him or me at all.

A few evenings after my arrival, I had a phone call from a man who said Albuquerque was his home town too, and could he come up? When he arrived, he turned out to be a sailor. His name was Hoyt Tomlinson and his mother and sister lived at 510 West Roma. Hoyt had been in the Navy for two years and was on his ninth round trip across the Atlantic, with a couple of invasions thrown in. He was a cook, first class, and liked it. He used to work in the soda fountain in the Triangle Café out near my home, then he worked for the Rainbow Baking Company.

Tomlinson loved to see people from Albuquerque. One time, while on liberty in New York, he was sitting in a doughnut place on Broadway when he recognized a man's back in the sidewalk crowd. He dashed out and chased the man down the street, knocking people over as he went. The man was a Mr. Baccachi of the Sunny State Liquor Company in Albuquerque. Sailor Tomlinson said he was so homesick at the time that he started to cry. And he was so delighted at seeing somebody from home that he kept Mr. Baccachi up till 3 a.m.

Tomlinson was clean-cut and bighearted, and he insisted on going back to his ship and bringing me stuff like a roast chicken, canned ham, and so on. But since I was just leaving for the front and already overloaded, I had to forgo his western hospitality. Before very many days I knew I'd probably be willing to give a week's pay for half a roast chicken.

I had intended to work back into the war gradually. I'd see how things were in Naples, and whether the island of Capri was as pretty as they say. I don't know what happened. But something did. I hadn't been in Naples two hours before I felt I couldn't stand it, and by the next evening there I was—up in the mud again, sleeping on straw and awakening throughout the night with the old familiar crash and thunder of the big guns in my reluctant ears.

It was the artillery for me this time. I went with an outfit I had known in England during the fall of 1942, made up largely of men from the Carolinas and eastern Tennessee. The regiment shot 155-

millimeter howitzers. They were terrifically big guns and, Lordy, did they make a noise! The six-ton gun fires a shell so big it is all an ammunition carrier can do to lug one up to the gun pit. The regiment had all new guns then. I can't tell you how far they shot, but as the Carolina boys said, "It's awful fur."

The commanding officer was a good-natured former textile-plant executive who fought all through the last war and had already spent nearly a year in the front lines in this one. He was humorous, as southern as magnolia, and he loved being alive. He called every soldier around him by his first name.

He lived in a two-man tent with his executive officer. When I first joined the outfit the tent was pitched on a hillside, and they had put big rocks under two legs of their cots to make them level. They washed from gasoline tins, and slogged a quarter of a mile through deep mud for their meals. Both were men of refinement and accustomed to good living back home. The colonel was fifty years old—proof that middle-aged men of the right frame of mind can take it at the front.

When I came puffing up the muddy hillside late one afternoon between showers, the colonel was sitting in a canvas chair in the door of his tent reading a magazine. When I got within about fifty yards he looked up, let out a yell, and called out, "Well, I'll be damned if it ain't my old friend Ernie Pyle! Goshamighty, am I glad to see you! Ansel, this calls for a drink."

He reached under his cot and brought out a square bottle of some white Italian fluid full of what looked like sugar Christmas trees. It was a very thick, sweetish substance—which shows what a Southerner can come to who's been without mint juleps for a year.

The colonel's tentmate was Lieutenant Colonel Ansel Godfrey, who used to be principal of the high school at Abbeville, South Carolina, but he called Clinton his home. He and I and the colonel sat for two hours while they pumped me about America and told me about Italy.

The colonel said, "Boy, are you a welcome sight! You don't know how wonderful it is to have somebody new to talk to. Ansel and I have been boring each other to death for months. Today we tell each other what we are going to do tomorrow, and then tomorrow we tell each other we're doing it. The next day we tell each other we did it. That's what we've been driven to for conversation."

After supper and a couple of hours with these friends I told them I wanted to go live with one of their gun crews. They said all right, but since it was raining again there might not be much shooting. They promised that if they did get any orders during the night, they'd have whatever battery I was with do the firing.

So I went down and introduced myself to a gun crew and warned them I probably was going to cause them to overwork, for which I apologized. Then I settled gradually in mud up to my knees.

It wound up that I stayed three days and three nights with those boys and got so I felt like a cannoneer myself. Only once did I hear anybody singing the famous artillery song about the caissons rolling along. A cannoneer hummed it one day during a lull, "Over hill, over dale, as we hit the dusty trail . . ."

What a sardonic line that was in Italy, with our guns hub-deep in black, sloshy, gooey, all-encompassing mud and not a grain of that longed-for dust within a thousand miles.

Our artillery played a huge part all through the Mediterranean fighting. It was good even in the spring of 1943, and it had grown better all the time. The Germans feared it almost more than anything we had. There was plenty of it, and plenty of ammunition too.

The artillery was usually a few miles back of the front-line infantry, although there were times in Italy when artillerymen were actually under machine-gun fire.

In ninety-nine cases out of a hundred an artilleryman never sees what he's shooting at, and in nine cases out of ten he never even knows what he's shooting at. Somebody just gives him a set of figures over his telephone. He sets his gun by those figures, rams in a shell, pulls the lanyard and then gets ready for the next one.

He usually shoots over a hill, and there in Italy the men said they were getting sick of going around one hill and always finding another one just like it ahead of them. They sure wished they could get out in the open country and just once shoot at something that didn't have a hill in front of it.

The country where we were fighting then was fertile in the valleys and farmed up as far as the lower slopes of the hills, but it was wild and rocky on the upper ridges. The valleys were wide, flat, well-populated and well-farmed. Little stores, farmhouses and sheds dotted the valley and the hillsides. I never saw more beautiful country; I'd had no idea southern Italy was so beautiful.

It rained almost constantly and everything was vivid green. When we looked out across our valley, rimmed around in the distance by cloud-bound mountains—all so green in the center and lovely—even the least imaginative soldier was struck by the uncommon beauty of the scene.

Refugee Italians returned to their homes as soon as the fighting moved beyond them, and resumed their normal business right under the noses of the big guns. Women drove huge gray hogs past the gun pits, and the crews had to yell at them when they were about to fire. Small herds of gray cows that looked like Brahmans, except that they had no humps, wandered up and down the trails. Little children stood in line at the battery kitchen with tin pails to get what was left over. Italian men in old ragged uniforms moseyed through the arbors. Now and then we stopped one and questioned him, but mostly they just came and went and nobody paid any attention. Like the Arabs, they seemed unconscious and unafraid of the warfare about them. That is, all except the planes. When German planes came over they ran and hid and quivered with absolute terror. It was that way in Sicily too. They remembered what our bombers did.

Those lovely valleys and mountains were filled throughout the day and night with the roar of heavy shooting. Sometimes there were uncanny silent spells of an hour or more. Then it would start up again across the country with violent fury. On my first night at the front I slept only fitfully—never very wide awake, never deeply asleep. All night long the valley beside us and the mountains and the valleys over the hill were dotted and punctured with the great blasts of the guns.

We could hear the shells chase each other through the sky across the mountains ahead, making a sound like cold wind blowing on a winter night. Then the concussion of the blasts of a dozen guns firing at once would strike the far mountains across the valley and rebound in a great mass sound that was prolonged, like the immensity and the fury of an approaching sandstorm. Then the nearer guns would fire and the ground under our bedrolls would tremble and we could feel the awful breath of the blast push the tent walls and nudge our bodies ever so slightly. And through the darkened hodgepodge of noise we could occasionally pick out the slightly different tone of German shells bursting in our valley.

It didn't really seem true. Three weeks before I had been in Miami, eating fried chicken, sleeping in deep beds with white sheets, taking hot baths and hearing no sound more vicious than the ocean waves and the laughter of friends. One world was a beautiful dream and the other a horrible nightmare, and I was a little bit in each of them.

As I lay on the straw in the darkness they became mixed up, and I was confused and not quite sure which was which.

Artillery batteries are "laid in," as artillerymen say, in all kinds of positions, but my "Battery E" was probably typical. Our four guns were set in and around a grape arbor. On one side a ridge rose steeply four or five hundred feet. A broad valley spread out below us.

The four guns formed a rough square about the size of a city block, and they were so close under the brow of a bill that it was almost impossible for the German artillery to reach us. Each gun was planted in a pit about three feet deep, and the front of the pit was lined, shoulder-high, with sandbags. Over the entire pit a camouflage net had been stretched on poles. The net, just head-high, gave you a sense of having a roof overhead. When the guns were quiet we could yell from one gun pit to another.

A few feet on one side of the gun pit was a stack of black cases about three feet long, clipped together in triple clusters. These were the powder charges. On the other side of the pit lay a double row of rust-colored shells. The ammunition carriers kept a supply of ten or twelve shells inside the pit, but the powder charges were brought in one at a time, just before the shooting, because of the danger of fire.

The floor of the gun pit was muddy and we had to move carefully to stay on our feet. One day one of the ammunition carriers, a slight fellow, slipped with his heavy shell and let out an irritated "Goddammit!" Whereupon the sergeant said sarcastically, "Hush. The devil will get you for talking like that."

Several times a day an ammunition truck came plowing through the muddy field, backed up to the gun pit and unloaded another truckload of shells. It was a game with the gun crew to try to get the truckers to carry the shells inside the pit instead of stacking them outside, and sometimes, when in good humor, they would do it.

All four guns were connected to the battery's executive post by telephone, and the chief of each crew wore a headphone all the time he was in the pit. An executive post might be anything from a telephone lying on the ground under a tree, clear up to the luxury of an abandoned cowshed. But it was always within a few yards of the battery.

An officer in the executive post gave the firing directions to the four guns of his battery. He got his instructions from the regimental command post half a mile or so to the rear, which in turn received its firing orders from the division command posts and from its own observers far ahead in the mountains.

The men of the gun crew lived in pup tents a few feet from the gun pit. Since an artillery unit usually stays in one place for several days, the men had time to pitch their tents securely and dig little drainage ditches around them. They covered the floors of the tents with straw and kept themselves dry inside the tents, at least. For each two gun crews there was also a larger pyramidal tent, empty except for the straw on the ground. Nobody lived in there, but the ground crews used it for a loafing place in the daytime when they weren't firing, and for playing poker at night by candlelight. They sat or lay on the ground while they played, since there was no furniture.

There was a kitchen truck for each battery. Our truck was full of battle scars. There were holes in the walls and roof from bomb fragments, and the stove itself had a huge gash in it, yet nobody in the kitchen had ever been hurt.

The battery's three officers ate standing up at a bench inside the truck while the men ate outside, either sitting on their steel helmets in the mud or standing up with their mess kits resting on a farmer's stone wall. They didn't all eat at once. Three went at a time from each crew, since the guns were never left, day or night, without enough men to fire them.

Our crew claimed it could fire faster with three men than the others could with ten, but of course all crews say that. Actually the crews didn't stay at the alert inside the gun pit all the time. But they were always close enough to get there in a few seconds when the whistle blew.

Supper was at 4:30, and by 5:30 it was dark. There was nothing to do, no place to go, and even inside the big tents the candlelight wasn't conducive to much fun, so usually the crews were asleep by 8:30. Some took off their pants, but most of the men just removed their shoes and leggings. Each crew posted a guard, which was changed every two hours throughout the night, to stand by the field telephone and listen for firing orders. Most of the cannoneers got so they could sleep through anything. Steady firing, even fairly close, didn't keep a man awake after he got used to it. It was the lone battery that suddenly whammed away after hours of complete silence that brought us awake, practically jumping out of our skins.

My gun crew had fought through four big Mediterranean campaigns. The men had been away from America for nearly seventeen months and it had been more than a year since any of them had slept in a bed. A few weeks before I joined them, they turned in their old gun for a brand-new one. The old howitzer had fired more than six thousand rounds.

Originally the whole crew was from South Carolina and they were a closely knit bunch, but transfers and illnesses over the months had whittled the Carolinians down to five. People from such strange and unorthodox places as California and Missouri had infiltrated. But Carolina still set the pace, and a year of wrastling with French and Italian hadn't changed their accent a bit. Practically everybody had a nickname—such odd ones as "Rabbit" and "Wartime" and "Tamper" and "Mote." I noticed that most of the crew called their gun "howzer" instead of "howitzer," and they said "far" instead of "fire."

The officers were mostly southern too, and I must say that outfit came the nearest to being a real democracy of any I had seen in the Army. The battery officers worked, lived and played with their men. It was a team, rather than a case of somebody above giving orders and somebody below taking them.

Most of the men were from small towns or farms. They were

mainly hill people. There was something fundamentally fine and sound about their character that must have been put there by a closeness to their hills and their trees and their soil.

They were natively courteous. Most of them had little education, and their grammar was atrocious, but their thinking was clear and they seemed to have for all people a friendliness that much of America doesn't have. They accepted their hardships with a sense of gaiety and good humor that is seldom found in Army outfits.

The artillery lives tough, but it too, like nearly every other branch of the Army, bows in sympathy and admiration to the infantry. One day we were sitting on our steel hats, planted in the mud around a bonfire made of empty pasteboard powder cases, when one member of the gun crew said, "We live like kings in comparison to the infantry."

"What's that you say?" burst in another cannoneer. The sentence was repeated.

"Oh, I thought you said we live like kings," the questioner said. "I thought you must be crazy in the head. But if you compare us with the infantry, that's all right. Those poor guys really have to take it."

The average artilleryman's outlook on life can be summed up, I think, by saying that he's uncompromisingly proud of his battery, he's thankful and glad because he's in the artillery, and he wants to go home so bad he talks about it nearly twenty per cent of the time.

The artillery doesn't live in as great danger as the infantry. For example, not a single officer out of that regiment had been lost in more than a year of combat. They always tried to lay in their guns behind a hill where the enemy's long-range guns couldn't reach them. Also, they were heavily protected by antiaircraft concentrations to drive off German bombers. But casualties were bound to happen anyway. During the few weeks they had been in Italy, tragedy had struck twice in my battery. Number 2 gun blew up from a premature explosion as they were putting in a shell. Three men were killed and half a dozen wounded.

Not long before that some German raiders did get through and a bomb explosion killed three men and wounded nearly a dozen others. Over and over I was told the story of one of the three who had died. His legs were blown off clear up to his body. He stayed conscious.

When the medical men went to help him he raised what was left of himself up on his elbows and said: "I'm done for, so don't waste time on me. Go help the other boys."

He lived seven minutes, conscious all the time.

Things like that knock the boys down for a few days. But if they don't come too often they can take it without serious damage to their fighting spirit. It's when casualties become so great that those who remain feel they have no chance to live if they have to go on and on taking it—that's when morale in an army gets low.

But the morale was excellent in my battery. The men griped, of course, but they were never grim or even mad about the toughness of their life. They were impatient only for movement; they would have been willing to fire all day and move all night every day and every night if only they could keep going forward swiftly.

Because everywhere in our army "forward," no matter in what direction, is toward home.

The conversation that went on in our gun pit during a lull in the firing ran anywhere from the number of flies in a bottle of local vino clear up to conjecturing on what the war was all about. Although profanity was a normal part of their language, the boys in the artillery seemed less profane than the infantry. The rougher a man lives the rougher he talks, and nothing can touch the infantry for rough and horrible living.

The impending arrival of galoshes occupied a good part of the conversation in our howitzer crew. Galoshes had been promised for weeks, day after day, but the rains were two months old and the galoshes had not arrived.

"I'd give my pay roll for a pair of galoshes," one soldier said.

"They're supposed to be on a ship already in the harbor," another cannoneer said. "And sure as hell the Jerries will sink it before they get them unloaded."

Dozens of times a day the subject of galoshes came up.

"My feet haven't been dry for six weeks," one soldier said.

And another one spoke up: "If you take a shot of that lousy

cognac they sell in Naples, it will dry your socks as soon as it hits bottom."

Little Corporal John C. Graham, from Dillon, South Carolina, sat on a water can before a bonfire, scraping the mud off his shoes before putting on his leggings. He too got off on the subject, and one of the other boys said: "Oh, for God's sakes, stop talking about overshoes; that's all I've heard for weeks and I'm sick of listening to it."

"Well," said Corporal Graham, "you got to talk about something and it might as well be overshoes."

Corporal Graham was nicknamed "Peewee." He was short and chubby and round-faced, and his eyes squinted with good humor and friendliness. He was only twenty years old and had been in the Army since he was seventeen. He weighed 117 pounds when he went in but had put off 43 more in those three years. Peewee lived on a farm before he enlisted. He was very conscientious and always on the job. He was the gunner, which means second in command to the sergeant. When the sergeant was away he ran the gun.

The other boys liked to kid Peewee about swearing mildly and smoking occasionally, since he was so young, but he always had some good-natured retort for them and never got mad.

Three boys in the crew were only twenty. They had nothing but fuzz on their faces and only shaved once a week—and didn't need it then. Another of the crew was Pfc. Lloyd Lewman, from Ottumwa, Iowa. He went by the nickname of "Old Man." That's because he was thirty-five, which was ancient to most of the crew. Actually, he didn't look much older than the rest and it seemed odd to hear him called Old Man. He used to be a farmer, and then he had worked for a long time as a section hand on the railroad. He was quiet and pleasant and everybody liked him.

As soldiers do everywhere, the gun crews killed time by gambling. Our battery got paid for the first time in two months while I was with them, and immediately a poker game started in every crew.

Our crew even brought a shelter half and spread it on the floor of the gun pit and played right there while waiting for firing orders. As Sergeant McCray said, the best way to bring on a firing mission is to start a hand of poker. And sure enough, they hadn't played five minutes when the firing order came and everybody grabbed his cards and money and scrambled for the shells.

While they were playing one of the boys said, "I wonder if the Germans got paid today."

And another one said, "Do you suppose the Germans play poker too?"

To which another answered, "Hell no, them guys ain't got enough money to play poker," which was probably a slight misconception on his part, since most of the prisoners I saw had money in their pockets.

The boys bet on anything. While I was home in the United States, they said they had bet on whether I would go to the Italian front or to the Pacific theater. They made bets on when we would get to Rome, and when the war would be over, and a couple of them were betting on whether Schlitz beer was sometimes put in green bottles instead of brown. They came to me to settle this but I didn't know.

The regiment, incidentally, had had a payday just before leaving America more than a year before. They left the States with around $52,000, and when they arrived in England and turned in their money for foreign exchange, they had $15,000 more than they started with. They had taken it away from other outfits on the ship, playing poker.

Dumb, these hillbillies.

Every morning a medical aid man made the rounds of all the gun pits in our battery. He carried a little satchel of bandages and had some instruments hooked to his belt. When he arrived at our pit one day he said: "Any sick, lame or lazy in this crew today?"

Nobody was sick but they all admitted being lazy.

The only business the medic could drum up was doling out some cotton for their ears and painting the cracked fingers of one boy. He carefully spread the vivid purple ointment around the cracked cuticle, and then proceeded to paint the entire nail on all ten fingers, as though he were a manicurist.

Despite the dampness the boys' fingers would crack open from the dirt and from always washing in cold water.

The medic, Private Clarence C. Upright, was a farmer from

Statesville, North Carolina. Incidentally, he ate razor blades. For $25 he offered to eat a double-edged razor blade, wash it down with a glass of water, and let us examine his mouth afterwards. He said he used to do it for less, but since the Italians had raised the price on everything he decided he would also. He tried to get me to buy a performance but I told him I'd wait till I got home again and see it in a carnival for two bits.

One night about eight of our crew were lying or kneeling around a blanket in the big tent, playing poker by the light of two candles. Our battery wasn't firing, but the valley and the mountains all around us were full of the dreadful noise of cannon. There was a lull in the talk among the players, and then out of a clear sky one of the boys, almost as though talking in his sleep, said, "War, my friends, is a silly business. War is the craziest thing I ever heard of."

And another one said, mainly to himself, "I wish there wasn't no blankety-blank war no more at all."

Then complete silence, as though nobody had heard. When somebody finally spoke it was something about the game, and no one talked about war. Weird little snatches like that stand out in your mind for a long time.

We were sitting in the gun pit one dark morning when word came over the field telephone that a delegation of Russian officers might be around that day on an inspection trip. Whereupon one of the cannoneers said, "Boy, if they show up in a fighting mood I'm taking out of here. They're fighters."

Another one said, "If Uncle Sam ever told me to fight the Russians, I'd just put down my gun and go home. I never could fight people who have done what they have."

The powder charges for our guns came in white sacks about the size of two-pound sugar sacks. Three of them tied together make one charge, and that was the way they arrived in their cases. The type and number of each charge was printed on the bag.

One day the sergeant calling out instructions asked for a charge of a certain size. When the powderman brought it, it was only half as big as it should have been.

The whole crew gathered around and studied it. They read the printing, and there it was in black and white just as it should be, and yet it was obviously a short charge. So the boys just threw it aside and got another, and that started a long run of conversation and wisecracks along this line: "Some defense worker who had to work on Sunday made that one," they'd say. "He was just too tired to fill it up, the poor fellow."

"If we'd shot that little one the shell would have landed on the battery just ahead."

"Guess somebody had worked eight hours already that day and made twenty or thirty dollars and had to work overtime at time and a half and was just worn out."

"Or somebody who had to drive all of three or four miles after work to a cocktail bar and he was in too big a hurry to finish this one. It sure is tough on the poor defense workers."

The boys were more taken with their own humor than by any bitterness. As Peewee Graham said, "You can't stand around all day with your trap hanging open, so you got to talk about something. And practically anything new for a subject is mighty welcome."

Late one dark night we were all in the gun pit on a firing mission. During one of those startling silences that sometimes came in the midst of bedlam, we could hear ever so faintly a few lovely, gentle strains of music.

One of the cannoneers said, "Hey, listen! That's music! It can't be. We're all going crazy."

Another man said, "Sure it's music. Don't you know?—it's one of those musical shells the Germans send over once in a while."

None of us really believed we had heard music, but a little nosing around next morning disclosed that an antiaircraft gun crew high up the hillside had a portable radio, and we had heard it playing.

One night in the tent a soldier brought out a box from home and passed around some pecans that had been sent from his own farm. "Just think," he said. "Three years ago I had my hands on the very trees these nuts came from."

"If you're lucky," another replied, "you can have your hands on them again in another three years—maybe."

That's the way conversation at the front went all the time. Rarely

did ten minutes elapse without some nostalgic reference to home—
how long they'd been away, how long before they'd get back, what
they'd do first when they hit the States, what the chances were
for going back before the war was over.

In one gun crew I ran onto there was a cannoneer who used to
be a photographer for Harris & Ewing in Washington, back in
the days when I worked in Washington. He was Private Francis
J. Hoffman, 608 Tennessee Avenue, N.E. He had been in the Army
about ten months, and overseas only two months. He was a perfect example of the queer things the Army can do. Hoffman had
had eighteen years' experience as a photographer, yet they listed
him as a cook at first and then changed their minds and made him
a cannoneer. He didn't think he was a very good cannoneer, but
if they wanted him to be a round peg in a square hole he was going
to do the best he could at it.

If a person wanted to be romantic he could drum up in his
imagination an artillery crew absolutely falling in love with its
gun. He could imagine a gunner who wouldn't sleep anywhere
but in the gun pit. I think I've seen it that way in the movies, and
of course it undoubtedly has happened but not, I think, often.
Certainly not with my crew.

Once during a lull, one of our boys said, "That damn gun is
driving me crazy."

And another one said, "I even dream about the damn thing at
night."

At least half the gun crews, I'd say, wanted to get transferred
to some other kind of work in the battery, such as cooking, running the switchboard, or driving.

Pfc. Frank Helms, from Newburg, West Virginia, was one of the
more articulate members of our crew. He was twenty-eight years
old, married, and had a two-year-old baby at home. He was a coal
miner. Frank had ideas on everything, and comments to make.
He thought the government ought to take over the coal mines and
end the strike trouble. He said he'd like working in a government-
operated mine. He called the Italian campaign a "mudaneering"
campaign. He carried a four-leafed clover inside a plastic disk
about the size of a watch. Somebody from home had sent it to him.

Frank told me he had the damnedest quirk—he didn't smoke a great deal, but the moment the crew was called to the guns and was just about ready to put the shell in, he went crazy for a cigarette. It was all right to smoke in the gun pit, and everybody did, but when that urge hit him he couldn't always take time to light up. He was one of the boys who said the gun was driving them crazy, but if that was true he was mighty good-natured about it.

The man who dreamed about the gun was Pfc. Raymond Wilson of 29 East General Robinson Street, North Pittsburgh. He was the No. 1 cannoneer, the one who closed the breech and pulled the lanyard. He was about the only member of the crew who didn't play poker. He said he'd rather waste his money some other way. He was only twenty.

It was an odd thing about both those boys hating the gun, for they seemed to be almost the two most conscientious ones in the crew.

Our artillerymen in the front lines didn't try to keep themselves looking very pretty. As they said, "There ain't nobody going to see you that amounts to a damn unless the colonel should happen to come around."

Their clothes were muddy and greasy and often torn. Some of them wore coveralls, but most of them wore regular o.d. pants, jackets and leggings.

It was funny to see them when they were routed out on a firing mission just before dawn. They jerked on their shoes and waded through the mud to their guns. Naturally they didn't take time to put on leggings. Then when it got light and the firing mission was over they sat around scraping the mud off their shoes and putting on their leggings.

It was a very strict military regulation in the combat zones that everybody must wear the leggings, but the average soldier, just like myself, was careless about it. Along this line one of the boys said the worst trouble they had was with new officers.

"One morning we were firing," he said, "and one of them asked over the telephone if we had our leggings on. It made me so damn mad that I just called this gun out of action while we all sat down and put on the leggings."

The artillerymen were also indifferent about wearing their corporal's and sergeant's stripes. Everybody knew everybody else in the battery so it seemed a waste of time to put stripes on their ordinary workclothes. One time an order came around that everybody had to get his stripes on. All that day during the lulls the men sat around on piles of shells or water cans, sewing at their shirts and jackets—like a bunch of old women.

The men didn't get a chance to take a bath very often. Once in a while the Army set up some portable showers in the woods a few miles away and the gunners could go, a few at a time, in a truck and get a bath. But most of them hadn't had a bath in more than two months.

One night the battery commander, Captain Robert Perrin of Union, South Carolina, got to arguing with one of his officers, Lieutenant Heath Stewart of Columbia, South Carolina, about how the home front should be conducted.

Lieutenant Stewart said he thought labor should be drafted for the defense plants and Captain Perrin said, "Why, that's just what we're fighting for, the freedom not to be drafted for labor. That's slavery the way Germany does it. If you feel that way about it there's no use fighting at all."

He saw he had Lieutenant Stewart whipped, so then they changed to the subject of civilization.

"I don't know whether we've advanced so much or not," Captain Perrin said. "Take baths, for instance. We think we're civilized because we take so damn many baths at home. Well, I've just had my first bath today in two months and I can't see a bit of difference in the way I feel."

Next day all the argument was relayed, as such things usually were, down to the gun pit, and the soldiers themselves got into the same discussion. They were divided about fifty-fifty on whether we should draft labor or not. On the bathing question they must have agreed with the captain, because I noticed that when the call came for the men to go on the truck to take showers nobody went.

Then I told them about my bath experience back in America. For months I had dreamed about how wonderful it would be to take a hot bath every day in a real bathtub in a warm bathroom. Yet when I got there I found myself almost allergic to baths. I'm almost ashamed to admit it, but I don't think I averaged more than one bath a week all the time I was home.

"Taking baths is just a habit," said Pfc. Frank Helms. "If our mothers hadn't started giving us baths when we were babies we would never have known the difference."

So maybe what we're fighting for is the right to be as dirty as we please. It suits me.

The commanding officer of the regiment did what seemed to me a pretty smart thing. Since most of the boys couldn't get to a city to buy souvenirs, he had a Special Service officer go to Capri and buy souvenirs for anybody who wanted them. Lieutenant Don H. Poston, of Logan, Ohio, who used to be a theater manager in Columbus, was the Special Service officer. He was helped out by Private Joe Pacucci, of 1805 South 15th Street, South Philadelphia. Joe had lived for seven years in Naples and didn't go to America until he was twenty years old, so he knew all the ins and outs.

They made two trips to Capri, and they spent over $3,000. They bought seven hundred ladies' cigarette boxes, five hundred cameo brooches, nearly a hundred vivid little paintings on wood, and scores of rings, bracelets, necklaces and other gadgets.

Prices went up more than a hundred per cent between their first and second trips. This was partly due to inflation, induced by the American soldiers' willingness to pay practically any amount for practically anything. Also there were some sounder justifications— the electric current was off in the cities and Italian craftsmen had to run their jigsaws and do their welding by hand, thus cutting down production.

All this in the heart of a bitter war. It's a funny world. As one of our gun crew remarked, "The Germans fight for glory, the British for their homes, and the Americans fight for souvenirs."

My regiment ran a lottery, and the grand prize was a bottle of Coca-Cola.

It all started when a former member, then back in the States— Pfc. Frederick Williams of Daytona Beach, Florida—sent two bottles of coke to two of his old buddies—Corporal Victor Glover of Daytona Beach and Master Sergeant Woodrow Daniels of Jacksonville, Florida. Nobody in the outfit had seen Coca-Cola in more than a year. The recipients drank one of the bottles and then began having ideas about the other. At last they decided to put it up in a raffle, and use the proceeds to care for children whose fathers had been killed serving in the regiment. The boys hoped the Coca-Cola company would match whatever amount they raised.

The lottery was announced in the little mimeographed newspaper, and chances on the coke were put on sale at twenty-five cents apiece. Before the end of the first week the cash box had more than $1,000 in it. The money came in quarters, dollars, shillings, pounds, francs and lire. They had to appoint a committee to administer the affair. At the end of the third week the fund exceeded $3,000.

Then Private Lamyl Yancey, of Harlan, Kentucky, got a miniature bottle of Coca-Cola and he put it up as second prize. Just before the grand drawing the fund reached $4,000. All the slips were put in a German shell case, and the brigade commander drew out two numbers.

The winnah and new champion was Sergeant William de Schneider of Hackensack, New Jersey. The miniature bottle went to Sergeant Lawrence Presnell of Fayetteville, North Carolina. Sergeant de Schneider was appalled by what had happened to him. That one coke was equal in value to eighty thousand bottles back home. "I don't think I care to drink a $4,000 bottle," he said. "I think I'll send it home and keep it a few years."

The Rome radio picked up the item, completely distorted it, and used it for home-front propaganda. The way it came out was that our soldiers were so short of supplies they were paying as high as $10,000 for just one bottle of Coca-Cola. Not only did they give the story a completely false meaning, but they deftly added $6,000 to the kitty. Well, that's one way to fight a war.

Shells and big guns cost money, but it's better to spend money than lives. Along that line a bunch of us were sitting around conjecturing about how much it costs to kill one German with our artillery. When you count the great price of the big modern guns, training the men, all the shipping to get everything over, and the big shells at $50 each, it must cost, we figured, $25,000 for every German we killed with our shelling. "Why wouldn't it be better," one fellow said, "just to offer the Germans $25,000 apiece to surrender, and save all the in-between process and the killing? I bet they'd accept it too."

It's a novel theory, but personally I bet they wouldn't.

One forenoon a nice-looking young soldier walked up and sat down on the earthen ledge behind our gun pit. He was Corporal Bubble Perritt, of Peedee, South Carolina, and his job was stringing telephone wires.

The other boys were kidding him about having a soft job, and he was saying he walked more in one day than they did in a month. Finally he said in a soft southern accent, "Say, I've been in the Army three years and ain't fard a gun yet. Why don't you let me shoot off that thing?"

"All right, come on," said Sergeant Jack McCray. "You can shoot the next one."

So Bubble went over, pulled the lanyard, and sent the big shell on its way. He dusted off his hands and said, surprised-like, "Hell, I always thought you boys had something to do."

They chased him out of the gun pit.

When the battery moved, each gun was pulled by a huge Diamond-T truck. It was no picnic moving those guns over the mountains and through the deep mud. On one move our gun turned over twice in a single night, when it skidded off the road.

When they arrived at a new position the whole crew turned to with shovels, dug a pit for the gun and brought up logs to keep the gun from kicking itself out of position. I had thought it took hours to lay in the gun mathematically, get it all braced and everything, but the boys said that on extreme occasions they could fire eight minutes after reaching a new position.

Army powdered eggs were usually no bargain. I think the worst I ever ate were those I had in England, and the best were the work of Mess Sergeant Clifton Rogers of Mullins, South Carolina, who cooked for our artillery battery. Rogers cooked with imagination. Here's how he made powdered eggs for approximately a hundred men: He took two one-gallon cans of egg powder, poured in sixteen cans of condensed milk and four quarts of water, mixed it up into a batter, then dipped it out with a ladle and fried it in boiling lard.

The result looked like a small yellow pancake. It was frizzled and done around the edges like a well-fried egg, and although it tasted only vaguely like an egg still it tasted good. And that's all that counted.

Speaking of powdered eggs and all the various other forms of dehydrated stuff we got, one of the soldiers said he had heard we were now getting dehydrated water from America.

The cannoneers led a life that was deadly with monotony and devoid of any comfort or diversity or hope of diversity. Ordinarily they were firing the guns only a small part of any one day. The rest of the time they either played poker, did their washing, sewed buttons, wrote letters, or just sat around doing absolutely nothing, talking the same kind of small talk day after day after day.

If they had had a comfortable place to loaf in it wouldn't have been so bad, but there was never anything but a helmet, a water can or a sandbag to sit on, and a little straw on the ground to lie on. There was no place to put anything, and a man's castle was the cramped confines of his pup tent. And yet the average cannoneer was in good spirits and apparently resigned to going on and on that way indefinitely.

The regiment had recently begun a rotation system of giving a few men in each battery leave to go to Naples for five days. Naples is a nice city, and the boys could get a bath and a good bed, go sightseeing, drink some vino, and maybe even have a date. The boys, incidentally, cut cards to see who would go on the Naples junkets.

The rotation plan of sending one per cent per month of each outfit back to America also came in for a lot of discussion. It wasn't working very well up to that point, and the quota had been cut to half of one per cent. It was an optimist indeed who figured the quota would ever get around to him personally.

Sergeant Jack McCray had his own chances all figured out. He said the way things were going he would get his five days in Naples around the following July, and he would get to go back to America seventeen years from then.

The shell they fired from those 155-millimeter howitzers had a single metal band around it. Two or three times a day in every battery one of those bands would fly off as a shell left the gun. On its own, the band was liable to go in any direction, careening and screaming through the air. They were called "rotating bands," and they made a variety of noises, one of which sounded like a whipped dog yowling in terror.

I was standing one morning with a bunch of cannoneers when a rotating band of the whipped-dog type cut loose from another battery, whereupon one of the soldiers said, "We've run out of ammunition so we're shootin' dogs at 'em now."

Dogs also figured in the conversation about food. Every day or so somebody brought up the suggestion that the cook was putting Italian dogs in the chow. One of the boys said, "As soon as I don't see no more dogs around I'm gonna quit eatin'."

One day an ammunition truck drove past and it had a little black-and-white dog standing on top of the hood. His ears and tail stood straight up, and he looked so damned important we had to laugh. When the truck came back the little dog was running ahead of it, nosing around into everything, still acting awfully important. When he saw us he came bounding into the gun pit, walked right across a row of shells lying there, and continued busily on his way.

I don't know why that struck the soldiers as so odd, but they kept talking about the dog walking right across those shells as though there might have been some danger of his setting them off, which of course there wasn't. In fact the men themselves walked and sat on them all the time.

Lots of soldiers had picked up local dogs as pets. The dogs in Italy were better and healthier-looking than those in Africa. Some of the pups were absolutely indifferent to a blast from the heavy guns, while others were scared to death. At night, after a salvo, we could hear the farmers' dogs all around yelling in fright as though they had been kicked. And the cannoneers said that sometimes a dog would just stand and shake all over with fright after a big gun had gone off.

In that respect there was a lot of similarity between a dog and me.

During one of my last nights with the battery we were routed out of our blankets an hour before dawn to put down a barrage preceding an infantry attack. Every other battery for miles around was firing. Batteries were dug in close together and we got the blasts and concussions from other guns as well as our own. Every gun threw up a fiendish flame when it went off, and the black night was pierced like a sieve with the flashes of hundreds of big guns.

Standing there in the midst of it all, I thought it was the most violent and terrifying thing I'd ever been through. Just being on the sending end of it was staggering. I don't know how human sanity could survive on the receiving end.

When it was all over and daylight came with a calm and unnatural quiet, a rainbow formed over the mountain ahead of us. It stood out radiantly against the moist green hillsides and drifting whitish-gray clouds. One end of it was anchored on the mountain slope on our side of the valley, while the other disappeared behind a hill on the German side. And, as we watched, that other end of the rainbow became gradually framed by a rising plume of white smoke—caused by the shells we had just sent over. The smoke didn't obscure the rainbow. Rather it seemed to rise enfoldingly around it, like honeysuckle climbing a porch column.

Men newly dead lay at the foot of that smoke. We couldn't help thinking what a strange pot of gold that beautiful rainbow was pointing to.

TEN

PERSONALITIES AND ASIDES

The little towns of Italy that had been in the path of the war from Salerno northward were nothing more than great rubble heaps. Of most of them there was hardly enough left to form a framework for rebuilding. When the Germans occupied a town we rained artillery on it for days and weeks at a time. Then after we moved in the Germans would shell it heavily. The town got it from both sides.

Along the road for twenty or thirty miles behind the fighting front I passed through one demolished town after another. Most of the inhabitants took to the hills after the first shelling. Some went to live in caves, some went to relatives in the country. In every town there were people who refused to leave no matter what happened, and many of these were killed by the shelling and bombing from both sides.

A countryside is harder to disfigure than a town. You have to look closely to find the destruction wrought upon the green fields and the rocky hillsides. It is there, but it is temporary—like a skinned finger; time will heal it. In a year the countryside covers its own scars.

Wandering on foot and observing very carefully, you could see the signs: the limb of an olive tree broken off, six swollen dead horses in the corner of a field, a strawstack burned down, a chestnut tree blown clear out, roots and all, by a German bomb, little gray patches of powder burns on the hillside, scraps of broken and abandoned rifles and grenades in the bushes, grain fields patterned with a million crisscrossing ruts from the great trucks that had crawled frame-deep through the mud, empty gun pits, and countless foxholes, and rubbish-heap stacks of empty C-ration cans, and now and then the lone grave of a German soldier.

The apple season was on then, and in the cities and those towns that still existed there were hundreds of little curbside stands selling apples, oranges, and hazelnuts. In Italy the apples were to us what the tangerines had been in North Africa the year before, and the tomatoes and grapes in Sicily the previous summer.

From the time he landed the average soldier liked Italy a great deal better than he did Africa. As one soldier said, "They seem more civilized."

Our soldiers were slightly contemptuous of the Italians and didn't fully trust them; yet with typical American tenderheartedness they felt sorry for them, and little by little they became sort of fond of them. They seemed to us a pathetic people, not very strong in character but fundamentally kind and friendly.

A lot of our Italian-American soldiers took to the land of their fathers like ducks to water, but not all of them. One night I was riding in a jeep with an officer and an enlisted man who was of Italian extraction. The officer was saying that there were plenty of girls in Naples—most of the soldiers there had girls.

"Not me," said the driver. "I won't have anything to do with them. The minute they find out I speak Italian they start giving me a sob story about how poor and starved they are and why don't the Americans feed them faster?

"I look at it this way—they've been poor for a long time and it wasn't us that made them poor. They started this fight and they've killed plenty of our soldiers, and now that they're whipped they expect us to take care of them. That kind of talk gives me a pain. I tell them to go to hell. I don't like 'em."

But our average soldier didn't hold a feeling of animosity for very long. We couldn't help liking a lot of the Italians. For instance, when I pulled back of the lines to do some writing for a few days, I stayed in a bare, cold room of a huge empty house out in the country. My roommates were Reynolds Packard, of the United Press, and Clark Lee, of the International News Service.

We had an Italian boy—twenty-four years old—who took care of the room. I don't know whether the Army hired him or whether he just walked in and went to work. At any rate, he was there all day and he couldn't do enough for us. Every day he swept the room six times and mopped it twice. He boarded up blown-out windows, did our washing, and even picked up the scraps of wood and built a little fire to take the chill off the room. When he ran out of anything to do he just sat around, always in sight, awaiting our pleasure.

His name was Angelo. Every time we looked at him he smiled. He and I talked to each other all the time without either of us knowing what the other was saying. He admired my two-fingered speed on the typewriter. It drove me crazy the way he used to stand and look over my shoulder while I was writing, but he was so eager and kind I couldn't tell him to go away. It's hard to hate a guy like that.

As far as we could observe, the Italian people had more to eat, and more goods, than the French did when we hit North Africa. There was more to buy in the shops and the better-off people seemed to have a greater variety of food. Of course the poorest people of both countries were pretty close to starvation, but that was not a new experience for them.

The first American troops to hit Naples could buy fine watches and sweaters and carpenter's tools and real silk stockings—I know of one officer who bought fifty pairs for $1.50 a pair. Before long, good liquor was almost exhausted and in the cities there was considerable bootlegging of very dangerous booze. But as time went on other types of merchandise came out of hiding and went on sale. Apparently the Italians had hidden a great deal of stuff while the Germans were there. Not that the Germans would steal it, but the German Army regulated prices strictly, and the German price standard was below what the Italians wanted. So they waited until we came. They said the Germans didn't go in much for buying souvenirs and jewelry as much as we did, but instead bought clothing and food to send home to their families.

Out of their fear of the Germans these people concealed strange things in strange places. One day I talked with a soldier who said he had helped clean out the sewing machine an Italian family had buried in the bottom of the manure pile in their barnyard.

One night I went to a USO show given in a rest area and was put in the bald-headed row up front, next to a two-star general. As part of the program a girl came out and sang "Pistol-packin' Mama." The applause was scattered, and I could tell the tune was not too familiar. The general turned and said, "That's a new one on me; I never heard that before."

To which I replied, "You're a fortunate man. I never heard it either until I went home last fall, and then I had to listen to it thirty times a day. It was coming out of trees and water faucets. Even my dog was howling it at night."

So, you see, there's one advantage in being overseas and out of touch with things.

Just before Christmas I ran into the Tennessee twins, Arlie and Charlie Pass. I had met them in England, back in the fall of 1942. Well, there they were in Italy, still going strong, both still driving for colonels, still looking exactly alike. But one very special thing had happened: Arlie had captured himself a German.

It seems Arlie was driving a couple of colonels up in the front lines one day when they came to a 20-mm. gun sitting in the middle of the road. Beyond it was a bridge that was obviously mined. So the officers left Arlie waiting in the jeep while they went ahead on foot. While they were gone, a German soldier came out of the nearby woods with his hands up. Arlie just pointed his gun at him and kept it pointed till the officers got back.

Ordinarily Charlie might be expected to feel bad about the extraordinary distinction that had come to Arlie, but I don't think he worried much, since practically nobody could tell the boys apart. At least half the people they met thought Charlie was the one who captured the German. Charlie's cue was just to keep his mouth shut and blush modestly at the proper time.

Shortly after leaving the artillery outfit, I stopped in at an evacuation tent hospital to see Dick Tregaskis, war correspondent for International News Service. He had been badly wounded a few weeks before. A shell fragment had gone through his helmet and ripped his skull open. That he was alive at all seemed a miracle. Even after he was wounded, other shells exploded within arm's length of him; yet he escaped further injury.

He still had his battered steel helmet. It had a gash in the front two inches long and a smaller one at the left rear where the fragment came out. The blow had knocked off his glasses but not broken them. Even with such a ghastly wound Dick had walked half a mile down the mountain by himself until he found help. Late that night he arrived at the hospital, was put to sleep on morphine, and Major William Pitts performed the brain operation.

It was Major Pitts's fourth head operation that night. He took more than a dozen pieces of bone and steel out of Dick's brain, along with some of the brain itself. He and the other doctors were proud of pulling Dick through—as well they might be.

At first Dick had little use of his right arm, he couldn't read his letters, and he couldn't write. Also, he couldn't control his speech. He would try to say something like "boat" and a completely different yet related word like "water" would come out.

But he was making rapid progress. During my visits he made only a couple of small mistakes such as saying "flavor" when he meant "favorite." But he always kept trying until the word he wanted came forth. The doctors said he was a marvel. While other patients usually lay and waited for time to do the healing, Dick worked at it. He constantly moved his arm to get it back into action, and he read and talked as much as he could, making his mind practice.

While I was visiting him the second time, a corporal in the Medical Corps came in with a copy of *Guadalcanal Diary*, which Dick wrote, and asked if he would autograph it. Dick said he'd be glad to except he wasn't sure he could sign his name. He worked at it several minutes, and when he got through he said, "Why, that looks better than the way I used to sign it." And after the boy left he said, "I always like to be asked to sign a book. It makes you feel important."

Dick Tregaskis was the quiet and scholarly type of newspaperman. His personal gear was in the same room I had been living in back at the base camp, and I had noticed that his books were Shakespeare and the like. He wore tortoise-shell glasses and talked slowly and with distinctive words. He was genuine and modest. His manner belied the spirit that must have driven him, because he had by choice seen a staggering amount of war. He had been through four invasion assaults in the Pacific and the Mediterranean. His famous *Guadalcanal Diary* sold half a million copies in America and was made into a movie. He was a very thoughtful person and was as eager to know about my book as if it had been his own.

Dick was married and his home was in Elizabeth, New Jersey. He was the tallest correspondent over there—six feet five. General Mark Clark, who is six feet two, always said he was glad to see Tregaskis because he was one of the few men he could look up to. One of the surgeons laughingly remarked that if Dick had been short like me he might never have been wounded, but Dick said no. Where they were that day, with no cover anywhere, even "the tallest midget in the world would have got it." He meant the shortest midget, but we understood.

Dick wore a size fourteen shoe and once had to travel all the way from Guadalcanal to New Caledonia to find a new pair. He was strong and muscular but very thin, and his health was not too rugged. The night he was wounded, the last thing he did before the morphine put him to sleep was to warn the doctors against using any drugs that would stimulate his diabetes.

The hospital where he spent the first three weeks was only a few miles behind the lines. It was deep in mud, and Dick lay on a cot in the middle of a dirt-floored ward tent crammed with other patients. A few days after I saw him he was moved to a general hospital farther in the rear, and in a short time the Army was going to send him back to America for final recuperation. The surgeons had taken a big patch of skin off his left leg and grafted it onto his head, to cover the wound. They predicted he would be ready for the front again within six months.

You'd think that after as much war as he had seen, and after such a hairbreadth escape, he might have been ready to call it a day. If I'd had his wound I would have gone home and rested on my laurels forever. But not Dick; he expected to be back in action in 1944. (And he was—in France.)

He was no adventurer, but a deeply sincere and conscientious man who did what he did because he felt he should. His next ambition was to make a combat parachute jump.

One day I dropped into a prisoners-of-war collecting point and picked up a little lore about the super race.

German prisoners those days were on the whole a fairly crummy-looking lot. Most of them were very young. A great many were still in summer uniform and wearing light underwear.

The prisoners were much more talkative then than they used to be. It was only the dyed-in-the-wool Nazis who got on their high horses and refused to talk. The others seemed so relieved to be out of the war that they just opened their traps and let it run. Lots of the prisoners were Poles and Austrians, and many who weren't Poles insisted they were. They figured they would get better treatment if we thought them Poles. But they couldn't fool the examiners, because most of our Army men who examined prisoners could speak German like natives and could tell an accent a mile away.

The German officers knew we treated prisoners well, but apparently they fed their troops horror stories to discourage desertion. Lots of prisoners came in obviously fearful about what we might do to them.

A great many German soldiers captured in Italy still felt that Germany would win the war. That is, they thought so at the time they were captured. But as they were brought to the rear they were astounded to see the amount of Allied equipment and supplies along the roads and in the fields. Some of the more sensitive ones were actually crying when brought to collecting points— overwhelmed by the sudden realization that we had enough stuff to beat them. The examiners said that by the time the prisoners reached the rear areas, seventy-five per cent of them were doubtful of Germany's winning.

The examiners often asked prisoners what made them think Germany was going to win. Some of them said that the Allies would simply collapse. Some thought Germany would soon sweep back over Russia. Others talked wishfully about a new secret weapon, due in the spring, that would bring quick victory. Still others, almost in desperation, said that some miracle was going to happen— Germany just couldn't, just didn't dare lose the war—and so they wouldn't let themselves think of defeat.

As far as I could gather, the German soldiers in Italy were pretty well aware of their disasters in Russia and on the bombing front at home, and I was surprised that the German censors allowed so much gloom from home to seep through in the soldiers' letters. Many letters found on German soldiers, from their families in Germany, had fright in them, or bitterness, and all that I heard of were tinged with war weariness, and fervently hopeful for quick victory.

But on the whole the letters showed no general tendency to give up. Some of them rang with the same wordy sort of confidence in victory that our own family letters and editorials carry. In other words, the Germans weren't admitting that they were whipped.

One of the German kids who came through seemed terribly depressed. When the examiners strike a case like that, they try to find out the trouble, other than the normal depression over being captured. But they couldn't seem to get at this boy.

Finally, just to make light conversation, one of them said, "Well, cheer up, at least you'll be able to spend Christmas with us."

Thereupon the boy sat up and said eagerly, "Do you celebrate Christmas too?"

He didn't know that we knew about Christmas, and apparently he had been brooding over the prospect of spending it with a heathen people. After that he was bright and chipper.

Our prisoner-collecting points were staffed, of course, with American soldiers who spoke perfect German. Mostly they were German-born men who had emigrated and become American citizens. They said that often when a prisoner was brought in and heard nothing but good old German flying around the place he was utterly bewildered, and could hardly be made to believe he was in American hands.

I had a talk with two of the examiners of enemy personnel, as they are called. Both had worked all through the previous day and all night too, examining a steady flow of prisoners. It was then three in the afternoon and they hadn't slept since the morning before. One of them, a sergeant, was a short, slight man of scholarly appearance who seemed out of place in uniform. He had been a student most of his life. He had gone to America nine years before because he sensed that he might get into trouble with the Nazis. In America he had tutored for a living.

The other, also a sergeant, was a real-estate man in private life. He was born near Hamburg and went to America when he was twenty-one years old, over seventeen years back. He still talked English with a slight accent—said "v" for "w." He had just passed his thirty-eighth birthday; he didn't know whether to apply for a discharge or not, but guessed he wouldn't, since his work was pretty important. He said it was almost impossible for a German prisoner to lie to him, because, having examined thousands of prisoners, he knew so much about the German Army. He knew every unit, where it was, and who commanded it. If a prisoner lied and told him his company commander was So-and-so, the sergeant said, "Oh, no, he isn't," and then gave the right name. Which was disconcerting to the prisoner, to say the least.

"Actually I know a great deal more about the German Army than I do about the American Army," he said, "for all I do alt day long is sit here behind this desk in this battered old building, talking to Germans, and I never get out to see the American Army."

Practically everybody I ran into in the Army got Christmas packages. I know of one captain—Frank Knebel, of Pottsville, Pennsylvania—who got twenty-four boxes from home. Nearly every soldier's package had in it at least one ironic item, such as brushless shaving cream or Life-Savers, with which we were flooded. But most of them were pretty nice collections.

It sounds silly, but there were men who actually got cans of Spam. Others got fancy straw house slippers, and some got black silk socks—as though the boys were likely to put on full dress and spend an evening in a night club. But the funniest gift I saw was a beautiful blue polka-dot necktie.

I didn't get any Christmas packages, but then I hadn't been back from America very long. Besides, my packages had a way of getting lost, whatever the season.

One of the meanest stunts I heard of was a Christmas envelope full of clippings that a practical joker back home sent a soldier. The clippings consisted of colored ads cut out of magazines, and they showed every luscious American thing, from huge platters of ham and eggs to vacationists lolling in bright bathing robes on the sand, surrounded by beautiful babes. There ought to be a law. On second thought, I remember an even meaner trick. In fact, this one would take first prize in an orneriness contest at any season, Christmas or otherwise. The worst of it was that it happened to a front-line infantryman. Some of his friends at home sent him three bottles of whisky for Christmas. They came separately, were wonderfully packed, and the bottles came through without a break. The first bottle tasted fine to the cold kids at the front, but when the second and third ones came the boys found they had been opened and drained along the way, then carefully resealed and continued on their journey. Of course, mailing them in the first place was illegal, but that's beside the point. The point is that somewhere in the world there is a louse of a man with two quarts of whisky inside him who should have his neck wrung off.

Right after Christmas some of our front-line troops, for the first time in many months, were not getting enough cigarettes. In the middle and latter days of Tunisia we were issued up to five or seven packs a week. One outfit I talked with said that since hitting Italy they had been averaging only three and a half packs per man per week. Another unit, not five miles away, was getting more than a carton a week. Nobody seemed to know the reason for it.

And speaking of cigarettes, the boys wondered why, after all those months, they still were cursed with three obscure brands nobody liked. Washington could have done several million soldiers a favor by either cutting cigarettes out entirely or else explaining why the unpopular ones had to be included. This was later corrected until there was almost no kick at all about cigarettes.

In the last war the *Stars and Stripes* had many men on its staff who later became prominent in the literary world. It is too early yet to tell what the various Army newspapers in this war will produce, but we had a couple of likely candidates in Italy. Soldiers and correspondents both would have cast a willing vote for them right then. One was a reporter, the other a cartoonist. The reporter was Sergeant Jack Foisie of Berkeley, California; the cartoonist was Sergeant Bill Mauldin of Phoenix, Arizona. Both were very young, both were quiet and earnest, both had genuine talent, and that ephemeral and intuitive ability to express the soldiers' viewpoint.

Sergeant Foisie had only been on the staff of *Stars and Stripes* since the invasion of Sicily, but already he was the man for whom the paper got the most requests when units wanted somebody to write about them. He had been overseas almost fifteen months. Before transferring to the paper he was in a tank-destroyer unit. He drove a half-track and ran a 50-caliber machine gun. He fought all through Tunisia. He was never wounded, but in the Battle of Sidi-bou-Zid, in February, 1942, he lost his half-track by a hit from an 88-mm. cannon. Along with it he lost everything he had, including his portable typewriter.

Before the war, Foisie was a reporter on the *San Francisco Chronicle*. When he went into the Army he was determined not to lose the writing touch, so he took his typewriter with him and wrote scads of letters to the folks back home, just to keep his hand in. He said his folks couldn't understand how he was able to write them so often in combat and then got to be such a bad correspondent after he took the quieter job on the paper. The answer was, of course, that he didn't have to write letters for practice any more.

Toward the end of the Tunisian campaign Jack wrote to *Stars and Stripes* and asked if there was any chance of getting on the staff. Captain Bob Neville, the editor, wrote back a two-word letter: "Why not?"

Jack thought Bob was being facetious and supposed that was the end of it. But ten days later there came official transfer papers with travel orders calling for transportation by airplane. The airplane business so astounded and impressed Jack's company commander that he cleaned up, put on his dress blouse for the first time since he had left America, and personally drove Jack the fifty miles to the nearest airdrome to see him off.

Among correspondents Foisie had the reputation of always being willing to go anywhere and do anything. But he was shy, and for months he kept in the background, just filling his job and saying nothing. After he knew everybody he joked and kidded as much as the rest. When I first met him, the previous summer in Sicily, he had had a fairly marked hesitation in his speech. But on rejoining him in Italy I noticed that it was gone. I spoke to him about it and he said he thought it was because he had gained more confidence in himself.

Although he was a good soldier, Foisie went up and down in rank six or eight times before joining *Stars and Stripes*, owing largely to the whims of various commanders. His ups and downs destroyed all his regard for rank, and finally he truly didn't care whether he was a private, a sergeant or a lieutenant. He actually argued against it when they made him a sergeant on *Stars and Stripes*, and he wouldn't wear his chevrons until forced to.

Jack Foisie was twenty-four years old, darkish blond, with hair starting to thin in spots. He had a big chin, and his eyes were set back in his head, giving him the appearance of looking out of two narrow slits. He was left-handed, and did not smoke. Although of French extraction, he spoke little French. He was born and raised in Seattle and went to the University of Washington for two years—until his folks moved to Berkeley. His father, Frank P. Foisie, was head of the waterfront employers of the Pacific Coast, which meant he was the man who sat across the table and argued with Harry Bridges.

After the war Jack had two ambitions—to finish school and to get married. The marriage business came first. Her name was Florence McTighe and she lived in Trenton, New Jersey. The big question would be how to make a Californian out of her. (Foisie was transferred to America in the spring of 1944 and they were married.)

Foisie had lived a rugged life both as a combat soldier and as a reporter. For a while he was put on special assignment, living in town and making trips out to the airfield by jeep. He found it interesting but he began to get a little frightened.

"I'm getting soft," he said. "The life is too nice. It would be better to be back at the front living with doughboys and writing about them."

Sergeant Bill Mauldin seemed to us over there to be the finest cartoonist the war had produced. And that's not merely because his cartoons are funny, but because they are also terribly grim and real. Mauldin's cartoons aren't about training-camp life, which is most familiar to people at home. They are about the men in the line—the tiny percentage of our vast Army who are actually up there doing the dying. His cartoons are about the war.

Mauldin's central cartoon character is a soldier, unshaven, unwashed, unsmiling. He looks like a hobo; he looks, in fact, exactly like a doughfoot who has been in the lines for two months. And that isn't pretty. In a way his cartoons are bitter. His work is so mature that I had pictured him as a man approaching middle age.

Yet he was only twenty-two years old, and he looked even younger. He himself could never have raised the heavy black beard of his cartoon dogface. His whiskers were soft and scant, his nose was upturned good-naturedly, and his eyes had a twinkle. His maturity came simply from a native understanding of things, and from being a soldier himself for a long time. He had been in the Army three and a half years.

Bill Mauldin was born in Mountain Park, New Mexico. Although he called Phoenix, Arizona, home base, we of New Mexico could claim him without much resistance on his part. Bill had drawn ever since he was a child. He always drew pictures of the things he wanted to grow up to be, such as cowboys and soldiers— not realizing that what he really wanted to become was a man who draws pictures. At seventeen he graduated from high school in Phoenix, took a year at the Academy of Fine Arts in Chicago, and at eighteen was in the Army. He did sixty-four days on KP duty in his first four months. That fairly cured him of a lifelong worship of uniforms.

Mauldin belonged to the Forty-fifth Division. Their record has been a fine one, and their losses have been heavy. Mauldin's typical grim cartoon soldier is really a Forty-fifth Division infantryman, and he is one who has truly been through the mill. Bill was detached from straight soldier duty after a year in the infantry, and put to work on the division's weekly paper. His true war cartoons started in Sicily and continued on through Italy, gradually gaining recognition.

Captain Bob Neville, *Stars and Stripes* editor, shook his head with a veteran's admiration and said of Mauldin, "He's got it. Already he's the outstanding cartoonist of the war."

Mauldin worked in a cold, dark little studio in the back of the *Stars and Stripes* Naples office. He wore silver-rimmed glasses when he worked. His eyes used to be good, but he damaged them in his early Army days by drawing for too many hours at night with poor light. He averaged about three days out of ten at the front, then came back and drew up a large batch of cartoons. If the weather was good he sketched a few details at the front. But the weather was usually lousy.

"You don't need to sketch details anyhow," he said. "You come back with a picture of misery and cold and danger in your mind and you don't need any more details than that."

His cartoon in *Stars and Stripes* was headed "Up Front with Mauldin." One day some soldier wrote in a nasty letter asking what the hell did Mauldin know about the front. *Stars and Stripes* printed the letter. Beneath it in italics they ran a short editor's note: "Sergt. Bill Mauldin received the Purple Heart for wounds received while serving in Italy with Private Blank's own regiment."

That's known as telling 'em.

Bill was a rather quiet fellow, a little above medium size. He smoked and swore a little and talked frankly and pleasantly. He was not eccentric in any way. Though he was just a kid, he was a husband and father. He married in 1942 while in camp in Texas, and his son was born in August of '43, while Bill was in Sicily. His wife and child were living in Phoenix. Bill carried pictures of them in his pocketbook.

After the war he planned to settle again in the Southwest, our mutual love, then to go on doing cartoons of those same guys who fought in the Italian hills; except that when peace comes the men will be in civilian clothes and living as they should be.

Fortunately for everybody, including Mauldin, the American public has had an opportunity to see his daily drawings. Syndication of them to newspapers was arranged early in 1944.

There was an Army hospital where I went occasionally to see one of my wounded friends, and I got acquainted with several of the other patients. One of these was Walter Jentzen, of Carlsbad, New Mexico. Like the rest, he was in hospital pajamas, and I thought all the time he was a private—he seemed so quiet and humble. When I went to write down his name it turned out he was a lieutenant. Back in Carlsbad he had a two-month-old baby whom he had never seen.

It was the second time Jentzen had been wounded. In Sicily he got shot in his behind when a German tank let loose on him. And then, very early in the Italian campaign, he got a shell fragment in his chest. A notebook which he always carried in his left shirt pocket was all that saved him. He had been in the hospital more than a month and was just about ready to go back to duty.

Jentzen used to manage creamery plants in Albuquerque, Portales, and Las Cruces. So, having come from Albuquerque recently, I tortured him by telling him what the New Mexico sun felt like, how the air smelled, and how beautiful the Sandias were at sunset.

The only trouble with torturing a guy that way was that I tortured myself at the same time.

There for a spell, I was really starting to worry. I'd been in Italy more than a month and I was continuing to feel fine. What was going to become of my record of being sick in every country I'd ever set foot on? Could I be slipping in my old age?

But I saved the day. I knew how to fix it. I just took a bath, and sure enough I started to sniffle right off. By neglecting the sniffles for the next two days, I promoted myself a first-class cold. And then everything was fine. The only trouble with the cold was that I couldn't find anything funny to write about it. I moved into town for my convalescence, had a nice room in an apartment house, had good food and several friends, and didn't even feel too badly.

The only reason I mention it at all is just to keep my record intact. I'm ashamed not to have had a really bad sickness, but maybe I can do better when we hit Germany.

All the highways north from Naples were thick with speeding convoys of supplies day and night. Lights were used right up to the combat zone. Both British and American trucks crowded the roads. Drivers pounded the big trucks along at forty and fifty miles an hour, and the main highways were no place for a nervous Nellie. Originally the highways were good macadam, but they became filled with holes from the intensity of the traffic. Engineers worked on them constantly.

At the edges of the cities the roads were wide and lined with stately sycamore trees. It was like driving through a beautiful tunnel.

Both American and British armies had put up thousands of stenciled and painted signs along the way, directing drivers to the numerous units. When we came to a central crossroads we could see anywhere up to a hundred signs clustered on top of small stakes, like a flower garden in bloom. If we were really puzzled about our destination we'd have to pull off and study the hodgepodge for five minutes before finding out anything.

Somebody in our Army must have been a roadside advertising man before the war, for we had all kinds of signs along the highways in addition to the direction signs. They were tacked onto trees, telephone poles and posts. There were many in the Burma Shave poetic style, the several phrases being on separate boards about fifty yards apart, such as: "If you leave—good clothes behind—you may need them—some other time." That was an admonition against the American soldier's habit of abandoning gear when he got more than he could carry.

Another one in Burma Shave fashion, and of dubious rhyme, said, "Some like gold—some like silver—we like salvage—bring it, will you?"

There were also frequent warnings against venereal disease, and one sign far out in the country said, "Is your tent clean?" A lot of front-line soldiers who hadn't even been in a pup tent for months used to get a laugh out of that one.

As we advanced mile by slow mile across the Italian mountains and valleys, our many command posts were set up wherever possible in Italian farm or village houses. The houses were mostly all alike. They were very old and substantial-looking, yet they shook all over from the blast of our nearby guns.

Sometimes an Italian family still lived in one room of the house while the Americans occupied the rest. At other times the family had gone—nobody knew where—and taken with it everything but the heaviest furniture.

Often faded pictures would still be hanging on the walls— wedding-group pictures of forty years back, a full-face picture of some mustachioed young buck in the uniform of the last war, and old, old pictures of grandpa and grandma, and always a number of pictures of Christ and various religious scenes and mottoes. I billeted in dozens of Italian homes on the farms and little towns of our front lines, and invariably the faded pictures on the walls were of the same sort.

In one house nothing was left except the big cupboards and two heavy suitcases stored on top of the cupboards. We didn't nose into the suitcases, but I noticed that one bore the label of a big Italian steamship line and underneath the label it said, in English, "Steerage Passenger." Somebody in that poor family had been to America and back.

One day I heard a soldier say, "I'd sure like to see just one good old-fashioned frame house. I haven't seen a wooden building since we came to Italy." There were frame buildings farther north, but in that part of Italy everything was brick or stone. We almost never saw a building afire.

The pitiful towns like Vairano and San Pietro and San Vittore and Cervaro and even Cassino, which had been absolutely pulverized by exploding shells and bombs, had gone down stone by stone and never from flame. They died hard, but they died.

Came a day when Major Ed Bland got fed up with flying for a living and I got fed up with writing for a living and Corporal Harry Cowe got fed up with being a corporal for a living, so the three of us said, "To hell with it," and we got into Major Bland's jeep and went touring out to Pompeii.

The only thing in all Italy I had really wanted to see was the Leaning Tower of Pisa, but that was up north. I left Italy before we got that far. So Pompeii was the first and last real sightseeing I got to do in Italy.

Someone had told me he was disappointed in Pompeii because so little of the ruins had been uncovered, but he must have got on the wrong side of the mountain; there's certainly plenty uncovered. The buried city originally had twenty-five thousand inhabitants, and two-thirds of the whole city has been dug out. The reclaimed part surely must be almost a mile square. The volcanic eruption which covered Pompeii twenty to twenty-four feet deep and smothered everybody to death didn't come from Vesuvius, as most people think, but from Vesuvius's sister volcano, named Somma, now extinct. The catastrophe took place in AD 79 and the ruins weren't rediscovered until the eighteenth century.

When we stopped the jeep in the little barren square in front of the main gate to Pompeii, we were assaulted by a swarm of Italian urchins so grabby and insistent that we had to choose one as a watcher for our jeep. Then we bought tickets for ten cents apiece and went through the turnstiles. A few Italian men in civilian clothes tagged along, asking if we wanted a guide.

We picked one out. Many of the guides spoke fruit-stand English, such as "Dissa ees da bedaroom." But ours spoke with quite a cultured accent. He said he had once lived in New York, but that he'd been a guide in Pompeii since long before the war. His name was Ugo Prosperi. He was tall and thin and looked American. He wore a fedora hat and a long dark overcoat—with a fur collar—and gray trousers and gray spats. He smoked a thin cigar and addressed us constantly as "sir."

About a hundred bombs had fallen within the old Pompeii during the war. The ruins, of course, were never aimed at deliberately by either side. The bombs that fell inside the walls were strays, and not much real damage was done. But our guide, spotting Major Bland as an Air Force man, made four or five deadpan yet subtle digs about the bombings. All we could do was wink at each other. Major Bland had dive-bombed a lot of Italy, but never around Pompeii.

Dozens of small parties were wandering around the ruins, each with a guide and all composed of military people on leave. Down the street came a British brigadier smoking a pipe and a Scots officer wearing kilts. We turned a corner and met a group of British naval ensigns in from the sea, all carrying canes just as though they were on the college campus back in England. There were gay young American fliers in leather jackets and groups of crumpled-looking doughboys on leave from the front lines, eating peanuts.

War hadn't made much difference in the scribbling habits of the Americans and British. On the walls of Pompeii we saw hundreds of names written in pencil—Private Joe Doakes from Kansas City, Sergeant Jock McLean from Glasgow.

Pompeii is noted for the dirty pictures on the walls of certain houses. In peacetime the guides had to be discreet with mixed groups of tourists, but in wartime they didn't have to pull their punches except when a bunch of nurses or WACs happened along. As always, they offered to sell us obscene little good-luck emblems in silver or bronze, and books of "feelthy" photographs. Whether or not we bought any is a military secret.

Major Bland from Oklahoma and Corporal Cowe from Seattle and I from Indiana and New Mexico spent three hours in the ruins of old Pompeii and decided we enjoyed it. But we hoped the next time we went sightseeing it could be through the less ancient ruins of Berlin.

Italian trains were running again, and they had some electric trains out of Naples that were as modern as ours at home. But no transportation was back to prewar proportions, and everything was packed with masses of humanity. People rode on top of the cars and hung all over the sides.

The funniest thing about this was that whenever a train approached a tunnel it stopped in order to let the hangers-on get off, so they wouldn't be raked off by the tunnel walls.

One of the items on the Naples black market those days was American Army C ration. Where the black market got them I don't know, but a can of C-ration meat-and-vegetable hash sold for twenty-five cents. An Italian housewife whom I knew slightly bought three cans of C-ration hash, but when she got home she discovered she had been hoodwinked, for the cans were filled with sand.

Some smart operator had simply gathered up a batch of empty cans and lids, put sand in the cans, and then neatly crimped the lids back on.

At the entrance to an airfield which I visited occasionally, a ragged Italian woman sat on the ground selling apples, hazelnuts and English walnuts to the soldiers. These roadside merchants preferred not to sell to the Italians at all, because our soldiers willingly paid higher prices than the natives. But one day another Italian woman stopped in front of this vendor and gathered up an apron full of apples. Then she started to pay for them. The vendor woman unfortunately quoted her the soldier price. The prospective customer looked at her a moment, and then in a rage threw all the apples right in her face.

Sergeant Bill Mauldin, the Army cartoonist, bought a pair of rubber panties in Naples and sent them home to Phoenix for his six-month-old baby. Evidently his wife spread the word, for Bill had about twenty requests from young mothers in America wanting rubber pants for their babies. Apparently this article was extinct back home. Bill was in a spot, and had to declare rubber panties extinct in Italy too.

Sherman Montrose was the boss of all the civilian photographers in Italy. He worked for NEA Service and had covered the Solomons, the Aleutians and Italy, which made him one of the real veterans among war correspondents.

Monty had one piece of equipment which everybody wanted to steal. It was a pure eider-down sleeping bag, a thin envelope which he crawled into, and so wonderfully warm he didn't need anything else except a shelter half to keep the rain off. Monty had it made back in the days when eider down was still available. It cost $60. He packed it into a little drawstring bag, and carried it in his hand the way a woman carries a shopping bag.

Late in January, the British Army announced a new system of wound and foreign-service stripes, similar to ours of the last war. The new British wound insigne was a straight up-and-down gold strip an inch and a half long on the left forearm, one for each wound. Similar stripes of red were to be granted for each year of service in the war. Ours of the last war was a golden V on the right sleeve for each wound, and the same on the left sleeve for each six months of service abroad.

A little thing like a stripe can do wonders for morale. And certainly it's pointless to wait to give them until everybody goes home, for the average soldier will get into civvies the moment he is discharged. Over there and right then was when wound and service stripes would have given a guy a chance to get a little kick out of wearing his record on his sleeve.

In fact, I said I wouldn't mind parading a few stripes myself. I had spent a total of nearly two years overseas in World War II, and since I was at the age where hardening of the arteries might whisk me off at any moment, I would have liked somebody to see my stripes before it was too late.

A thing I had always feared in war zones happened at last—my typewriter broke down. A certain metal bracket cracked right in two, and I could no longer turn the cylinder and start a new line by hitting the little lever on the side. Fortunately I could still turn the cylinder the old-fashioned way, but that was like a soldier with a machine gun who had to stop and load every bullet separately. However, I finally got so used to it that it became automatic, and almost a year later I was still turning the cylinder by hand.

Imagination occasionally got the best of some of our letter writers. I heard about a soldier who wrote to his girl that he had been wounded, and then wrote his mother and tipped her off that he had just made it up. And another one who didn't fly at all wrote home that he had just shot down three Zeros. That was really good going, especially in Italy, and topped my own record. The most I was able to destroy in one day was two Spitfires and an Italian vegetable cart.

Mount Vesuvius developed a couple of streaks of red lava running down the side from the cone. They showed up wonderfully at night and were fascinating. The volcano smoked continually.

One night in Naples we had a couple of small earthquake shocks which shook our cots and scared us half to death.

It seems all America was worrying about whether the soldiers were going to get to vote. It sounded as if Congress were practically in fist fights about it.

Well, if you'll let me have the platform a moment, I think I can tell you how it was. I can't answer for that part of the Army which was either in training or in behind-the-lines routine jobs, but I think I can speak for the front-line combat soldier. Sure he wanted to vote. If you had asked him he would have said yes. But actually he thought little about it, and if there was going to be any red tape about it he would say nuts to it. The average combat soldier was so preoccupied with the job of merely keeping alive and with contributing what little he could to his own miserable existence, that he had scant time for thinking about the ballot. If you had offered him his choice between voting in November and finding a dirty cowshed to lie down in out of the rain, the cowshed would have won.

If the Army could have set up the machinery and told every soldier in the combat zone to step up on the proper day and mark his "X" if he wanted to, then ninety-nine per cent of the front-line troops would have voted. But if voting meant that soldiers would have to fill out long questionnaires from their home states, sign affidavits, and fuss around with reading and writing out complicated lists, then I think ninety-nine per cent of those same front-line troops would have said, "To hell with it, we'd rather have a cigar ration at suppertime instead."

One of the most fabulous characters in that war theater was Lieutenant Rudolf Charles von Ripper. He was so fabulous, a man might have been justified in thinking him a phony until he got to know him. I had known him since the previous summer in Algeria. Most of the other correspondents knew him. One whole fighting infantry division knew him. He was no phony.

Von Ripper was the kind they write books about. He was born in Austria. His father was a general in the Imperial Austrian Army, his mother a baroness. They had money. He could have had a rich, formal, royal type of existence. Instead he ran away from home at fifteen, worked in the sawmills, collected garbage, was a coal miner for a while, and then a clown in a small traveling circus. At nineteen he went into the French Foreign Legion, served two years, and was wounded in action. After that he went back to Europe and studied art. He was first of all an artist.

He traveled continuously. He lived in London and Paris. He lived in Shanghai during 1928. Then he returned to Berlin, joined liberal groups, and did occasional cartoons. Because he helped friends hiding from the Nazis, he was arrested in 1933, accused of high treason, and sent to a concentration camp. Dollfuss of Austria got him out after seven months. Then he went to the Balearic Islands off the coast of Spain and hibernated for a year, doing political, satirical drawing.

During his entire life he had fluctuated between these two extremes of salon intellectualism and the hard, brutal reality of personal participation in war. You don't think of an artist as being tough or worldly; yet von Ripper had been shot in battle more than twenty times. In 1936 he went to Spain as an aerial gunner in the Loyalist air force. He got sixteen slugs in his leg during that adventure, and barely came out alive.

Back in Austria in 1938, he saw that there was no possibility of organizing even a token resistance against Hitler, so he left for America. He became an American citizen five years later. By that time he was a private in the United States Army.

His Army career was a curious one. First he was a hospital laboratory technician. Then he was transferred to the newly formed Army Arts Corps, and left for North Africa in May of 1943 to paint battle pictures for the War Department. I happened to meet him a few days after he arrived overseas. He had hardly got started on his art work when Congress abolished the whole program. So he went back to being a regular soldier again, this time as an infantryman. He was transferred to the Thirty-fourth Division.

In the fall of '43 he was put in a front-line regiment, and in October he was wounded by shell splinters. He didn't seem to mind being shot at all. A month later, while leading a night patrol, he got four machine-pistol slugs in him. One slug split his upper lip just where it joined his nose. Another ripped a deep groove in the back of his hand. Another shot one finger clear off at the first joint. The fourth went through his shoulder. Before all his bandages were off he was back patrolling again.

Up to that time he had been a sergeant, but then he was given a battlefield commission as second lieutenant, and transferred to the division's engineers. Later it was possible for him to resume his art work in his spare time.

When I ran into him again, Lieutenant von Ripper had a nice little room on the top floor of a Naples apartment building which had been taken over by the Army. There he worked at a huge drawing board, doing water colors and pen-and-ink sketches of war. He slept on a cot in the same room. Around the walls were tacked dozens of his sketches. Now and then he returned to the front with his old outfit. Whenever he did, he was out in front getting shot at before you could say scat.

Von Ripper was quite a guy—a soldier of fortune in a way, yet he didn't look or act like one. He was intelligent, and his manner was simple. He was thirty-nine, but seemed younger. He was medium tall, slightly stooped, and one eye had a cast that made it appear to be looking beyond you. His face was long and thin, and his teeth were prominent. His knowledge of the English language was profound and his grammar perfect, but he still pronounced his words with a hissing imperfection. He swore lustily in English. He was as much at home discussing philosophy or political idealism as he was describing the best way to take cover from a machine gun. He was meticulous about his personal appearance, but he didn't seem to care whether he slept between satin sheets or in the freezing mud of the battlefield.

It was hard to reconcile the artist with the soldier in von Ripper, yet he was obviously professional at both. It may be that being a fine soldier made him a better artist. His long experience at warfare had made him as cunning as a fox. I couldn't conceive of his being rattled in a tight spot; he seemed to have been born without the normal sense of fear that dwells in most men. He was so calm and so bold in battle that he had become a legend at the front. High officers asked his advice in planning attacks.

He would volunteer for anything. Being wounded four times hadn't affected his nerve in the slightest. In fact, he became so famous as an audacious patrol leader that his division finally forbade his going on patrol unless by specific permission.

One night von Ripper, returning from patrol, was stopped by an itchy-fingered sentry who called, "Who goes there?" The answer came back in a heavy German accent, "Lieutenant von Ripper." He was wearing lieutenant bars, but his dog tag showed him to be a sergeant. It took an hour to get it straightened out. Some sentries would have shot first and then investigated.

Out of this background as a proven fighting man, von Ripper was painting the war. He had produced more than a hundred pictures. His work went to the War Department in Washington, but he hoped that an arrangement might be made whereby a book of his war drawings could be published.

Von Ripper, like most of us over there, had finally become more interested in the personal, human side of war than in the abstract ideals for which wars are fought. He said that in his paintings he was trying to take the applesauce out of war, trying to eliminate the heroics with which war is too often presented. From what I saw of the work of other artists, von Ripper was not alone in this sincerity. It's hard to be close enough to war to paint it, and still consider it heroic.

Von Ripper's dead men look awful, as dead men do. His live soldiers in foxholes have that spooky stare of exhaustion. His landscapes are sad and pitifully torn. His sketches aren't photographic at all; they are sometimes distorted and grotesque, and often he goes into pen-and-ink fantasy.

He gave me one of these, labeled "Self-Portrait in Italy," which shows himself and another wounded man, against a background of wrecked walls and starving children, being led downhill by the bony arms of a chortling skeleton.

You get to seeing things like that when you've been a soldier for a long time.

ELEVEN

MOUNTAIN FIGHTING

The war in Italy was tough. The land and the weather were both against us. It rained and it rained. Vehicles bogged down and temporary bridges washed out. The country was shockingly beautiful, and just as shockingly hard to capture from the enemy. The hills rose to high ridges of almost solid rock. We couldn't go around them through the flat peaceful valleys, because the Germans were up there looking down upon us, and they would have let us have it. So we had to go up and over. A mere platoon of Germans, well dug in on a high, rock-spined hill, could hold out for a long time against tremendous onslaughts.

I know the folks back home were disappointed and puzzled by the slow progress in Italy. They wondered why we moved northward so imperceptibly. They were impatient for us to get to Rome. Well, I can say this—our troops were just as impatient for Rome. But on all sides I heard: "It never was this bad in Tunisia." "We ran into a new brand of Krauts over here." "If it would only stop raining." "Every day we don't advance is one day longer before we get home."

Our troops were living in almost inconceivable misery. The fertile black valleys were knee-deep in mud. Thousands of the men had not been dry for weeks. Other thousands lay at night in the high mountains with the temperature below freezing and the thin snow sifting over them. They dug into the stones and slept in little chasms and behind rocks and in half-caves. They lived like men of prehistoric times, and a club would have become them more than a machine gun. How they survived the dreadful winter at all was beyond us who had the opportunity of drier beds in the warmer valleys.

That the northward path was a tedious one was not the fault

of our troops, not of the direction either. It was the weather and the terrain and the weather again. If there had been no German fighting troops in Italy, if there had been merely German engineers to blow the bridges in the passes, if never a shot had been fired at all, our northward march would still have been slow. The country was so difficult that we formed a great deal of cavalry for use in the mountains. Each division had hundreds of horses and mules to carry supplies beyond the point where vehicles could go no farther. On beyond the mules' ability, mere men—American men—took it on their backs.

On my way to Italy, I flew across the Mediterranean in a cargo plane weighted down with more than a thousand pounds beyond the normal load. The cabin was filled with big pasteboard boxes which had been given priority above all other freight. In the boxes were packboards, hundreds of them, with which husky men would pack 100, even 150, pounds of food and ammunition, on their backs, to comrades high in those miserable mountains.

But we could take consolation from many things. The air was almost wholly ours. All day long Spitfires patrolled above our fighting troops like a half dozen policemen running up and down the street watching for bandits.

What's more, our artillery prevailed—and how! We were prodigal with ammunition against those rocky crags, and well we might be, for a $50 shell could often save ten lives in country like that. Little by little, the fiendish rain of explosives upon the hillsides softened the Germans. They always were impressed by and afraid of our artillery, and we had concentrations of it there that were demoralizing.

And lastly, no matter how cold the mountains, or how wet the snow, or how sticky the mud, it was just as miserable for the German soldier as for the American.

Our men were going to get to Rome all right. There was no question about that. But the way was cruel. No one who had not seen that mud, those dark skies, those forbidding ridges and ghostlike clouds that unveiled and then quickly hid the enemy, had the right to be impatient with the progress along the road to Rome.

The mountain fighting went on week after dreary week. For a while I hung around with one of the mule-pack outfits. There was an average of one mule-packing outfit for every infantry battalion in the mountains. Some were run by Americans, some by Italian soldiers.

The pack outfit I was with supplied a battalion that was fighting on a bald, rocky ridge nearly four thousand feet high. That battalion fought constantly for ten days and nights, and when the men finally came down less than a third of them were left.

All through those terrible days every ounce of their supplies had to go up to them on the backs of mules and men. Mules took it the first third of the way. Men took it the last bitter two-thirds, because the trail was too steep even for mules.

The mule skinners of my outfit were Italian soldiers. The human packers were mostly American soldiers. The Italian mule skinners were from Sardinia. They belonged to a mountain artillery regiment, and thus were experienced in climbing and in handling mules. They were bivouacked in an olive grove alongside a highway at the foot of the mountain. They made no trips in the daytime, except in emergencies, because most of the trail was exposed to artillery fire. Supplies were brought into the olive grove by truck during the day, and stacked under trees. Just before dusk they would start loading the stuff onto mules. The Americans who actually managed the supply chain liked to get the mules loaded by dark, because if there was any shelling the Italians instantly disappeared and could never be found.

There were 155 skinners in this outfit and usually about eighty mules were used each night. Every mule had a man to lead it. About ten extra men went along to help get mules up if they fell, to repack any loads that came loose, and to unpack at the top. They could be up and back in less than three hours. Usually a skinner made just one trip a night, but sometimes in an emergency he made two.

On an average night the supplies would run something like this—85 cans of water, 100 cases of K ration, 10 cases of D ration, 10 miles of telephone wire, 25 cases of grenades and rifle and machine-gun ammunition, about 100 rounds of heavy mortar shells, 1 radio, 2 telephones, and 4 cases of first-aid packets and sulfa drugs. In addition, the packers would cram their pockets with cigarettes for the boys on top; also cans of Sterno, so they could heat some coffee once in a while.

Also, during that period, they took up more than five hundred of the heavy combat suits we were issuing to the troops to help keep them warm. They carried up cellophane gas capes for some of the men to use as sleeping bags, and they took extra socks for them too.

Mail was their most tragic cargo. Every night they would take up sacks of mail, and every night they'd bring a large portion of it back down—the recipients would have been killed or wounded the day their letters came.

On the long man-killing climb above the end of the mule trail they used anywhere from twenty to three hundred men a night. They rang in cooks, truck drivers, clerks, and anybody else they could lay their hands on. A lot of stuff was packed up by the fighting soldiers themselves. On a big night, when they were building up supplies for an attack, another battalion which was in reserve sent three hundred first-line combat troops to do the packing. The mule packs would leave the olive grove in bunches of twenty, starting just after dark. American soldiers were posted within shouting distance of each other all along the trail, to keep the Italians from getting lost in the dark.

Those guides—everybody who thought he was having a tough time in this war should know about them. They were men who had fought all through a long and bitter battle at the top of the mountain. For more than a week they had been far up there, perched behind rocks in the rain and cold, eating cold K rations, sleeping without blankets, scourged constantly with artillery and mortar shells, fighting and ducking and growing more and more weary, seeing their comrades wounded one by one and taken down the mountain.

Finally sickness and exhaustion overtook many of those who were left, so they were sent back down the mountain under their own power to report to the medics there and then go to a rest camp. It took most of them the better part of a day to get two-thirds of the way down, so sore were their feet and so weary their muscles.

And then—when actually in sight of their haven of rest and peace—they were stopped and pressed into guide service, because there just wasn't anybody else to do it. So there they stayed on the mountainside, for at least three additional days and nights that I know of, just lying miserably alongside the trail, shouting in the darkness to guide the mules.

They had no blankets to keep them warm, no beds but the rocks. And they did it without complaining. The human spirit is an astounding thing.

The little Italian mules were smaller and weaker than the average American mule. Also, they had been taken around in trucks from one place to another and a lot of them were sick from their travels.

At first we misjudged and put too heavy a load on them. In fact, we put on more than an American mule could carry over such a trail. We lashed on four cans of water and two cases of rations, making a load of about 240 pounds. The mules just couldn't take it; they'd all be sick next day. So then we loaded them with only two cans of water and one of rations, cutting the weight in half.

They said the Italians were cruel to their mules on the trail but took good care of them when they were not working. The Italian method of saying "giddap" to a mule was to go "brrrrrrr," the way we do when we are cold. When I stood along the pack trail at night and listened to the skinners "brr-ing" their mules upward, it sounded as if the whole population was freezing to death.

In the beginning there were some white mules in the pack train, but they were too easy to see by moonlight, so we stopped using them. A few horses were used in some of the outfits, and several were discovered with the brand of the Italian royal family.

When the mules first arrived from Sardinia, the most pressing problem was to get them shod. It took days to scour the country and dig up shoes for them. Then horseshoe nails were lacking, but finally they found enough race-track nails to do the job. Horseshoe nails were so scarce and so precious in Italy that the nails had to be counted out to the civilian blacksmiths. If a smith broke a nail, he had to bring the pieces back before he could get another one.

Some of the pack trains were run exclusively by Americans. I was told the Americans were better mule skinners than the Italians, and I was also told the opposite, so I don't know which is right. But as one soldier said about the Americans, "Them old city boys hadn't never fooled around with mules before, so they didn't do so good at first."

In emergencies, some pack trains were sent up the mountains

in the daytime, but it was dangerous business, for the Germans kept the trail pretty well plastered with shells.

Luckily there were no casualties on the trail in my outfit, but seven Italian soldiers were wounded in the mule park in a dive bombing. The Italians were very nervous about bombs and shells. Any night the shells started dropping too close to the mule park, the Italians disappeared into their foxholes as if by magic. The men fared much better than the mules, for unfortunately a mule doesn't know about foxholes. My outfit alone lost fifty mules in shellfire and bombing, and another hundred became sick from overwork.

The Italian mule outfit was under two Italian lieutenants who wore plumed Tyrolean caps and looked sort of romantic. Neither of them spoke English, but in the American Army you only had to yell twice to find a soldier who spoke Italian, so the little group had an interpreter. Everybody had to depend so heavily upon him that he practically ran the show. He was Corporal Anthony Savino, 262 14th Avenue, Newark, New Jersey. His job would have driven anybody crazy. The Italians were not so quick and efficient as we were, and about the time Savino got a pack train all ready, everything collapsed and chaos reigned. Then he caught it from both sides.

The officer in charge of this mule park was Lieutenant Harmon W. Williams, of Flint, Michigan. He was named after General Harmon, who won fame in the last war. Some nights Lieutenant Williams was up till 3 a.m. seeing that all the skinners got back down the mountain. Other nights he got to bed as early as 7 p.m. He slept whenever he could, for it was an unusual night when he wasn't routed out to get some emergency supplies to the top. He slept in a stone cowshed along with a dozen of his enlisted men. He had been an undertaker in civil life, and was an antitank man in the Army, but just then he was a mule expert.

Corporal Savino took his interpreting job so seriously that he even talked about it in his sleep. I slept in the same cowshed with the boys, and one night when I happened to wake up about three o'clock I heard Savino saying, "Well, if we can't use them as interpreters, let's make guides out of them."

He thought that was pretty funny when I told him about it. He had never known before that he talked in his sleep.

The human packers interested me much more than the mule trains, partly because their job was much harder and partly because they talked instead of heehawing. The magnitude of this human freight service was really astonishing. In one ten-day period American soldiers packed up this one mountain nearly a hundred thousand pounds of supplies for their battalion. That was just *one* outfit. The same thing was being done in a dozen or more places during the same time. More than half the trail was out in the open, across bare rocks exposed to German artillery fire. The top part of the trail was so steep that ropes were anchored alongside the path for the men to pull themselves upward with.

We tried to hire Italians to do the job, but after the first day they were never seen again. I heard a report that on one mountain Italian women had volunteered and were carrying up five-gallon cans balanced on their heads, but I was never able to verify this story. I think it was a myth.

Some of the soldiers carried the water cans on their shoulders, while others lashed them onto packboards. At first some of the packers would cheat a little and pour out some of the precious water when the can became too heavy. But the laws of physics soon put a stop to this, for with the can only partly filled the water would slosh around inside, throw the packers off balance and make it doubly hard to walk.

From the bottom of the mountain to the top a good walker carrying nothing whatever could make it in three hours. Carrying a heavy load it took longer than that, and yet there were some fantastic exhibitions of human strength.

The champion packer in our outfit was Pfc. Lester Scarborough, but he had left the area when I got there and I never did see him. He was from somewhere in West Virginia, and he was a miniature Paul Bunyan. He had been sick and was supposed to be convalescing, yet he could take a full can of water to the top and be clear back down again in two and a half hours; others took three hours and longer just to get up. He didn't do this just once, but day after day. He reached the climax of his carrying career when he made four round trips in one day—the fourth one being an emergency dash to the mountaintop to help beat off a German counterattack.

Scarborough was no giant. He was 18 years old, stood 5 feet 7-1/2 inches, and weighed only 135 pounds. I never heard of so much strength in such a small package.

When I went up the trail my guide was Pfc. Fred Ford, of 3037 North Park Drive, East St. Louis. He was a tall, rugged fellow, and he had two weeks of whiskers and grime on his face. He looked sort of ferocious but turned out to be pleasant and friendly. Like practically all the regular packers, he was a line soldier who had fought for weeks on top and was supposed to be down for a rest. He was a Browning automatic rifleman in an infantry company. And there was a funny thing about that.

"I threw dozens of hand grenades, and even rocks, and I guess I killed plenty of Germans," Ford said. "But I never had a single chance to shoot that automatic rifle."

On the back of his jacket Ford had printed in purple ink his serial number, the name "Betty," and, underneath that, "East St. Louis, Ill." His wife, Betty, was a chemist in a defense plant. His feet were all taped up because of blisters, and he walked on his toes to save his heels from rubbing. "Sometimes going up the mountain you get to the point where you know you can't make it," he said, "but somehow you always do."

Actually some of them didn't. I saw packer after packer report back in at the bottom of the trail saying he "couldn't make her." He'd dumped his load and come back down. A few of these may have been malingerers, but most of them were genuinely exhausted. Their feet were broken out, and infirmities such as arthritis, hernia or heart weakness would leap to the fore on those man-killing climbs.

When we started back down, German shells began dropping quite a way behind us.

"If I get to going too fast for you, just yell," Ford said. "When they start shelling we practically fly down the mountain. We don't stop for nothing."

But I didn't have any pressing business engagements along the way to detain us, so Ford and I flew down the mountainside together, going so fast the rocks we kicked loose couldn't even keep up with us.

You've heard of trench mouth and athlete's foot, but still another occupational disease of warfare sprang up on both sides in the Italian war. It was called "trench foot," and was well known in the last war. The Germans as well as the Americans had it.

Trench foot comes from a man's feet being wet and cold for long periods and from not taking off his shoes often enough. In the mountains the soldiers sometimes went for two weeks or longer without ever having their shoes off or being able to get their feet dry. The tissues gradually seem to go dead, and sores break out. It is almost the same as the circulation stopping and the flesh dying. In extreme cases gangrene occurs. We had cases where amputation was necessary. And in others soldiers couldn't walk again for six months or more. In a way it was much like frostbite, and as with frostbite, it was the wrong thing for a man to put his feet in hot water when he got an opportunity.

Sometimes the men let trench foot go so long without complaining that they were finally unable to walk and had to be taken down the mountain in litters. Others got down under their own power, agonizingly. One boy was a day and a half getting down the mountain on what would normally be a two-hour descent. He arrived at the bottom barefooted, carrying his shoes in his hand, his feet bleeding. He was in a kind of daze from the pain.

The fighting on the mountaintop almost reached the caveman stage sometimes. Americans and Germans were frequently so close that they actually threw rocks at each other. Many more hand grenades were used than in any other phase of the Mediterranean war. And you have to be pretty close when you throw hand grenades.

Rocks played a big part in the mountain war. Men hid behind rocks, threw rocks, slept in rock crevices, and even were killed by flying rocks.

When an artillery shell bursts on a loose rock surface, rock fragments are thrown for many yards. In one battalion fifteen per cent of the casualties were from flying rocks. Also, now and then an artillery burst from a steep hillside would loosen big boulders which went leaping and bounding down the mountainside for thousands of yards. The boys said such a rock sounded like a windstorm coming down the mountainside.

When soldiers came down the mountain out of battle they were dirty, grimy, unshaven and weary. They looked ten years older than they were. They didn't smile much. But the human body and mind recover rapidly. After a couple of days down below they began to pick up. It was a sight to see a bunch of combat soldiers after they had shaved and washed up. As one said, "We all look sick after we've cleaned up, we're so white."

It was funny to hear them talk. One night in our cowshed I heard one of them tell how he was going to keep his son out of the next war. "As soon as I get home I'm going to put ten-pound weights in his hands and make him jump off the garage roof, to break down his arches," he said. "I'm going to feed him a little ground glass to give him a bad stomach, and I'm going to make him read by candlelight all the time to ruin his eyes. When I get through with him he'll be double-4 double-F."

Another favorite expression of soldiers just out of combat ran like this: "Well, let's go down to Naples and start a second draft." Meaning let's conscript all the clerks, drivers, waiters, MPs, office workers and so on that flood any big city near a fighting area, and send them up in the mountains to fight.

The funny thing is they wouldn't have had to draft many soldiers down there. A simple call for volunteers would have been enough, I really believe. One of the paradoxes of war is that those in the rear—no matter what their battle experience—want to get up into the fight, while those in the lines want to get out.

In one of the outfits I noticed the boys always used the word "uncle" when they meant the powers that be. They said, "You do whatever Uncle tells you" or "I wish Uncle would hurry up with those overshoes." Another term was "eyeballing," which meant viewing and gandering around, such as "eyeballing into Naples."

At the front one morning I heard an expression which may be old but which sounded funny at the time. About a dozen soldiers and I were sleeping in a goatshed. The soldiers hadn't shaved for weeks, or washed either. And they always slept with their clothes on. When they first came out of their blankets on a cold morning they were enough to frighten children.

It was at that early-morning moment when one soldier looked for a long time at another one and then said, "Cripes, you look like a tree full of owls."

There was an old stone building sitting on the bare mountain-side at the top of the mule trail. It was used as a medical-aid station, but even so the Germans put a few score shells around it every day. While I was there once, we were standing around outside—a dozen or more medics, telephone linemen, packers and slightly injured men—and all of a sudden came that familiar and rapid whine. We all ducked.

The shell exploded with a terrific blast about a hundred yards away, and for twenty seconds afterward big and little pieces of shrapnel tinkled and clattered down upon the rocks around us with a ringing metallic sound.

One day, when I was at the top of the trail, a wounded para-trooper captain walked into the aid station in the old stone building. He was Captain Francis Sheehan, of 22 North Grey Street, Indianapolis, a man with a finely sensitive face, who almost seemed out of place in such a rugged outfit as the paratroopers. He stood out among the other wounded because he was cleanly shaven, and although his face was dirty it was recent dirt, not the basic grime that comes of going unwashed for weeks and weeks. He had gone up the mountain the day before, to relieve a battalion medical officer who had been wounded. Captain Sheehan was on the mountain only a few hours when he too was wounded, although not seriously. He got a machine-gun bullet in his right shoulder, but it apparently missed the bones. He walked on down the mountain without help, and said that the wound didn't actually hurt much.

Captain Sheehan graduated from Indiana University Medical School in 1938, and had a residency at City Hospital in Indianapolis before he went into the paratroops. We happened to get together because he used to read my column in the *Indianapolis Times*.

Imagine my surprise and delight when after several days of C and K rations we wandered into a division command post and sat down to a luncheon of fresh, crisp, American-style fried chicken, the kind we have in Indiana. Texas' famous Thirty-sixth Division was the provider.

One of the jovial mess sergeants in the Thirty-sixth Division was Charles Morgan of Gladewater, Texas. His wife was in Mexia, Texas, and she would have had trouble recognizing him if she had been there. When the sergeant went into the Army he weighed 189 pounds. He had now upped his weight to 235.

One day on the mountain trail I met three German prisoners coming down, and one dogface trailing behind them with a tommy gun.

Some Signal Corps movie photographers were on the trail, and they stopped the little cavalcade for pictures. They asked the soldier to take the Germans back up about fifty feet, then march them down again past the cameras. At first the Germans were puzzled, but when they sensed what was happening they began primping and sprucing up. They fixed their overcoat collars snugly, and straightened their pants, and came marching past with big grins on their faces, as vain as children.

Speaking of vanity, one regiment of the Thirty-sixth Division had some fine photographs of me taken at their outdoor box toilet on the hillside. They thought it was a great joke, and no doubt planned to blackmail me into buying the film from them. But I had them whipped. I had lived the war life so long, where everything is public, that I just didn't care. In fact, I told them I might even pay them to publish the pictures.

During my time with various parts of the Thirty-sixth Division I fell in with one of the regimental surgeons—Captain Emmett L. Allamon, of Port Arthur, Texas. He was slight in build, talked with a direct look and a flattering smile, and had an acute, analytical mind. An idiosyncrasy of his was hesitating a couple of seconds between phrases; then when he spoke he rattled the phrase off so fast I felt I was being left behind.

Captain Allamon had distinguished himself a couple of times in Italy. His regimental commander had shortly before commended him for running his jeep right down to the edge of a battlefield and pulling out the wounded. And before that he had had the interesting experience of being a German prisoner for six days.

He and his first sergeant, Frank T. Holland of West, Texas,

were captured shortly after we struck Italy. They weren't really treated as prisoners, but as fellow medics. About thirty American wounded were captured at the same time, and the Germans let Captain Allamon do all the operating and the dressing of their wounds. Then after two days the Germans had to retreat. Apparently the German medical officers didn't want to turn in the captain and sergeant as regular prisoners, so they held a conference, finally took the question to their colonel, and came back with the verdict that the two Americans should retreat with them.

None of the Germans spoke English, but Captain Allamon spoke just enough French to get along. They retreated for four days, and then early one morning they found the sentry asleep and just walked away. An Italian farm family hid them for several days. The Italian grapevine carried the word of their presence to the nearest town in Allied hands, and one morning an Italian arrived saying they could come with him. The two Americans walked with him for nine miles, found a British scout car waiting for them, and eventually landed back with their own outfit.

Captain Allamon said he learned from the Germans that it's best to put a medical-aid station in a building, even if it's only an old goatshed, rather than in tents. There is something psychologically comforting about having rigid walls around you in the combat zone. Also, he had a theory that the best medicine you can give a wounded man is some warmth and comfort. So he always put his aid stations into a building if possible, had a fire going in the fireplace day and night, and hot coffee was always ready. The minute a man was carried in, or walked in, he was given coffee and a cigarette, he warmed himself before the fire, he felt a sense of security again, and his spirits rose. I know it works, for I saw it in one of Captain Allamon's aid stations night after night.

Like all front-line medical officers, he was touched by what he called the "mental wreckage" of war—the men whose spirits break under the unnatural strain and incessant danger of the battlefield. He felt that American children in recent generations have had too much parental protection and too little opportunity for self-sufficiency, and that as a result a man crumbles when faced with something he feels he cannot bear. He said that if he were to pick a company of men best suited for warfare he'd choose all ex-newsboys. He thought they would have shifted for themselves so early in life that they would have built up the inner strength to carry them through battle.

Personally, I am sort of on the fence. I hate to think of an America of one hundred thirty million people so hard inside that nothing could touch them. On the other hand, comparatively few men *do* crack up. The mystery to me is that there is anybody at all, no matter how strong, who can keep his spirit from breaking in the midst of battle.

In this war I have known a lot of officers who were loved and respected by the soldiers under them. But never have I crossed the trail of any man as beloved as Captain Henry T. Waskow, of Belton, Texas.

Captain Waskow was a company commander in the Thirty-sixth Division. He had led his company since long before it left the States. He was very young, only in his middle twenties, but he carried in him a sincerity and a gentleness that made people want to be guided by him.

"After my father, he came next," a sergeant told me.

"He always looked after us," a soldier said. "He'd go to bat for us every time."

"I've never known him to do anything unfair," another said.

I was at the foot of the mule trail the night they brought Captain Waskow down. The moon was nearly full, and you could see far up the trail, and even partway across the valley below.

Dead men had been coming down the mountain all evening, lashed onto the backs of mules. They came lying belly-down across the wooden packsaddles, their heads hanging down on one side, their stiffened legs sticking out awkwardly from the other, bobbing up and down as the mules walked.

The Italian mule skinners were afraid to walk beside dead men, so Americans had to lead the mules down that night. Even the Americans were reluctant to unlash and lift off the bodies when they got to the bottom, so an officer had to do it himself and ask others to help.

I don't know who that first one was. You feel small in the presence of dead men, and you don't ask silly questions.

They slid him down from the mule, and stood him on his feet

for a moment. In the half-light he might have been merely a sick man standing there leaning on the others. Then they laid him on the ground in the shadow of the stone wall alongside the road. We left him there beside the road, that first one, and we all went back into the cowshed and sat on water cans or lay on the straw, waiting for the next batch of mules.

Somebody said the dead soldier had been dead for four days, and then nobody said anything more about it. We talked soldier talk for an hour or more; the dead man lay all alone, outside in the shadow of the wall.

Then a soldier came into the cowshed and said there were some more bodies outside. We went out into the road. Four mules stood there in the moonlight, in the road where the trail came down off the mountain. The soldiers who led them stood there waiting.

"This one is Captain Waskow," one of them said quietly.

Two men unlashed his body from the mule and lifted it off and laid it in the shadow beside the stone wall. Other men took the other bodies off. Finally, there were five lying end to end in a long row. You don't cover up dead men in the combat zones. They just lie there in the shadows until somebody comes after them.

The unburdened mules moved off to their olive grove. The men in the road seemed reluctant to leave. They stood around, and gradually I could sense them moving, one by one, close to Captain Waskow's body. Not so much to look, I think, as to say something in finality to him and to themselves. I stood close by and I could hear.

One soldier came and looked down, and he said out loud, "God damn it!"

That's all he said, and then he walked away.

Another one came, and he said, "God damn it to hell anyway!" He looked down for a few last moments and then turned and left.

Another man came. I think he was an officer. It was hard to tell officers from men in the dim light, for everybody was bearded and grimy. The man looked down into the dead captain's face and then spoke directly to him, as though he were alive, "I'm sorry, old man."

Then a soldier came and stood beside the officer and bent over, and he too spoke to his dead captain, not in a whisper but awfully tenderly, and he said, "I sure am sorry, sir."

Then the first man squatted down, and he reached down and took the captain's hand, and he sat there for a full five minutes holding the dead hand in his own and looking intently into the dead face. And he never uttered a sound all the time he sat there.

Finally he put the hand down. He reached over and gently straightened the points of the captain's shirt collar, and then he sort of rearranged the tattered edges of the uniform around the wound, and then he got up and walked away down the road in the moonlight, all alone.

The rest of us went back into the cowshed, leaving the five dead men lying in a line end to end in the shadow of the low stone wall. We lay down on the straw in the cowshed, and pretty soon we were all asleep.

TWELVE

DIVE BOMBERS

The Mediterranean Allied Air Force, under the command of Lieutenant General Ira Eaker, covered everything in the whole Mediterranean theater from Casablanca on the Atlantic almost to Cairo at the edge of Asia. It was a gigantic force. Although there were many British planes and pilots in it, and even a few squadrons of Frenchmen, still it was predominantly an American air theater.

The main geographical objective of our push into Italy was to get heavy-bomber bases near enough to start pounding Germany from the south. The great plains around Foggia were capable, they said, of basing all the air forces in the world. Our heavy-bomber force was still being built up, and had not yet really begun on its program of blasting Germany proper, but planes had been flowing across the South Atlantic all winter.

Meantime, the 12th Air Support Command bore the burden of the close-in fighting there in Italy. The 12th was composed of fighters, dive bombers and light bombers, which worked over the front line, helping our ground troops, bombing supply dumps and strafing roads just back of the enemy lines.

I had to make some psychological adjustments when I switched from the infantry to the Air Forces. Association with death was on a different basis.

A man approached death rather decently in the Air Forces. He died well-fed and clean-shaven, if that was any comfort. He was at the front only a few hours of the day, instead of day and night for months on end. In the evening he came back to something approximating a home and fireside. He still had some acquaintance with an orderly life, even though he might be living in a tent. But in the infantry a soldier had to become half beast in order to survive.

Here is a subtle difference between the two: When I was with the infantry I never shaved, for anyone clean-shaven was an obvious outsider and liable to be abused. But in the Air Forces if I went for three days without shaving I got to feeling self-conscious, like a bum among nice people, so I shaved in order to conform.

I spent some time with a dive-bomber squadron of the 12th Air Support Command. There were about fifty officers and two hundred fifty enlisted men in a squadron. They all lived, officers and men too, in a big apartment house built by the Italian government to house war workers and their families. It was out in the country at the edge of a small town and looked like one of our own government housing projects. The Germans had demolished the big factories nearby, but left the homes intact.

When our squadron moved into this building it was their first time under a roof in six months of combat. They had wood stoves in their rooms, slept in sleeping bags on folding cots, had shelves to put their things on, ate at tables and had an Italian boy to clear the dishes away. They had an Italian barber, and their clothes were clean and pressed. They had a small recreation room with soldier-drawn murals on the walls. They could go to a nearby town of an evening and see American movies, in theaters taken over by the Army. They could have dates with nurses. They could play cards. They could read by electric light in a warm room.

Don't get the wrong impression. Their life was not luxurious. At home it wouldn't be considered adequate. It had the security of walls and doors, but it was a dog's life at that.

The toilets didn't work, so we had to flush them with a tin hat full of water dipped out of an always-filled bathtub. The lights went out frequently and we had to use candles. It was tough getting up two hours before daylight for a dawn mission. The floors were cold, hard tile. There were no rugs. Some of the windows were still blown out.

And yet, as the airmen unblushingly admitted, their life was paradise compared with that of the infantry. They were fully appreciative of what the infantry goes through, because the 12th

Command had started a program of sending pilots up to the front as liaison officers for a few days at a time. When they came back they told the others what they had learned, so that the whole squadron would understand the ground problem and know how their brothers were living up there in the mud. The result was a touching eagerness to help out those ground kids. On days when the squadron dive-bombed the Germans just ahead of our own lines it wasn't as academic to them as it used to be. The pilots were thinking of how much that special bomb might aid the American boys down below them.

It was teamwork with a soul in it, and we were fighting better than ever before.

The dive bomber has never been fully accepted by the Allied armies. The British have always been against it—they call the German Stuka a vastly overrated instrument of war—and America has more or less followed suit. Our Navy used the dive bomber to good effect in the Pacific. But in the Mediterranean it didn't show up until the beginning of the Sicilian operation, and it was never built up in great numbers.

In the dive-bomber groups in Italy we had several hundred pilots and mechanics who believed with fanatical enthusiasm that the dive bomber was the most wonderful machine produced in this war. I never wanted to enter into this argument, since I was in no position to know; but certainly those dive-bomber boys were a spectacular part of our Air Forces.

Their function was to work in extremely close support of our infantry. For instance, suppose there was a German gun position just over a hill which was holding us up because our troops couldn't get at it with their guns. They called on the dive bombers and gave them the location. Within an hour, and sometimes much quicker, they would come screaming out of the sky right on top of that gun and blow it up.

They could do the same thing to bunched enemy troops, bridges, tank columns, convoys, or ammunition dumps. Because of their great accuracy they could bomb much closer to our own troops than other kinds of planes would dare. Most of the time they worked less than a thousand yards ahead of our front lines—and sometimes even closer than that.

The group I was with had been in combat six months. During that time they had flown ten thousand sorties, fired more than a million rounds of 50-caliber ammunition, and dropped three million pounds of bombs. That's more than the entire Eighth Air Force in England dropped in its first year of operation.

Our dive bombers were known as A-36 Invaders. Actually they were nothing more than the famous P-51 Mustang equipped with diving brakes. For a long time they didn't have any name at all, and then one day in Sicily one of the pilots of the squadron said, "Why don't we call them Invaders, since we're invading?"

The name was carried home in newspaper dispatches, and soon even the company that made them called them Invaders. The pilot who originated the name was Lieutenant Robert B. Walsh, of Felt, Idaho. I didn't meet him because he had completed his allotted missions and gone back to the States. His younger brother was then a replacement pilot in the same squadron.

The P-51 Mustang was a wonderful fighter. But when it was transformed into an A-36 by the addition of diving brakes it became a grand dive bomber as well. The brakes were necessary because of the long straight-down dive on the target. A regular fighter would get to going too fast, the controls would become rigid, and the pilot would have to start pulling out of his dive so early that he'd have to drop his bombs from too great a height.

Those boys dived about eight thousand feet before dropping their bombs. Without brakes their speed in such a dive would ordinarily build up to around seven hundred miles an hour, but the brakes held them down to about 390. The brakes were nothing but metal flaps in the form of griddles about two feet long and eight or ten inches high. They lay flat on the wings during ordinary flying.

The dive bombers approached their target in formation. When the leader made sure he had spotted the target he wiggled his wings, raised his diving brakes, rolled on his back, nosed over, and down he went. The next man behind followed almost instantly, and then the next, and the next—not more than a hundred fifty feet apart. There was no danger of their running over each other, for the brakes held them all at the same speed. They flew so close together that as many as twenty dive bombers could be seen in a dive all at once, making a straight line up into the sky like a gigantic stream of water.

At about four thousand feet the pilot released his bombs. Then he started his pull-out. The strain was terrific, and all the pilots would "black out" a little bit. It was not a complete blackout, and lasted only four or five seconds. It was more a heaviness in the head and a darkness before the eyes, the pilots said.

Once straightened out of the dive, they went right on down to "the deck," which means flying close to the ground. For by that time everything in the vicinity that could shoot had opened up, and the safest place to be was right down close, streaking for home as fast as they could go.

If you ever heard a dive bombing by our A-36 Invader planes you'd never forget it. Even in normal flight that plane made a sort of screaming noise; when this was multiplied manifold by the velocity of the dive the wail could be heard for miles. From the ground it sounded as though they were coming directly down on us. It was a horrifying thing.

The German Stuka could never touch the A-36 for sheer frightfulness of sound. Also, the Stuka always dived at an angle. But those Invaders came literally straight down. If a man looked up and saw one a mile above him, he couldn't tell where it was headed. It could strike anywhere within a mile on any side of him. That's the reason it spread its terror so wide.

However, our pilots had to hand it to the Germans on the ground. They had steeled themselves to stand by their guns and keep shooting. Pilots said the Italians would shoot until the bombs were almost upon them, then dive for their foxholes; then they'd come out and start shooting again after the bombs had exploded. But not the Germans—they stuck to their guns.

My friend Major Edwin A. Bland, Jr., a squadron leader, told me about flying suddenly over a hilltop one day and finding a German truck right in his gunsights.

Now it's a natural human impulse, when you see a plane come upon you, to dive for the ditch. But the German gunner in that truck swung a gun around and started shooting at Bland. German and American tracer bullets were streaming back and forth in the same groove, almost hitting each other. The German never stopped firing until Bland's six machine guns suddenly chewed the truck into complete disintegration.

For several reasons our dive bombers didn't have much trouble with German fighters. First of all, the Luftwaffe was weak over there at that time. Then too, the dive bombers' job was to work on the infantry front lines, so they seldom got back to where the German fighters were. Also, the Invader itself was such a good fighter that the Jerries weren't too anxious to tangle with it.

There were pilots in this squadron who had finished their allotted missions and gone back to America without ever firing a shot at an enemy plane in the air. And that's the way it should be, for their job was to dive-bomb, not to get caught in a fight.

For several months the posting period back to America was set at a certain number of missions. Then it was suddenly upped by more than a score. When the order came, there were pilots who were within one mission of going home. So they had to stay and fly a few more months; some of them never lived to finish the new allotment.

There is an odd psychological factor in the system of being sent home after a certain number of missions. When pilots got to within three or four missions of the finish, they became so nervous they almost jumped out of their skins. A good many were killed on their last allotted mission. The squadron leaders wished there were some way they could surprise a man and send him home with six or eight missions still to go, thus sparing him the agony of those last few trips.

Nowhere in our fighting forces was cooperation closer or friendship greater than between Americans and British in the air. I never heard an American pilot make a disparaging remark about a British flier. Our pilots said the British were cooler under fire than we were. The British attitude and manner of speech amused them, but they were never contemptuous.

They liked to listen in on their radios as the RAF pilots talked to each other. For example, one day they heard one pilot call to another, "I say, old chap, there is a Jerry on your tail."

To which the imperiled pilot replied, "Quite so, quite so, thanks very much, old man."

And another time, one of our Invaders got shot up over the target. His engine was smoking and his pressure was down and he was losing altitude. He made for the coast all alone, easy meat for any German fighter that might come along. He was just barely staying in the air, and he was a sad and lonely boy indeed. Then suddenly he heard over his earphones a distinctly British voice saying, "Cheer up, chicken, we have you."

He looked around and two Spitfires, one on either side, were mothering him back to his home field.

Although our dive-bomber pilots were largely spared the worry of German fighter planes, they were plenty concerned over the antiaircraft flak and other ground fire. The German ack-ack over the front lines was smothering.

Suppose our planes made a big circle back of the German lines in order to approach the target from a new angle, which they did every day. The Germans might pick them up forty miles from their target. Our men would have to fly every inch of that through heavy flak.

It was a game of wits. By that time, the pilots in the air and the gunners on the ground knew each other's actions so well that it was almost impossible for either side to do anything new. If our pilots did think of a novel evasive maneuver one day, the Germans had it figured out by the next; and, vice versa, if the German gunners shot a different pattern, our pilots had it figured out before the next mission.

The planes had to fly in constant "evasive action," which meant going right, going left, going up, going down, all the time they were over enemy territory. If they flew in a straight line for as long as fifteen seconds, the Germans would pick them off.

A pilot sat up there and thought it out this way: "Right now they've got a bearing on me. In a certain number of seconds they'll shoot and in a few more seconds the shell will be up here. It's up to me to be somewhere else then."

But he also knew that the Germans knew he would turn, and that consequently they would send up shells to one side or the other, or above or below his current position. Thus he never dared make exactly the same move two days in a row. By constantly turning, climbing, ducking, he made a calculated hit almost impossible. His worst danger was flying by chance right into a shell burst.

I asked one of the pilots, "Why wouldn't it be a good idea to fool them about once every two weeks by just flying straight ahead for a while?"

He said, "Because they've got that figured out too. They always keep the air dead ahead of you full of shells, just in case."

Pilots experienced some freakish escapes from shell blasts. Several had shells explode within a foot or two of their planes without getting hurt. They said it sounded as if somebody had fired off a dozen shotguns in the cockpit. The concussion tossed the plane around like a cork, yet often those close bursts didn't damage the plane at all. A friend of mine, Lieutenant Jimmy Griswold, of 4709 East 56 Street, Maywood, California, was thrown violently into a dive by a shell that must have exploded within a foot of the tail of his plane, but there wasn't a mark on it when he got home.

The German gunners were canny. For instance, on a bad day when there was a high layer of clouds with just a few holes through which the bombers might dive, they would fill up those holes with flak when they heard planes overhead. Or sometimes the smoke of their gunfire formed a thick layer through which the planes had to dive. If there was a hole or two in that layer they would put up a few shells and cover them up.

It wasn't the heavy flak up above or the medium flak on the way down that worried the pilots so much as the small-arms fire from the ground after they had finished their dives. If you'd ever been in a raid, you'd understand. I know that when German planes came over our line the whole valley for miles and miles around became one vast fountain of flying lead with bullets going up by the thousands. It was like a huge water spray, filling the air as far as the eye could see.

Our dive-bomber pilots had to fly through that every day. They "hit the deck" the minute they pulled out of their bombing dive, because it's harder to see a plane that is close to the ground. Also because, when they were almost down to earth, the Germans fir-

ing at them might shoot their own troops. But even that didn't
stop the Jerries—they kept banging away.

The pilots said it was the accidental bullet they feared the most;
nine times out of ten it was some goof—standing out in a field,
shooting wildly into the air—who hit them.

When a big push was on, our dive-bomber pilots sometimes
had to go through this sort of thing three times in a single day.
So, although they lived well when at home base, they weren't on
any picnic when they went out to work.

Before this, while I was keeping my sick record intact, I stayed
at the apartment of some Air Forces friends. Pilots from the various fields dropped in there when they were in town on leave. Then
it was that I met Major Bland.

It was during the summer of 1941 in Albuquerque that I decided to get a new car and as usual I wanted a convertible. The
Pontiac dealer there didn't have a convertible but said that one
could be sent from the district agency in Pueblo, Colorado. So
three days later the shiny convertible arrived. It was a beauty
and still is a beauty, even though it has spent half its life sitting
in storage.

Now what does a convertible coupé in Albuquerque have to
do with a dive-bomber pilot in Italy?

Well, when Major Ed Bland came to the apartment he told me
about that car. It seems that in the spring of 1941 he was a salesman for the Pontiac people in Pueblo. They had only one convertible left, and Salesman Ed had already sold it and was ready
to make delivery next day. Then came word that the Albuquerque dealer wanted that car to deliver to me. So they took it away
from Ed and he thereby lost his $80 commission. He was so dis-
gusted that he joined the Army a month later.

"Well, it looks as if I owe you eighty bucks, to be real ethical
about it," I said.

But Ed just laughed, and I didn't have eighty bucks with me
anyhow. So despite the past, we became good friends.

Ed Bland was a tall, friendly fellow with blond hair cut in crew
style. He never knew what to say when people asked where he
was from. Sometimes he said Oklahoma and sometimes Colorado.
He was raised in Waurika, Oklahoma, where his parents still lived.

But he married a girl from Fort Morgan, Colorado, and home to almost any soldier is wherever his wife is. Ed's plane was named "Annie Jane" in her honor. He had seen their baby only once— he got home for a few hours when it was four days old, and then went right overseas.

His father was agent for the Rock Island Railway. Ed often thought how ironic it was that his father had spent a lifetime making trains run and now his son was overseas shooting up trains so they couldn't run. But he loved to fly and was torn between flying after the war or going back to Colorado and settling down to enjoy the mountains.

He almost got his'n a couple of weeks before I visited his squadron. That day Ed couldn't get his plane out of a dive. The tab on his rudder had either been shot or torn loose by the pressure of the dive. The stick vibrated so violently that it flew out of his hands and he lost control.

The only chance of saving himself was to get hold of that stick again. I asked him if it was vibrating so fast he couldn't grab it. He said, "Hell, it was going so fast I couldn't even see it."

So Ed clasped his hands, reached clear up to the dash, then lowered his hands toward the cockpit floor and drew them back toward him. He knew the stick had to be somewhere inside the circle of his arms.

As he gradually pulled back, the stick beat upon his hands and arms with killing pain, but he kept pulling until finally he had hold of it. The infernally flailing thing hit with such fury it literally pulled a big hunk of flesh out of the palm of his hand, but he finally got the plane out of the dive, just by will power and brute strength.

He was only four hundred feet above the ground when he leveled off—as narrow an escape as a man ever wants to have. "I thought it was my time," Ed said. "I figured my number had come up, and I sort of said good-bye to everybody." (After I left Italy late in the spring for England, Ed Bland, by then a lieutenant colonel, was shot down behind the German lines. Later we got word that he was a prisoner.)

The youngest pilot in the squadron was Lieutenant Robert L. Drew, who was nineteen years old and came from Fort Thomas,

Kentucky. Young as he was he outranked his own father; he was
a first lieutenant while his dad was only a shavetail. The father,
Robert W. Drew, was in the Navy in the last war, and ran a
flying-boat service on the Ohio River in recent years. Now he
was a Ferry Command pilot back home. Lieutenant Drew was
shot down while I was with the squadron. Nothing at all was
heard from him. But the story had a happy ending. After three
and a half months behind the enemy lines he escaped and returned to the squadron. Then he was sent back to America. One
day he walked into his own home. His father, by now a lieutenant of equal rank, got a week's leave, and what a time the Drew
family had!

One of my friends in that squadron was Corporal Adolph Seeger,
who owned a farm two miles outside of Evansville, Indiana. Seeger
was a driver. Although most of the other enlisted men lived in the
same apartment building the pilots lived in, Seeger voluntarily
slept at the motor pool in a tent in order to be near at hand in
case of emergencies.

Seeger thought it was odd that he should be over there driving
a car—which didn't seem to him a very important job—while at
home his 64-acre farm lay idle because there was no one left to
farm it. His mother lived there all alone.

Around a fighter or dive-bomber airdrome there is always talk
about low-flying missions. That means jobs on which a pilot
flies so low he is practically on the ground. Often the planes go
so low they can hit a person standing on the ground.

On such a mission a flier went out "looking for things." He
would shoot at practically anything he saw. He would go whipping up over a slight rise, then zip down the other side, and in his
gunsights there might be a gun, a truck, a train, a whole line of
German soldiers, a supply dump. Whatever he found he shot up.

The squadron of A-36 Invader dive bombers had some freakish experiences on those missions. For example, Lieutenant Miles
C. Wood, of Dade City, Florida, almost shot himself down one
day. He was strafing, and he flew so low that his bullets kicked
up rocks and he flew into the rocks. They dented his propeller and
punched holes in his wings. He was lucky to get home at all. Even
a hunk of mud will dent a wing at that speed.

Another pilot flew right through an eight-strand steel cable the Germans had stretched on poles above some treetops. It was one of their many tricks, and that one almost worked. The pilot landed at his home field with the cable still trailing from his wing.

Ed Bland was so interested in his strafing one day that he didn't notice a high-tension line just ahead. When he did see it, it was too late to pull over it. So he flew under it—at about three hundred miles an hour.

Another of the pilots was diving on a truck and got so interested in what he was doing that he ran into a tree. The plane somehow stayed in the air, although the leading edge of the wing was pushed up about eight inches and crumpled like an accordion. He got the plane back over our lines, but finally it went into a spin and he had to bail out. He broke his leg getting out of the cockpit, hit his head on the tail as he went past, and then smashed his leg up some more when he hit the ground.

He was the luckiest man the squadron had. Everybody was concerned about him, and grateful that he lived. Yet when Ed went to see him in the hospital, the first thing the injured pilot did was to start apologizing for losing the plane.

Sometimes the pilots flew so low they even had German tracer bullets coming down at them from the hillsides. They flew so low that Italians behind the German lines would often come running to their doors and wave, and now and then some dirty guy who had different sentiments would run out and take a shot at them.

A man on a low-flying mission was justified in shooting at anything. One day one of our pilots, after a dull time in which he saw nothing worth destroying, decided to set a haystack afire. He came diving down on it, pouring in bullets, when suddenly he saw his tracers ricocheting off the haystack. Now you know bullets don't ricochet off ordinary haystacks, so our pilot gave it the works— and thus destroyed a brand-new pillbox.

As I have said, the Germans were full of tricks. They sent up all kinds of weird things from their ack-ack guns. They had one shell that looked, when it exploded, as if someone had emptied a wastebasket full of serpentine. They shot all kinds of wire and link "daisy chains" into the air to snag our propellers.

But the weirdest one I heard of was described by a pilot who was on the tail of a Messerschmitt one day. Just as he was pulling the trigger, the fleeing German released out of the tail of his plane a parachute with a long steel cable attached to it. By fast maneuvering, the American pilot got out of its way, but he did lose his German.

One time an artillery observer saw three big German tanks pull into a field several miles back of the German lines. The crews jumped out and began pitching straw over them, and in a few minutes they resembled a strawstack.

Not five minutes later our dive bombers came over. Their target was a gun position in an adjacent orchard. But their aim was bad, and their bombs landed directly on the three straw-covered tanks. It was just an accident, but the Germans probably wondered what the world was coming to when Americans could have planes over blowing up tanks five minutes after they had hidden them.

Another time our dive bombers couldn't find their principal target because of bad weather. They were on their way home when they picked up their alternate target, a supply dump at a crossroads.

The first plane dived in and dropped its bombs. Instantly a gigantic flame shot fifteen hundred feet into the air. Before the last plane had finished its dive—a matter of only a few seconds—the pillar of smoke was four thousand feet high. They had really hit the jackpot, but they never knew what the jackpot was. They couldn't conceive of anything that would flame that high so quickly.

Still another time a pilot went out on a reconnaissance mission. Because of hazy weather, and because two adjacent passes in the mountains looked exactly alike, he took the wrong one and got lost, although he didn't know he was lost.

He kept on flying by his map for a long time, although actually he was far north of where his map ran out. At last it began to dawn on him that something was wrong. Just as he was getting good and worried he looked down and directly under him saw an airfield with a dozen or more small German planes lined up alongside the runway. So down he went in a surprise dive, set the German planes afire, and then headed rapidly south.

He found his home field just as he ran out of gas. When the

boys asked where he'd been he didn't know. It took the pilot and his squadron commander two hours of intense map study to figure out what field he had shot up so beautifully. He had been two hundred miles north of where he intended to be.

At one of our airdromes a German plane sneaked over and plastered the field with five-pronged steel spikes. Our fliers called it a "jacks raid," since the spikes resembled the jacks kids play with, only they were much bigger. Those vicious spikes would have punctured the tires when our planes taxied out.

So the field engineers got a huge magnet, attached it to the front of a truck, and swept the field free of the spikes. Then they loaded them into our planes and dropped them on German airfields. That was the end of the jacks raids.

Before the squadron moved into the big apartment house, they had flown from ten different fields in the previous six months. They had lived in tents, under trees, and in foxholes. They had lived in mud so deep the planes had to be towed to the runway, and in dust so thick they had to take off by instruments.

They had flown from fields so close to enemy lines that they could go out on a bombing mission and be back in ten minutes. So close, in fact, that ground crews could stand on the field and watch their own planes going into their bombing dives.

Once the air over one of their fields was so full of wounded planes from other stations that the squadron commander himself had to get out and act as traffic manager, deciding which planes were in greatest danger and should be allowed to come in first.

The turnover of pilots was high—partly owing to casualties but mainly because of the system of relieving pilots after a certain number of missions. It was unusual for a combat airman to be overseas more than a year.

The squadron had come into combat just six months before, yet only three of the original fifty pilots were left. Twelve had been casualties, and the rest had finished their missions and gone home. The three originals were due to be homeward bound shortly.

Those dive-bomber boys had compiled some statistics about their operations. They found that a new pilot, starting in to build up the required missions for going home, had about a seventy-five per cent chance of coming through safely, and if shot down he had almost a fifty-fifty chance of becoming a prisoner.

A dozen times during my stay, pilots voluntarily brought up the subject of how wonderful the enlisted men were. These men took a terrific personal pride in their planes, and they worked like dogs to keep them in good shape. They were a really high-class bunch. Being trained technicians, most of them were at least twenty-five years old. You could have put officers' uniforms on half of them and no one would have known the difference.

While I was on the field they pumped me about conditions and politics at home, and about the end of the war and the peace, as though I were an information bureau. They were certainly one group of soldiers who did some thinking about the war.

These mechanics were fully aware of three things about their jobs: that their life was immeasurably better than that of the infantrymen and that they should be grateful; that the pilot who flew out to battle was the one of their family who really took it; and that pilots' lives often depended on their work. The result was that they were enormously conscientious.

When a favorite pilot failed to come back the enlisted men took it as hard as the officers did. A mechanic whose plane had been shot down was like a boy who has lost his dad.

There was quite a spirit of rivalry among the ground crews. For a while there two ships were running a neck-and-neck race for the most missions flown. Then one of the ships came back so badly damaged it had to be worked on for several days, and it fell behind in the race. It almost broke the crew chief's heart.

Here are two little examples of the zeal with which the enlisted men worked. Once as the planes were taxiing out for their daily mission, it was discovered that the tire on the tail wheel of one of them was flat. Ordinarily the plane would have been just left behind. But the crew came running, other crews pitched in to help, and they had a new wheel on the plane by the time the next-to-last ship of the squadron was taking off.

Another time a plane came in full of holes, but not basically damaged. Usually it would have taken a day or two to mend the holes but, in their excitement and pride of accomplishment, the crews had that plane patched and ready to go on the next mission an hour and a half later. It was during a hot time, and the squadron was flying two and three missions a day.

Around the airdrome they joked about how one pilot won his victory over an enemy plane. It seems he caught a tiny observation plane, similar to our Cubs, while he was out on a low-level mission. As soon as the frightened little enemy saw our ships, he got as near to the ground as he could. One of our planes pulled up and came down at him in a dive. The little plane was so slow that our pilot misjudged its speed and completely missed him. But as he shot on past, his propeller blast caught the little ship, threw it upside down, and it dived into the ground—quite fatally.

As they say, there's more than one way to skin a cat.

You laugh at some very sad things in wartime. For instance, the pilots told with merriment about the fate of a German motorcyclist. Our planes were strafing a mountain road one day. They saw this German motorcyclist who kept looking back over his shoulder in terror at the approaching planes, and consequently rode right off the highway and over the edge of a 400-foot cliff.

In describing what it feels like to fly one of our high-powered fighting planes, one of our pilots said, "You're just sitting there with a thousand horses in your lap and a feather in your tail."

One night I went into a little Italian town with some pilots to see the movie *This Is the Army*. The Air Forces had taken over a local theater, and as long as a man was in uniform all he had to do was to walk in and sit down. About a third of the audience were pilots and the rest mechanics. I couldn't help being interested in their reaction to the picture. On the whole, they applauded, but every time the action got a little gooey or mushily patriotic, a combination boo and groan went through the audience. Soldiers at the front can't stomach flag-waving from back home.

I've already mentioned that interesting psychological thing accompanying the "rubbing out" process of the last few missions a combat airman went on before he completed that final one and returned to America. It interested not only the man himself but everybody on the field from cook to crew chief. When a pilot got within five missions of the finish everybody knew and watched his total. If one plane was missing when the group got back, the first thing on everybody's mind was the question: Was it the guy who was about finished?

For the pilot nearing the finish, most squadron leaders deliberately picked missions that were expected to be easy. There were so many ironic cases of men "getting it" on their last flight that the leaders were as nervous about it as the pilots.

When a pilot came back from his last trip he turned out of formation as he neared the field and came down wide open and screaming, to "buzz" the field just above the ground. It was a gesture of elation similar to that of a fighter pilot doing a snap roll over the home field after shooting down a Nazi plane.

While I was at the airdrome, I saw the pilots do all kinds of things after their last flights. A friend of mine—Captain Dean Schuyler of 144–55 87th Avenue, Jamaica, Long Island—felt so good the night he got down that he canceled a $300 debt another pilot owed him.

Another one who finished the same day—Lieutenant Swithin Shortlidge of West Grove, Pennsylvania—shaved off the beard he had been growing for months. The previous fall Lieutenant Shortlidge had fallen down, knocked out his upper front teeth and cut his chin. He started the beard then because he couldn't shave for a while, and he finally decided to keep it until he had finished his missions. The dentist made him a false plate to cover up the gaping hole in his mouth, but he refused to wear it. With a long beard and a big grin and no teeth he was a sight to behold.

When Lieutenant Jimmy Griswold finished his missions I asked if his last one was the hardest. He said, "No, it was all right once I got in the air, but thinking about it ahead of time almost had me in the asylum."

We were sitting around the mess-hall table, and Dean Schuyler said, "Yes, we thought this flying business was going to be very romantic. And it was, for the first few missions when everything was new and strange and we were just learning. But since then it's been a job to do, just a job of muddy, hard work." And all the others agreed.

Most dive-bomber pilots went home without any enemy planes

to their credit, since attacking enemy planes wasn't their job. Jimmy Griswold said the first thing his younger brother was going to ask him was how many planes he shot down, and when he said "None at all" the kid was going to give him an awfully funny look.

Some pilots finished and went home in as little as five months, while others were overseas more than a year before completing their missions. Occasionally sickness or wounds would keep one out of the air for weeks, and he fell behind.

There was one hard-luck pilot—an excellent one too—who was laid up a long time with a bad flak wound in the leg. Then just after he started flying again the jeep he was riding in was strafed by an enemy fighter and he went back to the hospital with another bad leg wound. As a result, he was far behind on his missions and while all his pals had gone home he was just starting to fly again.

The saddest thing about the strafing was that the pilot driving the jeep had just finished his last mission and had his orders home—and he was killed.

The airdrome was lousy with Hoosiers. I thought I'd take down their names, but the list got so long I realized it would sound like discrimination and the forty-seven other states might get mad at me.

So I decided to compromise and name only one. He was Lieutenant James F. Short of Clinton, Indiana. He had been in the Army four years, and was a sergeant up until the time he got his commission a year before. He called himself "one of the ninety-day wonders." He was only twenty-two years old, and he was the assistant operations officer of his squadron.

The reason I picked Lieutenant Short out of all the Hoosiers was that he was born and raised five miles from that proud metropolis from which I sprang—Dana, Indiana.

One afternoon we had an exciting half hour. On our field were two full groups of dive bombers plus a menagerie of night fighters, day fighters, photo planes, light bombers and cargo ships. We were all standing out waiting for our squadron to come back from a mission, when, lo and behold, the entire caboodle came back at once! It was the damnedest melee in the sky you ever saw. It was just as though somebody had broken open a hornets' nest.

One group of dive bombers approached the field from one direction, and the other from the opposite direction, at exactly the same time. They both came over the field at about four hundred feet, and when they met at mid-runway they all channeled off in a thousand directions. Before that I had thought there were only 360 points on the compass, but now I know better. Planes were going in at least three times that many directions.

Of course everybody knew what he was doing and it was actually well-regulated, but it looked like a madhouse even to the pilots on the ground. Our squadron leader stood there putting on an act of alternately tearing his hair and hiding his face.

In the midst of all this confusion a Flying Fortress flew over the field and we saw white parachutes begin to spring out behind it. At first we thought they must be having a practice jump, but nobody makes practice jumps over a front-line airdrome. The plane was in trouble.

One by one those scores of dive bombers got themselves successfully landed, and in the meantime seven parachutes had come out of the Fortress. That meant three still inside, and she was still flying.

Finally the air was clear and the Fortress approached for a landing. The entire complement of the field, several thousand men, were standing on top of anything they could find to see the excitement, and the ambulance and fire trucks were ready. As the Fort approached the field we could see that the bomb-bay doors were still open.

The big plane touched the runway as softly as down, rolled straight in and gradually came to a stop. We all heaved sighs of relief. The fliers on the ground began acting out comically exaggerated scenes of how the ambulance drivers' faces would look as they'd reach over in disgust and turn off their switches.

A little later we got the story on the Fortress. It was one of those unbelievable things that sometimes occur in the best-regulated wars. A fellow Flying Fortress had dropped its bombs on this one in mid-air.

Fortunately, that day the unintentional enemy was carrying only 25-pound fragmentation bombs instead of large ones. A couple of these bombs had blown the victim's left wing full of great jagged holes, had knocked out one engine and the radio, and jammed the bomb-bay doors. But that's the mildest part of the story. The pay-off was that one bomb hadn't gone off and was still lodged inside the Fortress's wing, liable to explode at any moment and blow the wing clear off.

When we finally left, the plane was roped off, the field engineering officer had brought out a tall stepladder, had climbed up to the wing, and for an hour had been standing there looking down at the bomb—wondering why the hell he ever chose to be an engineer anyway.

Later that evening some of our pilots and I went to a neighboring field to see some friends. They were complaining about the traffic on their field and said they believed they'd bring their fifty planes over to our field. At which we all howled and said, "Sure, come on over. In the confusion over there you wouldn't even be noticed."

One evening Sergeant James E. Knight, a flight chief from McAlester, Oklahoma, took me in tow and we spent the evening gabbing with about fifty of the mechanics. The men lived in the same big apartment building as the officers. Their quarters were exactly the same, except that the men had their places fixed up more comfortably and kept them neater.

I found that true in almost any Air Forces group in the combat area, because the men, being craftsmen, could make things that the average officer didn't know how to make. They fixed up stoves and lights and shelves, and little gadgets that gave a homey touch to their quarters.

Sergeant Charlie Bennett, a youngster on the maintenance crew, from York, South Carolina, had worked up a beautiful ash tray from the base of a German 88-millimeter shell, with American machine-gun bullets sticking out of it. It was too heavy to lug around for a year or more of war, so Charlie decided to send it home.

One of Charlie's roommates was Sergeant Mintford Blair of Spokane, Washington, a crew chief. In the same group was Blair's uncle, Sergeant Ted Chapman, an electrical specialist. Uncle and nephew were about the same age. They had enlisted together two years before, and had been lucky enough to stay together ever since.

Sergeant Knight, being a flight chief, had charge of about six planes. Another flight chief was Sergeant Orville Reeves of Fittstown, Oklahoma. Sergeant Reeves was one of the few superstitious people I encountered in the Air Forces. Superstition was rare even among the pilots. The last war's phobia against three-on-a-match was almost unheard-of.

Sergeant Reeves normally had six planes in his charge, but sometimes he would have more. His idiosyncrasy was that he wouldn't accept seven. He didn't mind the work, and he would accept two extra planes, but not one. The reason was that on three different occasions after they arrived overseas he had had an extra plane shoved onto him—making a total of seven—and each time his flight had lost a plane the following day. So he would have none of it after that, and you can't blame him.

Sergeant Knight carried a whole walletful of pictures of his wife and year-old baby. He had seen his son only once, when he was a week old. Knight said he was "sweating out" a picture of his youngster in the Italian colonel's suit he sent him for Christmas.

Sergeant Knight was one of the many mechanics who felt they were not personally doing enough to help win the war. For instance, Knight said all the men under him were then so well trained that he had almost nothing to do, that he could go back and take flight training and hardly be missed. You'd think that after seeing what the combat pilots went through, the mechanics would be content to stay put. Yet when applications for flight training were reopened ten per cent of the ground crew applied.

Always in the combat area I heard soldiers on ground jobs talking earnestly along this line: Why couldn't well-trained 4-Fs do their jobs and release them for combat? They knew that a man didn't have to be a Samson to stand ordinary Army life, and they pointed out such cases as that of the soldier who was discharged from the Army on physical grounds, yet was capable of playing swell football when he got back into civil life.

Constantly, also, the Air Forces boys paid tribute to the infantry. In two weeks around the airfield I think I heard the subject brought up two hundred times. Pilots and mechanics both felt the same way—their hats were off to the infantry.

One pilot said to me, "What must you think of us, anyhow,

knowing as you do what the infantry goes through, and then finding that all we talk about is when we can get our missions in and go home?"

I told him I thought they were acting like very normal human beings, and that, furthermore, bad as infantry life is, I believed the average infantryman looked on the combat pilot's job as too dangerous to be envied.

One night I was gossiping in a tent with a bunch of dive-bomber pilots, and one of them sitting next to me said in a sudden off-hand way, "I wonder what those Germans in that truck are doing tonight?"

He was referring to a truck he had strafed and blown up the afternoon before. Such things sometimes got under their skins. The pilots liked to go on a hunt, and it was thrilling to sweep down and shoot hell out of something, the same as it is to shoot a running deer, but they really didn't relish the idea of killing people who weren't trying to kill them.

The pilot said to himself, "Some of them aren't doing anything tonight," and then the subject was changed.

Every time I went to an airdrome it seemed as if I always slept on the cot of the last pilot who had been shot down. It was quite natural, since there were usually just enough cots to go around, and I slept on whichever one was empty. I didn't mind it, because I'm not superstitious. But it did impress me after it happened several times in a row.

I found that almost every combat unit had (1) one pilot so nerveless that he thought his narrow escapes were funny, and meant it; (2) a majority who truly loved to fly and at times found a certain real exhilaration in combat, but who on the whole existed only for the day when they could do their flying more peacefully; and (3) one pilot who absolutely hated airplanes and kept going, if at all, only through sheer will power. I knew of two pilots who developed such neuroses against airplanes that they had to be sent to a rest spot where they wouldn't see a plane for six months.

But I suppose pilots as a class are the gayest people in the Army. When they came back from a mission they were usually full of high spirits. And when they sat around together of an evening, nine-tenths of their conversation was exuberant and full of howling jokes. There was no grimness in their conduct to match that of the infantrymen in the line.

For example, one night during supper we heard some terrific shouting in the adjoining room, as though a politician were making a Fourth of July speech. Finally we moved to the door to see what it was all about, and there sat a roomful of pilots before their finished supper plates, giving rapt attention to another pilot who was on his feet delivering a burlesque harangue on the merits of snake-oil hair tonic.

This pilot was Lieutenant Robert J. Horrigan, of 1443 South Cheyenne Avenue, Tulsa, Oklahoma. He had an infectious grin and a perpetual sense of mimicry. It turned out that his father, a banker in Tulsa, was for many years on the stage as a magician, and his uncle was a famous juggler. The two even toured Europe with their act. Bob Horrigan wanted to go on the stage himself after the war, but he supposed he wouldn't. His current ambition was to land an airplane at the Tulsa airport, with his family and friends all out to meet him. He said he wouldn't even object to a small brass band.

The nicest thing about Horrigan's impromptu acting was that he got as tickled as his audience did. His final act was a hundred per cent sound imitation of the unconventional scene of a Messerschmitt shooting down a Spitfire. The audience of pilots yelled their delight as though they hadn't a care in the world.

Our Army worried some because the soldiers didn't have a very good idea of what the war around them was all about. This was largely because the Army never told them. But finally a definite program of making our combat troops better informed was inaugurated, and it was taking effect. I saw one example of it in the Air Forces.

In my dive-bomber group, pilots went down to the enlisted men's mess hall every evening and told them what had happened on their missions that day. Our squadron had flown three missions on this particular day, so three pilots went down that night—one to describe each mission. They brought maps with them and told the soldiers exactly what they had been trying to bomb, how successful they were, how much flak they ran into, how many enemy fighters they saw, and what road strafing they did on the way home. They also told the men why each point was selected to bomb, and what its destruction would mean.

The pilots made it informal, and one of them who had had a rather tough mission wound up by saying, "I think I earned my pay today."

The next one got up and said, "Well, I didn't earn mine."

His flight had had an easy ride, encountering no fighters and little flak.

Later I was with a squadron of A-20 bombers and sat in on their early-morning briefing. The briefing officer, before starting on the details of the forthcoming mission, gave the crews a complete summary of the ground war throughout the Italian and Russian fronts in the previous twenty-four hours, as brought in over the teletype system.

All this was a good thing. It's easier to fight when you know what the other fellow is doing and how he is getting along.

One of the enlisted gunners in this A-20 outfit finished his allotted number of missions the day I got to his field. He was Sergeant Lester C. Eadman, of Wiyaumega, Wisconsin. Sergeant Eadman had been overseas fifteen months and was wounded in the leg by flak the winter before in one of the raids over Tunis. Eadman just cleaned up and loafed all the next day after his last mission, and he looked mighty satisfied with everything.

A lot of pilots and enlisted men who finished their missions got married as soon as they hit home. Three gunners in this same group went home together and all three were married within two days after they got to the States.

There was a controversy in *Stars and Stripes* over the pin-up girls versus the girl back home. One soldier wrote in and said that the picture of his one-and-only was good enough for him and to hell with pin-up pictures. But he had a lot of dissenters. Personally I couldn't see that there was much conflict. I never heard of a soldier writing to his real girl to break off the engagement because he had fallen in love with a picture.

Looking at a pin-up girl is pleasant, and sort of academic. Everybody carried pictures of his own family anyway, and got them out on the slightest pretext. I looked at thousands of pictures of wives and three-month-old babies, and said "Hmm!" and "Ah, beautiful!" and "My, what a strapping youngster!" until I was red in the face. Not that I minded it. Not at all. It gave me an excuse to haul out my own pictures and show them right back.

But from that vast experience of looking at pictures of other men's wives I got one definite cross-section impression, and that was how much alike so many women in the world look. (Don't shoot, boys, I didn't mean YOUR wife.)

There was one pin-up gallery in a room occupied by six mechanics of my dive-bomber squadron. Tacked on the walls were three dozen of the most striking pin-ups I ever saw. Before long the squadron had to move and give up its nice quarters. I suggested that the pin-ups be left there and the room roped off by the Italian government as a monument to the American occupation. I'll bet the place, if given a few centuries' time, would become as historic as Pompeii.

THIRTEEN

THE FABULOUS INFANTRY

Knowing my weakness for the foot soldier, you won't be surprised to learn that my next port of call was an infantry company of the Thirty-fourth Division. The Thirty-fourth was the oldest division on that side of the Atlantic. It had been away from home two full years.

Two years is a long time overseas, even if a division did nothing but travel around and work hard. But when in addition those two years meant campaign after bitter campaign, a division became wise and worn and old, like a much-read book, or a house that wears its aging stone stoutly, ignoring the patchwork of new concrete that holds it together.

Out of any front-line rifle company of around two hundred men in the Thirty-fourth, there were usually fewer than a dozen men who had first shipped overseas with the division. In one battalion not a single one of the original officers was left. Not that they had all been killed; but through casualties of all sorts, plus sickness and transfer and some small rotation back to the States, the division had had almost a complete turnover in two years of fighting. Only its number remained the same. But even a number can come to have character and life to those who are familiar with its heritage. I had been with the Thirty-fourth as far back as June of 1942, in Ireland, and I had a feeling about it.

I went to the regimental command post in a jeep after dark one night. Regimental handed me down to battalion, and battalion on down to the company I was to stay with. The company commander was Lieutenant John J. Sheehy, of 520 Audubon Avenue, New York City. The division had originally been all Iowa and Minnesota men, but now there were men from everywhere. The Iowans were the veterans, however, and they still stood out.

Jack Sheehy was tall and thin and quite young, and of course he was Irish. In the regiment he was considered pretty remarkable. Any time his name was mentioned among higher officers, they would nod and say, "Yes, Sheehy is a case." I gathered from innuendo that in the pinches he used his noggin in spectacular ways, and that he feared neither German soldiers nor American brass hats. He was an extremely likable and highly respected company commander.

Lieutenant Sheehy used to be a clerk for American Airlines in New York. He said that after the war he was going into salesmanship of some kind, because he figured his gift of gab would carry him through—which surprised me, because during all the time I was with him he was far from garrulous. Actually he seemed very reserved.

I've never seen a man prouder of his company than Lieutenant Sheehy, and the men in it were proud too. I've been around war long enough to know that nine-tenths of morale is pride in your outfit and confidence in your leaders and fellow fighters.

A lot of people have morale confused with the desire to fight. I don't know of one soldier out of ten thousand who wants to fight. They certainly didn't in that company. The old-timers were sick to death of battle, and the new replacements were scared to death of it. And yet the company went on into battle, and it was a proud company.

When I joined the outfit it was during one of those lulls that sometimes come in war. The company was still "in the lines," but not actually fighting. They had taken a town a few days before, and since then had been merely waiting for the next attack. Those intervals gave the soldiers time to restore their gear and recuperate their spirits. Usually such intervals came weeks apart.

The regiment was bivouacked over an area a mile or more square, with the men in foxholes under olive trees, and the company, battalion, and regimental command posts set up in farmhouses. It was the first time our company command post had been inside walls since they hit Italy five months before.

In areas where there had been recent battles the towns were largely evacuated—in fact, practically all of them were mere heaps of rubble from bombing and shelling—and no stores were open. There was little chance of buying wine. But my regiment had gone sniffing into cellars in a depopulated town and turned up with all kinds of exotic liquors which they dug out of the debris.

The result was, you could make a tour of a dozen company and battalion command posts around the perimeter of the town and in nearly every one discover a shelf full of the finest stuff imaginable. It was ironic to walk into a half-demolished building and find a command post set up in the remaining rooms, with soldiers sitting in front of a crackling fireplace, and—at ten o'clock in the morning, with enemy shell bursts making the old building tremble—be offered a choice of cherry, peach, apricot, and half a dozen other varieties of fine brandy out of fancy bottles. But I must say a windfall like that didn't come often.

Our company command post consisted of one table, one chair and one telephone in a second-story room of a stone farmhouse. In most of those two-story farmhouses the stairway went up the outside. We hung blankets at the door for blackout, and burned candles.

Five platoons of the company were bivouacked in olive orchards in a circle around the farmhouse, the farthest foxhole being not more than two hundred yards away. Some soldiers just dug regular foxholes and put their blankets at the bottom. During the day they would sit at the edge of the hole cleaning guns, writing letters or just talking, and at night they would sleep at the bottom of the foxhole.

Others dug more elaborate places. I was always struck by the work some men would put into a home as temporary as a foxhole. I saw men in that company arrive at a new bivouac at midnight, dig a hole just big enough to sleep in the rest of the night, then work all the next day on a deep, elaborate, roofed-over foxhole, even though they knew they had to leave the same evening and would never see that hole again.

In the olive groves throughout that Cassino area there were pitiful reminders of close-up warfare. In our grove I don't believe there was a single one of the thousands of old trees that hadn't at least one bullet scar in it. Knocked-off branches littered the ground. Some trees were cut clear down by shells.

Stone walls had shell gaps every so often, and every standing thing was bullet-pocked. We couldn't walk fifty feet without hitting a shell or bomb crater, and every house and shed had at least a corner knocked off.

Some soldiers were sleeping in the haymow of a stone barn. They had to get up into it via a stepladder they had pieced together, because the steps had been blown away.

Between the house and the barn ran a footpath on a sort of ledge. Our men had been caught there that first night by a tank in the valley below firing at them point-blank. One soldier had been killed instantly. As we walked along the path a few days later we saw his steel helmet still lying there, bloody and riddled with holes.

Another soldier had a leg blown off, but lived. The men were telling me of a replacement—a green soldier—who joined the company the day after, when the leg was still lying in the path. The new soldier stopped and stared at it and kept on staring.

The other boys watched him from a distance. They said that when anyone came along the path the new man would move off to one side so as not to be seen. But when the coast was clear, he would come back and stare, sort of hypnotized. He never said anything about it afterward, and nobody said anything to him. Somebody buried the leg the next day.

Of the nearly two hundred men who came overseas in my company, only eight were left. Those eight men had everything a military man would want in a soldier. They had all been in the Army nearly three years—away from America two years. They had served in Northern Ireland, Scotland, England, Algeria, Tunisia and Italy. They had been at it so long they had become more soldier than civilian.

Their life consisted wholly and solely of war, for they were and always had been front-line infantrymen. They survived because the Fates were kind to them, certainly—but also because they had become hard and immensely wise in animal-like ways of self-preservation. None of them liked war. They all wanted to go home, but they had been at it so long they knew how to take care of themselves and how to lead others. Around a little group like them every company was built.

I wouldn't go so far as to say those boys hadn't changed since they left America. Of course they changed—they had to. And yet when I sat and talked with them they seemed just like ordinary human beings back home.

Take Sergeant Paul Allumbaugh, for instance. He was an Iowa boy and a great soldier, yet so quiet, kind and good-natured that you couldn't imagine him ever killing anybody. He was only twenty-one—after all those years of fighting—and when shaved and cleaned up after battle he didn't look a bit older. At first I thought he looked too small to be a soldier, but then I realized how well-built he was. He was good-looking, and his face was the kind people like instinctively.

Sergeant Allumbaugh's nickname was Tag. He had gone through the whole thing without a wound, although his narrow escapes had been countless. He had one bullet scratch across his hand and another across a foot. Those were not counted as wounds.

Tag served for three months in the British Commandos when volunteers were asked for out of his company in Scotland. He fought with them in Africa too, then came back with his buddies—and his relatives. At one time the outfit was practically the Allumbaugh family, with Tag and his brother and five cousins in it, all from Shenandoah, Iowa. All seven of them were still alive, but their luck had varied.

Tag's brother Donald had been captured in 1943 and was still a German prisoner. Two cousins were also captured, but one of them had escaped. Of the remaining three, one was due to go home on rotation, another was in the engineers, and the third was still in the division.

While my company was in its brief olive-grove bivouac, Tag was living in a captured German dugout with his close buddy, Sergeant William Knobbs of Keokuk, Iowa. They had such a battle getting the place that they decided to live in it for a while. Sergeant Knobbs's nickname was Knobby, and he too had had some close shaves. Once a bullet went right through his helmet, across the top of his head. It burned the hair off in a groove just as though it had been shaved, yet it never broke the skin.

Knobby said his wife never knew he had been in combat. Then he corrected himself. He said actually she did know, through friends, but not from him. He had never once written her of any of his experiences or said he was in battle. (Knobby was killed a few days after this.)

Some of the remarks the men made in fun were pathetically revealing. There was the thing Sergeant Jack Pierson said one day in battle.

Jack was a wonderful guy, almost a Sergeant Quirt, except that he was good-looking, smart and friendly. But he was tough. As the other men said, "Jack is really a rough man. He would be rough even back home." He had been in the Commandos with Tag Allumbaugh.

He came from Sidney, Iowa, and was older than most of the others. For many years he ran a pile driver, doing construction work along the Missouri and Mississippi rivers. He called himself a river rat. The boys called him a "one-man army." He had been wounded once.

Jack was married and had three children. He had a girl nine, a boy seven, and then he had Junior. Junior was going on two and Jack had never seen him. Jack pretty much doted on Junior, and everybody in the company knew about Junior and how badly Jack wanted to see him.

One day in battle they were having it tough. There were rifle fire, mortars, and hand grenades all around, and soldiers on both sides getting knocked off like flies. Tag Allumbaugh was lying within shouting distance of where Jack was pinned down, and he yelled over, "How you doin', Jack?"

And then this man who was hard in peacetime, and was hard in war, called back a resigned answer that expressed in a general way every combat soldier's pathetic reason for wanting to live and hating to die.

He called back—and he wasn't joking, "It don't look like I'm gonna get to see Junior." (But he did. He survived, and went back to America in rotation, so I guess he saw Junior after all—and how he deserved to!)

The handful of old-timers had been together so long that they formed a little family of their own. Somehow they stood apart from the newer members of the company. They knew how to seek out the best place to settle down in a new bivouac. They were the first to find an abandoned German dugout, or a cozy pigshed, or a case of brandy in the cellar of a bombed building. And by right of seniority they took it.

Most of them were sergeants and platoon leaders by that time. Such men as Tag Allumbaugh and Knobby Knobbs and Jack Pierson, and Sergeant Ed Kattelman, of 735 Epworth Avenue, Cincinnati, and Buck Eversole, of Twin Falls, Idaho, and First Sergeant Bill Wood, of Council Bluffs, Iowa, and Sergeant Pete Conners, of Imogene, Iowa, and Pfc. Eddie Young, of Pontiac, Michigan.

So much depended on this little group of noncoms, and war is such a familiarizing force, that they were almost on the same basis as the officers. The officers ate separately when they were in bivouac, but that was about the only class distinction.

There was little military formality. I had to laugh one afternoon when Lieutenant Tony Libertore, of Charleston, South Carolina, was lying on the ground with several of the sergeants sitting around him, just gabbing about this and that.

Lieutenant Libertore made some remark—I forget what it was—and Jack Pierson rocked back and forth with his hands locked around his knees, and said, "Why, you horse's behind, it ain't that way at all."

Even in fun you don't talk that way to an officer until you've been through that famous valley of death and out again together.

Then Lieutenant Libertore started telling me all that he had to put up with: "Now take Tag and Knobby. They treat me like dirt. They browbeat me all the time. But word came around this afternoon that six men were to be picked for rest camp and, boy, they've been sirring me to death ever since, bringing me gifts and asking if I needed anything."

Tag and Knobby just sat there listening with appreciative grins on their faces.

The old-timers in the company sort of took me in and made me feel a part of their group. One afternoon Lieutenant Sheehy asked if I'd ever shot a carbine and I said no, but that I'd always wanted to. So he said, "Well, let's go out and shoot at something."

At the time we were a couple of miles back of the fighting. Our company was to march that night and start its own attack next day. That afternoon they had nothing to do, and they were just like men who take a day off from the office to lie around home. The artillery fire was in the distance, and the day was warm and sunny and lazy.

The lieutenant went to get his gun, and by common consent the little circle of veterans went after theirs too. When they came back they had carbines, tommy guns, Garands, .45s, and the German automatic known as the P-38, similar to the Luger. We walked about a quarter mile from our olive orchard down into a broad, protected gully.

Then with seasoned eyes they looked around for a place to do some target shooting. They'd look at one slope and say, "No, that's too rocky. The bullets will ricochet, and they might hit some of our artillery batteries over the hill." They looked at another slope and turned it down because we'd seen some Italian children running across it a little while before. Finally they picked a gravelly bank that seemed to have nothing behind it, and we started shooting. There weren't any tin cans or anything, so we'd pick out tiny white rocks in the bank. The distance was about seventy-five yards.

I'd been joking and bragging on the way down about what a crack rifle shot I was, so I had to make good or else. And I did! Nothing could make me any prouder than the way I picked off little white rocks right along with those veterans.

We must have shot for half an hour. We traded guns all around, so I could try them all. Buck Eversole showed me how they held a tommy gun and sprayed a slope full of krauts. Finally the lieutenant said: "We better stop or the colonel might raise hell about wasting ammunition."

Toward the end the boys were clowning, holding the guns out at arm's length and shutting their eyes like girls, and pressing down the trigger and just letting the gun jump.

It was really an incongruous interlude—war is full of them. Eight of the finest and most hardened soldiers in the American Army out in picnic fashion, having fun shooting at rocks two miles behind the line where the next day they would again be shooting to kill.

Most infantry companies then in the American front lines were composed largely of replacements, as happens in all armies after more than a year of fighting. Some of those replacements had been there only a few weeks. Others had been there so long that they were almost as seasoned as the original men of the company.

The new boys were afraid, of course, and very eager to hear and to learn. They hung on the words of the old-timers. I suppose the anticipation during the few days before a man's first battle is one of the worst ordeals in a lifetime. Now and then a soldier would crack up before he ever went into action.

One day I was wandering through an olive grove talking with some of the newer kids when I saw a soldier sitting on the edge of his foxhole, wearing a black silk opera hat. That's what I said— an opera hat.

The wearer was Private Gordon T. Winter, a Canadian. His father owned an immense sheep ranch near Lindbergh, Alberta, two hundred miles northeast of Edmonton. Private Winter said he'd found the top hat in a demolished house in a nearby village and just thought he'd bring it along. "I'm going to wear it in the next attack," he said. "The Germans will think I'm crazy, and they're afraid of crazy people."

In the same foxhole was a thin, friendly boy who seemed hardly old enough to be in high school. There was fuzz instead of whiskers on his face, and he had that eager-to-be-nice attitude that marked him as one not long away from home. He was Private Robert Lee Whichard, of 3422 Leverton Avenue, Baltimore, and he turned out to be just eighteen. He had been overseas only since early winter but had already seen action. He laughed when he told me about his first time in battle.

Apparently it was a pretty wild melee, and ground was changing hands back and forth. Private Whichard said he was lying on the ground shooting, "or maybe not shooting, I don't know," because he admitted he had been pretty scared. He happened to look up and there were German soldiers walking past him. Bob said he was so scared he just rolled over and lay still. Pretty soon mortar shells began dropping and the Germans decided to retire. So they came back past him, and he still lay there playing dead, until finally they were gone and he was safe.

Bob also told me about a dream he had had a few nights back. He dreamed his feet were so cold that he ran to the battalion aid station, and there were his mother and sister fixing him some hot food over a wood fire, and poking up the fire so he could warm his feet. But before he could eat the food or warm his feet, he woke up—and his feet were still cold.

Corporal Carnal Meena spoke up at that point and said he'd dreamed the night before that he was home and his mother was cooking tubfuls of pork chops for him to eat. He too had waked up before he could get a mouthful of food.

The post-office system had broken down so far as Carnal was concerned. He had been overseas five months and had never received a letter. He had never been in combat, either, but he was ready for it. The corporal couldn't decide about the future, whether or not he was going to be a minister, like his father—a Syrian minister back in Cleveland. But he admitted he had recently taken to reading his Bible.

Corporal Meena wanted me to visit Cleveland after the war and have a good old Syrian meal at his house. He said I wouldn't have to remember his name—just remember that his father was the only Syrian preacher in town, and I'd find him that way.

During another of my rambles, I ran onto a soldier under a tree, cleaning a sewing machine. He was Private Leonard Vitale of Council Bluffs, Iowa—one of the old-timers in the division. As I looked around I saw a couple of other sewing machines sitting on boxes. "Good Lord, what are you doing?" I asked. "Starting a sewing-machine factory?"

Vitale said no, he was just getting set to do altering and mending for division headquarters. The first two sewing machines he had bought from Italians, and an AMG officer had given him the newest machine. It was a Singer, in an elaborate mahogany cabinet.

Vitale said he wasn't an expert tailor but that during his three and a half years in the CCC he had picked up some of the rudiments of tailoring. He thought he would do all right and make a little money on the side. As I walked away he called out, "I'll have this war sewed up in a couple of months."

I grabbed a rifle from a nearby MP and shot the punster through and through before he had me in stitches.

Sometimes a person says the silliest things without being able to account for them. For example, one night our command post made a night move of about five miles. I went in a jeep, perched high on top of a lot of bedrolls.

The night was pure-black and the road was vicious. We were in low gear all the time, and even that was too fast. Many times we completely lost the trail, and would wander off and bump into trees or fall into deep ditches.

It was one of those sudden nose dives that undid me. We were far off the trail, but didn't know it. Suddenly the front end of the jeep dropped about three feet and everything stopped right there. That is, everything but me.

I went sailing right over the driver's shoulder, hit the steering wheel, and slid out onto the hood. And as I flew past the driver I said, "Excuse me."

Our company had a mascot which had been with it more than a year. It was an impetuous little black-and-white dog named Josie, a native of North Africa. Josie's name had gradually been transformed into Squirt.

Squirt was extremely affectionate, and when she came romping back to camp after a whirl with some gay Italian dog she would jump all over the old-time sergeants and lick their faces until they had to push her away. She had been wounded twice, which is an unusual experience for a dog. But more of a source of wonderment to the soldiers was how, unchaperoned and free-reined as her life was, she managed to survive all this time without becoming a mother.

And speaking of dogs, there was a story about a demonstration, back of the lines, of a new type of rifle grenade. A lot of high-ranking officers, including generals and colonels, were invited. Rows of chairs were placed for them out in the open.

Then a soldier fired the new grenade. It landed about a hundred fifty yards ahead of the officers, and failed to go off. No sooner had it hit the ground than a big black dog, doubtless with retriever blood in him, dashed out, grabbed the grenade in his mouth, and started back toward the assembled brass.

They said you never saw such a scramble as the visiting dignitaries made, getting out of their chairs and heading rapidly to the rear. Fortunately the grenade was so hot the dog had to drop it. From the dog's standpoint the demonstration was entirely successful—the grenade never did go off.

While I was with my company, we had one afternoon that was beautifully sunshiny and warm. Incessant but distant artillery walled the far horizons, yet nothing came into our area, and the day seemed infinitely peaceful.

We ate supper about an hour before dark in the grove back of a stone farmhouse. We had just started eating when all of a sudden "Whyyyeeeoooowww—Bang" came a shell right over our heads and whammed into the hillside beyond us. It was so close and so unexpected that even the veterans ducked, and the soldiers took to their foxholes pronto. Jack Sheehy ducked too, but then he immediately said, "There won't be any more. That one was a mistake."

He figured out that the Germans had pulled a tank out of the woods a mile or so away, and were trying to shell the hillside ahead of us. And their first practice shot had gone high and come over the ridge.

His theory was proved right a few moments later, when shells began pounding steadily on the other hillside just over the ridge. Which shows how wise a man can become in the ways of a world utterly foreign to a ticket desk in the dimly remembered city of New York.

A small white pill was discovered in captured German combat rations. It was a "fire" pill which produced heat without either flame or smoke, sufficient to warm a cup of coffee or a can of ration. I forgot to ask how the pill was set going. I do know our troops wished they had something similar for front-line mountaintop work. Just one warm meal a day would have meant a great deal.

Ray Clapper's passing hit us hard. He had many friends in the war theater. He traveled to all the wars because he felt it his duty to inform himself, and everywhere he went he was liked for himself and respected for his fine mind. We had known each other for twenty years. He was always generous and thoughtful of me. Time and again he went out of his way to do little things that would help me, and to say nice things about me in his column, and I cannot remember that I ever did one thing for him. Those accusing regrets come when it is too late.

War correspondents tried not to think of how high their ratio of casualties had been in this war. At least they tried not to think of it in terms of themselves, but Ray Clapper's death sort of set us back on our heels. Somehow it always seemed impossible that anything could ever happen to him. It made us wonder who would be next.

When *Stars and Stripes* announced Ray Clapper's death, I think the most frequent comment in that area was one that would have made Ray proud. People said: "The old story again. It's always the best ones that get it."

One night in a group of soldiers and officers, the question came up whether or not it was a good idea to yell when making a close-in attack.

An officer thought it was good psychology because the Germans were afraid of night attacks, and a good barrage of Indian yells would further demoralize them. But the soldiers mainly disagreed. They said Jerry didn't scare as easily as all that, and when an attacker yelled he just gave his position away.

Speaking of noise, you've probably heard the term "screaming meemies," meaning a certain noisy type of German shell. The boys called them "screaming meanies" instead and, brother, they were bad indeed to listen to.

The Germans called the gun the "*Nebelwerfer.*" It was a six-barreled rocket rack which fired one rocket after another, electrically. The gun didn't go off with a roar, but the shells swished forward with a sound of unparalleled viciousness and power, as though gigantic gears were grinding. Actually it sounded as though some mammoth man were grinding them out of a huge machine.

Whenever a shelling started we always stopped and listened, and somebody made a remark like, "Grind 'em out, boy; keep on turning!" or "Boy, Jerry's gettin' mad again!"

The screaming meanies made a frightful noise when they were coming head on, and even when they were going off at an angle some distance away they made a long-drawn-out moaning sound that was bloodcurdling.

At an Army chow line near a village or close to farms, there were usually a few solemn and patient children with tin buckets— waiting to get what was left over.

One soldier said to me, "I just can't bear to eat when they stand and look at me like they do. Lots of times I've filled my mess kit and just walked over and dumped it in their buckets and gone back to my foxhole. I wasn't hungry."

Lieutenant Sheehy was tremendously proud of the outfit. He told me, "Every man in the company deserves the Silver Star."

We were walking around the bivouac where the men of the company were sitting on the edges of their foxholes, talking or cleaning their gear.

"Let's go over there," he said. "I want to introduce you to my personal hero."

I figured that the lieutenant's own "personal hero," out of a whole company of men who deserved the Silver Star, must be a real soldier indeed.

And that is how I was first introduced to Sergeant Frank ("Buck") Eversole, one of the old-timers. He shook hands sort of timidly and said, "Pleased to meet you," and then didn't say any more. I could tell by his eyes, and by his slow, courteous speech when he did talk, that he was a Westerner. Conversation with him was rather hard, but I didn't mind his reticence, for I know how Westerners like to size people up first. The sergeant wore a brown stocking cap on the back of his head. His eyes were the piercing kind. I noticed his hands too—they were outdoor hands, strong and rough.

Later in the afternoon I came past his foxhole again, and we sat and talked a little while alone. We didn't talk about the war, but mainly about our West, and just sat and made figures on the ground with sticks as we talked. We got started that way, and in the days that followed I came to know him well. He was to me, and to all those with whom he served, one of the great men of the war.

Buck was a cowboy before the war. He was born in the little town of Missouri Valley, Iowa, and his mother still lived there. But Buck went west on his own before he was sixteen, and worked as a ranch hand. He was twenty-eight years old, and unmarried. He worked a long time around Twin Falls, Idaho, and then later down in Nevada. Like so many cowboys, he made the rodeos in season. He was never a star or anything. Usually he just rode the broncs out of the chute, for pay—$7.50 a ride. Once he did win a fine saddle. He rode at Cheyenne and the other big rodeos.

Like any cowboy, he loved animals. There in Italy one afternoon, terrific German shellfire pinned Buck and some other boys down inside a one-room stone shed. As they sat there, a frightened mule came charging through the door. There simply wasn't room inside for men and mule too, so Buck got up and shooed the critter out the door. Thirty feet from the door a direct hit killed the mule. Buck still felt guilty about it.

Another time he ran onto a mule that was down and crying in pain from a bad shell wound. Buck took his .45 and put a bullet through its head. "I wouldn't have shot him except he was hurtin' so," Buck said.

Buck Eversole had the Purple Heart and two Silver Stars for bravery. He was cool and deliberate and very effective in battle. His commanders depended more on him than on any other man. He had been wounded once, and had had countless narrow escapes. A person instinctively felt safer when he was around. He was not helpless like most of us. He was practical. He could improvise, patch things, fix things.

His grammar was the unschooled grammar of the plains and the soil. He used profanity, but never violently. Even in the familiarity of his own group his voice was always low. It was impossible to conceive of his doing anything dishonest. He was such a confirmed soldier by then that he always said "sir" to any stranger.

After the war Buck wanted to go back west to the land he loved. He wanted to get a little place and feed a few head of cattle, and be independent. "I don't want to be just a ranch hand no more," he said. "It's all right and I like it all right, but it's a rough life and it don't get you nowhere. When you get a little older you kind a like a place of your own."

Buck Eversole had no hatred for Germans, although he had killed many of them. He killed because he was trying to keep alive himself. The years rolled over him and the war became his only world, and battle his only profession. He armored himself with a philosophy of accepting whatever might happen.

"I'm mighty sick of it all," he said quietly, "but there ain't no use to complain. I just figure it this way, that I've been given a job to do and I've got to do it. And if I don't live through it, there's nothing I can do about it."

His job was platoon sergeant. That means he had charge of about forty front-line fighting men. He had been at the front for more than a year. War was old to him and he had become almost the master of it, a senior partner in the institution of death.

The personnel of his platoon had turned over many times as battle whittled down the old ones and the replacement system brought up the new ones. Only a handful were veterans.

"It gets so it kinda gets you, seein' these new kids come up," Buck told me one night in his slow, barely audible western voice, so full of honesty and sincerity. "Some of them have just got fuzz on their faces, and don't know what it's all about, and they're scared to death. No matter what, some of them are bound to get killed."

We talked about some of the other old-time noncoms who could take battle themselves, but had gradually grown morose under the responsibility of leading green boys to their slaughter. Buck spoke of one sergeant especially, a brave and hardened man, who went to his captain and asked to be reduced to a private in the lines.

"I know it ain't my fault that they get killed," Buck finally said, "and I do the best I can for them. But I've got so I feel like it's me killin' 'em instead of a German. I've got so I feel like a murderer. I hate to look at them when the new ones come in."

Buck himself had been fortunate. His one wound was a bullet through the arm. His own skill and wisdom had saved him many times, but luck had saved him countless other times.

One night Buck and an officer took refuge from shelling in a two-room Italian stone house. As they sat there, a shell came through the wall of the far room, crossed the room and buried itself in the middle wall, with its nose pointing upward. It didn't go off.

Another time Buck was leading his platoon on a night attack. They were walking Indian file. Suddenly a mine went off and killed the entire squad following Buck. He himself had miraculously walked through the mine field without hitting a single one.

One day Buck went stalking a German officer in close combat, and they wound up with the German on one side of a farmhouse and Buck on the other. They kept throwing grenades over the house at each other without success. Finally Buck stepped around one corner of the house, and came face to face with the German, who'd had the same idea. Buck was ready and pulled the trigger first. His slug hit the German just above the heart. The German had a wonderful pair of binoculars slung over his shoulders, and the bullet smashed them to bits. Buck had wanted some German binoculars for a long time.

The ties that grow between men who live savagely together, relentlessly communing with Death, are ties of great strength. There is a sense of fidelity to each other in a little corps of men who have endured so long, and whose hope in the end can be so small.

One afternoon Buck's turn came to go back to rest camp for five days. He knew the company was due to attack that night. Buck went to Sheehy and said, "Lieutenant, I don't think I better go. I'll stay if you need me."

The lieutenant said, "Of course I need you, Buck, I always need you. But it's your turn and I want you to go. In fact, you're ordered to go."

The truck taking the few boys away to rest camp left just at dusk. It was drizzling and the valleys were swathed in a dismal mist. Artillery of both sides flashed and rumbled around the horizon. The encroaching darkness was heavy and foreboding.

Buck came to the little group of old-timers in the company with whom I was standing. You'd have thought he was leaving forever. He shook hands all around. "Well, good luck to you all." And then he added, "I'll be back in just five days." He was a man stalling off his departure. Another round of good-byes, and he slowly started away. But he stopped and said good-bye all around again, and again he repeated, "Well, good luck to you all."

I walked with him toward the truck in the dusk. He kept his eyes on the ground, and I think he might have cried if he had known how, and he said to me very quietly, "This is the first battle I've ever missed that this battalion has been in. Even when I was in the hospital with my arm, they were in bivouac. This will be the first one I've ever missed. I sure do hope they have good luck." And then, "I feel like a deserter."

He climbed in, and the truck dissolved into the blackness. I went back and lay down on the ground among my other friends, waiting for the night orders to march. I lay there in the darkness thinking—terribly touched by the great simple devotion of that soldier who was a cowboy—thinking of the millions of people far away at home who would remain forever unaware of the powerful fraternalism in this ghastly brotherhood of war.

We had been alerted for the night march just before suppertime. Word was passed around to collect twenty-four hours' field rations and a full supply of ammunition. At chow time each soldier held his tin hat in his left hand while holding his mess kit in his right. Five C-ration cans were put into each man's hat, and one bar of D ration.

After supper, while there was still light, each man rolled his one blanket inside his one shelter half. Early darkness had come before 5:30. It was chilly. A misty rain began to fall. The men just lay or sat in their foxholes under the doubtful shelter of the olive trees.

Full darkness came over the olive grove, the artillery raged and flashed around half the horizon, and the concussion crashed and ran across the sky along the sounding board of the low clouds.

We of our little company were swallowed in a great blackness, connected to the war by one field telephone which ran to the battalion command post a quarter mile away. Nobody knew when the marching order would come. We just had to sit there and wait. There were only two places to get out of the rain. Both were pigsheds an Italian farmer had dug into the side of a bank. They were stacked over with straw. Lieutenant Jack Sheehy and four enlisted men and I crawled into one and dragged the phone in after us. A few sergeants went into the other.

We lay down on the ground there in the pigshed. We had on our heavy coats but the chill came through. The lieutenant had an extra blanket which he carried unrolled when not actually in battle, so he spread it out and he and I both lay under it. We huddled against each other and became a little warmer.

The lieutenant said, "When I read your column back home, I never supposed we'd ever meet. Imagine us lying together here on the ground in Italy." Then we talked a little while in low tones, but pretty soon somebody started to snore and before long all of us were asleep, although it was still only seven o'clock.

Every now and then the lieutenant would phone battalion headquarters to see if any orders had come yet. Finally he was told that the line to the regiment was cut. Linemen were out of the darkness feeling with their hands, tracing the entire length of the wire, trying to find the break. Around nine o'clock it was repaired, but still no marching orders came.

A dark form appeared faintly silhouetted in the open end of the shed, and asked if Lieutenant Sheehy was there. The lieutenant said he was. "Can the men unroll their blankets?" the form asked. "They're wet and cold."

The lieutenant thought a moment and then he said, "No, better not. We should get the word to go any minute now, certainly within half an hour. They'd better keep them rolled."

The form said, "Yes, sir," and faded back into the darkness.

By ten o'clock everybody in the shed had awakened from his nap. Our grove was deathly still, as though no one existed in it, although the night was full of distant warfare. Now and then we'd get clear under the blanket and light a cigarette and hide it under the blanket when we puffed. Over on the far hillside where the Germans were we could see a distant light. We finally decided it was probably a lamp in some unwitting Italian's farmhouse.

For a little while there was a sudden burst of flares in the distance. The first was orange, then came some in green, then a white, and then some more orange ones. Our soldiers couldn't tell whether they were German or ours.

Between flashes of artillery we could hear quite loud blasts of machine guns. As usual you could distinguish between a German machine gun and ours, for theirs was much faster. Machine guns were rarely fired except in flashes, so the barrel wouldn't get too hot, but once some Jerry just held the trigger down and let her roll for about fifteen seconds. "Boy, he'll have to put on a new barrel after that one," a soldier said.

The time dragged on and we grew colder and stiffer. At last, nearly at midnight, the phone rang in the stillness of our pig-shed. It was the order to go.

One of the boys said, "It's going to be a bitch of a thing to move. The ground is slick and you can't see your hand in front of you."

One sergeant went out to start the word for the company to assemble. Another disconnected the field telephone and carried it under his arm. Everybody wrestled into the harness of his heavy pack.

"Assemble down by the kitchen tent," the lieutenant told the first sergeant. "Platoons will form in this order—headquarters, third, first, second, and heavy weapons. Let's go."

The sergeant moved off. I moved after him. The first two steps were fine. On the third step I went down into a ditch and said a bad word.

The night was utterly black. It was the dark of the moon, and thick, low clouds further darkened the sky. "In two years over-seas, this is the blackest night we've ever moved," one soldier said.

With a couple of others, I felt my way from our pigshed down to where we thought the kitchen tent was. We knew we were near it, but we couldn't see it.

"It's up ahead about fifty feet," one soldier said.

I butted in and said, "No, it's over to the right about thirty feet."

Just at that moment a flash of fire from one of our nearby can-non brightened the countryside for a split second, and we saw the tent. It was six inches in front of us. That's how dark it was.

One by one the platoon leaders felt their way up to the head of the column, reported their platoons ready in line, and felt their way back. Finally the lieutenant said, "Let's go."

There's no military formality about a night movement of in-fantry. Men don't try to keep step. Nobody says "Forward march," or any of that parade-ground stuff. After a rest the leader says, "All right, let's get along." And everybody gets up and starts.

In trying to get out of the orchard we lost our various places. Finally everybody stopped and called out to each other in order to get reassembled. The lieutenant and the sergeant would call for me occasionally to make sure I was still along.

When we fell in again, I was marching behind Sergeant Vincent Conners of Imogene, Iowa. His nickname was "Pete." We hadn't gone far before I realized that the place behind Pete was the best spot in the column for me, for I had discovered a little trick. He had a rolled-up map about two feet long stuck horizontally through the pack harness on his back. By keeping close to it, I could just barely make out the vague white shape of the map. And that was my beacon throughout the night.

It was amazing how I could read the terrain ahead by the movement of that thin white line. If it went down a couple of inches, I knew Pete had stepped into a hole. If it went down fast, I knew he had struck a slope. If it went down sideways, I knew his feet were sliding on a slippery slope. In that split second before my own step followed his, I could correct for whatever had happened to him. As a result I was down only once the whole night.

Going along we were suddenly startled to hear some magnificent cussing down at one side. It was Jack Sheehy's voice. He had stepped right off into a narrow ditch about two feet deep and gone down on his back. Bundled as he was with packsacks, he couldn't get out of the ditch. He finally made it on about the third try.

The thing that always amazed me about those inhuman night movements of troops in war areas was how good-natured the men were about it. A certain fundamental appreciation of the ridiculous carried them through. As we slogged along, slipping and crawling and getting muddier and muddier, the soldier behind me said, "I'm going to write my congressman about this."

Another soldier answered, "Hell, I don't even know who my congressman is. I did three years ago, but I don't now."

The first voice was that of Pfc. Eddie Young, of Pontiac, Michigan, the company's runner and message carrier. A person gets to know voices very quickly. Newcomer that I was, there were a dozen men I could name in the blackness. Eddie Young's voice especially haunted me. It was soft, and there was a tolerant and gentle humor in it. It was a perfect duplicate of the voice of my friend Ben Robertson, the correspondent who was killed in the clipper crash at Lisbon the year before. Whenever Eddie spoke, I could not help feeling that Ben was marching behind me.

The company's first sergeant was Bill Wood, a tall man who

carried a heavy pack, and when he fell there was a lot of him to go down. Whenever Bill fell we'd hear him and stop. And then we could hear him clawing with his feet and getting partway up, then hitting the mud again, and cussing more eloquently with each attempt. It sounded so funny we all had to laugh. When Bill finally got back in line he was good and mad, and he said he couldn't see anything funny about it. A few days later he was wounded, and I saw him next in a hospital.

It took us half an hour to feel our way out of the big orchard and down a few feet onto the so-called road, which was actually not much more than a furrow worn by Italian mule carts. There were knee-deep ruts and bucket-sized rocks.

Once on the road, the column halted to let a train of pack mules pass. As we stood there, the thought occurred to all of us: "it's bad enough to be floundering around on the ground and mud, but now it'll be like groveling in a barnyard."

The trail was never straight. It went up and down, across streams, and almost constantly around trees. How the leaders ever followed it was beyond me. The trees on each side had been marked previously with white tape or toilet paper, but even so we did get lost a couple of times and had to backtrack.

Our pace was miserably slow. The rain had stopped, but the mud was thick. We literally felt each step out with the toes of our boots. Every half hour or so we'd stop and send runners back to see how the tail end of the column was doing. Word came back that they were doing fine, and that we could step up the pace if we wanted to.

Somewhere in the night, both ahead of us and strung out behind us in files, was the rest of our battalion. In fact, the whole regiment of more than three thousand men was on the move. But we knew nothing about the rest of the outfit.

Throughout the night the artillery of both sides kept up a steady pounding. When we started, our own guns were loud in our ears. Gradually we drew away from them, and finally the explosion of their shells on German soil was louder than the blast of our guns.

The German shells traveled off at a tangent from us, and we were in no danger. The machine-gun and rifle fire grew louder as our slow procession came nearer the lines. Now and then a front-line flare would light up the sky, and we could see red bullets ricocheting.

The gun blasts made a continuous crashing in the night, yet they were always so brief they didn't give a revealing view of the trail ahead.

The nagging of artillery eventually got plain annoying. Accentuated by the cloudy night, the sounds crashed and reverberated against the low ceiling. A single gun blast set off a continuous rebounding of sound, against clouds and rocky slopes, which would keep going for ten seconds and more.

In fact, that cloudy night the rustle of the shells, as they went tearing above our heads, was so magnified that when we stopped to rest and tried to talk we couldn't hear what the other fellow said. The shells were passing almost constantly.

At last we passed through a village and stopped on the far edge to rest while the column leader went into a house for further directions. We had caught up with the mules and drawn alongside them. Out in the darkness, one of the mule skinners kept up a long monologue on the subject of the mules being completely done up. Nobody answered him, and he went on: "They're plumb done in. They can't go another foot. If we try to go on, they'll fall down and die."

Finally, some soldier in the darkness told him to shut up. We all privately endorsed his suggestion. But the monologist got huffy and wanted to know who that was. The voice said it wasn't anybody, just a new replacement soldier.

Then the mule skinner waxed sarcastic and louder. He had an objectionable manner, even in the dark.

"Oh, oh!" he said. "So we've got a baby right from the States telling me how to run mules! A tenderfoot, huh? Trying to talk to us veterans! A hero right from the States, huh?"

Whereupon one of the real veterans in our company called out to the gabby skinner, "Aw, shut up! You probably haven't been overseas two months yourself."

He must have hit the nail on the head, or else his voice carried command, for that was the last we heard of the mule skinner.

It was almost midnight when the company reached its bivouac area and dug its foxholes into the mud. Always that was the first thing to do. It became pure instinct. The drippy, misty dawn found us dispersed and hidden in the bottom of shallow, muddy depressions of our own digging, eating cold hash from C-ration cans.

The men attacked just after dawn. The Germans were only a short distance away. I stayed behind when the company went forward.

In the continuously circulating nature of my job, I might never again see the men in that outfit. But to me they would always be "my" company.

FOURTEEN

LIGHT BOMBERS

To keep some sense of proportion about the various fighting units, I shifted next to a light-bomber group—the 47th. They flew the fast twin-engined Douglas-built plane known as the A-20 Boston. The 47th was a veteran outfit. It fought through Tunisia, and helped beat the Germans back at Kasserine Pass. It flew from Souk el Arba and Cape Bon and Malta and Sicily, and then it was on the front in Italy.

Like most air groups of long service, it had almost no flying personnel left who had come overseas with it. Its casualty rate had been low, but the crew men had all reached or passed their allotted number of missions and gone home. In fact, some of its members had gone home so long before that they were then back overseas on their second tour of combat duty, fighting out of England or in the South Pacific. The ground-crew men got letters from them sometimes.

I stayed with a certain squadron of the 47th. It changed commanders while I was with it. The outgoing commander was Major Cy Stafford, a brilliant young pilot-engineer from Oak Park, Illinois. He had been promoted to the group staff, and his place as squadron commander was taken by Lieutenant Colonel Reginald Clizbe, of Centralia, Washington.

Colonel Clizbe was a veteran in combat, but for several months had been on staff duty. He was pleased to get back to the small and intimate familiarity of a squadron. As he said, "Squadron commander is the best job in the Air Corps."

On his first day, Colonel Clizbe got a plane and went out and practiced while the rest went on their mission. I was staying in the same tent with him, and although at that time I didn't know him very well I could tell he was worried and preoccupied. He wasn't afraid. Everybody knew that. But he was rusty, everybody's eyes were on him and he was scared to death he would foul up on his first mission.

He flew the morning mission on his second day in command. He flew a wing position, and he did all right. He was in good spirits when they came back before lunch.

There was another mission that afternoon. Instead of resting, Colonel Clizbe put himself on the board for that one too, this time leading a flight of three. I was at his revetment when the planes came back just before dusk. When they got out, Colonel Clizbe was a changed man. He was just like a football player after winning a game.

It had been a perfect mission. The bomb pattern had smothered the target. They'd started fires. Their breakout from the bomb run was just right, and the planes got only a little flak. The new man had his teeth into the game again, and he was over the hump. He was all elation and enthusiasm. "We'll give 'em hell from now on," he said.

All evening he kept smiling to himself, and he was like somebody released from a great oppression. That night he went to bed around nine o'clock, for he was tired, and he had assigned himself to lead the mission early next morning. Just before he went to sleep, he happened to think of something. He raised up and said, "Say, this is my birthday! I'd forgotten about it. Boy, I couldn't have had a better birthday present than those two missions today."

The colonel was back in the war. He was doing a job again in person, with his own hands and brain, and he went to sleep with a fine satisfaction.

Our pilots laughed about some of their accidental successes. A light-bomber outfit was making a run with a brand-new replacement pilot, out on his first mission. Their target was very close to our own lines. As they were making their turn this new pilot lost formation and swung way out on the outside of the others.

Realizing his mistake, and seeing he was about to get left behind, he just salvoed his bombs and went streaking to catch up with the formation.

The squadron leader saw it and felt sure this neophyte had dropped his bombs on our own troops. When he got home he sat there by the telephone, sweating, waiting for the inevitable phone call.

Pretty soon the phone rang. A voice announced itself as General So-and-so. The squadron leader's heart sank. When a general phones it bodes no good. The general boomed, "Say, who is that crazy pilot that left your formation and dropped his bombs off to the side?"

The squadron leader got ready to faint. He knew the next sentence would be that those bombs had killed three hundred American troops. Instead, the general shouted, "Well, whoever he was, give him my congratulations. He got a direct hit on a gun we've been trying to get for two weeks. Wiped it out. Excellent work."

The group was based on a magnificent field that had been bulldozed by British engineers out of a gigantic vineyard in three days' time. The dark earthen runway was more than a mile long, and scores of crooked taxi paths led out to where each plane was individually parked among the grapevines. The field never got really muddy, for the soil was volcanic and water drained through it. Every morning the ground was lightly frozen and the grass and the shoulder-high grapevines were covered with white frost. In sunny weather it was warm at midday, but by four in the afternoon the evening chill had set in and our breath showed as we talked.

Guards theoretically kept Italians out of the airfield area, but there was always a little knot of them standing behind some plane, watching the mechanics work. And all through the vast vineyards which engulfed the tents of the Americans, there were Italians tying up their grapevines and digging in the earth.

It was an odd sensation to walk along a narrow path and hear a dirty and ragged Italian girl singing grand opera as she worked on the vines. Or to go to an outdoor toilet and suddenly discover a bunch of Italian peasant women looking over the low canvas wall as they walked past. They didn't seem to care, and we didn't either.

Everybody lived in square, pyramidal tents, officers and men alike. The tents were scattered throughout the vineyard, fifty or so yards apart, and they were hard to see at a distance.

From four to six men lived in a tent. They all slept on folding cots, and most of them had the big, warm, Air Forces sleeping bags. They lived comfortably.

The inside of each tent depended on the personality of its occupants. Some of them were neat and bright and furnished with countless little home comforts of the boys' own carpentering. Others were shoddy and cavelike, offering little more than the bare requirements of life.

All the tents had stoves in the middle. They were homemade from twenty-gallon oil drums. Back of each tent was a can of 100-octane gasoline, set on a waist-high stool. A metal pipe led under the tent wall and across the floor to the stove. It was the old siphon system, pure and simple. A man had to suck on the pipe, and get a mouthful of gasoline, before the flow started. After that he controlled it with a petcock. Stoves blew up frequently, but seldom did any damage.

An electric light hung down from the middle of each tent. The blackout was not terribly strict, and when we wandered around the area at night we used a flashlight. Some of the tents had wooden floors—made by knocking apart the long boxes that frag bombs come in, and nailing them into sections. Others had only dirt floors.

Many tents had radios. The boys listened to all kinds of stations—our own Naples broadcast, the BBC, the distorted Rome radio, Axis Sally still cynically admonishing us that we would go home (if we were lucky) only to find our jobs gone and our girls married to other guys. But most of all they listened to the sweet music from German stations and to the American swing music from our own.

The day began early. Just before dawn the portable generators, which were scattered among the grapevines, began to put-put and lights went on everywhere. Nobody ever turned a light on or off. The generators stopped at ten each night, and the lights simply went out. Thus when the generators started again at six in the morning our lights automatically went on and our radios started.

One man in each tent would leap out of his sleeping bag and get the stove going, and then leap back for a few minutes. Little strings of oily gray smoke soon began to sprout upward out of the vineyard.

In a few minutes came the sound of engines barking on the other side of the runway, and then with a deep roar that seemed to shake the whole silent countryside the planes would thunder down the runway and take to the air. They were out on early test hops. A few unfortunates had to crawl out of their sacks at 4 a.m. to get them going.

Everybody was up by 6:30 at the latest. Guys clad only in long gray underwear dashed out under the nearest olive tree and dashed shivering back into the tent.

A little cold water—out of a five-gallon can—was splashed onto their faces, they jumped into their clothes in nothing flat, and were on the way to breakfast as full daylight came. Breakfast was finished at 7:30. But even before that the squadron commanders and operations officers had driven in jeeps around to the other side of the field to get briefed by the group staff on the morning's mission.

Each squadron in the group lived in a separate area. They formed three distinct families, which fused into one big unit only when they were in the air.

The plane crews assembled around the operations tent immediately after breakfast. From a nearby tent, they picked up their parachutes and their new flak vests. They stood around outside zipping on their heavy flying clothes while they waited the call to briefing. When it came, they crowded into the tent and sat on rows of frag-bomb boxes, as in a little school. The squadron intelligence officer got up on a low platform and started talking.

They said this particular officer's briefings were the best in the group. I sat in on scores of briefings in England and Africa, and usually they were repetitious and dull. But that squadron's briefings were interesting. The intelligence officer was intensely thorough. The crews got a detailed picture of what they were to do. And above all he was honest.

One of the gunners said to me, "Some briefing officers will tell you flatly you won't get any flak, and then when you get there it just pours up. Now our intelligence officer, he'll say, 'I don't think you'll get much flak today, but you know the Germans have mobile ack-ack, and they can concentrate it overnight, so watch out.'"

Part of the talk was a résumé of the war news. The officer gave the whole Italian war situation, both ground and air, of the previous twenty-four hours. He told them also any news that had come from England or Russia.

Then he went into the briefing. Behind him were a big map and two big blackboards. The map was of Central Italy, and he would point out the target. Then on the blackboard he chalked a detailed sketch of the target area, which covered an area forty or fifty miles square. It invariably included the coast line, so that crews could orient the target with the coast.

The second blackboard had a "blown-up" sketch of the target area, covering territory only a couple of miles square. It contained full details for helping the crews identify the target when they got there, such as exact towns and roads, little lakes, groves of trees, and even an isolated white farmhouse.

When the intelligence officer had finished, the flight leader got up. Usually that was Captain Gene Vance, from Pueblo, Colorado, who used to be a newspaperman himself.

Captain Vance told them what type of bomb they were carrying, and how many and what kind of fighters would be escorting them. He also went into great detail on just how each flight would "break away" out of the bomb run, plus a few methods to avoid flak. He advised what route to take home if anybody got lost. Sometimes they had to throw out bundles of pamphlets as well as drop bombs, and he advised the exact formation to fly so that the bundle wouldn't hit the following plane.

At the end he gave them a time set. Everybody looked at his watch and Captain Vance said: "It is now 23 seconds till 10 minutes to 9. It is now 20 seconds—15 seconds—10 seconds—5—4—3—2—1. Check. Ten minutes to 9."

The crews, looking sober, filed out and got into their trucks.

Pilots fly planes, and mechanics fix planes, and bombardiers drop bombs out of planes, and they've all been written about. But I've never heard anybody mention the guys who put the bombs in the planes. They are called armorers. They not only "bomb up" the planes, but it is their job to keep all the planes' guns in tiptop working order. In the 47th Group of A-20 light bombers there was theoretically one armorer to each plane. But they were short then, and each armorer usually had two planes to care for.

An armorer was as proud of his plane as the pilot. He called it "my plane," and when "his" plane failed to come back he felt horrible. Among the armorers, everybody knew whose plane had the most missions.

The armorers lived in tents, the same as all the other men in the squadron. Each morning a truck took them to the area where their planes were dispersed. They started bombing up about an hour and a half before take-off time.

For really heavy bombs, the planes were equipped with a lifting device. Smaller bombs, even up to 300-pound ones, were lifted by hand. To do this, the armorers of several planes formed themselves into a team of four or five men, and went from one plane to another helping each other until their little family was all bombed up.

I went around one day with a team composed of Sergeant Steve Major of Monessen, Pennsylvania; Corporal Vincent Cline of Paragould, Arkansas; Corporal John Peoples of Alameda, California; Corporal Robert Gerrie of Chicago, and Corporal James La Barr of Dallas, Pennsylvania. Corporal La Barr's plane, incidentally, had more missions than any other—123—and was piling them up by one and two a day.

The bombs had already been hauled out, and were lying on the ground alongside the planes, when the armorers arrived. This day they were loading 250-pound demolition bombs. These were about three feet long and ten inches thick, and tapered at both ends.

The boys rolled them to the planes by kicking them along with their feet. Six were rolled under each plane. The bomb-bay doors were already hanging down open. The armorer crawled under and then he could stand erect with his head inside the bomb bay. An 18-inch clamp was taken from the bay wall and hooked into two steel rings in the back of the bomb. Then two of the men grabbed the bomb and heaved it up. As it rose, a third man got under it and lifted with his shoulders. The two others put it into position.

It was good heavy heaving. Only the rugged ones stayed on as armorers. Now and then somebody slipped and a bomb fell on an armorer, but serious accidents were rare.

After the bombs were clamped inside the bomb bay, they put in the fuses. The bomb had a steel plug in each end. The boys unscrewed these plugs, and screwed the fuses into the hole. I never knew before that our bombs had fuses on both ends. I asked what it was for. The boys said, so that if one fuse didn't work the other one would. Each fuse had a little metal propeller on it. When the bomb was dropped the propeller started whirling, and after dropping about five hundred feet it unscrewed itself enough to become a plunger and "arm" the bomb, as they called it. Then when the bomb hit the ground, this plunger was forced back and the bomb was discharged.

Of course, there had to be some guarantee that propellers didn't get to whirling inside the planes. So the boys took a piece of wire and fastened it into the clamp from which the release hung. Then they ran each end of the wire through two small holes in the propellers, thus locking them. When the bomb was released, this wire remained fastened to the plane and the ends slipped out of the little propellers, freeing them.

If the pilot had to salvo his bombs over friendly territory, where he didn't want them to go off, he could pull a different lever which released the wire and let it fall still attached to the bomb, thus keeping the little propellers locked.

The armorer's job was really not a hard one, except for the heavy lifting which lasted only a few minutes a day. What disgusted armorers the most was when the command kept changing its mind about what kind of bomb load was to be carried on the next mission.

Sometimes they would get an order to bomb up with 500-pounders, then the order would be changed to frag bombs, then changed again to 250-pounders. On every change they had to unload and reload.

The boys said the all-time record was one day when they changed bombs twelve times, and it finally wound up that the planes never went out after all.

Armorer Sergeant Steve Major of Monessen, Pennsylvania, was six feet six inches tall and weighed 222 pounds. Despite that weight he looked slim, because of his great height. He was good-looking and good-natured, and always had something to say. As he rode along in a truck he would shake his fist at some tough-looking crew chief and yell at him, "You ugly bastard!" Nobody could possibly get mad at him.

Steve had been in the Army nearly six years, and was an excellent soldier. He quit high school and enlisted when he was seventeen, and served one shift in Panama. When his first three years were up, he stayed out just six days and then re-enlisted on the condition that they send him to California. They did. Steve liked to see the world.

I asked him if he would stay in the Army after the war. He said, "No, the Army's all right, but I've had enough of it. I've got three thousand coconuts in the bank, and I'm going to get some education after the war and be a salesman."

"Yeah, I'll bet," said another soldier. "You look like a thirty-year man to me."

Steve had a good, calm philosophy about everything. He was even philosophical about his part in the war. He said, "I tried to be a pilot—too big. Tried to be a gunner—too big. So I'm an armorer. Okay, I'm happy. What the hell."

He said further, "This job is easy. We work hard for a little while every day, and then the rest of the day we don't do much. Any civilian could do this work after a little training. It's just like a regular job, only we're away from home.

"It's not like last winter in Tunisia when we lived on British rations and damned near froze to death and got raided every day. Everything's different now. We're living good here. Why, this is better than it was back home in camp."

Steve didn't go on missions. He was so big he would have been in the way. The plane of which he was armorer had been lost several weeks back, so then he was helping out the other boys. He slept in a tent right out on the line in order to be near his job.

Steve was cool in the pinches. One day his plane came back with its full load of bombs. When they dropped the unexploded bombs down to the ground, he discovered that one of the fuses was on. A few of the fuses that day had been set for forty-five seconds' delay, but he didn't know how much of the forty-five seconds had been used up before he made his discovery. The natural impulse would have been to run as fast and as far as he could before the bomb went off. But Steve just sat there on the ground and unscrewed the fuse with his hands and then tossed it aside just as it went off—harmlessly.

Big Steve loved to travel. And I believe he got more out of it than any soldier I met. He might have been dropped down at a new field in any old country, and within a week he would have known half the natives in the adjoining village. Steve's parents were Austrian and Yugoslav, and he spoke four Slav dialects. In Panama he learned Spanish, and in Italy he wrote down twenty new Italian words every night and memorized them. He got along fine in Italian.

On his afternoons off he hopped a train or bus and went out by himself seeing the country. Invariably he got into conversation with the people. Half the time he wound up going to somebody's home for a meal. He said, "I've been in rich homes and poor homes over here. These are pretty good people, but they're so damned emotional. They get into the wildest arguments with each other over the most trivial things. But they're goodhearted."

Steve wasn't obsessed like the average soldier about getting home. He took the war as it came, and didn't fuss. He looked forward to seeing home again, but he didn't want to stay even when he got there. His big worry was that he would meet some woman who would have him married to her before he knew what had happened. He didn't want to be tied down. He wanted to travel and be free and roam around the world, talking to people, as soon as the little bombing job of his was finished.

Most of my time with the group was spent with the gunners. All the gunners were sergeants. Each plane carried two, who rode in the rear compartment of the plane.

The top gunner sat in a glass-enclosed bubble rising above the fuselage. The bottom gunner sat on the floor during take-off, and after they were in the air he opened a trap door and swiveled his machine gun down into the open hole.

Owing to the nature of their missions and to the inferiority of German fighter strength in Italy, the A-20 gunners seldom had a battle in the air. Their main worry was flak, and that was plenty to worry about.

Like everyone else in the squadron, the men lived in pyramidal tents, four and five to a tent. Some of their tents were fixed up inside even nicer than the officers'. Others were bare.

The gunners had to stand in chow line the same as other soldiers, and eat out of mess kits. Now and then they even had to go on cleanup detail and help pick up trash throughout their area. They had to keep their own tents clean, and stand frequent inspection.

I found them a high-class and sincere bunch of boys. Those who really loved to fly in combat were the exceptions. Most of them took it in workaday fashion, but they kept a fanatical count on the number of missions flown, each one of which took them a little nearer to the final goal—the end of their tour of duty.

Ordinarily a gunner went on only one mission a day, but with the increased air activity they sometimes went both morning and afternoon, day after day. There were boys there who had arrived only in December and had already almost finished their missions, whereas it used to take six months and more to run up the allotted total.

Life in the combat air forces was fairly informal. On that field I seldom saw a salute. But that was all right, for the Air Forces didn't need the same type of discipline that less specialized branches required. The enlisted gunners and the commissioned pilots worked so closely together that they felt themselves in the same boat.

Gunners didn't like braggarts, among either commissioned officers or their own fellows. After I got to know them they told me of some of their own number who talked too big, and of some with the bad judgment to tell "whoppers" even to their gunners.

Gunner Sergeant Alban Petchal, who came from Steubenville, Ohio, said that if I would come over to their tent after supper they'd see if they couldn't drum up a snack before bedtime. He said they often cooked just to pass the time.

So I went over about eight o'clock and Sergeant Petchal said, "I haven't put the potatoes on yet. We were afraid you weren't coming."

The potatoes were already peeled. Petchal sliced some thin and dropped them into a skillet on top of the fiery gasoline stove. When he got them a crispy brown he said, "Have you ever eaten eggs scrambled right in with potatoes?"

Sergeant Petchal said that was the way his mother always fixed them, so he broke up a few eggs in the skillet, scrambled them with the potatoes, and served them in the mess kits. They were wonderful.

The eggs cost twenty cents apiece.

There were seven boys in that tent, all aerial gunners. We sat and talked for a long time about things in general. Finally I started to put down their names, and one by one I discovered that—with one exception—every boy in that tent had been through at least one violent experience.

Sergeant Robert Sweigert was from Williamsport, Pennsylvania. The others good-naturedly called him "Pretty Boy," because he was sort of suave-looking. He had on nothing but shorts, and while I was there he shaved and then took a sponge bath out of a washpan.

Sergeant Sweigert was wounded once by flak and spent two months in a hospital. Another time his plane made a crash landing after being badly shot up, and it broke in two and caught fire when it hit. Yet the crew escaped. The boys showed me snapshots of the demolished plane.

Then we turned to Sergeant Guadalupe Tanguma, of San Antonio, Texas. He had just got his orders home, and was feeling wonderful about it. Sergeant Tanguma was of Spanish blood, spoke fluent Spanish, and therefore got along fairly well in Italian. His experience was a gruesome one, although it turned out fine. His pilot was killed in the air and the plane went into a dive. Tanguma couldn't get to the pilot's compartment, so all he and the other gunner could do was try to get out. They finally made it.

Tanguma landed upside down in a tree. Italians came running and got him down. He gave the parachute to the crowd. Forty-five minutes after his jump he was in a farmhouse eating fried eggs. An Italian volunteered as guide and showed him the way back to base. The Italians wouldn't take money for their help. The other gunner landed safe too.

Next I put down Sergeant Charles Ramseur, of Gold Hill, North Carolina. Sergeant Ramseur used to fly with my dive-bombing friend Major Ed Bland, and Ed said he was tops. Ramseur was about to shave off a half-inch growth of whiskers. He was feeling a little abashed because the first sergeant had spoken sharply about it that afternoon. When Ramseur did shave, he left a mustache and a straggly little goatee. He was the quiet, courteous, unschooled but natively refined sort so often found in the hill country in the South. He hoped to go home shortly, although his orders had not been put through.

After getting into the Army, Ramseur had taught himself engraving. At least it was a form of engraving. With a penknife, he pricked out designs on all his medals. His canteen top was covered with names and flight insignia. He had a photo album with aluminum covers made from a German plane, and all over it were engraved names and places. On the fiber lining of his steel helmet he had chronicled his missions, a small bomb representing each one. They covered the entire front of the helmet, and he looked at them with relief. Sergeant Ramseur hoped maybe this talent might lead to an engraver's job after the war.

Sergeant Robert Fleming, of Cambridge, Massachusetts, and Sergeant Steve Ujhelji—pronounced You-haley—of Salem, Ohio, had flown together as gunners in a foray that won their pilot the Distinguished Flying Cross.

The pilot was Lieutenant George Gibson, also from Salem, Ohio. Lieutenant Gibson's nickname was "Hoot," and that had gradually been warped into "Hooch" for reasons beyond my power to fathom. Hooch had finished his missions and gone home. I knew him before he left, and he was a wonderful pilot. He was another of those great, good-natured people whom everybody liked. He would tell you seriously, and I know he meant it, that he was the world's worst combat pilot, that he had balled up half the missions he had gone on, that he was scared to death, and that he was just hanging on by the skin of his teeth, trying to finish.

But he did finish, and before doing so he crash-landed his badly shot-up plane one day so expertly that he saved not only the lives of his crew, but also that of a fighter pilot who was landing his damaged plane from the opposite direction and running directly into Hooch.

He got the DFC. If you should ever run into him back home, just ignore the DFC and ask him to tell you the story about the British motorcyclist.

Finally we got around to my host, Sergeant Alban Petchal of Steubenville, Ohio. When he stepped out the tent door to dispose of a washpan of water, the other boys told me he had the worst experiences of all.

The previous summer Petchal was flying as gunner in a flight of bombers coming over from America. They had reached Central Africa, and were flying north toward the combat zone. Somehow Petchal's plane got separated from the rest of the flight and wound up far out over the Sahara Desert and out of gas.

They rode the plane into the sand dunes, which were everywhere, and about two stories high. They bounced across the tops of four of them and slammed head on into the fifth. All three men were painfully hurt. They crawled out, made a shelter out of their life raft under the wings, and patched up their wounds as best they could.

They stayed there for three days and nights. On the third day Sergeant Petchal walked eight miles on a reconnaissance and then walked back. He thought he saw trees and camels, but it turned out to be the old storybook mirage.

Despite their pitiful condition, they all started walking on the fourth day. They sprinkled the wrecked plane with gasoline and set it afire. It was sad to see it burn. They carried a five-gallon can of water between them, slung from a stick. Their wounds pained them constantly. They almost froze at night. Petchal kept getting sick at his stomach. The two officers became semidelirious and quarreled violently. One day they saw three planes in the distance, too far away to attract.

Finally they found tracks, and the same day ran onto a camel caravan. The Arabs fed them and took them with them. The boys tried to ride the camels, but it was so rough and horrible that they finally had to walk.

On the night of the tenth day they came to the end of their rainbow. Soldiers from a French desert outpost rode up to the caravan and took charge of them. They had by then walked more than a hundred miles. They were in the hospital for several weeks. After such a harrowing start as that, Sergeant Petchal finally arrived at the front. And since that day he had flown more than sixty combat missions. He was nearly due to go home.

Petchal had been wounded by enemy flak, but we never got around to that.

The only man without an "experience" was Sergeant John McDonnell of Cedarhurst, Long Island—a good-looking, friendly, hospitable fellow. For Christmas, friends at home had sent him some brown liquid in a G. Washington coffee bottle. It looked like coffee, but it wasn't coffee. Sergeant McDonnell was saving it to celebrate his last mission. He offered to open it for me, but some hidden nobility in me reared its ugly head and I told him to save it.

Sergeant McDonnell had gone more than four-fifths of the way through his allotted missions, and had never laid eyes on an enemy plane. Furthermore, there had been only one tiny flak hit on his plane in all that time. "That suits me fine," the sergeant said. "I hope it stays that way."

And so did I.

A junior and miniature edition of W. C. Fields was Sergeant Gilford Muncy. Not much over five feet, Muncy was sort of pudgy, with very narrow shoulders, and a face that had a wise, devilish, old look like one of the Seven Dwarfs. He was twenty-nine, came from Hyden, Kentucky, up in the hills, and he didn't at all mind being called a hillbilly. In fact, he sort of traded on it. He talked just like the mountaineers in the cartoons. I think it sort of hurt his pride that he couldn't claim to have been a moonshiner.

Everybody laughed at Muncy and with him, and everybody thought he was great. He liked people, and was uncommonly generous and kind. It was a poor day when he didn't survive at least one escapade that was slightly out of this world.

The gunners' tent which Muncy dominated was a sight to behold, probably the most tired-out tent in all Italy. It was often the scene of rioting and devilry. The top was full of holes, caused by the frequent blowing up of the gasoline stove. One wall had big adhesive patches on it where a happy guest had tried to carve his initials in the canvas. The back wall bore the marks of a nervous visitor who went right through it one night during an air raid.

The two outstanding features of Muncy's tent were the late evening meals cooked there and the fabulous stove, which had been known to blow up seven times in one day. Once it exploded just as a guest entered, and he was blown clear out into the grapevines.

The other boys had told me all about Muncy's stove, so one morning just as he was starting on a mission (he was an aerial gunner) I introduced myself, and said I'd like to drop past that evening and see his stove blow up. Muncy said, "We'd sure like to have you, but the stove's liable to get contrary and not blow up tonight. Lots of times when we have company it don't blow up at all." I went over that night.

The tent had a dirt floor which was swept out whenever they figured inspection was about due. Muncy had once had a fastidious streak and decided to levy a fifty-cent fine on anybody who threw anything on the floor, such as cigarette butts, apple cores, walnut shells, etc. Before the first evening was over he had fined himself $11.50.

They had great feasts in the Muncy tent. Fried chicken was their special dish. They bought chickens from the village at $5 each. "I reckon there's been $300 worth of chickens cooked on that old stove there," Muncy said.

One night Sergeant Jack Bohn of Scranton, Pennsylvania, made chicken soup while Muncy did the rest. All the guests said they thought the soup was wonderful. But Jack couldn't quite get it down. Eventually he discovered the reason—he had put half a cake of GI soap in it, thinking it was butter.

Now and then they had steak. One night Muncy was in bed when one of his soldier friends came in from town, feeling fine. He had with him three or four big steaks.

"Where's your sledge hammer?" the friend asked.

"Over there in that pile of stuff, I reckon," Muncy said, and went back to sleep.

Pretty soon he was awakened and there was this guy with all the steaks lying on the dirt floor, and just beating hell out of them with an eight-pound sledge. Then he threw them into the skillet, and Muncy had to get up and share the feast.

"I've still got rocks and mud in my teeth," said Muncy.

To Muncy and his tentmates all Italians were "gooks." They couldn't remember how they started that. It wasn't a term of contempt at all, for Muncy loved the Italians and they loved him. "I don't care where I go to, people like me," Muncy said. "Why, when we moved from our last place all them gooks around there cried when I left."

He dressed up and played Santa for them at Christmas, and he was always giving them stuff.

We sat and talked and laughed until almost lights-out, and finally I said, "Well, if the stove isn't going to blow up, I guess I have to go."

So Muncy jumped up and said, "Wait a minute." He turned off the gasoline, let the fire in the tin-bellied stove die out and cool, then turned the gas on again. They let it sit that way a little while. Then all the boys crouched behind boxes and things, and Sergeant Bohn got off as far as he could and threw a lighted match at the stove door.

But as Muncy had feared, the stove was contrary and wouldn't blow up that night. They were all very humiliated.

Our bomber group had more dogs than any outfit I ever saw. It was hard for an infantryman to take care of a dog, but the Air Forces men were often based at the same field for weeks or months, and could live a more or less permanent life.

One of the soldiers told me about an order that had been issued some months before by the doctors, requiring that all dogs in camp be shot. For some reason it was never carried out.

Then the soldier said, "Boy, I'd like to see any doctor try to have our dogs killed now, with Colonel Clizbe around."

The colonel had a coal-black Labrador retriever named Tarfu. That's one of those mystic military names which you'll have to get somebody else to explain to you. Colonel Clizbe got Tarfu in England when he was so tiny that the colonel carried him inside his shirt. He had grown as big as a German shepherd. He was wonderfully smart, and good too, but so black that Colonel Clizbe couldn't get a good snapshot of him. He was raised on the treeless and wind-swept plains around two airdromes in Tunisia, and he still hadn't learned to use a tree.

There was a great communion between man and dog. Tarfu almost went frantic when it was time for the colonel to return from a mission.

Colonel Clizbe had a large doghouse for Tarfu, built out of frag-bomb boxes, and he kept it right in the tent with him. Any time he said "Bed," whether it was day or night, Tarfu went reluctantly into his doghouse and lay down. In the morning when Colonel Clizbe got up, Tarfu would wait about fifteen seconds, then slip out of his doghouse, get into Colonel Clizbe's sleeping bag, and burrow clear down out of sight. If he had been a little dog it wouldn't have seemed so funny, but he was so big he practically filled the bag.

Unlike most dogs, he loved to have his face washed. After Colonel Clizbe got through washing his own face, he washed Tarfu's.

I actually got jealous when I saw some of the soldiers over there with dogs deeply attached to them. It was the nearest thing to civilization in that weird foreign life of ours.

Major Burt Cochrane was executive officer of the squadron. He was not a flier, but he took most of the onerous duties off the shoulders of the squadron commander, who was always a flying man.

Major Cochrane was the perfect example of a man going all-out for his country. He didn't have to be over there at all. He was fifty-five, and a grandfather. But he fought through the last war, kept his commission in the reserve, and just couldn't picture himself not being in this one. He had been away from home three years. In civil life he was what you might call a gentleman cattle raiser. He owned about three hundred acres in the beautiful rolling country north of San Francisco, not far from Jack London's famous "Valley of the Moon." He turned out about seventy-five head of beef cattle a year, had a lovely home, beautiful riding horses, and lived an almost utopian life. He had left the city eight years before, and said he never knew what happiness was until he got out into the hills.

Major Cochrane was quiet and courteous. Enlisted men and officers both liked and respected him. He was so soldierly that he continually said "sir" even to me, although I was a civilian and much younger than he.

One of the newer and much-trusted pilots in my squadron was a good-natured, towheaded youngster named Lieutenant Leroy Kaegi (pronounced Keggy). He was from Ashland, Oregon.

Lieutenant Kaegi's life was not uneventful. One day he flew two missions, morning and afternoon. Returning from his morning mission, he couldn't get one of his wheels down. He had to fly around for an hour and finally stall the plane in order to shake the wheel loose.

Then just as he was ready to take off on his afternoon mission, some major came rushing up to the plane in a jeep, jumped out and yelled, "Hey, wait a minute. This girl wants to kiss you good-bye."

Lieutenant Kaegi had never seen the girl before, but she was American and she was beautiful. So out he popped and gave her a great big smackeroo, and then dashed into his plane again. When he got back, all he could talk about was the strange and wonderful thing that had happened to him. He said he was so excited he took off with his upper cowl flap open. The girl was Louise Allbritton of Hollywood, over with June Clyde, entertaining troops for the USO. They were both swell gals.

After Lieutenant Kaegi's adventure I hung around the planes at take-off time for a week, just hoping, but nothing came of it except that I got a large quantity of dirt blown in my face.

One day I was standing around an A-20 bomber when the crew chief came up and pulled a clipping out of his pocket. It was a piece about his plane written more than a year before by my friend Hal Boyle of the Associated Press.

Hal wrote that the plane was the most shot-up ship in the squadron, with more than a hundred holes in it. The crew chief, Sergeant Earl Wayne Sutter of 1129 Lombardy Avenue, Oklahoma City, had had that same ship since just before they left England nearly a year and a half before. He was very proud of its record. And it still held the record. By then it had more than three hundred holes in it. But Sutter and his gang just patched them up, and it kept on flying. With all that riddling only one crew member had ever been hurt, and he only slightly.

Crew members had begun to wear "flak vests." They looked something like life jackets and were made of steel strips covered with heavy canvas. They weighed about twenty-five pounds.

Already there were several instances in which those vests had saved men from being wounded by flak. The oddest instance was of one gunner who took his vest off because it felt too heavy, and threw it on the floor. By chance it happened to fall across his foot. A moment later a piece of flak came through the side and smashed into the flak vest. If it hadn't been lying where it was, he would have had a bad foot wound.

As I got to know the A-20 gunners better and better, they gradually began to tell me their inner feelings about a life of flying in combat.

Several had just about completed their missions, yet they said they were willing to stay if needed and fly extra ones. In any squadron were many men willing to fly beyond the stated missions if it was put up to them, although the average man was not eager to go on. In our squadron I found such a gunner in Sergeant John D. Baker, of 839 Park Avenue, Indianapolis. He was twenty-one. He had flown more missions than anybody else in the squadron, men or officers. He said it was his ambition to fly a hundred.

Many men in our squadron had gone beyond the required goal. Some were still flying, and others had gone on to the breaking point and been grounded. The flight surgeons tried to sense when the strain was beginning to get a man.

Some of them seemed to have nerves that were untouchable. One of my pilot friends told me that on one mission, when the flak was breaking all around, he didn't think much of the danger but kept thinking that if a fragment should break the Plexiglas nose and let the below-zero air rush through the plane, he would be one mad pilot.

Another told of the funny reflexes he had. For example, he knew he needn't worry about the flak he saw, for if he saw it the danger was over and he hadn't been hit. Yet this pilot, after a harmless puff of smoke ahead of him, always went around it.

One of the gunners—a man with a fine record—told me he had not only become terrified of combat but had actually become afraid to fly at all. He said that when the generators came on in the morning, and the radio in their tent started crackling, it made him dream they were being attacked in the air. He dreamed that a bullet came up through the fuselage and hit him in the throat.

Another one told me he felt he just couldn't go on. He had completed his allotted missions, and nobody could doubt his courage. He wanted to go and ask to be grounded, but just couldn't bring himself to do it.

So I urged him to go ahead. Afterward I got both sides of the story. The officers told me that they were kicking themselves for not noticing the gunner's nervousness in time and for letting it go until he had to hurt his pride by asking to be grounded.

But those were men's innermost feelings. They didn't express them very often. They didn't spend much time sitting around glooming to each other about their chances.

Their outlook and conversation were just as normal as that of men in no danger at all. They played jokes on each other, and wrote letters, and listened to the radio, and sent gifts home, and drank a little vino, and carried on just like anybody else.

It was only when a man "had had it"—the combat expression for anyone who had had more than he could take—that he sat alone and didn't say much and began to stare.

Sergeant Petchal never heard of Buck Eversole, and yet the morning I left Petchal spoke about his place in the war with the same sort of sadly restrained philosophy and even in almost the same words that Buck had used at the front. He said, "The job has to be done, and somebody has to do it, and we happen to be the ones that were picked to do it, so we'll go on doing it the best we can."

And Sergeant Ramseur said, "I don't ever want to fly again, but if they tell me to keep on flying then I'll just keep on flying, that's all. You can't do anything else."

FIFTEEN

LST CRUISE

A correspondent who wanted to go to Anzio simply drove to the dock where the ships were loading, told the Army captain in charge, and the captain said, "Okay, get on this boat here." Since it was a very front-line kind of war at the beachhead, isolated and horny-handed like the early old days in Tunisia, there was little red tape about it. Our troops were supplied and replaced by daily ship convoys.

I went on an LST (landing ship tank)—a type of vessel being considerably publicized at home then and probably the outstanding ship of our amphibious forces.

It was the second time I had been on one. The first time was the previous June at Bizerte, a few days before we took off on the invasion of Sicily. At that time I was living on a warship, but took a run around the harbor one day going aboard various types of landing craft, just to see what they were like. I spent about half an hour on an LST that day, and had never been on one since.

So imagine my surprise when I climbed aboard for the Anzio trip, checked in with the captain, and suddenly realized that it was the very same LST, still commanded by the same man. He was Lieutenant Joseph Kahrs, of Newark, New Jersey—a 37-year-old bachelor and the product of two universities. Before the war he was a lawyer in practice with his father in Newark. After Pearl Harbor he went into the Navy. His sum total of seafaring had been several trips in peacetime.

Exactly one year to the very day after he enlisted, Lieutenant Kahrs and a crew just as landlubberish as himself took over a brand-new LST and pointed her bow toward Africa. Only two men of the crew of more than sixty had ever been to sea before.

Just before my Anzio trip, they celebrated their ship's first birthday and everybody aboard had a turkey dinner. In that one year of existence their LST had crossed the Atlantic once, taken D-day roles in three invasions, and made a total of twenty-three perilous trips between Africa, Sicily, and the Anzio beachhead.

They were almost blown out of the water once, and had had countless miraculous escapes, but they were never seriously damaged. Most of the original crew were still with it, but instead of being green landlubbers they were tried and true salts.

Long lines of soldiers, loaded down with gear, marched along the dock to enter adjoining ships. They were replacements to bolster the fighters at Anzio. A person could tell by their faces that they were fresh from America. They carried a new type of barracks bag, which few of us over there had seen before. The bags were terrifically heavy, and it was all the boys could do to handle them.

One of the passing replacements remarked, "Hell, I've got more clothes than I had when we left America. I don't know how we accumulate so much."

Italian children scampered along with the marching soldiers, insisting on helping with the heavy bags. Some soldiers shooed the children away, but others accepted their help.

We were due to sail a few hours after I got aboard, but at the last minute there came a warning of a storm of gale force brewing in the Mediterranean. We laid over for twenty-four hours.

Some of the sailors took the opportunity next day to go ashore, and asked if I didn't want to go along. But I said, "What for? I've been ashore for three months already." So I stayed aboard, and just killed a full day doing nothing.

We were tied up along the waterfront street of a small port city near Naples. All day long the dock was a riot of Italians grouped below to catch cookies and chocolates and knickknacks the sailors and soldiers threw down to them. There must have been two hundred people on the dock, either participating in the long-shot chance of actually catching something or just looking on. Many of them were children, boys and girls both. Mostly they were ragged and dirty, but they were good-natured.

Every time a package of crackers went down from above, they

scrambled and fought over it like a bunch of football players. Now and then some youngster would get hurt, and make a terrible face and cry. But mostly they'd laugh and look a little sheepish, and dash back in again after the next one.

All Italian children called all American soldiers "Hey, Joe," and all along the dock was a chicken-yard bedlam of "Hey, Joe, bisueet," each boy crying at the top of his lungs to call attention to himself, and holding up his hands.

The soldiers' favorite was a stocky little fellow of about eight, with coal-black hair and a constant good humor. He was about the only one of them who wasn't ragged, the reason being that he was entirely clad in military garb. He had on a blue Navy sweater and the biggest pair of British tropical shorts I ever saw. They came clear below his knees. His legs were bare, with gray Army socks rolled down to his shoetops, and on his feet were a pair of brand-new American GI shoes which must have been at least size eight. To top it all off, he had a beguiling grin with a tooth out in the middle of it.

This youngster was adept at walking on his hands. He spent hours walking around the muddy stone street on his hands, with his feet sticking straight up in the air. The soldiers and sailors were crazy about him, and every time he finished his little performance he'd get a flood of crackers. I finally figured out that he walked on his hands so much because it was easier than walking in those gigantic shoes.

Pretty teenage Italian girls in red sweaters came and stood at the edge of the throng watching the fun. The sailors and soldiers at the rail were quick to spot them, and the play for them was on. Reluctant and timid at first, the girls finally obeyed the sailors demand that they try to catch something too, and in they went battling for broken crackers.

Most Americans were touched by the raggedness and apparent hunger of the children. But it was hard to feel sorry for those kids, for although maybe some of them really were hungry, the rest of them were just having a wonderful mob-scene sort of good time.

It was the old women in the crowd that I could hardly bear to look at. Throughout the day there must have been a couple of dozen who came, tried for half an hour to catch something, and finally went dejectedly away. They were horrible specimens of poverty and uncleanliness. They were old and pitiful and repulsive. But their hunger most surely was genuine.

One elderly woman, dressed in tattered black and carrying a thin old shopping bag on her arm, stood at the far edge of the crowd, vainly beseeching a toss in her direction. Finally one sailor, who had just started on a large box of Nabiscos, piece by piece, changed his mind and threw the entire box toward the old woman.

It was a good throw and a good catch. She got it like an outfielder. But no sooner did she have it in her arms than the crowd was upon her. Kids and adults both tore at the box, scratched and yelled and grabbed, and in five seconds the box was empty and torn.

The poor old woman never let go. She clung to it as though it were something alive and precious. And when the last cracker was gone she walked sort of blindly away, her head back and her eyes toward the sky, weeping, her face stricken just like that of a heartbroken child, and still gripping the empty box.

It was a spectacle, watching that foreign riot of childish emotions and adult greed that day. But some of it was too real—greed born of too great a necessity—and I was glad when word came that we would sail that night.

The sailors aboard the LST had the same outlook on life as the average soldier overseas—they devoted a good part of their conversation to home and to when they might get there.

They were pretty veteran by then, and had been under fire a lot. They had served the hot beaches of Sicily, Salerno, and Anzio. They knew a gun fired in anger when they heard one. On the whole, although the boys who manned those beachhead supply ships were frequently in great danger, they did live fairly comfortably. Their food was good, their quarters were fair, and they had such facilities as hot baths, new magazines, candy, hot meals, and warmth.

An LST isn't such a glorious ship to look at. It is neither sleek nor fast nor impressively big—no bigger than an ocean freighter—and yet it is a good ship and the crews aboard LSTs are proud of them.

The sailors slept in folding bunks with springs and mattresses. The officers slept in cabins, two or so to a cabin, the same as on bigger ships. The engines and crew's quarters and bridges are all aft. The rest of the ship is just a big empty warehouse sort of thing, much like a long, rectangular garage without any pillars in it.

Two huge swinging doors open in the bow, and then a heavy steel ramp comes down so that trucks and tanks and jeeps can drive in. The ships can land at a beach for loading and unloading, or run nose-first to a dock.

They have flat bottoms and consequently they roll when there is no sea at all. The sailors said, "They'll even roll in drydock." They roll fast, too. Their usual tempo is a round-trip roll every six seconds. The boys said that in a really heavy sea they could stand on the bridge and actually see the bow twist, like a monster turning its head. It wasn't an optical illusion either, but a result of the "give" in these ships. The sailors also said that when they ran across a sand bar the ship seemed to work its way across like an inchworm, proceeding forward section by section.

My LST had handled every conceivable type of wartime cargo. It had carried a whole shipload of fused shells, the most dangerous kind. Among the soldiers of many nationalities that had been on the ship, the crew found the Indian troops of Johore the most interesting. The Indians were friendly, and as curious as children. The Americans liked them; in fact, I've found that Americans like practically anybody who is even halfway friendly.

The Indian soldiers base practically every action on their religion. They brought their own food, and it had to be cooked by certain of their own people. They made a sort of pancake out of flour that was full of weevils and worms. But it was sacred, and if an American cook tried to help out and touched the pan, the whole batch had to be thrown away. Even going to the toilet was a religious ritual with them. They carried special toilet-seat covers previously blessed by some proper person, and would no more think of using an unblessed toilet than you would think of committing murder.

Lieutenant Joseph Kahrs told me of one touching incident that happened when the Indian troops were put ashore. One of them had fallen ill and had to be taken back to Africa. He was the only Indian left on the ship. The tragedy of his pitiful case was that the poor unfortunate was caught without a sacred toilet seat, and he had dysentery.

"What did he do?" I inquired.

"I never did ask," Lieutenant Kahrs said. "I couldn't bear to know. To me it is the most frightful incident of the war."

It was after dark when we backed away from the dock. We nosed out to sea for a mile or so, then dropped anchor for a couple of hours—waiting for other ships to finish loading and join us.

There was always the danger of submarines, and once off the beachhead the ships were frequent targets for aerial bombing and shelling from the land. Quite a few had been hit by all three methods, yet the supplies kept going through, and were often piled on the beachhead a day ahead of schedule.

One night the Germans hit a gasoline dump and burned up some five thousand gallons. An officer said, "At home, where gas is rationed, that would seem like an awful lot, but up here it's just a drop in the bucket and makes no difference at all."

Our fleet of supply ships was manned by Americans, British and Greeks. As we lay at the dock before sailing, a British LST was on one side of us and a Greek on the other.

When we finally got under way for good, I went to the open-air deck just above the bridge to see how a convoy formed up at night. On LSTs the bridge is completely enclosed with heavy armor plating which has little slits of thick, bullet-proof glass to look through. Since visibility is thus limited, the officer in charge stays on the open-air deck above and calls his instructions down through a tube to the bridge.

The moon was swathed in clouds, but it gave a faint light. I could see landmarks silhouetted against the horizon, but not much more.

"Have you ever looked through night binoculars?" the captain asked. "Try these."

The view was astonishing. Those binoculars seemed to take twenty-five per cent of the darkness out of the night. With them I could see several ships in line, where I could see none before.

Far ahead of us, directly out to sea, we saw occasional flashes of gunfire. I asked what that could be, but no one knew. It seemed unlikely that a naval battle could be going on out there, and yet there were the flashes.

"That's one of the things I've found out about the sea," Lieutenant Kahrs said. "You're always seeing and hearing things which are completely mysterious and unexplainable. You go on your way and never do find out the answer."

The wind began to come up and the air grew chilly. It was straight sailing for the rest of the trip, so I went to bed. The night passed with nothing more exciting than the ship doing some violent rolling. I could hear considerable sliding and breaking in the galley, and out on deck several half-tracks broke their moorings and charged back and forth with a frightening sound of steel scraping on steel. We landlubbers aboard slept rather fitfully.

The officer of the deck sent a sailor to awaken me just at dawn. I got up sleepily and went back to the deck above the bridge. Anzio and Nettuno were in sight off to our right. We could see an occasional golden flash of artillery fire on shore.

The day was gray. Heavy clouds covered the sky, and rain occasionally drenched the landscape. That meant another day for our troops on the beachhead to go without air support, but it also meant the Germans would be grounded too and our ships could land without being bombed. And for that we were selfishly glad.

Our convoy eased along until we were just off Anzio harbor. Everything was as peaceful as could be. I was walking along the deck just looking at the shore, when suddenly a shell smacked the water about a hundred yards away. It was so close we heard the whine after the blast. At that the captain moved us farther out. The shells continued to come at about ten-minute intervals, none quite so close as the first. We all wore our steel helmets then.

Finally the signal came to enter the harbor. Lieutenant Kahrs stood on a little platform on the open deck, steering the ship to its moorings. I stood just behind him to watch. The morning was raw, yet he wore only summer khaki trousers, a light Army field jacket and, of all things, tennis shoes. He was shivering.

Shells continued to sing through the air, some landing ahead of us, some behind. One hit the end of the stone mole just before we got to it. Another one screamed right over our heads and hit behind the mole. At each sound we'd all duck instinctively. And the captain laughed and said, "We sure get a lot of knee-bending exercise on these trips."

We were all pretty silent and tense during those last few minutes of entering the harbor. The captain had to maneuver into a tiny space just barely the width of the ship. Yet he put it in there as though he were using a pointer, and he put it in fast too, no monkeying around. I couldn't help admiring this new skill of a man whose profession was so alien to the sea.

There he stood, far from home, worming his ship into a half-wrecked harbor with shells passing a few feet over his head. And he did it with complete absorption and confidence. Men can do strange and great things when they have to do them.

SIXTEEN

ANZIO-NETTUNO

I didn't waste any time getting off the boat, for I had been feeling pretty much like a clay pigeon in a shooting gallery. But after a few hours I wished I was back aboard. No one could have described Anzio as any haven of peacefulness.

In our first day ashore, a bomb exploded so close to the place where I was sitting that a fragment came through the window of the room next to mine. On our second evening a screamer slammed into the hill so suddenly that it almost knocked us down with fright. It smacked into the trees a short distance away. And on the third day ashore, an 88 went off within twenty yards of us.

I wished I was in New York.

When I write about my own occasional association with shells and bombs, one thing must be remembered: Other correspondents were in the same boat—many of them much more so. There were correspondents there on the beachhead, and on the Cassino front also, who had dozens of close shaves. I know of one who was knocked down four times by near-misses on his first day there. Two correspondents, Reynolds Packard of the United Press and Homer Bigart of the *New York Herald Tribune*, had been on the beachhead since D-day, without a moment's respite. They were by that time such veterans that they didn't even mention a shell striking twenty yards away.

On the beachhead every inch of our territory was under German artillery fire. There was no rear area that was immune, as in most battle zones. They could reach us with their 88s, and they used everything from that on up.

I don't mean to suggest that they kept every foot of our territory drenched with shells all the time, for they certainly didn't. They were short of ammunition, for one thing. But they could reach us, and we never knew where they would shoot next. A man was just as liable to get hit standing in the doorway of the villa where he slept at night as he was in a command post five miles out in the field.

Some days they shelled us hard, and some days hours would go by without a single shell coming over. Yet nobody was wholly safe, and anybody who said he had been around Anzio two days without having a shell hit within a hundred yards of him was just bragging.

People who knew the sounds of warfare intimately were puzzled and irritated by them. For some reason, we couldn't tell anything about anything. The Germans shot shells of half a dozen sizes, each of which made a different sound on exploding. We couldn't gauge distance at all. One shell might land within our block and sound not much louder than a shotgun. Another landing a quarter-mile away made the earth tremble as in an earthquake, and started our hearts pounding.

We couldn't gauge direction, either. The 88 that hit within twenty yards of us didn't make much noise. I would have sworn it was two hundred yards away and in the opposite direction.

Sometimes we heard them coming, and sometimes we didn't. Sometimes we heard the shell whine after we heard it explode. Sometimes we heard it whine and it never exploded. Sometimes the house trembled and shook and we heard no explosion at all.

But one thing I found there was just the same as anywhere else—that same old weakness in the joints when they got to landing close. I had been weak all over Tunisia and Sicily, and in parts of Italy, and I got weaker than ever in Anzio.

When the German raiders came over at night, and the sky lighted up with flares bright as day, and ack-ack guns set up a turmoil and pretty soon a man heard and felt the terrible power of exploding bombs—well, his elbows got flabby and he breathed in little short jerks, and his chest felt empty, and he was too excited to do anything but hope.

Anzio and Nettuno run together along the coast, forming practically one city. There is really only one main street, which runs along the low blocks just back of the first row of waterfront buildings. The two cities stretch for about three miles, but extend only a few blocks back from the waterfront. A low hill covered thick with tall cedar trees rises just back of them, and along some of the streets there are palm trees.

I had supposed these two places were just ancient little fishing villages. Well, they are old, but not in their present form. Anzio is where Nero is supposed to have fiddled while Rome burned, but in more recent years he would doubtless have been sprawling in a deck chair in the patio of his seaside villa drinking cognac.

These two towns are now (or, rather, were until the war) high-class seaside resorts. They've been modernized within the last twenty years, and they are much bigger and much more up-to-date than I had supposed. At one point, the towns extend two hundred yards from the water's edge, forming a solid flank of fine stone buildings four and five stories high. Most of these are apartment houses, business offices, and rich people's villas.

When we landed there was no civilian life in Anzio-Nettuno. The Germans had evacuated everybody before we arrived, and we found the place deserted. A few Italians straggled back in, but they were few indeed.

In the path of warfare, "business as usual" seems to have been the motto of the natives. Adult civilians stayed in some places despite the fall of heaven and earth upon them. They stayed and dealt with the Germans while we were blasting their towns to bits, and those who survived stayed and dealt with us when the town changed hands and the Germans began showering the same death and destruction back upon us. The ties of a man's home are sinewy and strong, and something that even war can hardly break.

But in Anzio and Nettuno the expensive villas were deserted—the swanky furniture wrapped in burlap and stored all in one room or two. The little hovels were empty also, and so were the stores. Scarcely a door or a window with whole shutters remained. There was no such thing as a store or shop doing business in those two towns.

When our troops first landed they found things intact and un-damaged, but the Germans changed that. Little by little, day by day, those cities were reduced to destruction by the shells and bombs of the enemy. It happened slowly. The Germans shelled spasmodically. Hours would go by without a single shell coming in, and then all of a sudden a couple of shells would smack the water just offshore.

A few buildings would go down, or the corners would fly off some of them. One day's damage was almost negligible. But the cumulative effect after a couple of weeks was heartbreaking. You couldn't walk half a block without finding a building half crumpled to the ground. The sidewalks had shell holes in them. Engineers repaired new holes in the streets. Military police who directed auto traffic were occasionally killed at their posts.

Broken steel girders lay across the sidewalks. Marble statues fell in littered patios. Trees were uprooted, and the splattered mud upon them dried and turned gray. Wreckage was washed up on shore. Everywhere there was rubble and mud and broken wire.

Yet that German shelling and bombing had only the tiniest percentage of effect on our movement of supplies and troops into the beachhead. One day of bad weather actually harmed us more than a month of German shelling. It was a thrilling thing to see an LST pull anchor when its turn came, to watch it drive right into the harbor despite shells all around. And it was thrilling, too, to see the incessant hurry-hurry-hurry of the supply trucks through the streets all day and night, despite anything and everything.

From all indications we were supplying our troops even better by sea than the Germans were supplying theirs by land.

The land of the Anzio beachhead is flat, and our soldiers felt strange and naked with no rocks to take cover behind, no mountains to provide slopes for protection. It was a new kind of warfare for us. Distances were short, and space was confined. The whole beachhead was the front line, so small that we could stand on high ground in the middle of it and see clear around the thing. That's the truth, and it was no picnic feeling either.

Back in the days of desert fighting around Tebessa, the forward echelons of the corps staff and most of the hospitals were usually more than eighty miles back of the fighting. At Anzio everybody was right in it together. From the rear to the front was less than half an hour's drive, and often the front was quieter than the rear.

Hospitals were not immune from shellfire and bombing. The unromantic finance officer counting out his money in a requisitioned building was hardly more safe than the company commander ten miles ahead of him. And the table waiter in the rear echelon mess got blown off his feet in a manner quite contrary to the Hoyle rules of warfare.

Though the beachhead land was flat, it did have some rise and fall to it; it was flat in a western Indiana way—not the billiard-table flatness of the country around Amarillo, Texas, for example. A person would have to go halfway across the beachhead area from the sea before the other half of it came into view. Rises of a few score feet, and little mounds and gullies, and groves of trees cut up the land. There were a lot of little places where a few individuals could take cover from fire. The point is that the general flatness forbade whole armies taking cover.

Several main roads—quite good macadam roads—ran in wagon-spoke fashion out through the beachhead area. A few smaller gravel roads branched off from them. In addition, our engineers bulldozed miles of road across the fields. The longest of these "quickie" roads was named after the commanding general. It was such a superboulevard that we had to travel over it in super-low gear with mud above our hubcaps, but still we did travel.

Space was at a premium. Never had I seen a war zone so crowded. Of course, men weren't standing shoulder to shoulder, but I suppose the most indiscriminate shell dropped at any point on the beachhead would have landed not more than two hundred yards from somebody. And the average shell found thousands within hearing distance of its explosion. If a plane went down in No Man's Land, more than half the troops on the beachhead could see it fall.

New units in the fighting, or old units wishing to change positions, had great difficulty finding a place. The "already spoken for" sign covered practically all the land. The space problem was almost as bad as in Washington.

Because of the constant extreme danger of shelling, our Army had moved underground. At Youks and Thelepte and Biskra, in Africa the year before, our Air Forces lived underground. But there in Italy was the first time our entire ground force had had to burrow beneath the surface. Around the outside perimeter line, where the infantry faced the Germans a few hundred yards away, the soldiers lay in open foxholes devoid of all comfort. But everywhere back of that the men had dug underground and built themselves homes. On that beachhead there must have been tens of thousands of dugouts, housing from two to half a dozen men each.

As a result of the digging-in, our losses from shelling and bombing were small. It was only the first shell after a lull that got many casualties. After the first one, all the men were in their dugouts, and you should have seen how fast they got there when a shell whined.

In addition to safety, those dugouts provided two other comforts our troops had not always had—warmth and dryness. A dugout is a wonderful place to sleep. In our Anzio-Nettuno sector a whole night's sleep was as rare as January sun in sunny Italy. But shortly after my arrival I spent three consecutive nights in various dugouts at the front, and slept soundly. The last two nights I slept in a grove that was both bombed and shelled; men were killed each night, and yet I never even woke up. That's what the combination of warmth, insulation against sound, and the sense of underground security can do for a man.

The Anzio beachhead area is practically all farms. Much of it lies in the famous old Pontine marshes. I consulted a Baedeker, and found that the Romans had been trying to drain them since three hundred years before Christ. Caesar took a shot at it, and so did many Popes. Mussolini was the last one to give the marshes a whirl, and as far as I could see he did a pretty good job of it.

On these little farms of the Pontine marshes Mussolini built hundreds of modern (in the Italian manner) stone farmhouses. They're all exactly alike, except for color, and they stipple the countryside like dots on a polka-dot dress. Despite its flatness, the area is rather pretty. It doesn't look like marshland. It was green when I was there, and wheat was coming through the ground. There were rows of cedars throughout the area. Spots of uncultivated ground were covered with waist-high scrub oak, resembling our hazelnut bushes in the fall, crisp and brown-leafed.

Now and then I saw a farmer plowing while German shells landed right in his field. We tried to evacuate the people, and did

evacuate thousands by boat. Daily I saw our trucks moving down
to the dock with loads of Italian civilians from the farms. But some
of them simply refused to leave their homes. Sometimes the Germans would pick out one of the farmhouses, figuring we had a
command post in it, I suppose, and blow it to smithereens. Then,
and then only, did some Italian families move out.

One unit told me about a family they had tried in vain to move.
Finally a shell killed their tiny baby, just a few days old.

There in the battle zone, as in other parts of Italy, our Army
doctors were constantly turning midwife to deliver bambinos.

Farmers frequently did dry cleaning for our officers, and I understand that the job they did would pass inspection in any New
York tailoring shop. Soldiers throughout the area also got the
Italians to do their washing. Practically every inhabited farmhouse had a gigantic brown washing hanging in the back yard.

One outfit of tankers that I knew sent all its spare clothes to
one farmhouse to be washed. Shortly afterward the Germans
picked out that house for the center of a barrage. The Italians
abandoned the place and were unhurt. But next morning, when
the soldiers went to see about their clothes, they found dozens of
American shirts and pants and socks torn into shreds by shell
fragments.

In the fields were small herds of cattle, sheep, horses and mules.
Many of the cattle were slate-gray, just like Brahman cattle. And
they had wide, sweeping horns very much like the majestic head-
gear of the famous longhorn steers of Texas. Now and then I saw
an Army truck radiator decorated with a pair of those horns.

Most of the livestock could graze without human attention,
but being an old farmer I worried about the cows that had nobody
to milk them when the farmers left. As you may or may not know,
a milch cow that isn't milked eventually dies a painful death. An
officer friend of mine, who had been at the front almost since D-
day, said he had seen only one cow in trouble from not being
milked, so I suppose somebody was milking them.

One unit I heard of took the milking proposition into its own
hands, and had fresh milk every day. Of course that was against
Army regulations (since the cattle might have been tubercular),
but Army regulations have been known to be ignored in certain

dire circumstances. Much of the livestock was killed by German shellfire. On any side road we couldn't drive five minutes without seeing the skeleton of a cow or a horse.

And of course some cows committed suicide, as the saying used to go in Tunisia. It was the damnedest thing, but one cow stepped on a mine, a very odd mine indeed, for when it exploded it hit her right between the eyes. And there on the beachhead we saw an occasional cow deliberately walk up and stick her head in front of a rifle just as it went off.

There wasn't as much of that, to my mind, as there might have been. We were fighting a horrible war that we didn't ask for, on the land of the people who started it. Our supply problems were difficult. K rations got pretty boring, and fresh meat was something out of Utopia.

One day Wick Fowler, war correspondent of the Dallas *News*, and I were walking along the road in Nettuno. I saw a jeep coming with a one-star plate on the front bumper, indicating that the occupant was a brigadier general. I peered intently, trying to make out who the general was.

While I was absorbed in this endeavor, the jeep drew abreast and the general suddenly saluted us. I don't know why he saluted— maybe he thought I was the Secretary of War. At any rate I was so startled, and so unaccustomed to being saluted by generals, that I fumbled a second and then returned the salute with my left hand.

Wick said he would be glad to appear at my court-martial and put in a plea of insanity for me. On the other hand, I did try, while Wick never raised an arm. So I don't think even a plea of insanity would have saved him. Wick was a nice fellow, too.

Incidentally, we never did find out who the general was.

You read about the little Cub planes that flew slowly around over the Anzio front lines doing artillery spotting for us. They were a wonderful little branch of the service, and the risks they took were tremendous.

The Germans tried to shoot them down with ack-ack, and occasionally a German fighter sneaked in and made a pass at them. But the Cub was so slow that the fighters usually overshot, and the Cub could drop down and land immediately.

One of the worst strokes of fate I ever heard about happened to a Cub there on the Fifth Army beachhead. A "Long Tom"—or 155 rifle—was the unwitting instrument. This certain gun fired only one shell that entire day—but that one shell, with all the sky to travel in, made a direct hit on one of our Cubs in the air and blew it to bits. It was one of those incredible one-in-ten-billion possibilities, but it happened.

The headquarters of a regiment I knew well had a beautiful police dog named "Sergeant." He belonged to everybody, was a lovable dog, liked to go through a whole repertoire of tricks, and was almost human in his sensitiveness. He had even become plane-raid conscious, and when he heard planes in the sky he would run into his own private foxhole—or any foxhole, if he was away from home.

Sergeant was dutifully in his foxhole when he died. Shrapnel from an air burst got him. He wasn't killed instantly, and they had to end his suffering.

The outfit lost two officers, four men and a dog in that raid. It is not belittling the men who died to say that Sergeant's death shared a big place in the grief of those who were left.

There on the Anzio beachhead nobody was immune. It was not only a standing joke but a standing fact that a lot of front-line people would not voluntarily return to the hot Anzio-Nettuno area for a small fortune. People whose jobs through all the wars of history have been safe ones were as vulnerable as the fighting man. Bakers and typewriter repairmen and clerks were not immune from shells and bombs. Table waiters were in the same boat.

When I was back in the harbor area writing, I ate at a mess for staff officers. Twice within ten days big shells demolished buildings on either side of that mess.

The four boys who served us asked if I would write about them. I said I certainly would, not only because they were doing a dangerous job but also because they were four of the most courteous and best-dispositioned men I ever met. They were: Corporal Harold Gibson, of Boothbay Harbor, Maine; Private Lloyd Farlee, of Pierce, Nebraska; Private Herb Wullschleger, of 815 South

Sycamore Street, Wichita, Kansas, and Private Charles Roderick, of 13 Hibert Street, Salem, Massachusetts.

More than a year ago I wrote an item about the numerous uses we'd found for the brushless shaving cream issued to front-line troops. Its virtues were legion. It was perfect for sun- and windburn, nurses shampooed their hair in it, it soothed fleabites and softened chapped hands and cracked fingers. And there at Anzio the soldiers discovered that if they massaged their feet with it once a day, it went a long way toward preventing the dreaded trench foot.

It's a shame somebody didn't shave with it once in a while.

Some soldiers told about running onto another soldier stretched out in the back seat of a jeep, way up front, almost in No Man's Land. His helmet was down over his eyes, and he had a half-smoked cigar in his mouth. They were in dangerous territory, and they went to take a closer look at a soldier so nonchalant.

He was dead. A sniper had shot him through the back of the helmet. He was just lying there, looking perfectly relaxed, the cigar still in his mouth. He had been dead two days.

I was riding through the wreckage of Anzio and saw a big bulldozer in a vacant lot. On it was the name "Ernie," spelled out in big blue metal letters wired to the radiator. So I stopped to look into this phenomenon. The displayer of this proud name was Private Ernie Dygert of Red Lodge, Montana. His father owned a big ranch there. Young Dygert had driven trucks, ducks and bulldozers in the Army. His main job there was filling up shell craters. He didn't seem to mind living in Anzio. The same couldn't be said for his namesake.

Again I ran onto Major Henry Frankel, of 357 Highland Boulevard, Brooklyn. I had been crossing his trail ever since July of 1942 in Ireland, and every time I saw him he had gone up a notch in rank. When I first knew him he was a lieutenant.

Major Frankel spoke about eight languages but, as far as I could see, a man with his luck didn't need to speak anything. Listen to this: He was digging a dugout in the back yard of a place he had picked out for billeting, and he dug up a case and a half of fine cognac, numerous bottles of Benedictine, anisette and old wines, a box of silverware, and a gallon of olive oil.

Being an honest man, Major Frankel hunted up the Italian owner who had buried it, and gave him back everything except the eighteen bottles of cognac. These he kept as a reminder of his own meticulous honesty, and shared them with other parched and deserving Americans.

It's funny how nicknames change from one war to the next, and even during wars. Last war, if I remember correctly, the Germans were almost always referred to as "Huns," but the word doesn't seem to be used in this war. For the first year or so it was always "Jerry." Then the term "Kraut" showed up, and it was used at the front more than any other, I guess.

Another name was "Tedeschi," the Italian word for Germans. The "ch" is hard, like the "k" in Kansas. About a third of the time our soldiers spoke of the Germans as "the Tedeschi."

One of the most practical pieces of equipment our Army got around to was the little Coleman stove for cooking. It's about eight inches high and burns gasoline. It comes in a round metal can which can be used to heat water in after the stove is taken out of it. The stove has folding legs and folding griddles which open up to hold a can or a canteen cup. It's easy to carry and burns without a lot of tinkering.

There at Anzio, almost every group of front-line soldiers had one. They heated their C rations on it, made coffee several times a day, heated water for shaving, and if they were in an enclosed place such as a dugout they even used it for warmth.

You have no idea what a big thing some practical little device like a successful stove is in the life of a man at the front.

Our Army canteen cup was pretty good, but it had one big drawback. The rolled-over rim collected so much heat we couldn't put it to our lips without burning them, hence we had to wait till our coffee was lukewarm before we could drink it. A few soldiers, I noticed, had partly solved the problem by cutting the rim off and filing the top smooth.

Another much-needed item that had at last shown up in good quantity was candles. It seems to take any nation a year or two to find out through experience all the little things needed at the front, and to produce them and get them there. The winter before, we had needed candles and they were as scarce as though made of gold. But at last they became plentiful. They were white and about nine inches long. We either dripped some tallow on a table and anchored them in it, or set them in empty cognac bottles. Of course if we had a full cognac bottle we didn't need a candle.

I've told you about the dogs our soldiers took as pets and mascots. Running second to dogs, I believe, were Italian kids. There's no way of estimating how many Italian boys were adopted by our troops, but there must have been hundreds.

An outfit would pick up some kid, usually one who had been orphaned by bombing and had no home and no place to go. The children went along of their free will, of course. And they began having the time of their lives.

The soldiers cut down extra uniforms and clothed them in straight GI. The youngsters picked up English at a terrific pace, and they ate better than they had eaten in years. The whole thing was exciting and adventuresome to them. When units went into action, they kept the children in areas as safe as could be found.

What will become of those kids when the war ends, I don't know. Probably many will be carried clear back to America and their collective godfathers will try to sneak them in.

I do know of Sicilian adoptees who were taken along on the invasion of Italy, just like the animal pets. And there were two adoptees who stowed away and joined in the Anzio beachhead landings on D-day.

As usual, whenever we had a radio, one of our diversions was listening to "Axis Sally." She was still going strong. Hers was one of several German propaganda broadcasts in English directed at our troops.

The thing was wonderful but, as far as I could see, a complete failure, because: In the first place, only a tiny few of our troops ever heard the radio. And secondly, for those who did, Sally's music was so good and her jokes so pathetically corny that we listened just to be entertained. We felt like cads for enjoying Sally's music while being unconvinced by her words.

Sally went on the air five or six times a day, starting around 6 a.m. and lasting through till 2 a.m. A guy named George served as Sally's end man. Some of the programs were directed at the British troops, some at ours. Actually, it wasn't the same girl on all the programs, although they all called themselves Sally. The program was entitled "Jerry's Front."

Early in each program they sang the great German war song, "Lili Marlene," which we all loved and which we practically took away from the Germans as our national overseas song. Then Sally read a list of prisoners' names, and just as she finished a female quartet would swing off into a snappy version of "Happy Days Are Here Again." The idea being, you see, that it was all over for those prisoners and they were safe and happy, so why didn't we all come and surrender and be happy too?

The rest of the program was divided up between the chatter of Sally and George and the playing of German and American music, including such things as "Stardust" and all of Bing Crosby's records.

The news was actually funny. They would tell us of ships sunk at Anzio that day. From where we sat, we could spit into the waters of Anzio, and we knew that what Sally said was not true.

Both Sally and George spoke good English and claimed to be Americans, but they did make odd mistakes. They pronounced Houston, Texas, as though it were "house-ton," and they spoke of Columbus Square in New York when they meant Columbus Circle. It's tiny little mistakes like that which nullify a propaganda program.

Small and shell-raked as our Anzio beachhead was, life in some respects seemed astonishingly normal. For example, the Fifth Army ran a daily movie. It started less than a month after our troops first landed. They put on two shows each night. I went occasionally, just to kill time at night, since the place where I wrote had no electricity, and I haven't enough Abe Lincoln in me to do my work by candlelight.

A funny thing happened at the movie one evening. I was standing outside the building with a big bunch of soldiers waiting for the first show to end. As we stood there, a shell suddenly whipped in, scared us out of our wits, and exploded behind the building.

When the boys came out after the first show ended, they were laughing about the odd timing in the picture's dialogue. The exploding shell made a big boom inside the theater, and just as it went off there was a pause in the film's dialogue, and the heroine slowly turned her head to the audience and said, "What was that?"

Also, our beachhead had a rest camp (ha-ha) for infantry troops. The camp was under artillery fire, as was everything else on the beachhead. But still it served its purpose by getting the men out of the foxholes, and as somebody said, "There's a hell of a lot of difference between getting shells spasmodically at long range and being right up under Jerry's nose where he's aiming at you personally."

Furthermore, our beachhead had a big modern bakery, which had been working under fire for weeks, turning out luscious, crisp loaves of white bread from its portable ovens, at a pace of around twenty-seven thousand pounds a day.

More than eighty soldiers worked in that bakery. It was the first draftee baking outfit in our Army. They had been overseas a year and a half, and had baked through half a dozen bitter campaigns.

They had casualties right there on the beachhead, both physical and mental, from too much shelling. Their orders were to keep right on baking through an artillery barrage, but when air raiders came over, they turned out the fires and went to the air-raid shelter.

Life seemed very quiet in the bakery when I visited there. The shift leader at the time was Sergeant Frank Zigon of 5643 Carnegie Avenue, Pittsburgh, who showed me around. The boys were glad to have a visitor, and they gave me a pie to take home.

They said they'd had shells on this side of them and that side of them, and in front and behind. It was believable, yet everything was running so smoothly that their stories of shells seemed quite academic. But after I left the bakery, we hadn't gone a hundred yards when an 88 smacked into the soft ground just the width of the road from our feet. If the ground hadn't been muddy, thus absorbing the fragments, we would have got some hot steel in our jeep and probably some in our persons, as the lawyers say.

The baker boys' story of shelling ceased to be academic right then, but I still held onto my pie.

One night, I ran onto two soldiers who had kindly volunteered to help lug my gear off the boat the day I arrived at the beachhead. They were Corporal Bert L. Hunter of Tonkawa, Oklahoma, and Private Paul Norman of 4133 Second Avenue, Des Moines, Iowa. Hunter was in the engineers, and Norman was in a signal company, and worked in the message center. The boys said they didn't mind it on the beachhead.

On the boat, they and some other soldiers had a frisky little brown puppy they'd bought in Naples for two packs of cigarettes and some gumdrops. They couldn't think what to name the dog, so I had suggested they call him "Anzio." So Anzio it was, and he lived there with them, having a fine time.

We correspondents stayed in a villa run by the Fifth Army's Public Relations Section. In that house lived five officers, twelve enlisted men and a dozen correspondents, both American and British.

The villa was located on the waterfront. The current sometimes washed over our back steps. The house was a huge, rambling affair with four stories down on the beach and then another complete section of three stories just above it on the bluff, all connected by a series of interior stairways.

For weeks long-range artillery shells had been hitting in the water or on shore within a couple of hundred yards of us. Raiders came over nightly, yet ever since D-day the villa had seemed to be charmed.

Most of the correspondents and staff lived in the part of the house down by the water, it being considered safer because it was lower down. But I had been sleeping alone in a room in the top part because it was a lighter place to work in the daytime. We called it "Shell Alley" up there because the Anzio-bound shells seemed to come in a groove right past our eaves day and night.

One night Sergeant Slim Aarons of *Yank* magazine said, "Those shells are so close that if the German gunner had just hiccuped when he fired, bang would have gone our house." And I said, "It seems to me we've about used up our luck. It's inevitable that this house will be hit before we leave here."

The very next morning I awakened early and was just lying there for a few minutes before getting up. It was only seven o'clock but the sun was out bright.

Suddenly the antiaircraft guns let loose. Ordinarily I didn't get out of bed during a raid, but I did get up that time. I was sleeping in long underwear and a shirt, so I just put on my steel helmet, slipped on some wool-lined slippers and went to the window for a look at the shooting.

I had just reached the window when a terrible blast swirled me around and threw me into the middle of the room. I don't remember whether I heard any noise or not. The half of the window that was shut was ripped out and hurled across the room. The glass was blown into thousands of little pieces. Why the splinters or the window frame itself didn't hit me, I don't know.

From the moment of the first blast until it was over probably not more than fifteen seconds passed. Those fifteen seconds were so fast and confusing that I truly can't say what took place. The other correspondents reported the same.

There was debris flying back and forth all over the room. One gigantic explosion came after another. The concussion was terrific. It was like a great blast of air in which my body felt as light and as helpless as a leaf tossed in a whirlwind. I jumped into one corner of the room and squatted down and just cowered there. I definitely thought it was the end. Outside of that I don't remember what my emotions were.

Suddenly one whole wall of my room flew in, burying the bed—where I'd been a few seconds before—under hundreds of pounds of brick, stone and mortar. Later when we dug out my sleeping bag we found the steel frame of the bed broken and twisted. If I hadn't gone to the window I would have had at least two broken legs and a crushed chest.

Then the wooden doors were ripped off their hinges and crashed into the room. Another wall started to tumble, but caught partway down. The French doors leading to the balcony blew out and one of my chairs was upended through the open door.

As I sat cowering in the corner, I remember fretting because my steel hat had blown off with the first blast and I couldn't find it. Later I found it right beside me.

I was astonished at feeling no pain, for debris went tearing around every inch of the room and I couldn't believe I hadn't been hit. But the only wound I got was a tiny cut on my right cheek, from flying glass, and I didn't even know when that happened. The first I knew of it was when blood ran down my chin and dropped onto my hand.

I had several unfinished dispatches lying on my table and the continuing blasts scattered them helter-skelter over the room, and holes were punched in the paper. I remember thinking, "Well, it won't make any difference now anyhow."

Finally the terrible nearby explosions ceased and gradually the ack-ack died down and at last I began to have some feeling of relief that it was over and I was still alive. But I stayed crouched in the corner until the last shot was fired.

When the bombing was all over, my room was a shambles—the sort of thing you see only in the movies. More than half the room was knee-deep with broken brick and tiles and mortar. The other half was a disarray covered with plaster dust and broken glass. My typewriter was full of mortar and broken glass, but was not damaged.

My pants had been lying on the chair that went through the door, so I dug them out from under the debris, put them on and started down to the other half of the house.

Down below everything was a mess. The ceilings had come down upon men still in bed. Some beds were a foot deep in debris. That nobody was killed was a pure miracle.

Bill Strand of the *Chicago Tribune* was out in the littered hall-way in his underwear, holding his left arm. Major Jay Vessels of Duluth, Minnesota, was running around without a stitch of clothing. We checked rapidly and found that everybody was still alive.

The boys couldn't believe it when they saw me coming in. Wick Fowler had thought the bombs had made direct hits on the upper part of the house. He had just said to George Tucker of the Associated Press, "Well, they got Ernie."

But after they saw I was all right they began to laugh and called me "Old Indestructible." I guess I was the luckiest man in the house, at that, although Old Dame Fortune was certainly riding with all of us that morning.

The German raiders had dropped a whole stick of bombs right across our area. They were apparently 500-pounders, and they hit within thirty feet of our house.

Many odd things happened, as they do in all bombings. Truthfully, I don't remember my walls coming down at all, though I must have been looking at them when they fell. Oddly, the wall that fell on my bed was across the room from where the bomb hit. In other words, it fell toward the bomb. That was caused by the bomb's terrific blast creating a vacuum; when air rushed back to the center of that vacuum, its power was as great as the original rush of air outward.

When I went to put on my boots there was broken glass clear into the toes of them. My mackinaw had been lying on the foot of the bed and was covered with hundreds of pounds of debris, yet my goggles in the pocket were unbroken.

At night I always put a pack of cigarettes on the floor beside my bed. When I went to get a cigarette, I found they'd all been blown out of the pack.

The cot occupied by Bob Vermillion of the United Press was covered a foot deep with broken tile and plaster. When it was all over somebody heard him call out plaintively, "Will somebody come and take this stuff off of me?"

After seeing the other correspondents, I went back to my shattered room to look around again, and in came Sergeant Bob Geake of Fort Wayne, Indiana, the first sergeant of our outfit. He had some iodine, and was going around painting up those who had been scratched. Bob took out a dirty handkerchief, spit on it two or three times, then washed the blood off my face before putting on the iodine. You could hardly call that the last word in sterilization.

Three of the other boys were rushed off to the tent hospital. After an hour or so, five of us drove out in a jeep to see how they were. They were not in bad shape, and we sat around a stove in one of the tents and drank coffee and talked with some of the officers.

By then my head and ears had started to ache from the concussion blasts, and several of the others were feeling the same, so the doctors gave us codeine and aspirin.

Much to my surprise, I wasn't weak or shaky after it was all over. In fact I felt fine—partly buoyed up by elation over still being alive, I suppose. But by noon I began to get jumpy, and by midaft-ernoon I felt very old and "beat up," as they say, and the passage of the afternoon shells over our house really gave me the willies.

We got Italian workmen in to clean up the debris, and by evening all the rooms had been cleared, shaky walls knocked down, and blankets hung at the windows for blackout.

All except my room. It was so bad they decided it wasn't worth cleaning up, so we dug out my sleeping bag, gathered up my scattered stuff, and I shifted to another room. But then the hospital invited Wick Fowler and me to move out with them, saying they'd put up a tent for us. We took them up on it. We thought there was such a thing as pressing our luck too far in one spot.

In the next few days little memories of the bombing gradually came back into my consciousness. I remembered I had smoked a whole pack of cigarettes that morning. And I recalled how I went to take my pocket comb out of my shirt pocket, to comb my hair, but instead actually took my handkerchief out of my hip pocket and started combing my hair with the handkerchief.

Me nervous? I should say not.

SEVENTEEN

BEACHHEAD FIGHTERS

The American infantry fighters on the Fifth Army beachhead were having a welcome breathing spell when I dropped around to leave my calling card.

There's nothing that suits me better than a breathing spell, so I stayed and passed the time of day. My hosts were a company of the 179th Infantry. They had just come out of the lines that morning, and had dug in on a little slope three miles back of the perimeter. The sun shone for a change, and we lay around on the ground talking and soaking up the warmth.

Every few minutes a shell would smack a few hundred yards away. Our own heavy artillery made such a booming that once in a while we had to wait a few seconds in order to be heard. Planes were high overhead constantly, and now and then we could hear the ratta-ta-tat-tat of machine-gunning up out of sight in the blue, and see thin white vapor trails from the planes.

That scene may sound very warlike to you, but so great is the contrast between the actual lines and even a short way back that it was actually a setting of great calm.

The company had been in the front lines for more than a week. They were back to rest for a few days. There hadn't been any real attacks from either side during their latest stay in the lines, and yet there wasn't a moment of the day or night when they were not in great danger.

Up there in the front our men lay in shallow foxholes. The Germans were a few hundred yards beyond them, also dug into foxholes, and buttressed in every farmhouse with machine-gun nests.

The ground on the perimeter line sloped slightly down toward us—just enough to give the Germans the advantage of observation. There were no trees or hillocks or anything up there for protection. A man just lay in his foxhole from dawn till dark. If he raised his head a few inches, he got a rain of machine-gun bullets.

During those periods of comparative quiet on the front, it was mostly a matter of watchful waiting on both sides. That doesn't mean that nothing happened, for at night we sent out patrols to feel out the German positions, and the Germans tried to get behind our lines. And day and night the men on both sides were splattered with artillery, although we splattered a great deal more of it in those days than the Germans did.

Back of the lines, where the ground was a little higher, men could dig deep into the ground and make comfortable dugouts which also gave protection from shell fragments. But on the perimeter line the ground was so marshy that water rose in the bottom of a hole only eighteen inches deep.

When a man was wounded, he just had to lie there and suffer till dark. Occasionally, when he was wounded badly, he would call out, the word would be passed back and the medics would make a dash for him. But usually he just had to treat himself and wait till dark.

For more than a week those boys lay in water in their foxholes, able to move or stretch themselves only at night. In addition to water seeping up from below, it rained from above all the time. It was cold too, and in the mornings new snow glistened on the hills ahead.

Dry socks were sent up about every other day, but that didn't mean much. Dry socks were wet five minutes after they were put on. Wet feet and cold feet together eventually resulted in that hideous wartime occupational disease known as trench foot. Both sides had it there, as well as in the mountains around Cassino. The boys learned to change their socks very quickly, and get their shoes back on, because once feet were freed of shoes they swelled so much in five minutes a man couldn't get his shoes on.

Extreme cases were evacuated at night. But only the worst ones. When the company came out of the lines some of the men could barely walk, but they had stayed it out.

Living like that, it was almost impossible to sleep. They finally got to the point where they couldn't stay awake, and yet they couldn't sleep lying in cold water. It was like the irresistible force meeting the immovable object.

I heard of one boy who tried to sleep sitting up in his foxhole, but he kept falling over into the water and waking up. He finally solved his dilemma. Alongside his foxhole there was a fallen tree. He tied some rope around his chest and tied the other end to the tree trunk, so that it held him up while he slept.

Living as those boys did, it seemed to me they should all be down with pneumonia inside of a week. But cases of serious illness were fairly rare. Maybe the answer lay in mind over matter. I asked if a lot of men didn't get sick from exposure and have to be sent back. I'll always remember the answer: "No, not many. You just don't get sick—that's all."

I had a chat with four front-line sergeants, as we loafed on a hillside one day. The four men were platoon sergeants of the Forty-fifth Division.

Sergeant Samuel Day of Covington, Kentucky, was a big guy. He weighed 257 pounds when he went into combat in January, and he still weighed 240 despite all the K rations he had eaten. Sergeant Day would have been hard on his feet in any circumstances, but when he got into a trench-foot world, 240 pounds was a lot of trouble for sore dogs.

We got to discussing trench foot, and Sergeant Day told about an incident that happened to him. It seems his feet got in pretty bad shape during a tour in the foxholes, so he went to the front-line medics for ointment or something.

The medics' solution for his troubles was simple. With a straight face, they told him, "Keep your feet dry and stay off them for two weeks!"

Sergeant Day went back to his watery foxhole, still sore-footed but unable to keep from chuckling over the irony of that advice. Their prescription for trench foot takes its place in history alongside W. C. Fields's sure cure for insomnia—get lots of sleep!

Sergeant Eugene Bender of Stroudsburg, Pennsylvania, was the company first sergeant. He was short and curlyheaded, and had a thin black mustache. He was sitting on a C-ration box, getting a between-battles haircut from a soldier barber. "You don't write news stories, do you?" the sergeant asked.

I told him no, that I just sort of tried to write what the war was like, and didn't even especially look for hero stories, since there were so many guys who were heroes without there being any stories to it.

"That's good," the sergeant said. "Hero stuff is all right, but it doesn't give people at home the whole picture. They read about something terrific a guy does over here, and his folks think that happens to him every day.

"Now take me. Once I was on patrol and was behind the German lines for thirty-six hours. We lay all day covered up with weeds in a ditch so close to Germans we could have reached out and touched them. When we finally got back, they had given us up for lost.

"Now if you just wrote that and nothing else, people would think that's what I did all the time."

Sergeant Vincent Mainente hailed from Astoria, Long Island, and was of Italian extraction. He wasn't voluble like most Italian-Americans, but friendly in a quiet and reserved way. He used to be a steam-heat inspector for the Pennsylvania Railroad, and he said, "I sure could use some of that steam heat in my foxhole these days."

Then one of the other boys said, "Vince, tell him about your raft."

"What do you mean, raft?" I asked. So Sergeant Mainente told me.

It seems the bottom of his foxhole was covered with water, like everybody else's. So the sergeant saved up empty wooden C-ration boxes, and one night he nailed them together and made a raft to float on top of the water in his foxhole. I gathered that it wasn't a hundred per cent successful in keeping him dry, but at least there wasn't any harm in trying.

Sergeant Michael Adams was from 1242 Girard Street, Akron, Ohio. He used to work for a trucking company. He had been with the regiment ever since it went overseas in the spring of 1943.

Adams seemed a little older than the others; his hair was beginning to slip back in front, and I could tell by his manner of speech that he thought deeply about things. He got to talking about soldiers who cracked up in battle or before; the ones who hung back or who thought they were sick and reported in as exhaustion cases.

I personally have great sympathy for battle neurosis cases, but not all the soldiers themselves share my feeling. For example, Sergeant Adams told me how some of the replacements, after only a few hours under fire, would go to the company commander and say, "Captain, I can't take it. I just can't take it."

That made Sergeant Adams's blood boil. He said to me, "They can't take it? Well, what the hell do they think the rest of us stay here for?—because we like it?"

And it's that spirit, I guess, that wins wars.

Our artillery was terrific. The beachhead being so small, it was no trick at all to train every gun in the Fifth Army forces on a single German target.

In my wartime life I've had a good many stray shells in my vicinity, but not until I went to that beachhead was I ever under an actual artillery barrage.

The Germans shelled us at intervals throughout the day and night, but usually there were just one or two shells at a time, with long quiet periods between.

One night, however, they threw a real barrage at us. It was short but, boy, it was hot. Shells were coming faster than we could count them. One guess was as good as another, but I estimated that in two minutes they put a hundred fifty shells into our area.

I was in bed, in a stone house, when it started, and I stayed in bed, simply because I was afraid to get up. I just reached out and put my steel helmet on, and covered my head with a quilt, and lay there all drawn up in a knot.

Shells came past the corner of the house so close their mere passage shook the windows. A shell that close doesn't whine or whistle. It just goes "whish-bang!" The whole house was rattling and trembling from constant nearby explosions. The noise under a barrage is muddling and terrifying. Of course we had casualties, but our own house came through unscathed.

The little barrage seemed awful to us, and it was awful; but I know of cases where our guns were fired incessantly hour after hour until we put thirty thousand shells into a single German area.

We had reports that the Germans were burying their dead with bulldozers, there were so many of them.

I had lunch with one of our artillery batteries which manned the big Long Toms. They had been in the thick of the fighting since December of '42—three phases of Tunisia, then Sicily, then through the Salerno-Cassino push. Yet sitting there in one spot on the Anzio beachhead they had fired more rounds than they did in the entire year before that. And they told me of another battery which fired more in four hours one night than in the previous eight months.

The Germans threw so much stuff back at them that the nearby fields were gradually being plowed up. Yet that battery had had nobody killed, and only a few wounded.

They told of a soldier who was standing in a ditch, with one foot up on the bank. An 88 shell went right between his legs, bored into the bottom of the ditch, blew an artillery range finder all to pieces, and never scratched the fellow. But after it was over, he was so scared he was sick for two days.

The men of the battery said that people who came to visit them, such as neighboring ack-ack crews, road patrols, and ammunition truckers, were always the ones who got hit. Being in the visitor category myself, I said a quick good-bye and was last seen going rapidly around an Italian strawstack.

One gun of that battery, incidentally, had a funny little superstition. It seems that on the very first shell they ever fired when they hit Africa, in 1942, they chalked a message—the kind you've seen in photographs—saying "Christmas Greetings to Hitler," and all put their names on it.

They sent the shell over, and immediately the Germans sent one back which exploded so close to the gun pit that it wounded seven of the twelve men who had signed their names to the holiday missive. From that day on, the crew wouldn't chalk anything on a shell.

One day an Army photographer came around to take some pictures of this gun crew firing. He asked them to chalk one of those Hitler messages on the shell. The crew obliged and he took the picture. But what the photographer didn't know was that the shell was never fired. After the photographer left, they carried it up the hillside, dug a hole, and buried it.

Practically everybody who was back of the outer defense line had his home underground. We correspondents didn't, but that's merely because we had no sense. Also, it could possibly be because we were lazy.

At any rate, the beachhead was so dug up that an underground cross section of it would have looked like a honeycomb. Even tanks and jeeps were two-thirds buried for protection.

The soldiers' dugouts were made by digging a square or rectangular hole about shoulder-deep, then roofing it with boards and logs, piling earth on top of that, and digging a trench out from it with steps leading up. The average dugout housed two men. It was just big enough for their blanket rolls, and they had to stoop when they got into it.

Digging was extremely easy, for the soil was almost pure sand. In an hour, two men could dig a hole big enough for their home. Two or three hours more, if they had the timbers ready, was enough to finish the simpler type of dugout.

It's pleasant to dig in sand, but it has its disadvantages. The sides of the dugouts caved in easily. Now and then a man was buried; even the concussion from our own big guns would start the walls sliding in.

A tank crew always dug in just a few feet from the tank, for which they also dug a hole. The boys then ran wires from their tank battery into their dugout, for electric lights. They had straw on the floor, and shelter halves hung at the entrance.

Most of the men slept on the ground, while most of the officers had cots. But it wasn't bad sleeping on the ground in a good dugout; a man could keep both warm and dry.

Some dugouts had board walls to keep the sand from caving in. Others had the more primitive construction of log supports in each corner with shelter halves stretched between them to hold back the sand. It took a lot of lumber to shore up all those thousands of dugouts. The boys rustled up anything they could find out of old buildings. The two most coveted pieces of equipment from deserted houses were wooden doors and wall mirrors. The doors were used for dugout ceilings, and it was a poor dugout indeed that didn't have a fancy mirror on the wall.

From the basic two-man dugout, which was usually bare except for a shelf, a mirror and some pin-up girls, those underground homes ran on up to the fantastic in elaborateness.

One of the best I saw was built by Lieutenant Edward Jacques, of 2730 Colchester Street, Cleveland Heights, Ohio, and his driver, Private Russell Lusher of Marion, Indiana. They had a wooden floor, shelves and nails on the wall for every item, a writing desk with table lamp, a washstand with a big mirror, porcelain lamp shades with little Dutch girls painted on them—and best of all, hidden on a shelf I noticed two nice brown eggs.

But the finest dugout I saw belonged to four officers of a tank company. Their dugout was as big as the average living room back home. They could stand up in it, and it had a rough wooden floor. A drawing table stood in the center, and there were numerous chairs. The four officers slept on cots around the walls.

Books and magazines and pipes and pictures were scattered on tables all over the place, just like home. They had a radio, and on the table was a sign listing the bets of various people on when the invasion of Western Europe would come.

The officers brewed hot tea or chocolate every afternoon and evening. The dugout was heated to the baking point by one of those funny Italian stoves, which for some reason are always painted pink. The officers chopped their own wood for the stove. To go with the pink stove, the boys had dug up from somewhere a huge overstuffed chair covered in old-rose upholstery. They named their dugout "The Rose Room."

They had several electric lights, and the crowning luxury of this palatial establishment was a Rube Goldberg arrangement of ropes and pulleys, whereby one of the lieutenants could switch off the light after he got into bed. They even had a big white dog, slightly shell-shocked, to lie on the hearth.

From all this you might draw the conclusion that war isn't hell, after all. Well, those men could and did go into battle twenty minutes away, and every day and every night shells and bombs fell around them. It was an unusual day when somebody wasn't killed within their own little village of dugouts.

Back in February of 1943, I struggled one forenoon into a cactus patch about halfway between Sbeitla and Faid Pass, in Tunisia.

Hidden in that patch was all that was left of an armored combat team which had been overrun the day before, when the Germans made the famous surprise break-through which led finally to our retreat through Kasserine Pass.

I found the men almost in a daze—and a very justifiable one, too, for they had been fleeing and groping their way across the desert for a day and a night, cut to pieces, and with the swarming Germans relentlessly upon them. The few who escaped had never expected to survive at all, and on that weary morning they were hardly able to comprehend that they were still alive.

I had good friends in that gang, and I saw them again at Anzio. Talk about your family reunions! It was like Old Home Week for a while.

I stayed with them two days, and we fought the Tunisian wars over and over again. I can just visualize us on some far day when we cross each other's paths back in America, boring our families and friends to distraction with our long-winded recountings and arguments about some happening in Tunisia.

Major Rollin Elkins, sometimes known in fact as R. Lafayette Elkins, used to be a professor at Texas A. & M., College Station, Texas. He was one of that old gang. His nickname was "Satch," and he went around in the green two-piece coverall of the infantry. Everybody loved him.

That memorable night in Tunisia I excitedly went away and left my helmet and shovel lying under a half-track in which Major Elkins was sleeping, and never saw them again. In our reminiscing I told the major how, when I was home, several people told me that my steel helmet was in somebody's house on Long Island. How it got there I haven't the remotest idea.

But I had another helmet then, and Satch Elkins had another half-track, "Bird Dog the Second," to replace the old one that was shot out from under him that awful Tunisian afternoon.

And there was Sergeant Pat Donadeo of Allison Park, a suburb of Pittsburgh, who was one of the best mess sergeants overseas. He had lived in the field for nearly two years, cooking in a truck on his portable kitchen, turning out excellent meals, and always having a snack for a correspondent, no matter what hour he showed up. Sergeant Donadeo looked a little thinner than he used to, but he was still all right. He spoke good Italian, and after hitting Italy he came into his own. He made little foraging trips and returned with such delicacies as fresh eggs, chickens, olive oil and cows.

Another old campaigner was Lieutenant Colonel Daniel Talbot, who owned a big cattle ranch outside Fort Worth, Texas. His nickname was "Pinky," and he didn't look like a warrior at all, but he was. Colonel Talbot used to have a driver named Manuel Gomez, from Laredo, Texas. One afternoon beyond Sidi-bou-Zid, the three of us drove up to the foothills so we could look down over the valley where the Germans were. Shells were falling in the valley, and every time we'd hear one we'd ditch the jeep and start for the gullies, although they'd actually be landing a mile away from us.

Private Gomez was still driving for the colonel, and the three of us laughed at our inexperience and nervousness back in those days. None of us had become brave in the meantime, but all of us had enriched our knowledge of shell sounds. By then we thought it was far away when a shell missed by two hundred yards.

Captain Jed Dailey, from Sharon, Massachusetts, was on hand too. He had avenged the loss of his camera back at Sidi-bou-Zid. He personally captured an even better one from the Germans, and added a Luger and a fine pair of binoculars for good measure. Jed Dailey was an unusual person. I think I liked him about as much as anybody I knew. He was a pure Bostonian, and talked with a Harvard broad "a." He was a far cry from the farm boy of the Kentucky hills, yet he commanded a company of such boys and they loved him.

Following the battle at Kasserine, Jed Dailey was switched from a desk job to the command of a company of tanks. The job of company commander, whether infantry or tanks or whatever, is the greatest job in the Army—the greatest and the toughest.

The boys themselves told me what they thought of Jed Dailey. When he first arrived, they were contemptuous of that cultured accent and had little faith in him. They told how he tried to speak in a flat accent whenever he gave them a talk, but without realizing it he would lapse back into his broad a.

But he lived that down, and all their other jokes about him. It wasn't long before they'd go anywhere with him, or for him. He had proved himself in many ways.

Whenever there was a battle he was in his own tank, directing his company. I had the pleasure of seeing him get the Silver Star for gallantry in action. He had been wounded twice after I saw him in Tunisia.

Whenever his company pulled back from battle, Jed Dailey threw the small details of military discipline out the back door and the men really got a rest. As they said, "He fights hard and he rests hard." That's the way the boys got the most out of it, and they appreciated it.

Captain Dailey was tall and his black hair stood up and roached back and you'd have to call him good-looking. He nearly always went bareheaded even in the danger zone. It was not an affectation; he simply liked to go bareheaded. He usually wore an Air Forces fleece-lined leather jacket that he once haggled out of some flier friend.

At the left shoulder of the jacket were two holes—one in front of the shoulder, one behind. The front hole was where a piece of shell fragment went in. The back hole was where it came out after going through his arm. They took a piece out of his leg to patch up his wounded shoulder.

The other officers laughed and said, "Jed wouldn't sew up those holes for $10,000."

And another one said, "Not only that, but you can see where he has taken his knife and made them bigger." You don't talk like that in front of a man when you mean it.

Jed just grinned and said, "Sure."

Before the shoulder hit, he was wounded in the face from an air burst. When he got out of the hospital from his second wound he had a week's leave at Sorrento, the beautiful resort city below Naples. He stayed one night and then returned to his company. Everybody at the rest camp thought he was crazy.

"It isn't that I am anxious to fight," Jed said, "but when you are commanding a combat unit your place is with your outfit. You feel like a heel if you are able to be there and aren't. I feel lots better since I got back."

The boys hadn't had much chance to do their stuff in the Italian war, because of the mountainous terrain and the incessant rains. But the tankers were ready, and they kept hoping. They were sure that sooner or later their big battle there on the beachhead would come. When I walked in, they laughed and said, "This must be it. Every time you'd show up in Tunisia, we'd have a battle. This must be the sign."

So you see I had my lifework cut out for me. I just went around the country starting battles, like a nasty little boy, and then immediately I'd run back and hide.

One night I bunked in the dugout of Sergeant Bazzel Carter, of Wallins Creek, Kentucky, which is just a short distance from the famous coal town of Harlan. In fact, Sergeant Carter's brother was a miner there.

Sergeant Carter was a tank commander. He had had two tanks shot out from under him and was then on his third. One was destroyed by bombing, the other by shellfire, but he didn't get a scratch either time.

I came to like Sergeant Carter a great deal. He was the typical man of the hills who doesn't say much until he gets to know you, and even then he talks very quietly and modestly. Gradually we got acquainted. Sergeant Carter told me about his folks at home and got out pictures of his father and mother and younger brother. He hoped his mother wasn't worrying too much about him.

He told me how he had gone to the University of Kentucky half a semester and then restlessly quit and joined the Army before we were in the war. Later he felt guilty about it, because his father had worked so hard to save the money for him to go to college. After the war Sergeant Carter was determined to go on with his schooling.

I hit his bailiwick at a propitious time—for me. He had just that day received a box from his mother and in it was a quart jar of good old American fried chicken.

We heated it on our little Coleman stove and ate it for breakfast. When the word got around that we'd had fried chicken for breakfast we were both the envy of the others and the butt of all "plutocrat" jokes for the day.

For once in my life I was able to reciprocate in sharing a gift. A friend of mine from Indiana University, Stew Butler, is connected with a candy factory which makes a bar called "Old Nick." The day before I left Washington, to return overseas, Stew called up long-distance to say he was going to send me a box of his candy every week. Never one to refuse anything, I told him to try if he wanted to, although I'd probably never get any of it.

A couple of months went by and nothing happened and I forgot about it, and then suddenly all that pent-up candy came pouring in, two and three big boxes at a time. Brother, did I have candy! I took it to the front with me, a box at a time, and passed it around. I had a box along on that trip, so I gave it to Sergeant Carter and his tank friends, and you should have seen them go for it. We got hard candy and plenty of gumdrops and Life Savers, and sugar too, but little chocolate.

Sergeant Carter fared pretty well himself on packages from home. Three were sent him every week, one by his mother, one by his sister, and one by his cousin. He got most of them. They didn't send fried chicken every time, but there was always something to eat.

Sergeant Carter's dugout was just a bare one, with straw on the floor, a tiny electric light in the ceiling, and a little shelf he had anchored into the dirt wall. He said that after he got his dugout finished and moved in he discovered a mole burrowing in the wall. So he killed it and skinned it, and the hide was still hanging on a nearby tree.

The sergeant slept in his overalls, but the dugout was so snug and warm I decided on the luxury of taking off my pants. Even so I was kept awake a long time by our own guns. Not by the noise, for it was rather muffled down there belowground, but the vibration of the earth was distracting. When the Long Toms, which were almost half a mile away, went off in battery salvo, the earth on which we were lying four feet below the surface trembled and jerked as though it were in an earthquake. But once asleep I never awakened, even though they said later that bombers were over during the night.

Sergeant Carter got up at six every morning, and the first thing he did was to slip out and start the engines of his tank, which was dug in about twenty feet from his dugout. It was a daily practice just to make sure everything was in readiness for a sudden mission.

After breakfast he showed me all through his tank. It was so spotless you could have eaten off the floor. He was very proud of it, and had me sit in the driver's seat and start the engines to hear them sing. I was proud too, just because he wanted me to.

Another night I stayed in an officers' dugout with Major Asbury Lee, of Clearfield, Pennsylvania, and Captain Charles H. Hollis, of Clemson, South Carolina. Major Lee was commander of a tank battalion. His nickname was "Az," and his father-in-law owned the "Lee-Hoffman's Famous Foods" restaurant in Cresson, Pennsylvania. Major Lee had a boy named Asbury Lee IV and a baby named Robert E. Lee.

Captain Hollis was Major Lee's executive, and was a good friend of the late correspondent Ben Robertson, who came from his home town.

It was very dark in the dugout when Captain Hollis got up to start the fire in the stove next morning. He fumbled around on the dirt floor for papers to use as kindling, threw in a handful, and finally got the fire going.

Soon after, he discovered that he had burned up three rolls of film that Major Lee had taken a few days before. Later he discovered that he hadn't burned up the film, after all. Life at the front is very confusing.

After breakfast Major Lee and I got in a jeep and drove a couple of miles up to where two companies of his tanks were bivouacked just back of the infantry. On the way up we were sailing along across a rise when, "Bang!", an 88 shell landed twenty yards to the side of us. Two minutes later we looked up and there came two planes falling earthward, with smoke swirling behind them. Both hit just over the rise from us, close together and only a few seconds apart.

Only one parachute came down. It took a long time, and the aviator lay very still when he hit the earth. Our medics ran out with a stretcher and got him. He was a German. A 20-millimeter bullet had hit him from behind and lodged in his stomach. An ambulance came and took him away.

The boys cut up his parachute to make scarves, and cut one off for me. But I told them I already had two—one American and one German—and to give it to somebody else.

After that exciting beginning of a new day, I went around picking up tank lore. I found that tankers, like everybody else, took their hats off to the infantry.

The average doughfoot or airman said no one could ever get him shut up in a tank. Once in a while there was a tankman who had a feeling of claustrophobia about being cooped up, but it was seldom. The boys said that more than half of them got safely out of damaged tanks, even the ones that caught fire. They told funny stories about how four and five men came out of a burning tank all at once, when actually it isn't possible for more than two to get through the turret at the same time.

They hated snipers worse than anything else. That is because visibility is pretty poor in a tank and the commander usually rides with his turret cover open and his head sticking out. Unseen snipers were always shooting at them.

The boys showed me all the little improvements that had come out on the newer tanks. And they also wondered why tank designers hadn't thought of some of the simplest things for making tank life more practical—such as putting racks for water cans on the rear, and a bracket where a bedding roll could be tied on. The men had welded on the necessary racks for their gear.

An armored unit's fighting usually came in spurts, with long intervals between. When the tank boys hit a lull they were used for emergency jobs. Ordinarily that would have been unusual, but there on the beachhead everybody had to do a little of everything.

Nearly every day the men of the tank crews back in bivouac had a detail starting just at dawn. They carried mines and barbed wire up to the front, for the engineers to put in place. They packed the stuff on their backs, and they didn't like it, but they did it without grumbling.

I suppose there is no custom in our Army more adhered to than the one of brewing some coffee or hot chocolate just before bedtime, whenever soldiers are in a place where it is possible. (Incidentally, coffee was one gift the boys always liked to receive.) It was especially the custom there on the Anzio beachhead, where nearly everybody was dug in, and they could have a fire safely. The little Coleman stove was perfect for that.

One night some of the tank-crew men asked me along to one of their dugouts to have coffee with them. Others followed until there were ten of us altogether, squatting on the floor.

This dugout was of the average size for two men, but three men were using it to sleep in. It was about shoulder-deep, and had straw on the floor, but no furniture at all.

The dugout was inhabited by Private Ruben Cordes, of Jasper, Alabama, and Pfc. Norman Cormier, of Leicester, Massachusetts, both assistant tank drivers, and Private Henry Sewell, of Buechel, Kentucky, a tank gunner.

Private Cordes was the company wit. The boys kidded him and he kidded himself. When I met him just before dark he was sitting on a kitchen chair tilted back against a tree trunk, in good southern style, whittling silhouettes out of a piece of board.

He whittled all the time. The boys laughed and said, "You should have been here a few minutes ago. The captain was right here under the tree, chopping his own firewood, and Cordes just sat there and whittled and let him chop."

Time was when Cordes never could find anything he owned, especially his whittling knife. But after they moved into the dugout he had a simple system. Whenever he lost anything he just got down on his knees and felt in the straw until eventually he found the missing item.

Some of the boys got packages from home the evening I was there. When the others saw that Cordes had a package they started giving him cigarettes, holding lights for him, brushing his shoes and sticking Life Savers in his mouth. It turned out his box contained seven pairs of heavy wool socks which he had written home for, and he intended to keep them.

Cordes was also the pin-up champ of the entire Army, as far as my investigations went. I had known a bunch of Air Forces mechanics who boasted thirty-four pin-ups in their room, but Cordes had thirty-eight on the walls of his little dugout. "I'm glad we're ahead of the Air Corps," one boy said.

In that feminine gallery there was one pin-up girl who meant more than the rest. That was Norman Cormier's wife. Somebody had done a pencil sketch of her at a party back home, and she had sent it to him. It hung in the place of honor among all his roommates' unknown beauties.

The boys were all good-natured. When I was taking down their names and ranks, Cormier laughed when he gave his as private first class, and somebody said, "What are the people of Massachusetts going to think about you being only a pfc.?"

The other tankmen in our little evening snack party were Sergeant Thomas Simpson, a tank commander, of 317 East Jacob Street, Louisville, Kentucky; Sergeant Ralph Sharp, a tank driver from Strathmore, California; Private Paul Cummins, assistant driver from Sharonville, Ohio; Corporal Max Hernandez, from Delmar, California; Sergeant Michael Swartz, a farmer from Scranton, Pennsylvania, and my own dugout mate, Sergeant Bazzel Carter.

Corporal Hernandez, a half-track driver, described himself as "one of those guys who wanted to see action, and now look at me." And the others chimed in that now he was "one of those guys who wanted to see home."

We sat there in the dugout for two or three hours, cooling our canteens with our hands and drinking sweet coffee and just gabbing. The boys pumped me about America and what I thought of the western invasion and what I knew about the authenticity of the latest crop of rumors, and how I found life on the beachhead.

They also related a sad story about a tank driver named Corporal Donald Vore, a farm boy from Auxvasse, Missouri. The corporal had a girl back home and he was crazy about her. After he got to Italy she sent him a beautiful new big photograph of herself. Like most tankmen, he carried it with him in his tank.

Not long after, a shell hit the tank. It caught fire, and the whole crew piled out and ran as fast as they could. Corporal Vore had gone a little way when he suddenly stopped, turned, and went dashing back to the tank. Flames were shooting out of it, and the heavy ammunition was beginning to go off. But he went right into the flaming tank, disappeared a moment, and came climbing out—with his girl's picture in his hands.

A few hours later the crew came trudging back to home base. Mail had arrived during their absence. There was a letter for Corporal Vore from his girl. He tore it open. The letter was merely to tell him she had married somebody else.

They said that if it hadn't been such a long walk back, and he hadn't been so tired, Corporal Vore would have returned to his tank and deposited the picture in the flames.

Finally it was getting late and Private Cummins stretched and said, "I feel like I was forty-five years old."

So I said, "Well, I feel like I was, too, and I damn near am."

Then Sergeant Swartz asked how old I was and I said forty-three, and he said he was thirty, and that if he knew he'd live to be forty-three he wouldn't have a worry in the world. But I said, "Oh, yes, you would, you'd be just like me—worrying whether you'd ever get to be forty-four or not."

And Private Cordes said he had nothing to worry about along those lines, since he didn't have sense enough to get killed.

That's the way the conversation went around a dugout at nighttime—rumors, girls, hopes of home, jokes, little experiences, opinions of their officers, and an occasional offhand reference to what might happen to a man in the end.

I visited another tank crew in emergency position just behind our front-line infantry. They had been there for eight days. They hadn't done anything. They were there just to help repel any attacks that might be coming. We keep lots of tanks located that way at all times.

This crew had its metal behemoth hidden behind a small rise, half obscured by scrub oak. The men were cooking a pot of dried beans when I got there in midforenoon. They had coffee boiling as usual, and we drank it as we talked.

When tankmen were out like that, 10-in-1 rations and C rations were brought up to them at night by jeeps. They did all their own cooking, and slept in the tank for safety. They weren't supposed to smoke inside the tanks, but everybody did. Some crews even burned their little cookstoves right in the driver's compartment. A tank and the territory around it were a mess after five men had lived that way for eight days. The ground was strewn with boxes and tin cans and mess gear. The inside of the tank looked as though a hurricane had hit it.

That particular tank had everything in it from much-handled comic books to a pocket edition of the Bible. I saw old socks, empty tobacco cans, half cups of cold coffee. The boys used the top of the tank for table and shelves, and this too was littered. But all the disorder didn't keep it from being a good tank, because that crew held the battalion record for firing its entire ammunition load in the shortest time.

Sleeping five nights in a tank isn't too comfortable, for space is very limited. They spread their blankets around the interior, slept in their clothes, and nobody got completely stretched out. The worst spot was around the gunner's seat, where a man really had to sleep half sitting up, so they took turns sleeping in that uncomfortable spot.

After they had stayed at the front eight to ten days, another company relieved them, and they moved back a couple of miles, dug in, then cleaned up and relaxed for a few days.

A medium tank carries a five-man crew. That one was commanded by Sergeant Speros Bakalos, a short, nice-looking ex-truck driver from 76 Arlington Street, Boston. Once the tank he was serving in was hit, and his tank commander's head shot clear off.

The driver was Sergeant Oscar Stewart of Bristol, Virginia. They called him "Pop" because he was in his middle thirties. He used to work for the State Highway Department.

His assistant driver was Private Donald Victorine of Crystal Lake, Illinois. He, incidentally, was a friend of Captain Max Kuehnert, whom I knew in Tunisia and whose baby I had the honor of naming Sandra, though Lord knows how I ever thought of that one.

The gunner was Corporal Bud Carmichael of Monterey, California, and his assistant was Private George Everhart, from Thomasville, North Carolina.

Carmichael's nickname was "Hoagy," after the famous composer of "Stardust." Carmichael used to be a pipe fitter for the gas company in Monterey. When I saw him he hadn't shaved or washed for a week. He wore a brown muffler around his neck, a stocking cap on his head, unbuckled overshoes, and was altogether the toughest-looking soldier I ever laid eyes on. But he belied his looks, for he was full of good nature and dry wit.

A few days later I saw the same gang again, and the boys were saying that after I left that day they talked about me. I'd remarked that I'd gone to college with the real Hoagy Carmichael, so this

"Hoagy" told the boys that if he'd been thinking fast he would have replied, "That's funny, Ernie. I don't remember you. What seat did you sit in?"

The men cooked in a big aluminum pot they took out of an abandoned house, and on a huge iron skillet that Carmichael got in barter for the equivalent of $20. They called it their "20 skillet," and were careful of it—even washed it sometimes.

Carmichael had a photo pasted on the barrel of his gun inside the turret—a dancing picture of Carmen Miranda and Cesar Romero. He said it gave him inspiration in battle, and then he grinned until his eyes squinted.

One day I was driving on a muddy lane alongside a woods, with an officer friend who had been at war a long time and had been wounded twice.

On both sides of the lane were soldiers walking, returning to the rear. It was the typical movement of troops being relieved after a siege in the front line. Their clothes were muddy, and they were heavily laden. They looked rough, and any parade-ground officer would have been shocked by their appearance. And yet I said, "I'll bet those troops haven't been in the line three days."

My friend thought a minute, looked more closely as they passed, and then said, "I'll bet they haven't been in the line at all. I'll bet they've just been up in reserve and weren't used, and now they're being pulled back for a while."

How can you tell things like that? Well, I based my deduction on the fact that their beards weren't very long and, although they were tired and dirty, they didn't look tired and dirty enough. My friend based his on that too, but more so on the look in their eyes. "They don't have that stare," he said.

A soldier who has been a long time in the line does have a "look" in his eyes that anyone who knows about it can discern. It's a look of dullness, eyes that look without seeing, eyes that see without conveying any image to the mind. It's a look that is the display room for what lies behind it—exhaustion, lack of sleep, tension for too long, weariness that is too great, fear beyond fear, misery to the point of numbness, a look of surpassing indifference to anything anybody can do. It's a look I dread to see on men.

And yet to me it's one of the perpetual astonishments of a war life that human beings recover as quickly as they do. For example, a unit may be pretty well exhausted, but if they are lucky enough to be blessed with some sunshine and warmth they'll begin to be normal after two days out of the line. The human spirit is just like a cork.

When companies were pulled out for a rest, they spent the first day getting dug into their new position, for safety against occasional shellings or bombings. Usually they slept little during their time in the line, so on their first night out they were asleep early—and how they slept!

The following day they got themselves cleaned up as best they could. They shaved, and washed, and got on some fresh clothes, if their barracks bags had been brought up. They got mail and they wrote letters, and they just loafed around most of the day.

On both second and third days, they took on replacements and began getting acquainted with them. All over the bushy slope where they bivouacked, you saw little groups of men squatting in tight circles. Those were machine-gun classes. The classes were for the new men, to make sure they hadn't forgotten what they had learned in training, and to get them accustomed to knowing their guns and depending on them.

Replacements arrived at many different stages of warfare. The best method was for replacements to come when a whole regiment was out of the line for a long rest. Then the new men could get acquainted with the older ones, they could form their natural friendships, and go into their first battle with a feeling of comradeship. Others arrived during those very short rest periods, and had only a day or so to fit themselves into the unit before going into the great adventure.

The worst of all was when men had to join an outfit while it was right in the line. That happened there on the Fifth Army beachhead. There were even times when a company had to have replacements instantly; that was in cases where no front-line movement whatever in daytime was possible. Hence the new men would have to be guided up at night, establish themselves in their foxholes in darkness, and inhabit those foxholes until it was all over.

I felt sorry for men who had to do that. All of us who have had any association at all with the imminence of death know that the main thing a man wants is not to be alone. He wants company, and preferably somebody he knows. To go up to the brink of possible death in the nighttime in a faraway land, puzzled and afraid, knowing no one, and facing the worst moment of your life totally alone—that takes strength.

EIGHTEEN

SUPPLY LINE

Perhaps the real drama of the Anzio beachhead campaign was the supply system. The supplying of the Fifth Army beachhead was one of the superlative chapters of our Mediterranean war.

The job was undeniably beautiful in execution. We had taken a port full of sunken ships and jumbled streets and wrecked buildings, and cleared enough paths through it for the movement of our ships and vehicles. Once our supplies reached the vicinity of beachhead waters they were under shellfire and bombing raids that might come any moment of the day or night. In addition, German E-boats and destroyers lurked on the edge of our concentration of ships, and naval forces had always to be on the lookout for them.

Our supplies were unloaded in many ways. Some few ships could go right up to a dock. Others went to nearby beaches. The bigger freight ships had to lie off the harbor and be unloaded into smaller boats, which in turn unloaded onto the docks or beaches.

All day long the waters in a great semicircle around Anzio, reaching to the horizon, were churned by big and little ships moving constantly back and forth. It resembled the hustle and bustle of New York Harbor. On the far edges lay cruisers and other battle craft. In the vicinity there was always a white hospital ship to evacuate our wounded and sick. Along toward dusk small, fast craft shot in and out of the great flock of ships, laying smoke screens, while smoke pots ashore put out a blinding cloud of fog.

At night when the raiders came over, a mighty bedlam of ack-ack blasted away on shore, and far out to sea the ships themselves let go at the groan and grind of German motors in the sky.

Sometimes the raiders dropped flares, and then the whole scene was lighted with a glare more cruel and penetrating than the brightest day, and every human being on the beachhead felt that the Germans were looking down at him individually with their evil eyes.

When the moon was full it threw its swath of gold across the lovely Mediterranean, and sometimes the nights were so calm and gentle that it was hard to remember or believe that the purpose of everything here was death. When there was no moon the night was so black we had to grope our way about, and even the ominous split-second flashes from our own big guns did not help us to see.

Sometimes the shelling and the raiding were furious and frenzied. At other times, hour after quiet hour went by without a single crack of an exploding shell. But always the possibility and the anticipation were there. There were times when I stood at a window with my elbows on the sill and my chin in my hand, and saw right in action before me a battlefield in the three dimensions of land, sea and air.

The streets and roads around Anzio were under a steady thundering flow of heavy war traffic. The movement was endlessly fascinating. One day I stood by the road just to watch for a while, and of the first twelve vehicles that passed each was something different.

There was a tank, and a great machine shop on heavy tractor treads that shook the earth as it passed, and a jeep of a one-star general, and a "duck," and a high-wheeled British truck, and a famous American six-by-six, and a prime mover trundling the great Long Tom gun with its slim, graceful barrel pointing rearward.

Then came a command car, and a stubby new gun covered with canvas—on four rubber-tired wheels—and an ambulance, and a crew of wire stringers, and a weapons carrier. Then a big self-propelled gun on tractor treads, and finally another duck to start the heterogeneous cycle over again.

Everywhere there was activity. Soldier-workmen sawed down trees and cut down concrete lampposts so that trucks might use the sidewalks of the narrow streets. Huge shovels mounted on trucks stood amid the wreckage of buildings, scooping up brick and stone to be hauled away in trucks for repairing damaged roads.

Allied military police stood on every corner and crossroads to highball traffic on through and, believe me, it was highballed. Everything moved with a great urgency. The less hesitation the better in that land where shells whistled and groaned. There was little hesitation anywhere around Anzio.

The beachhead was really like a little island. Everything had to come by water. Without a steady flow of food and ammunition, the beachhead would have perished. All the concentration of shelling and bombing against the Anzio-Nettuno area was for the purpose of hindering our movement of supplies. They did hinder it some, but certainly not much, for the supplies kept coming, and the stockpiles grew so great and so numerous that we almost ran out of room for establishing new dumps.

Many branches of the service deserve credit for the supply miracle—the Navy, the Merchant Marine, the Combat Engineers, the Quartermaster Corps. And the British were always there, too, always doing their part; in the case of shipping to Anzio, the Greeks and Poles helped as well.

American Army engineers were in command of all port facilities at the beachhead. The city of Anzio was a mess. Just off the waterfront, there was absolutely nothing but wreckage. And the wreckage grew day by day under German shelling and bombing. We called Anzio a "potential Bizerte," for it was approaching a state of complete wreckage. Yet our soldiers and sailors continued to live and work in Anzio. There wasn't a man in town who hadn't had dozens of "experiences." If you tried to tell a bomb story, anybody in Anzio could top it. Casualties occurred daily. But the men went on and on.

The American soldier's irrepressible sense of humor still displayed itself in Anzio. Down on the dock was a big, boxlike cart in which they picked up slop buckets and trash that got in the way on the dock front. The cart was freshly painted snow-white, and printed in neat blue letters on each side was "Anzio Harbor Department of Sanitation." A person had to see the bedlam of wreckage to get the full irony of the "Sanitation" part.

———

Probably the two outstanding features of our handling of supplies were the duck, or amphibious truck, and our system of carrying regular trucks fully loaded aboard many ships so they could be driven right off when they reached the beach. Without the ducks, some of our invasion landings would have been pretty close to impossible.

In one company all the ducks had been given names. The men stenciled the names on the sides, in big white letters, and every name started with "A." There were such names as "Avalon" and "Ark Royal." Some bitter soul named his duck "Atabrine," and an even bitterer one called his "Assinine"—misspelling the word, with two s's, just to rub it in.

Day and night, a thin, black line of the tiny boats moved constantly back and forth between shore and ships at anchor a mile or two out. They reminded me of ants at work. There were hundreds of ducks, each with a crew of one—the driver.

I hooked a ride with Private Paul Schneider of 1016 Madison Street, Seattle. He was only twenty-two, yet from appearances he could have been any age up to forty. His black whiskers were caked with dust, he wore green celluloid sun glasses, and all his upper front teeth were out, giving him a half-childish, half-ancient look. His teeth had been knocked out in an auto wreck before he left the States, and since then he had never been in one place long enough to get a plate made. I asked him if he didn't have trouble eating, and he said: "No. I get along fine. There's nothing to chew in C rations anyway."

As soon as we drove down into the water and got our truck officially turned into a boat I introduced myself, and Private Schneider said, "Oh, yes, I just finished reading your book. It was all right." From that moment Private Schneider was, for my money, the champion duck driver of the American Army. A man of great perspicacity and acumen, even without teeth.

Once in the water, Private Schneider shifted a few gears and pulled a lever to start the bilge pump. The engine made a terrific clatter, and we could hardly hear each other.

We had gone only a little way when Private Schneider yelled, "Would you like to drive it?"

I said, "Sure." So he took his foot off the throttle and we traded seats.

Driving a duck is funny. You turn the wheel, and about fifteen seconds later you get the reaction to it. You anticipate the waves, and steer toward them a little. I felt big and important, driving a rusty and battered-up old duck out through the shell-strewn waters of Anzio, out to get another load of the precious supplies that kept everything going on that tiny cameo of a beachhead. On that trip we carried back steel boxes of 20-millimeter machine-gun ammunition.

Some forms of unloading stopped at night, but the ducks worked right on through. Each driver did a twelve-hour shift; and the only rest he got was at the dump out in the country while he waited to be unloaded.

Private Schneider said their big worry was not being shelled, but being run down at night by the bigger and faster ships known as LCTs. We lost a few ducks that way. They also took an awful beating when the waves slammed them up against the sides of ships while they waited for winches to swing net loads of stuff down into them. Sometimes the swinging load hit the driver on the head.

The tires on a duck didn't last long. They had to be soft, for ease in climbing out onto the beaches, and they wouldn't take too much running around on land. Another trouble was that salt water got in the brakes. Every now and then I heard a story of a wreck caused by the brakes giving out. But on the whole the duck is almost as wonderful in this war as the jeep.

Private Schneider had worn out two ducks and was on his third. He had had some close shaves, but had never been hit. When a man goes a long time, as he had done, with fire all around him, without ever getting hit, he sometimes builds up a feeling of infallibility about himself. He doesn't worry too much about what might happen.

Private Schneider was just out of high school when he went into the Army, via the National Guard. His wife worked in a defense plant at Seattle. He had been through the invasions of Sicily, Salerno and Anzio. He said he would just as soon drive a duck as do anything else. This was exactly the fine philosophy you'd expect of a man who read good books.

———

Lieutenant Eugene Tousineau of Detroit was the official greeter for the new Anzio "Chamber of Commerce." He visited every ship as soon as it dropped anchor in Anzio waters, and "extended the keys of the city." Most of his guests would have preferred being ridden out of town on a rail.

He was the guy who checked the cargo of every incoming ship and checked daily on the progress and the quality of their unloading. All day long he rode around in an LCVP (landing craft, vehicles, personnel), climbing rope ladders up the sides of ships, snaking back down on single ropes—just holding on with his hands while his bouncing steel boat below tried to crush him. "I've got $10,000 insurance," he laughed.

All day he was out there on the water with shells speckling the whole area. I wouldn't have had his job for a million dollars. But he enjoyed it.

I rode around with him one day seeing how the ships unloaded. With us was Lieutenant John Coyle, of 2622 Swain Street, Philadelphia, who was learning the game. Our supply shipping had become so thick that the checking job was too much for one man, so the two planned to divide it between them. I wanted to see how it felt to sit at anchor aboard a ship full of explosives, within range of enemy artillery. It doesn't feel too good.

Lieutenant Tousineau had been on the job for six weeks. He was an ebullient fellow who got a great kick out of everything he did. He went aboard ships and served notice to ship's officers. He bawled out some people even though he was only a second lieutenant, and commiserated with others who had been bawled out by somebody that mattered. If things weren't going well enough on a certain ship, he would say to the Army officer in charge, "No excuse for this, sir," and never bat an eye. But that's the way wars are won.

Lieutenant Tousineau had had dozens of Hairbreadth Harry escapes. Shells had exploded near him in the water, bombs had dropped beside his house at night. He had even climbed off a ship just a few minutes before it was hit.

Before the war, Lieutenant Tousineau was a night-club manager, a sand hog, and numerous other things. He was tall and dark, with a long and narrow face and a little pencil mustache, and looked like the Anzio edition of Cesar Romero.

He called himself the "bad boy" of his regiment. "I get a commendation one day and a reprimand the next," he said. "The colonel will commend me for good work under dangerous conditions and then I'll go to Naples and get ticketed for having my hands in my pockets." But that's the Army, and Tousineau could take it.

The lieutenant had a crew of four soldiers who ran his boat. The former crew, according to the lieutenant, got "Anzio anxiety" and took off, so he picked his own men. Volunteers for the boat job were called for. Nobody volunteered, so four men were assigned. After they got the hang of it, they liked it and soon everybody else in the company was mad at himself for not volunteering. It was a soft job, nothing to do all day long but ride around in the boat and dodge a shell now and then.

Before Anzio, none of the crew knew anything about boats. They learned by trying. "We didn't know nothin' from sour apples about a boat," said Private James Davis, a farm boy from Covert, Michigan, "but we caught on."

Later, as we lay alongside a British ship, I heard Davis say, "Let's go ashore onto that boat." Such nautical sabotage as that would turn Admiral Dewey over in his grave.

The coxswain of the boat, the guy who drove it, was Pfc. Arthur Handy of Fellows, California, down in the oilfield district near Taft. Handy had spent years learning how to be a sailor, by driving a truck in the oilfields.

One of the "seamen" was Pfc. Nicholas Kardos, of 1702 North Damen Avenue, Chicago. His nickname was "Rabbit" and he used to be a punch-press operator.

The other was Pfc. William Lipiczky, of 7603 Rawlings Avenue, Cleveland. His ancestry was a combination of Russian and Hungarian, and the others called him "flunky." He used to be a welder.

When those soldiers first started learning how to run a boat they were sometimes seasick, but they got over that. And they became fairly indifferent to shells too. They didn't even wear their steel helmets half the time. When shells began coming too close, Private Davis would remark, "For a month I've been telling that fellow to take a furlough and go to Rome and have himself a time. But he doesn't seem to get my message."

———

The greatest apprehension I found in the Anzio-Nettuno area was not among the men on shore, who had been under it constantly for weeks, but among the crews of ships that sat out in the Mediterranean unloading.

It took several days to unload a big freighter, and during all that time they were subject to shelling from land and air raids from the sky. Their situation was hardly an enviable one.

You've never seen a shell hit the water? Well, a dud makes a little white splash only a few feet high. A medium-sized shell makes a waterspout about a hundred feet high. And one of the big shells makes a white geyser a couple of hundred feet in the air—a tall, thin, beautiful thing, like a real geyser, and out from it a quarter of a mile go little corollary white splashes as shrapnel gouges the surface.

Sometimes the whine of the shell, the geyser, the explosion, and the concussion come all at once. That's when they're landing only fifty yards or so away. And anyone would just as soon they didn't.

Few of the men were hit, considering the amount of shooting the Germans did. Yet there was always the possibility, and what gave our men the creeps was to be sitting on a ship full of ammunition or high explosive.

The crews of those big freighters were members of the Merchant Marine. They merely operated the ship. They didn't do the stevedore work of unloading. That was done by soldiers.

They had a good system for the job. At Naples a whole company of port-battalion soldiers were put on each ship just before it sailed. They made the trip up and back with the vessel, did the unloading at Anzio, and when they returned to Naples they went back to their regular dock jobs there. A different company went aboard for the next trip.

The result was that each one-time stevedore crew was so anxious to get unloaded and out of Anzio that everybody worked with a vim, and the material flew.

For a while previously all unloading was done by port-battalion groups based at Anzio. As soon as the crew finished one ship, they would have to go to work on another. There wasn't any end to it. The boys just felt they couldn't win. After the other system went into effect, efficiency shot up like a rocket.

The bigger ships were unloaded just as they would be at a dock, with winches hoisting out big netfuls of cargo from the deep holds and swinging them over the sides and letting them down—not onto a dock, however, but into flat-bottomed LCTs which carried the stuff to the beaches.

Each hold had a dozen or more men working down below, plus the winch crews and signalmen. They were all soldiers. They worked in twelve-hour shifts, but they got intervals of rest.

I was aboard one Liberty ship about 10 a.m. All five hatches were spewing up stuff. I could lean over and watch the men down below piling up ration boxes. And on the deck immediately below us I could see scores of other soldiers sound asleep, the deafening noise of the winches making no difference to them. They were the night shift. They slept on folding cots between blankets, with their clothes on.

One crew boss was Sergeant Sam Lynch, of 2411 West Street, Wilmington, Delaware. He was a veteran soldier, having served four months in the Arctic and fourteen months on this side. Before the war he was a fireman on the Pennsylvania Railroad and later a railway mail clerk. He was married and had one child.

I asked him how he liked coming to Anzio on a ship and he said he didn't like it any too well. "The trouble is," he said, "that you feel so damned defenseless. If you could just man a gun and shoot back it wouldn't be so bad."

But the Navy operated the gun crews aboard all those freight ships and the soldiers could only sit there idle and sweat it out when bombs or shells started flying.

You should have seen them work when a ship was about finished and it looked as if they might not get through in time to catch the next convoy.

They told a story about one ship which finished forty-five minutes after the convoy started. The skipper pulled anchor and started chasing the convoy. The Navy radioed him orders to stop and wait. But the fellow kept right on going. He simply figured he'd rather face disciplinary action at Naples than German bombers for one more night at Anzio.

But the Navy's premise was that he was in greater danger from

German subs and E-boats while running alone after the convoy than he would be from another night at Anzio. They had it all figured out by percentages, and they were right.

But that fellow was lucky and caught up with the convoy. I never heard what his superiors did when he got there, but I bet they didn't invite him out for a round of golf.

Once on shore, our supplies were taken over by the Quartermaster Corps (food and clothing) and the Ordnance Department (ammunition).

Traditionally the Quartermaster Corps is pretty much a rear echelon service and seldom in great danger. But at Anzio they had been under fire ever since the beachhead was established. Their casualties from enemy action had been relatively high. Around seventy per cent of the quartermaster troops on the beachhead were colored boys. They helped unload ships at the dock. They drove trucks. They manned the supply dumps. Hardly a day went by without casualties among them. But they took the bombing and shelling bravely.

The boss of the quartermaster troops was a former newspaper man—Lieutenant Colonel Cornelius Holcomb, of 3030 44th Street S.W., Seattle. He worked on *The Seattle Times* for twelve years before going into the Army. He was a heavy-built, smiling, fast-talking, cigar-smoking man who took terrific pride in the job his boys had done. He said there was one thing about having Negro troops—you always ate like a king. If you needed a cook you just said, "All cooks in this outfit step forward. Company halt!" And then picked out whoever looked best.

We drove out to one of the ration dumps where wooden boxes of rations were stacked head-high in piles for hundreds of yards, like planks in a lumberyard. Trucks from the waterfront added continually to the stock; other trucks from the various outfits continually hauled it away.

Our ration dumps were not at all immune from shellfire. This single one had had more than a hundred shells in it. Many of the soldier-workmen had been killed or wounded.

One of the main problems was how to keep gasoline fires from spreading when shells hit the dumps, which they did constantly.

But Colonel Holcomb had a brain throb. He ordered the gasoline dumps broken up into small caches, each cache about as big as a room and about two cans high. All our gasoline came in five-gallon American or British cans.

Then he had bulldozers push up a thick wall of dirt around every cache. That prevented the air from seeping in from the bottom and creating a draft. After that they had dozens of hits, but seldom a fire. It wasn't unusual to lose several thousand gallons in one night, without even a little flame starting.

Ration dumps seldom burned, because C rations aren't inflammable. But early in the beachhead's existence the Germans hit a dump of cigarettes and millions of them went up in smoke.

The local dumps of ammunition, food, and equipment of a thousand kinds were then so numerous that an enemy artilleryman could shut his eyes and fire in our general direction and be almost bound to hit something. Our dumps did get hit; but the fires were put out quickly, the losses were immediately replaced, and the reserve grew bigger and bigger.

The colonel himself had had many close squeaks. Just before I saw him a bomb had landed outside his bivouac door. It blew in one wall, and hurt several men.

Another time he was standing in a doorway on the Anzio waterfront talking to a lieutenant. Stone steps led from the doorway down into a basement behind him. As they talked, the colonel heard a bomb whistle. He dropped down on the steps and yelled to the lieutenant, "Hit the deck!"

The bomb hit smack in front of the door and the lieutenant came tumbling down on top of him. "Are you hurt?" Colonel Holcomb asked. The lieutenant didn't answer. Holcomb nosed back to see what was the matter. The lieutenant's head was lying over in a corner.

Soon a medical man came and asked the blood-covered colonel if he was hurt. Colonel Holcomb said no.

"Are you sure?" the doctor asked.

"I don't think I am," the colonel said.

"Well, you better drink this anyway," the doctor said. And poured a waterglassful of rum which put the colonel in a merciful stupor all day.

In the Quartermaster Corps they had begun a system of sending the key men away after about six weeks on the beachhead and giving them a week's rest at some nice place like Sorrento.

A man who went day and night on an urgent job under the constant strain of danger finally began to feel a little punchy, or "slug-butt," as the saying was. In other words, he had the beginning of Anzio anxiety, without even knowing it.

But after a week's rest he went back to the job in high gear, full of good spirits, and big and brave. It's too bad all forms of war can't be fought that way.

Major John C. Strickland of Oklahoma City was the area quartermaster. On his desk was a unique paperweight—a small can of Vienna sausage. His wife had sent it to him. He kept it as an ironic souvenir. He wrote her that as an Army quartermaster he handled millions of cans of it, and ate it in various forms a dozen times a week, but thanks anyway.

In addition to its regular job of furnishing food and clothing to the troops, the Quartermaster Corps ran the bakery, a laundry for the hospitals, a big salvage depot of old equipment, and the military cemetery.

Hospital pillow cases and sheets were the only laundry done on the beachhead by the Army. Everything else the individual soldier either washed himself or hired Italian farm women to do. People like me just got dirty and enjoyed it.

The Army laundry was on several big mobile trucks hidden under the sharp slope of a low hill. They were so well-camouflaged that a photographer who went out to take some pictures came away without any—he said the pictures wouldn't show anything.

The laundry could turn out three thousand pieces in ten hours of work. About eighty men were in the laundry platoon. They were well dug in and lived fairly nicely.

Laundrymen were killed in other campaigns, but so far they had escaped at Anzio. Their worst disaster was that the little shower-bath building they built for themselves had been destroyed three times by ducks which got out of control when their brakes failed, and came plunging over the bluff.

Our salvage dump was a touching place. Every day five or six truckloads of assorted personal stuff were dumped on the ground in an open space near town. It was mostly the clothing of soldiers who had been killed or wounded. It was mud-caked and often bloody.

Negro soldiers sorted it out and classified it for cleaning. They poked through the great heap, matched up shoes of the same size, picked out knives and forks and leggings and underwear and cans of C ration and goggles and canteens, and sorted them into different piles.

Everything that could be used again was returned to the issue bins as it was or sent to Naples for repair. They found many odd things in the pockets of the discarded clothing. And they had to watch out, for pockets sometimes held hand grenades.

It was best not to look too closely at the great pile. Inanimate things can sometimes speak so forcefully—a helmet with a bullet hole in the front, one overshoe all ripped with shrapnel, a portable typewriter irreparably smashed, a pair of muddy pants, bloody and with one leg gone.

The cemetery was neat and its rows of wooden crosses were very white—and it was very big. All the American dead of the beachhead were buried in one cemetery.

Trucks brought the bodies in daily. Italian civilians and American soldiers dug the graves. They tried to keep ahead by fifty graves or so. Only once or twice had they been swamped. Each man was buried in a white mattress cover.

The graves were five feet deep and close together. A little separate section was for the Germans, and there were more than three hundred in it. We had only a few American dead who were unidentified. Meticulous records were kept on everything.

They had to hunt quite a while to find a knoll high enough so that they wouldn't hit water five feet down. The men who kept the graves lived underground themselves, in nearby dugouts.

Even the dead were not safe on the beachhead, nor the living who cared for the dead. Many times German shells landed in the cemetery. Men were wounded as they dug graves. Once a body was uprooted and had to be reburied.

The inevitable pet dog barked and scampered around the area. The soldiers said at times he had kept them from going nuts.

Taking over a wrecked port and making it work is like everything else in successful warfare—a matter of thorough organization. At Anzio the British Navy and the American Army had the job down to a T. Soldier executives and clerks, sitting at regular desks in regular offices, did paper work and made telephone calls and kept charts and made decisions just as they would in a shipping office in New York.

Seldom did three hours pass without shells or bombs shaking the town around them, and everywhere there was wreckage. Yet they had fixed up their offices and quarters in a fairly business-as-usual way.

When I walked into the port commander's office, who should he be but the same man I rode into Licata with on the morning of D-day on the invasion of Sicily. Charles Monnier, an engineer from Dixon, Illinois, was a major then, but he had been promoted to lieutenant colonel. Ever since he hit Africa a year and a half before, he had been helping capture ports and then turning them from chaos into usefulness.

In their wisdom—built up through actual practice—such men as Colonel Monnier knew exactly what to look for, what to do, and how to do it when they went to work on the wreckage of a place like Anzio.

There was no guesswork about their progress. On the walls of the shipping room were big blackboards and charts and graphs. Hour by hour the total of the day's supplies brought ashore was chalked up. The big graph was brought up to date every evening. They could look at it, and translate the activities of the past three months day by day, and see what had happened and why.

Everybody joked about the perilous life in the Anzio-Nettuno area. I was with it long enough myself to appreciate the humor of nervousness. Some people had to leave because of nerves, and those who stayed liked to make fun of their own shakes.

The jitters were known as "Anzio anxiety" and "Nettuno neurosis." A person would hold out his hand and purposely make it tremble, and say, "See, I'm not nervous." Then there was "Anzio foot," where a man's feet were pointing in one direction and his face in another—the position sometimes momentarily assumed when he was going somewhere and the scream of a shell suddenly turned him on another course. Also, we had the "Anzio walk," a new dance in which the performer jumped, jerked, cowered, cringed, and twitched his head this way and that, something halfway between the process of dodging shells and just going plain nuts.

You wouldn't think that men could joke about the proximity of death; but they sometimes had to joke about it—or else.

And through it all they kept working and supplies kept coming in. I can't, of course, tell you in figures the total of that magnificent job they did. But I can say that daily the beachhead received nine times as much supplies as they had originally figured was possible. It was a thrilling privilege to have been there and have seen them do it.

NINETEEN

HOSPITAL SHIP

When the time finally came for me to leave the Anzio beachhead, I had a choice of going out by airplane, by LST supply ship, or by hospital ship. I chose the hospital ship, because I'd never been on one.

At the beachhead the hospital ships lay two or three miles out while loading. Ambulances brought patients from the tent hospitals to the waterfront. There they were loaded on the small, flat-decked LCTs, which had canvas over the top to keep off rain.

Usually more than half the men in each load were walking cases. They sat or stood at one end of the deck, while the litter cases lay in rows at the other. I went out to the hospital ship with such a load of wounded.

Once out there we had to lie off and wait for an hour or so while other LCTs finished unloading their wounded. As we lay at anchor, the officers in charge decided to transfer the walking wounded off another LCT onto ours. So it drew alongside, threw over a line, and the two ships came against each other. The slightly wounded and sick men jumped across whenever the ships hit together.

A heavy swell was running and the ships would draw a few feet apart and then come together with a terrific bang. It was punishing to the wounded men. I stood among them, and every time we hit they would shut their eyes and clench their teeth.

One man, nearly covered with a cast, looked at me pleadingly and said, "Don't those blankety-blank so-and-sos know there are men here who are badly hurt?"

Occasionally shells screamed across the town and exploded in the water in our vicinity. The wounded men didn't cringe or pay any attention to this near danger, but the pounding of the ships together made them wild.

Once alongside the big white hospital ship, the wounded were hoisted up by slings, just as cargo is hoisted. A sling was a wooden boxlike affair which held two litters on the bottom and two on top. Up they went as the winches ground. Litter-bearers waited on deck to carry the patients to their wards. The merchant seamen also pitched in and helped carry.

Each badly wounded man carried his own X-ray negative with him in a big brown envelope. As one load was being hoisted up, the breeze tore an envelope out of a wounded man's hand and it went fluttering through the air. Immediately a cry went up, "Grab that X-ray, somebody." Fortunately it came down on the deck of the smaller ship below, and was rescued.

It took about four hours to load the more than five hundred wounded and sick men aboard our ship. As soon as that was finished we pulled anchor and sailed. Hospital ships, like other ships, preferred to sit in the waters of Anzio just as short a time as possible.

Our hospital ships ran up to Anzio frequently, because we wanted to keep our hospitals there free for any sudden flood of new patients. Also, being in a hospital on the beachhead wasn't any too safe.

The hospital ships were mostly former luxury liners. Right then most of them were British, but the one I went on was American. Its officers and crew were all merchant seamen. Its medical staff was all Army—ten doctors, thirty-three nurses, and about eighty enlisted men. Major Theodore Pauli, of Pontiac, Michigan, was in command.

Those ships ferried back and forth on trips like that for a few months, then made a trip back to America with wounded. My ship had been back to the States three times since it first crossed less than a year before.

In a sense a hospital ship was the nearest thing to peacetime that I had seen in a war zone. The ship ran with lights on all over it, the staff had good beds and good cabins, there was hot water twenty-four hours a day, the food was wonderful.

I was given a top bunk in a cabin with one of the doctors. After nosing around into all the nice conveniences of the place, I discovered we also had a toilet and a shower.

I asked unbelievingly if the bath worked. They said, sure, it worked. So I took a bath for half an hour and felt very weak and civilized and wonderful afterward.

Part of two decks of the vessel remained just about as they were when it was a luxury cruise ship in the Caribbean. There the permanent staff of doctors and nurses lived, and also the officers of the ship. But the rest had been altered just as liners were altered when made into troopships. Cabin bulkheads had been cut out to form big wards. Double-deck steel bunks had been installed. The whole thing was fitted out like a hospital, with operating room and wards.

The wounded men got beautiful treatment. They lay on mattresses and had clean white sheets—the first time since going overseas for most of them. There was a nurse to each ward, and the bigger wards had more than one. Enlisted men served the meals and helped the nurses.

The doctors had little to do. On that run the wounded were on the ship less than twenty-four hours. Wounds had been thoroughly attended before the men were brought aboard, and it was seldom that anything drastic developed on the short voyage.

After supper, one of the doctors took me in tow and showed me the entire ship. He was Captain Benjamin Halporn, of 1500 State Street, Harrisburg, Pennsylvania. Captain Halporn's wife also was a doctor back in Harrisburg, practicing under her own name, Dr. Miriam R. Polk.

"We really have so little to do we almost forget how," Captain Halporn said. "My wife back home does more work in one day than I do in a month." But that was nobody's fault. The doctors had to be on the ship for advice and emergency.

As we went around the ship our trip turned into a kind of personal-appearance tour. When we left one ward, the nurse came running after us and said to me, "Do you mind coming back? The boys want to talk to you."

And while I stood beside the bunk gabbing with a couple of wounded men, another one across the ward yelled, "Hey, Ernie, come over here. We want to see what you look like." It occurred to me that maybe I should have had my face lifted. Nobody with a mug like mine has a right to go around scaring wounded men.

The boys had read about the proposal in Congress to give "fight pay" to combat troops, and they were for it. Most of them said it wasn't so much the money as to give them some recognition and distinction, and money seemed the only way to do it.

Some of the wounded would call to the doctor as we went around, and he would have a nurse attend to them. One boy with an arm wound was bleeding too much, and needed a new bandage. Another one, in a shoulder cast, said good-naturedly that he couldn't tell by the feel whether he was bleeding or just sweating under his cast.

A colored boy with a shattered leg said his cast was too tight and hurt his instep. So the doctor drew a curved line on it with his pencil and ordered the cast sawed off there. Each cast had written on it the type of wound beneath it. We stopped beside one man whose right leg was in a cast. The writing on it revealed that he was a British commando. The doctor asked him if he was in pain, and he smiled and said with some effort, "Quite a bit, sir, but not too much."

When I asked wounded men how they got hit, the majority of them were eager to tell in great detail just how it happened. But those in the most pain were listless and uninterested in what went on around them.

When the ship was overcrowded there weren't bunks enough for everybody. So those who weren't in bad shape—merely sick or with slight wounds—slept on mattresses on the floor of what used to be the salon. Everybody had a mattress, which was just so much velvet to any soldier.

The shock cases were down below in smaller wards. Actually most of them were what the doctors call "exhaustion" cases and would be all right after a few days' rest. Their wards had heavy screen doors that could be locked, but not a single door was closed, which showed that the boys weren't too badly off.

In addition, the ship had four padded cells for extreme shock cases. The steel door to each one had a little sliding-panel peephole. Only one cell was occupied. In it was a boy who refused to keep his clothes on. We peeped in and he was lying on his mattress on the floor, stark-naked and asleep.

There was a Red Cross worker on each hospital ship, not only to do anything she could for the wounded, but also to help keep the ship's staff and crew happy. On our ship the Red Cross girl was Percy Gill, of Palo Alto, California. She used to teach physical education at Castilleja School for Girls.

After supper she passed out a bottle of Coca-Cola to every man on the ship. It was the first time most of the boys had had one since leaving America. The Merchant Marine seamen in the crew always helped her pass the cokes around.

Miss Gill had a tiny office filled with books, toilet supplies, musical instruments, magazines. As soon as the wounded men were brought aboard she gave every one a pack of cigarettes and a toothbrush, for most of the boys had lost their gear.

As they were swung aboard, I saw some completely empty-handed and others carrying their pitiful little possessions in their tin hats, balanced on their stomachs. Some had on hospital pajamas, some just o.d. shirts, some only their dirty gray underwear.

Miss Gill did not intrude herself on the men, for she knew that the most badly wounded wanted to be let alone. Now and then she would give a boy a book and discover that he was still looking at the same page three hours later. Another boy might use his as a fan all afternoon.

Miss Gill had books in French, and in German too. Every shipload had a few wounded prisoners. We had two on my trip. One was a startled-looking German kid whose card showed him to be only seventeen. The prisoners were treated just the same as anybody else.

Miss Gill's musical warehouse included an accordion, four guitars, a violin, two banjos, two saxophones, a clarinet, a trombone, and two dozen harmonicas. She didn't have many requests for either the musical instruments or the books on those short trips between the beachhead and Naples, for there was hardly time. But on the long trip back to America they were a godsend, for the men were feeling better by then and time went slowly. On one sixteen-day trip across the ocean the wounded men read three thousand books—an average of six to a man.

It was a relief and a comfort for men to be on a hospital ship after their months of mud and cold and misery and danger and finally the agony of their wounding. It was a relief because the hospital ship was so little like war, and because those who operated it were in a world apart from the world those men had known.

There was no blackout at all. Nobody was ever dirty or cold.

Cabin windows had no shutters. A man could smoke on deck. Big spotlights slung on brackets pointed their dazzling beams at the big red cross painted on the ship's sides.

The ship took its course far outside the channels of regular war shipping, and instead of keeping radio secrecy we broadcast our position every fifteen minutes. The hospital ship wanted the enemy to know where it was, so no mistake could be made.

Our ship had had several "incidents." It had been stopped by surfaced submarines and been circled by enemy planes. But the enemy had always respected it. The greatest danger was going to such places as Anzio, or standing in ports during air raids.

Usually the ward lights were left on until 10:30 p.m. But on our trip they were turned off at 9:30, for we were to dock very early the next morning and the men had to be wakened by 5 a.m. to give the nurses time to get the wounded all washed and fed.

By ten o'clock the inside of the ship was dim and quiet. Nurses went about softly in the faint glow of the blue night light. The doctors, their rounds made, were playing chess and solitaire in the small salon on the top deck. A few soldiers strolled on deck or hung over the rail. It was warm and gentle outside. The lapping of the water seemed like a purring against the ship's sides.

It was wonderful to be going away from war instead of toward it. For the badly wounded there was a sense of completion of a task, for the others a sense of respite. And the sheets and the soft beds and the security of bulkheads lent a confidence in things present and to come.

There was intense suffering aboard that ship. But by 10:30 I could somehow feel the quiet, massed composure that comes to men of turmoil when they settle down for the night in the clasp of a strange new safety.

And early next morning we were in Naples.

TWENTY

FAREWELL TO ITALY

The morning I left Italy I had to get up at dawn to catch the plane. Sergeant Harry Cowe somehow managed to get both himself and me up right on the dot. It was so early I hadn't wanted or expected anybody else to get up. But while I was rubbing my eyes, in came Private Don Jordan with a beautiful breakfast tray of fruit juice, eggs, bacon, toast and coffee, just as if there weren't a war going on.

But that wasn't all. Our Italian boy, Reif, who ordinarily didn't come to work till eight o'clock, showed up just as it was starting to get daylight. Reif was a grand kid, smart and agreeable and full of good humor, and I'm sure he had never been so happy in his life as when working in our little madhouse. He had come voluntarily to help wrastle my luggage out to the airport.

And last but not least, in another minute there came prancing in my tiny friend Lieutenant Maxine Budeman, the nurse-dietitian from the nearby Army hospital. She was from Kalamazoo, Michigan, and everybody called her Goldilocks. She was just shoulder-high and weighed approximately ninety pounds. Back when I was wasting away with anemia, she kept sneaking me eggs and steak from the hospital. We had a lot of fun joking with the nurses about my meager hemoglobin and my one corpuscle, and it was Goldilocks who undoubtedly saved my life with her surreptitious calories.

At the airport Reif lugged in my bedroll and bags for me and I got all set for the plane. Then we started to say good-bye. We four were standing beside a command car. A group of officers and soldiers stood nearby, idly watching us, while they waited for their planes. Our little good-bye sequence must have given them a chuckle or two.

First I shook hands with Harry. And then, since pretty nurses don't come into one's life every day, I managed to inflict upon Goldilocks a good-bye kiss that must have shaken Rome. And then I turned to shake hands with Reif.

But Reif, instead, grabbed me by both shoulders and in true Continental fashion implanted a large Italian smack first on my right cheek and then on my left. Our audience was astonished, and so was I. And though slightly embarrassed, I must admit I was also sort of pleased. There are swell people in any nation, and I know that in our crazy little group there was a genuine fondness for many of our Italian friends.

Buoyed and puffed up by this international osculation, I floated onto the plane and we were off. On the way out we flew right past the magnificence of Vesuvius, but I was feeling badly about leaving and didn't want to look out, or even look back.

I had been in that Italian war theater so long that I thought of myself as a part of it. I was not in the Army, but I felt like a deserter at leaving.

There was some exhilaration there in Italy, and some fun along with the misery and the sadness, but on the whole it had been bitter. Few of us can ever conjure up any truly fond memories of the Italian campaign. The enemy had been hard, and so had the elements. Men had had to stay too long in the lines. A few men had borne a burden they felt should have been shared by many more. There was little solace for those who had suffered, and none at all for those who had died, in trying to rationalize about why things had happened as they did.

I looked at it this way—if by having only a small army in Italy we had been able to build up more powerful forces in England, and if by sacrificing a few thousand lives there that winter we would save half a million lives in Europe—if those things were true, then it was best as it was.

I wasn't sure they were true. I only knew I had to look at it that way or else I couldn't bear to think of it at all. Personally, I thought they were true.

And here I want to pay a kind of tribute to a small group I've never mentioned before. They were the enlisted men of the various Army Public Relations units who drove us correspondents around and fed us and looked after us. They were in the Army and subject to ordinary discipline, yet they lived and worked with men who were free and undisciplined. It is hard for any man to adjust himself to such a paradoxical life. But our boys did it, and retained both their capabilities and their dignity.

I wish I could mention them all. The few I can mention will have to represent the whole crew of many dozens of them.

There were drivers such as Delmar Richardson, of Fort Wayne, Indiana, and Paul Zimmer, of Oakland, California, and Jerry Benane, of Minneapolis. They took care of the bulk of the correspondents, and it was only a miracle none of these drivers had been wounded. Always they were courteous and willing, despite a pretty irritating sort of life.

Then there were such boys as Corporal Thomas Castleman, of my own town of Albuquerque, who rode his motorcycle over unspeakable roads through punishing weather to carry our dispatches to some filing point. And Private Don Jordan, probably the most remarkable of all the PRO men I knew. Don was a New England blueblood from Wells, Maine, and Attleboro, Massachusetts. He was a Brown University man, a dealer in antiques, a writer. He talked with a Boston accent, spoke French, and was at home in conversations about art and literature. And do you know what he did? He cooked. He not only cooked, but he cooked with an imagination that made eating at our place a privilege. On top of that, he ran the place as bookkeeper, house mother, translator, and fulfiller of all requests, working like a slave, with an unending good nature.

And there were such men as Sergeant Art Everett, of Bay City, Michigan, and my friend Harry Cowe, of Seattle, who missed being officers by the unfair Fates of war, and who went on—with an admirable acceptance—doing work of officer responsibility. To those few men and to all the others like them who made life at war possible for us correspondents—my salute.

As for all the rest in that Mediterranean Army of ours—it was wonderful in a grim, homesick, miserable sort of way to have been with them. There was not one single instance, from private to general, when they were not good to me.

I hated the whole damned business just as much as they did, who suffered so much more. I often wondered why I was there at all, since I didn't have to be, but I found no answer anywhere short of insanity, so I quit thinking about it. But I'm glad I was there.

Leaving Italy, we flew most of the day and far into the night. Crossing the Mediterranean I knotted myself up on top of a pile of mail sacks and slept half the trip away. And then, in a different plane, over western Algeria and Morocco, I got myself a blanket, stretched out on the floor and slept for hours. The sun was just setting when I woke up.

I've written many times that war isn't romantic to the people in it. But there in that plane, all of a sudden, things did seem romantic.

A heavy darkness had come inside the cabin. Passengers were indistinct shapes, kneeling at the windows—to absorb the spell of the hour. The remnants of the sun streaked the cloud-banked horizon ahead, making it vividly red and savagely beautiful. We were high, and the motors throbbed in a timeless rhythm. Below us were the green peaks of the Atlas Mountains, lovely in the softening shroud of the dusk. Villages with red roofs nestled on the peaktops. Down below lived sheep men—obscure mountain men who had never heard of a "*Nebelwerfer*" or a bazooka, men at home at the end of the day in the poor, narrow, beautiful security of their own walls.

And there high in the sky above and yet a part of it all were plain Americans incongruously away from home. For a moment it seemed terribly dramatic that we should be there at all amid that darkening beauty so far away, so foreign, and so old.

It was one of those moments impossible to transmit to another mind. A moment of overpowering beauty, of the surge of a marching world, of the relentlessness of our own fate. It made me want to cry.

ENGLAND

APRIL–MAY, 1944

TWENTY-ONE

THIS ENGLAND

It felt wonderful to be safe in England, for I had sort of dreaded the trip.

RAF and USAAF people saw us through the formalities. We ate breakfast in an RAE dining room. In an hour we were in another plane on the way to London. By noon we had landed at an airdrome where I had been many times before, and a big bus was waiting to take us into the city.

I had left London for Africa one dark and mysterious night a year and a half before. Many times since then I had never thought to see England again. But there it was, fresh and green and beautiful. And although I was still far from home and family it was a wonderful thing to be returning, for I have loved London ever since first seeing it in the blitz. It has become sort of my overseas home.

At first I couldn't seem to make up my mind about the state of things. Some people said they could see in people's conduct the strain of waiting on the invasion—that tempers were short and nerves taut. Yet the English seemed to me just as imperturbable as ever.

Some people said the English had been at war so long they had forgotten about peacetime life and were resigned, sheeplike, to the war dragging on and on. But I didn't sense any such resignation.

It was certainly true that Britain had adjusted herself to wartime life, but that didn't mean blind, perpetual acceptance. People had learned to get along. American aid, and years of learning how to do, had eased the meager war life of the early days. There was more food, and it was better than it used to be. There were more people on the streets, more shopping, more Sunday strollers in the parks.

I had supposed the people would look shabbier than before, but to me they looked neater. And the city itself seemed less dreary than in the fall of 1942.

As for short tempers, I didn't see any. Maybe it was just because I had been accustomed to the screaming outbursts of the emotional Italians. But from what I could see the English were as kind and polite to each other as always.

All in all, my first impression was that England was better, all around. Of course spring may have had something to do with it. The days were warm and the buds were out and flowers were blooming, and everything always seems kind of wonderful to me in springtime.

Every day the London papers quoted all the German rumors on invasion. They printed the predictions of the German radio and pieces from neutral countries saying the invasion would have to occur between 4:39 a.m. today and 4:41 a.m. tomorrow, or else be put off for a month. They printed pictures of German fortifications, and told of the sudden regrouping and rushing around of German troops. They conjectured about the thunderous explosions heard daily on the French side of the Channel.

Since the only invasion news we had was what the Germans predicted, this echo from Germany had the effect, upon me at least, of a war of nerves.

London was crawling with Americans, both Army and civilian. All headquarters cities were alike in their overcrowding, their exaggerated discipline, and what appeared to be military overstaffing.

There were those who said London was as bad as Washington. Others said it was worse. Certainly the section where American offices were most highly concentrated was a funny sight at lunchtime or in late afternoon. Floods of American uniforms poured out of the buildings. On some streets an Englishman stood out as incongruously as he would in North Platte, Nebraska. Desk officers and fliers and WACs and nurses abounded.

There were all kinds of cracks about the way Americans had flooded the island and nearly crowded the English off. Actually the Americans weren't bad and the English reception was good. But the little jokes helped to keep us from getting on each other's nerves. Americans told this one themselves. Said one American to another, "These English are beginning to act as if this country belonged to them."

Two things that amused the British were the "pink" trousers our officers wear and our perpetual saluting. The American Army was very strict about saluting there. Everybody had to salute. Second lieutenants saluted other second lieutenants. Arms flailed up and down by the thousands as though everybody were crazy. People jabbed each other in the eyes saluting. On one short street much traveled by Americans they had to make sidewalk traffic one-way, presumably to prevent salute casualties.

A friend of mine, a captain back from Africa, was stopped one day by another captain just over from America who bawled the living daylights out of him for not returning his salute. My captain friend said he couldn't because his right arm had become muscle-bound from waving it too much.

They were strict about dress too. We had to wear our dress blouses and either pinks or dark-green dress trousers. Everybody looked just so, and exactly like everybody else.

I thought I looked very pretty when I arrived, for all my clothes were clean for the first time in months. But I hadn't reckoned with the headquarters atmosphere. I have never been stared at so much in my life as during my first three days. I had on a British battle jacket, o.d. pants, and infantry boots. They had never seen anybody dressed like that before. Nobody knew what this strange apparition was, but they all played safe and saluted it anyhow— and then turned and stared belligerently at it. I think sheer awe was all that kept the MPs from picking me up.

Finally, I dug up a trunk I had stored when I went to Africa and got out my old brown civilian suit and gray hat, and after that I was all right. People just thought me a bedraggled bank clerk, and it was much better.

After going the rounds I decided that if the Army failed to get ashore on D-day there would be enough American correspondents to force through a beachhead on their own.

There were gray men who covered the last war, and men from the Pacific, and there were little girls and big girls and pretty girls, and diplomatic correspondents and magazine contributors and editors and cubs and novelists. I decided that if *Dog News* didn't get a man over pretty quickly to cover the dog angle of the invasion I personally would never buy another copy.

There were at least three hundred correspondents, and the report was that transmission facilities were set up to carry a maximum of half a million words a day back to America.

While in London we correspondents could wear either uniforms or civilian clothes, as we pleased. Some of the correspondents up from Italy had no civilian clothes and couldn't get any—since British coupons were not obtainable—so they had to wear uniforms constantly.

I was a civilian again for that little interlude, thanks to the old brown suit I had left in the trunk. The only trouble was, I got cold if the weather turned chilly. The only outer coat I had was a dirty old mackinaw. I couldn't wear that with my brown suit, since it's against the rules to mix military and civilian clothing. I couldn't wear it with my uniform, for it was nonregulation for city dress, and the MPs would have picked me up. And I couldn't buy a topcoat, for I couldn't get British coupons. So I just froze, brother, froze.

We could live where we pleased, and that was a problem. It was hard to find a place to live in crowded London. Some correspondents were lucky enough to find apartments or to share apartments with Army officers they knew. Others managed to get into hotels.

Through a friend I got into one of London's finest hotels. Ordinarily a person was allowed to stay there only a few days. But, again through the influence of this very influential friend, the hotel seemed to shut its eyes and let me stay, although nothing was actually said about it—and I was afraid to bring up the subject.

For the first two days in my luxurious hotel room I had an odd feeling of guilt. I felt ashamed, coming from Italy where so many lived so miserably, to be sleeping in a beautiful soft bed in a room so tastefully decorated and deeply carpeted, with a big bathroom and constant hot water and three buttons to press to bring running either a waiter, a valet, or a maid. But I found I have strong will power when it comes to readjusting to comfortable life. After a couple of days I said, "Boy, take it while you can get it," and didn't feel the least bit ashamed any more.

Incidentally, you just can't break down English traditions. For example, I registered as Ernie Pyle and then on another line gave my full three names, as the law requires. And do you know how my hotel bill came? It came weekly in a sealed envelope on which was typed "E. Taylor-Pyle, Esq."

Given time, if I had been a good boy I might have had "The Honourable" put in front of my name.

The good news that came from Italy was tinged with bad for some of us who still had strong roots and half our hearts in that cruel battleground.

The name of Roderick MacDonald may not have been familiar in America, but it meant much to many of us who marched with the wars in Tunisia, Sicily and Italy. Mac was one of our bunch—a war correspondent—and the report came that he had been killed at Cassino.

Mac was a Scot. His family emigrated to Australia and he was schooled there and eventually went to work for *The Sydney Morning Herald*. He left Australia in 1941 and followed the wars in China, the Near East, and all through Africa.

We first knew him in Tunisia. Just after Tunis fell he came down with a savage recurrence of malaria and spent three weeks in a hospital. Finally he got strong enough to get back to Algiers during that peaceful interval between Tunisia and Sicily.

During that time our Public Relations section was set up in a camp on the sandy and gentle shore of the Mediterranean, some twenty miles outside Algiers. That's where I used up those six weeks of peace—one of the grandest six weeks of my life, just lolling in my tent, eating well, working a little, reading a lot, mostly loafing and being wonderfully warm.

Roderick MacDonald sent word that he was in a hotel at Algiers, and I got a jeep and went and picked him up. He was so weak he couldn't even carry his bedroll. We brought him out to camp and put him in the tent next to mine.

For days he lay listless, with strength enough only to get up for meals. The sun was broiling and he would strip down to his shorts and lie there in the hot sand, baking his body a sleek brown. Gradually life began to flow into him again, his face filled out, the glaze left his eyes, and the famous MacDonald smile and Mac-Donald barbed retort began to return.

Mac had everything to live for, and he loved being alive. He was young, tall, handsome, brilliant, engaging. He had a sensitive mind, and he would have been a novelist had there been no war. Among Americans he was the best-liked British correspondent I have ever known. With his Scottish and Australian heritage he understood us. He would kid the pants off us about the way we talked, and mimic our flat pronunciation. He in turn took the same razzing about his Oxford accent. He had never been to America but it was his one ambition to go there.

Like most correspondents, Mac felt that he had to write a book. He had it about two-thirds finished when he came to our camp to recuperate. During the latter days of his stay, when his strength had returned, he tapped away belligerently on his little typewriter, cussing the day he ever started the book, resenting the deadline his London publishers were heckling him with. But he did finish it.

The day I arrived in London from Italy I went into a book-store, and I noticed Mac's book. I bought it just because I knew Mac, and brought it home and put it on the table, but did not get around to reading it.

After he was gone I read it. What an ironic world, that only the compulsion of death makes us do for our friends—in more ways than merely reading a book—what we should have done while they still lived.

Many of the correspondents who had gone through the campaigns in Africa, Sicily and Italy were in England, and we felt like a little family among all the newcomers.

Before I arrived they had a big banquet for the correspondents who had been in the Mediterranean. There was no general get-together after I got there, but a few of us occasionally called each other up and got together for a meal.

Most of the correspondents based in London and worked out to the camps or airfields, on trips of a few days each, and then came back to write up their stuff and wait on the invasion. A vast Army Public Relations branch occupied one huge four-story building and overflowed into several others. They had set up a "correspondents' room" as a sort of central headquarters for us. We got our mail there, and we went there to ask questions, and get various problems worked out, and meet each other.

The mail was a revelation. In the Mediterranean the average

letter took at least two weeks and a half to come from the States, and most of it much longer. In England half of my mail came through in a week. I even had one letter in five days, and the longest was only two weeks on the way.

Obviously no correspondent knew when the invasion would be or where. I imagine you could count on your fingers all the Army officers in England who knew. All we correspondents could do was to be ready.

Only a few were to go in on the initial invasion or in the early stages. Some of the eager ones tried to pull strings to get front seats in the invasion armada. Others with better judgment just kept quiet and let matters take their course. Personally, I tried to get accredited to the British Home Guard to help defend the Midland town of Burford from German attack.

The American contingent had acquired many new terms. The newest and most frequently heard was "SHAEF," the initials of Supreme Headquarters Allied Expeditionary Force. SHAEF was planning the invasion, and would direct it. Initials grew into words overseas just as they did back in Washington.

The word ETOUSA still existed. That stands for European Theater of Operation United States Army. That is, headquarters of the American Army as distinct from Allied Headquarters. It was two years old then and still functioning.

When we were there in 1942 ETOUSA was always pronounced "eetoosa." For some unexplained reason the pronunciation had changed to "eetowza." Being old-fashioned and set in my ways, I liked the first one best.

Not long after my arrival, I took a trip up to the Midlands to see a man from Albuquerque. He was, in fact, the man who built our little white house out there on the mesa, and who subsequently became one of our best friends. His name was Captain Arthur McCollum. He was a lieutenant in the last war. He spent twenty years regretting that he never got overseas the other time, and he was very happy that he had made it this time. He was attached to a big general hospital out in the country.

In January Captain McCollum had a reunion with his son, Lieutenant Ross McCollum. Ross was chief pilot of a Flying Fortress.

Father and son had two wonderful weekends together. And then on his second mission over Germany Ross didn't come back. Nothing had been heard from him since. That was nearly four months past.

Captain Mac and Ross were real companions—they played together and dreamed and planned together. After the war they were going to fish a lot and then start an airplane sales agency.

Captain Mac said he kind of went to the bottom of the barrel over Ross. For two months he was so low he felt he couldn't take it. And then he said to himself, "Look here, you damn fool. You can't do this. Get yourself together." And having given himself that command, he carried it out.

I found him the same life-loving, gay friend I had known in Albuquerque. We bicycled around the countryside, celebrated here and there, made fools of ourselves, and had a wonderful time.

Captain Mac talked a lot about Ross, and felt better for the talking, but he didn't do any crying on my shoulder. He felt firmly that Ross would come back, but he knew that if he never did he could take it. (Months later, when both of us were in France, word came that Ross was definitely dead. And Mac took that final news in the same brave way.)

The Zippo Manufacturing Company, of Bradford, Pennsylvania, makes Zippo cigarette lighters. In peacetime they are nickel-plated and shiny. In wartime they are black, with a rough finish. Zippos are not available at all to civilians. In Army PXs all around the world, where a batch comes in occasionally, there are long waiting lists.

While I was in Italy I had a letter from the president of the Zippo Company. It seems he is devoted to my column. It seems further that he'd had an idea. He had sent to our headquarters in Washington to get my signature, and then he was having the signature engraved on a special nickel-plated lighter and was going to send it to me as a gift.

Pretty soon there was another letter. The president of the Zippo Company had had another brainstorm. In addition to my superheterodyne lighter he was going to send fifty of the regular ones for me to give to friends.

I was amused at the modesty of the president's letter. He said, "You probably know nothing about the Zippo lighter."

If he only knew how the soldiers coveted them! They'll burn in the wind, and pilots say they are the only kind that will light at extreme altitudes. Why, they're so popular I had three of them stolen from me in one year.

Well, at last the lighters came, forwarded all the way from Italy. My own lighter was a beauty, with my name on one side and a little American flag on the other. I began smoking twice as much as usual just because I enjoyed lighting the thing.

The fifty others went like hot cakes. I found myself equipped with a wonderful weapon for winning friends and influencing people. All fifty-one of us were grateful to Mr. Zippo.

I was with an infantry company of the First Division in those bitter mountain battles west of Mateur, in Tunisia. For three days I lived in a tent with a British captain attached to us as a liaison officer. The night before an attack he and I marched up to the lines with separate battalions of the same regiment. Just after dawn the next day I saw a British officer being carried on a stretcher. When I ran over, sure enough it was my friend, Captain Jack Morris Enfield. He was badly wounded in the back and arm. Our stretcher bearers carried him to the rear and I did not see him again.

There in London I was having lunch in an officers' club when an American colonel I had known in Tunisia came over. He said he had a British girl at his table he'd like me to meet. And when he introduced us, it was Captain Enfield's sister.

She said her brother had recovered. He still had some pain in his back, but she guessed he was all right as he was then in the paratroops. I had missed him by only twenty-four hours.

I suppose to give this story the proper ending Miss Enfield and I should have been married and lived happily ever after. That occurred to me too, but when I asked her she said no. Oh, well, alackaday.

You probably heard about the frightful noise the English anti-aircraft rocket guns make. Well, we had a few minor raids after

I arrived. On the first one I found I was so scared, after our Anzio escape, that all I could do was just lie there trying to get my breath. A fellow has a kind of cumulative fright after he has had a really close one.

I think that I was so afraid to hear the awful noise of those rocket guns that I was practically paralyzed. Finally they did go off. I guess I had expected too much, for they didn't horrify me half so much as I had thought they would. The noise itself isn't so bad—it's what it sounds like that terrifies a person. For a rocket going up sounds like a bomb coming down. After I learned that and adjusted myself to it, rocket guns weren't bad.

During the noisiest raid of my stay, I slept through the whole thing. When the waiter came to the room next morning he started talking about the raid and I said, "What raid?"

He said, "Quit joking. Why, every gun in London was going last night." But I didn't wake up. I wish I could arrange it that way for all raids.

We Americans in London fared very well on post-exchange rations. We were allowed seven packs of cigarettes a week, two bars of chocolate, two razor blades, and a can of fruit juice. In addition we could buy soap, tooth paste, shaving cream, handkerchiefs, fountain pens, and dozens of other little things.

My family begged me to ask them for something, but truthfully there was nothing I wanted. Nothing, that is, except a dog and a sports roadster and a fireplace and my own easy chair and a dozen new books and lots of spare time. But unfortunately they all weigh over eight ounces.

TWENTY-TWO

BRASS HATS

The top commanders who toiled and slaved for months planning the second front were under a man-killing strain of work and responsibility. Thousands of men of high rank labored endlessly. They were up early, they worked all day, and after supper they went back to work far into the night. Seldom could you get one of them to take a day off.

Among the greatly conscientious ones in this category was Lieutenant General Omar Bradley, who was to lead all the American troops in the second front.

I ran into Sergeant Alex Stout, General Bradley's driver. The general was very fond of Alex, and in turn Alex was not afraid to look at his king or to plot in his behalf.

Alex kept saying, "General, you're working too hard. If you won't take a day off, why don't you get in the car and we'll just drive around the country for a couple of hours?" He was persistent. One day he put it to his boss again and the general said, well, as soon as he filled two more appointments he would go out for a half-hour ride. So Alex got him in the car and headed for the country.

"We drove for two hours," Alex says. "I told him I was lost and couldn't find my way back to town. But I knew where I was all the time, all right."

As you may know, I am concerned mainly with the common soldier—the well-known GI. I usually let the exalted high command shift for itself. But now I want to reverse things and write about an American general.

For three days, back in Sicily, I rode and I sat around with Lieutenant General Omar Nelson Bradley and at times I was so engulfed in stars I thought I must be a comet.

I make no bones about the fact that I am a tremendous admirer of General Bradley. I don't believe I have ever known a person to be so unanimously loved and respected by the men around and under him. It would be toying with the truth to call him hand-some, rather than good-looking. His face showed the kindness and calmness that lay behind it. To me General Bradley looked like a schoolteacher rather than a soldier. When I told him that, he said I wasn't so far wrong, because his father was a country schoolteacher and he himself had taught at West Point and other places. His specialty was mathematics.

The general didn't smoke at all. He took his cigarette rations and gave them away. He drank and swore in great moderation. There was no vulgarity in his speech. Back home, he said, he and Mrs. Bradley probably took one drink a month before supper. Over there where liquor was hard to get he drank hardly ever, but he did pour a dust-cutting libation for visitors who showed up at sup-pertime. He had three bottles of champagne that somebody gave him, and he saved those to celebrate the capture of Messina.

The general's voice was high-pitched and clear, but he spoke so gently a person couldn't hear him very far. His aides said they had never known him to speak harshly to anyone. He could be firm, terribly firm, but he was never gross nor rude. He always put people at their ease.

A quaking candidate for a commission in the officers' school at Fort Benning, Georgia, was once interviewed by General Brad-ley, and when the soldier came out he said, "Why, he made me feel like a general myself."

The general was just the opposite of a "smoothie." His con-versation was not brilliant or unusual but it was packed with sincerity. He still had the Middle West in his vocabulary—he used such expressions as "fighting to beat the band" and "a horse of another color." There was absolutely no pretense about him, and he hated ostentation.

He didn't fly his three-star flag except when formal occasions demanded it. And his aides were full of stories about how he stayed in the background rather than call attention to himself by pushing up where he had a right to be. He didn't even own a Sam Browne belt or a dress cap.

Oddly enough, for a man so quiet and modest, he didn't mind

public speaking. He was no ringing orator, but after a while his speech became powerful by its tone of intense sincerity. During vital periods of each campaign, the general always came to our correspondents' camp and, in front of a big map, gave us a complete fill-in on the situation. When he first did this back in Africa we all liked him but weren't especially impressed. But he grew on us just as he grew on everybody he worked with, and before long there wasn't a correspondent who didn't swear by him.

Despite his mildness the general was not what you would call easygoing. Nobody ran over him. He had complete confidence in himself, and once he made up his mind nothing swayed him. He was as resolute as rock, and people who worked with him had to produce or get out. They didn't get the traditional Army bawling-out from him, but they did get the gate.

He had a nice quality of respecting other people's opinions and of paying close attention to other people's conversation. I noticed that when he made a phone call he always said "If you please" to the Army operator. And on the road, when an Army truck pulled out to let his three-star jeep pass, he always turned and said "Thank you" to the driver.

When he passed a bunch of engineers toiling and sweating to create a bypass around a blown-up bridge he would call out, "You're doing a nice job here," to the startled lieutenant in charge.

The general rode around the front a great deal. During the campaign in northern Sicily he averaged five hours a day in his jeep, and sometimes ran it up to eight. He insisted that jeep riding was good for the liver. A few times he used planes. He hoped to have a small plane of his own that could land practically anywhere, as it would save him hours each day.

On the front bumper of the general's jeep was a red-and-white plate displaying three stars, and of course this drew a salute from every officer or soldier who was on his toes. In heavy traffic the general was returning salutes constantly. I told him that what he needed most was a little boy to do his saluting for him. He laughed and said, "Oh, that's the way I get my exercise."

When he drove through a town the Sicilians all yelled and waved, and the general waved back. Italian policemen, discharged soldiers, and even civilians snapped up to the salute, and the general always responded. Once in a while they'd give him the Fascist salute, out of old habit, and he returned that too, but in the American way.

He didn't affect a swagger stick, but he did sometimes carry an ordinary wooden cane with a steel spike in the end. It was given to him by former Congressman Faddis of Pennsylvania.

There in Sicily, General Bradley had around him at the front, in addition to his military staff of more than a hundred officers, a little official "family"—and it really was like a little family. It consisted of his two young captain aides, his sergeant driver, his corporal orderly, and his brigadier general chief of staff.

The two aides were Captain Chester Hansen of Elizabeth, New Jersey, and Captain Lewis Bridge of Lodi, California. Both were twenty-five, both were graduated from college in 1939, Hansen from Syracuse University and Bridge from California Aggies. Their nicknames were Chet and Lew and that's what the general called them.

Both captains went through Officers' Training School at Fort Benning when General Bradley was commanding there and both came right out of the officers' school into his family. They had been with him for sixteen months and considered themselves the two most fortunate young officers in the American Army. They slept in cots under a tree about fifty yards from the general's truck, which also was parked under a tree; the general had an aversion to occupying buildings and usually kept a command post in tents out in the open.

Around headquarters the two aides were on call constantly, but for jeep traveling with the general they took alternate days. Both were bright, understanding, likable fellows who worshiped at the general's feet and did a good job representing him, in the same thoughtful manner he used.

The general's driver, Sergeant Alex Stout, was from Port Barre, Louisiana, below Baton Rouge. Although he was only twenty-three, he had been in the Army six years. He didn't, however, intend to make it a career. Sergeant Stout had been driving for General Bradley for two and a half years. He was so good that when Bradley reached North Africa he sent back to the States for him.

Stout took meticulous pride in the general's jeep. He had it fixed up with sponge-rubber cushions, and a built-in ration box under the back seat, and kept it neat as a pin.

General Bradley said having a good driver was important, for he relaxed while he was riding and he couldn't have a driver who annoyed him by going too slow or one who kept him tense by reckless driving. One night the general had a blackout driver who was so cautious and creepy he had to take the wheel himself and drive half the night.

Sergeant Stout was another devoted fan of General Bradley. "He does everything for you," the sergeant said. "I go to him with my headaches, go to him for advice, go to him for money. He treats me just like my own father does."

The general's orderly was Corporal Frank Cekada of Calumet, Michigan. Frank was the most recent one of the general's family, having been with him only since the previous March.

Frank said a colonel in Oran picked him for the job because he always kept himself looking neat and clean. He was driving a truck before he got the assignment. He had never been an orderly before but soon caught on. Frank's duties were, as he put it, "to keep the general happy." He cleaned the quarters, looked after the luggage while moving, and whenever he couldn't find Sicilian women to do the general's washing Frank did it himself.

Frank was twenty-four, and before the war was, of all things, a bartender. He said the general treated him like a personal friend and he hoped nothing would happen to the job.

General Bradley lived in an Army truck which had been fixed up like a tourist trailer. In the front end was a nice wide bed running crosswise of the truck, with a blanket bearing the initials of the United States Military Academy. Along one side of the truck was a desk with drawers under it. On the other side were a closet and washbasin. A field telephone in a leather case hung on the end of the desk. There was a big calendar on the wall and each day was marked off with an X. There was a bookrack with four or five volumes of military textbooks, one called *Our Enemy, Japan*, and a French grammar which the general never found time to study.

On the front wall over the bed were painted the dates of the campaigns in North Africa, with the beginning and ending dates, and the Sicily invasion date.

We conjectured what date the Sicilian campaign would end on, and oddly enough the general's date turned out to be a little farther off than mine. There were no pictures in the truck, no gadgets on the tables. The general had not sent home any souvenirs, and had acquired only two for himself. One was a German Luger from Tunisia and the other a lovely Sicilian dagger with the Fascist emblem on the handle. On the wall opposite the table was a big map of that area of Sicily. It probably was the most important piece of equipment in the place.

The general sat there alone at night studying the map for hours, thinking and planning moves for the morrow over the frightful country ahead. There alone before his map many of the most important decisions were made.

It isn't customary for anybody as high as a corps commander to get too close to the actual fighting, but General Bradley insisted on keeping his command post up close, sometimes distressingly close, behind the front lines.

Once he moved into a bivouac from which the artillery was still firing, with the result that we got a good working over by German dive bombers which were after our artillery.

One day we were riding in a jeep through hilly country and just as we passed a hidden big gun at the roadside it let off a blast right over our heads. It almost burst our eardrums and practically knocked us out of our seats. For days, the general enjoyed telling how we almost got our heads blown off by our own gun.

Another day we were eating lunch at the command post of the First Infantry Division, then commanded by Major General Terry Allen. It was in a big, old building close to the front and General Allen had a whole battery of his big guns right alongside the building. They blasted away throughout lunch, and the noise was deafening. They were so close that at every volley the building shook, the table and dishes jiggled, the glassless window frames rattled, and we could feel the blast sweep through the room.

After a little of this, General Bradley turned to General Allen and said, "Terry, could you arrange to have those guns shoot over the building instead of through it?"

General Bradley had a separate mess at his own command post, in a tent a few feet away from the regular mess. He had this separate mess because at almost every meal there were visiting American or British generals there for discussions and they needed privacy and quiet while they ate. His table seated seven, and at each meal General Bradley had one junior member of his staff in as a guest. On duty the general was always spoken to as "general" or "sir" by other officers. But I noticed that on informal occasions, such as at dinner, all the general officers called him "Brad."

Almost every day he visited the headquarters of each division that was in the lines. He said he could do the work by telephone, but by going in person he could talk things over with the whole division staff, and if they were planning something he thought was not good he could talk them around to seeing it his way, rather than just flatly ordering it done.

I stood with him one day on a high observation post looking ahead at a town where we were having tough going. The Germans simply wouldn't crack. (They did later, of course.) All our officers, including the general, were worried. He said, "We've put enough pressure on already to break this situation, but still they hang on, so we'll have to figure out some other way. Some commanders believe in the theory of direct attack, accepting a thirty per cent loss of men and getting to your objective quickly, but I've tried to figure a plan for this to save as many lives as possible."

I said to him, "I never could be a general. I couldn't stand up under the responsibility of making a decision that would take human lives."

"Well," he said, "you don't sleep any too well from it. But we're in it now, and we can't get out without some loss of life. I hate like the devil to order the bombing of a city, and yet it sometimes has to be done." In speaking of being bombed and of enduring the sadness of our own casualties, he said, "It's really harder on some of the newer officers than it is on me. For although I don't like it, after all I've spent thirty years preparing a frame of mind for accepting such a thing."

As a result of all my hobnobbing with the high and mighty, I took considerable kidding from the other correspondents. When I returned to our camp the other boys said, "Uh, huh—Pyle, the doughboy's friend. Wait till all the mothers of privates hear you've started consorting with generals."

"Sure," I said, "from now on a mere colonel will have to do a couple of somersaults to get me to look at him."

Every time I passed Hal Boyle, of the Associated Press, he said out of the corner of his mouth so I could hear it, "There goes that social-climbing columnist."

And Chris Cunningham, of the United Press, conjectured that if matters kept up, in a few weeks I would be sitting around with the correspondents making such remarks as, "Well, I told Omar that his battle plan wouldn't work, but he insisted on trying it out anyhow."

And another one said, "We passed you on the road today and there you were riding with the big general, and bareheaded as usual when you know it's against the rules."

So I said, "Well, when I went with the general, I told him I couldn't find my leggings, and didn't like to wear a steel helmet, and was it all right? He said, 'Okay.'"

And then Chris chimed in and said, "That's the way. There you go, taking advantage of the power of the press. You ought to be ashamed."

So we had a lot of fun about my sad tumble from a long kinship with the common soldier down to the depths of associating with a general. Still, it was fine while it lasted and if I had to associate with generals I know I picked a pretty good one.

But whenever I was caught talking with anyone above the rank of major the other correspondents would say, "You're losing the common touch, Ernie."

I tried to excuse myself by saying, "Well, democracy includes the big as well as the little, so I have to work in a general now and then just to keep the balance."

Before I left Naples I had dinner with Lieutenant General Mark Clark. I had seen General Clark at a distance, but had never met him.

The most remarkable thing about our meeting was a letter I had received a few hours before, as I was setting out for General Clark's main headquarters in the country. I started reading my mail just before going over to meet him. And I almost fell over at the return address on one envelope.

It was from Mrs. Mark Clark. Within five minutes after opening the letter I walked over and showed it to her husband.

The general said that if his wife was going to start writing me, he'd better have me court-martialed. I said, "Hell, if I were running this Army I'd have her court-martialed." We compromised by drinking a toast to her.

Our dinner was in a small, one-room, collapsible building, and the wind was howling and blowing so hard we thought the building would really collapse. There were three other correspondents at dinner, and four officers of the general's staff. We just ate and chatted and leaned back in our chairs as if we were at home. The general told us some things we didn't know before, and some things I couldn't print, but he didn't tell us when the war would end.

Running the Italian war was a headache of terrific proportions, and I for one do not think it was General Clark's fault that the campaign went slowly. I thought that before meeting him, so no one can accuse him of charming me into saying it.

I found General Clark congenial, and straightforward too. He impressed me as a thoroughly honest man.

There was another lieutenant general in the Naples area whom I knew well. He was Ira Eaker, head of all the Mediterranean Allied Air Forces. We were friends of more than fifteen years standing.

I used to go up and have dinner with him now and then. He had four or five guests every evening. He would flatter me by saying to his guests, "I knew Ernie when he wasn't anybody."

I would flatter myself by saying, "I knew the general when he was a captain."

I never left the general's headquarters without his giving me some kind of present, and now and then he gave me something to send to That Girl back in America. He was one of the most thoughtful men about doing little things for people.

General Eaker was nearly bald, liked to smoke cigars, and sucked frequently at a pipe. He drank almost not at all. He talked with the slow clarity of a Texan and his voice was so low it was hard to hear him sometimes. For recreation, he liked to play volleyball late in the afternoon.

His driver was a British RAF sergeant who had been with him for two years. One of the general's greatest traits was love and loyalty to his old friends of early years.

The Air Forces staff lived in trailers and tents in a lovely grove, and ate in one big mess hall where the general also ate with his guests.

General Eaker lived in a wooden Dallas hut, fixed up with a big fireplace and deep lounges and pictures so that it resembled a hunting lodge—very nice indeed.

Every morning at 9:30 the general went to his "war room;" and in a space of twenty minutes received a complete history of the war throughout the world for the previous twenty-four hours. In order to provide this comprehensive briefing, many of his staff had to get up at five o'clock to collect the reports.

General Eaker's job in Italy was a tremendous one. Before that he ran the great Eighth Air Force in England with distinction, but in Italy he had to face some brand-new problems. In England it was purely an air war. In Italy it was air and ground both. Further, his command was stretched over thousands of miles and included fliers of three nations.

Integrating the air war with the ground war was a formidable task. Doing that was General Eaker's biggest job right then, for he already knew about the other side of his job—which was to bomb the daylights out of Fortress Europe.

There in England, while I was waiting for the invasion, I went gallivantin' around with lieutenant generals again. This time it was Jimmy Doolittle, who was still the same magnificent guy with three stars on his shoulder that he had been with a captain's bars.

General Doolittle ran the American Eighth Air Force. It was a grim and stupendous job, but he managed to keep the famous Doolittle sense of humor about it.

After arriving in England from Italy, Doolittle diabolically started a couple of false rumors circulating about himself. One was that his nickname used to be "Curly." He would occasionally throw his almost bald head back as though tossing hair out of his eyes. His other claim was that he used to be six feet tall but had worried himself down to his small height in the previous five months.

Jimmy Doolittle had more gifts than any one man has a right to be blessed with. He had been one of America's greatest pilots for more than twenty-five years. He was bold and completely fearless. He had a great technical mind and a highly perfected education in engineering. And he was one of the most engaging human beings I ever ran across. He talked with animation, his voice was dear and keen, and it carried a sense of quick and right decision.

The last time I had seen General Doolittle was some sixteen months before, down at the desert airdrome of Biskra on the edge of the Sahara. That was when he was running our African bomber force that was plastering the Tunisian ports.

General Doolittle flew in one afternoon from the far forward airdrome of Youks les Bains. The night before, his entire crew, except for the copilot, had been killed in a German bombing at the Youks field. His crew had manned their plane's guns until it got too hot, and then made a run for an old bomb crater fifty yards away. It was one of those heartbreaking freaks of hard luck. A bomb hit the crater just as they reached it, and blew them all to pieces.

General Doolittle had written hundreds, perhaps thousands, of letters to people who had lost sons or husbands in his air forces. But one of the men in that crew was the hardest subject he ever had to write home about.

When he led the famous raid on Tokyo, Doolittle had a mechanic who had been with him a long time. Doolittle was a colonel then. The mechanic went on the Tokyo raid with him. The details of that raid have gradually seeped out. The planes were badly scattered. Some were shot down over Japanese territory. Others ran out of gas. Some of the crews bailed out. Others landed in Russia. The remainder splattered themselves all over the rice paddies of China.

That night Doolittle was lower than he had ever been before in his life. There wasn't any humor in the world for him. He sat with his head in his hands and thought, "You have balled up the biggest chance anybody could ever have. You have sure made a mess of this affair. You've lost most of your planes. The whole thing was a miserable failure. You'll spend the rest of your life in Leavenworth for this, and be lucky to get out of it that easy."

As he sat there his sergeant-mechanic came up and said, "Don't feel so bad about it, colonel."

Doolittle paid no attention. But the sergeant kept at him. "It's not as bad as it seems. Why, I'll bet you that within a year you'll have a Congressional Medal for it and be a brigadier general."

Doolittle just snorted.

"Well, I'll bet you do," the sergeant said. "And I'd like to ask one thing. As long as you're flying I'd like to be your mechanic."

That finally got inside Doolittle's gloom. Somebody had confidence in him. He began to buck up. "Son, as long as I've got an airplane you're its mechanic, even if we live to be a thousand years old."

Doolittle did get a Congressional Medal of Honor, and received not one star only but the three of a lieutenant general. And that sergeant, who dedicated himself to Colonel Doolittle that miserable night out there in China, was still General Doolittle's mechanic the night they landed at Youks les Bains in February of 1943. He was one of the men who ran for the shell hole that night.

General Doolittle had to write the letter to his parents.

One day in England Jimmy Doolittle noticed in the roster of officers at his staff headquarters the name of a Captain Doolittle.

The name is not an ordinary one, and he made a mental note that someday he would look the fellow up for a little chat. Not long after, his phone rang and the voice at the other end said, "This is Captain Doolittle."

"Oh, yes," said the general. "I had noticed your name and I meant to call you up sometime."

"I'd like to come in and see you," said the voice at the other end.

"Why, yes, do that," the general said. "I'm pretty busy these days, but I'll switch you to my aide and he'll make an appointment for you. Glad you called, Captain. I'll look forward to seeing you."

He was just ready to hang up when the voice came back plaintively over the phone: "But, Dad, this is me. Don't you recognize me? I've got a package for you from Mom."

The general exploded, "Well, why in hell didn't you say so in the first place!"

It was Captain Jimmy Doolittle, Jr., a B-26 pilot in the Ninth Air Force. I don't know if the general ever got around to seeing the other Captain Doolittle. If he did it probably turned out to be his brother or something.

General Doolittle has always been a great storyteller. He was the only man I've ever known who could tell stories all evening long and never tell one his audience had heard before. He could tell them in any dialect, from Swedish to Chinese.

Above all he loved to tell stories on himself. One day he had his plane set up for a flight to northern England. The weather turned awful, and one of his crew suggested that they cancel the trip. As Jimmy said, he would probably have canceled it himself, but when the junior officer suggested it he sort of had to go ahead and go.

They were hanging around the operations room, getting the latest reports. The crew thought General Doolittle had left the room. The junior officers were talking about the dangers of making the trip in such weather. They didn't think the general ought to take the chance. And then he overheard one of them: "I don't think the bastard gives a damn about the weather."

The poor officer almost died when he discovered that the general had heard him.

Other passengers said that throughout the flight this benighted fellow just sat staring at the floor and now and then shaking his head like a condemned man.

The general thought it was wonderful. No, he didn't do anything about it—he was flattered by the compliment.

"But only one thing saved him," Doolittle said. "If he had used the word 'old' in front of bastard I would've had him hanged."

He told another one: He was at a Flying Fortress base one afternoon when the planes were coming back. Many of them had been pretty badly shot up and had wounded men aboard.

The general walked up to a plane from which the crew had just got out. The upper part of the tail gun turret was shot away. General Doolittle said to the tail gunner, "Were you in there when it happened?"

The gunner, a little peevishly, replied, "Yes, sir."

As the general walked away the annoyed gunner turned to a fellow crew man and said in a loud voice, "Where in the hell did he think I was?—out buying a ham sandwich?"

A frightened junior officer, fearing the general might have overheard, said, "My God, man, don't you know who that was?"

"Sure I know," the tail gunner snapped, "and I don't give a damn. That was a stupid question."

With which Jimmy Doolittle, the least stupid of people, fully agreed when he told the story.

Another time the general went with his chief, Lieutenant General Spaatz, to visit a bomber station which had been having bad luck and heavy losses. They thought maybe their presence would pick the boys up a bit. So they visited around awhile. And when they got ready to leave, a veteran Fortress pilot walked up to them. "I know why you're out here," he said. "You think our morale is shot because we've been taking it on the nose. Well, I can tell you our morale is all right. There is only one thing that hurts our morale. And that's having three-star generals coming around to see what's the matter with it."

Jimmy told those stories wonderfully, with more zest and humor than I can put into them secondhand. As he said, the heartbreaks and tragedies of war sometimes push all gaiety down into the depths. But if a man can keep a sense of the ridiculous about himself he is all right. Jimmy Doolittle could.

TWENTY-THREE

THE FLYING WEDGE

I visited some of the boys who had been blasting out our invasion path on the Continent of Europe. For nearly a year they had been hammering at the wall of defense the Germans had thrown up. They were a squadron of B-26 Marauder bombers—representative of the mighty weight of the tactical bombers of the Ninth Air Force. I went to spend a few days with them because I wanted to get a taste of the preinvasion assault from the air standpoint before we got a mouthful of the invasion proper from the ground.

The way I happened to go to that certain squadron was one of those things. One night in London I was sitting at a table with some friends in a public house when two boys in uniform leaned over from the next table and asked if I wasn't So-and-so.

I said yes, whereupon we got to talking and then we got to be pals and eventually we adjourned from one place to another, as Damon Runyon would say, and kept on adjourning throughout the evening, and a good time was had by all.

Those boys were B-26 bombardiers, and in the course of the evening's events they asked if I wouldn't come and live with their squadron awhile. Being nothing if not accommodating, I said sure, why not? The two boys were Lieutenants Lindsey Greene, 2630 Chestnut Street, San Francisco, and Jack Arnold, 603 North 14th Street, East St. Louis, Illinois. Being redheaded, Lieutenant Arnold went by the name of "Red Dog."

Their airdrome was a lovely place. Everything around it was wonderfully green, as was all England then. The station was huge, and the personnel was scattered for a couple of miles, housed in steel Nissen huts and low concrete barracks. The living quarters were spread through an old grove of giant shade trees. I walked from one barracks to another under elms and chestnuts, big-trunked and wide-branched, and it gave me a feeling of beautiful peace and contentment. The huts and barracks were painted green and everything blended together.

The station was a permanent one, and comfortable. Our B-26 group had been at that field ever since arriving overseas nearly a year before.

Within cycling or hitchhiking distance were several English villages—the lovely kind you read about in books—and our fliers had come to know them intimately. They liked the people, and I'm sure the people liked them.

There was more of understanding and harmony between those fliers and the local people of their neighborhood than in any other outfit I had ever seen. If you don't believe it, listen to this—fifteen of the boys from just one squadron had married English girls.

The boys said it was the best squadron in England. Nine out of ten squadrons, or infantry companies, or quartermaster battalions, or whatever, will say the same thing about themselves. It is a good omen when they talk like that.

The station seemed to me to have about the finest spirit I had run onto in our Army. It was due, I think, largely to the fact that the whole organization had been made into a real team. The boys didn't especially hate the Germans, and they certainly didn't like war, yet they understood that the only way out of the war was to fight our way out, and they did it willingly and with spirit and all together.

The commander of the group was Colonel Wilson R. Wood of Chico, Texas. Five years before he had been an enlisted man. There, at twenty-five, he was a full colonel. He was a steady, human person and he had what it takes to blend thousands of men into a driving unit.

The job of the B-26s was severalfold. For one thing, they had to rid upper France and the Low Countries of German fighters as far as possible, to clear the way for our heavy bombers on their long trips into Germany. They had done this not so much by bombing airdromes, which can be immediately repaired, as by blasting the enemy's reserve supply of planes, engines and propellers.

Their second job was to disrupt the enemy's supply system. As

the invasion neared, much of their work was on railroad marshaling yards, and along with A-20s and fighter-bombers they had
succeeded to a point where British papers said Germany could
not maintain a western front by rail.

And, third, they constantly worked on the enemy's military
installations along the Channel coast. They felt that they had
done a good job. I told them if they hadn't I was going to be plenty
sore at them some fine day, because I might be in the vicinity and
if there was anything that made me sick at the stomach it was an
enemy military installation in good working order.

The B-26 is a bomber that is very fast and carries a two-ton bomb
load. In its early stages it had a bad name—it was a "hot" plane
which took great skill to fly and killed more people in training
than it did in combat.

But the B-26 lived down the bad name. The boys said they
wouldn't fly in anything else. They liked it because it could take
quick and violent evasive action when the flak was bothersome,
and because it could run pretty well from fighters.

Its record in England was excellent. Bombing accuracy had been
high and losses had been extremely low. And as for accidents—
the thing that cursed the plane in its early days—they had been
practically nonexistent.

The boys so convinced me of the B-26's invulnerability that I
took my courage in hand and went on a trip with them. They got
us up at two in the morning. Boy, it was cold getting out of our
cots and into our clothes. We had gone to bed about eleven, but
I hadn't got to sleep. All night long the sky above us was full of the
drone of planes—the RAF passing over on its nightly raids.

"Chief" Collins, the pilot, "Red Dog" Arnold, the bombardier,
and I were the only ones in our hut who had to get up. We jumped
into our clothes, grabbed towels and ran out to the washhouse
for a quick dash of cold water on our faces. The moon was brilliant and we needed no flashlights.

Red Dog gave me an extra pair of long drawers to put on. Chief
gave me his combat pants, as I had given mine away in Italy. I
also put on extra sweaters and a mackinaw.

Then we walked through the moonlight under the trees to the

mess hall. It was only 2:30 a.m., but we ate breakfast before the take-off. And we had two real fried eggs too. It was almost worth getting up for.

We drove out to the field in a jeep. Some of the boys rode their bicycles. There were a couple of hundred crew men. At the field we went into a big room, brightly lighted, and sat on benches for the briefing. The briefing lasted almost an hour. Everything was explained in detail—how we would take off, how we would rendezvous in the dark, where we would make the turn toward our target.

Then we went to the locker room and got our gear. Red Dog got me a pair of flying boots, a Mae West life preserver, a parachute and a set of earphones. We got into the jeep again and rode out to the plane. It was still half an hour before take-off time. The moon had gone out and it was very dark.

We stood around talking with the ground crew. Finally, ten minutes ahead of time we got into the plane. One of the boys boosted me up through a hatch in the bottom of the plane, for it was high, and with so many clothes I could hardly move.

For the take-off, I sat back in the radio compartment on some parachutes. Red Dog was the only one of the crew who put on his chute. He said I didn't need to wear mine.

We were running light, and it didn't take long to get off the ground. I had never been in a B-26 before. The engines seemed to make a terrific clatter. There were runway markers, and I could see them whiz past the window as we roared down the field. A flame about a foot long shot out of the exhausts and it worried me at first, but finally I decided that was the way it was supposed to be.

It's a ticklish business assembling scores of planes into formation at night. Here is how they do it:

We took off one at a time, about thirty seconds apart. Each plane flew straight ahead for four and a half minutes, climbing at a certain rate all the time. Then it turned right around and flew straight back for five minutes. Then it turned once again, heading in the original direction.

By this time we were up around four thousand feet. We had not seen any of the other planes.

The flight leader had said he would shoot flares from his plane frequently so the others could spot him if they got lost. Red Dog was half turned around, talking to me, when the first two flares split the sky ahead of us. He just caught them out of the corner of his eye, and he almost jumped out of his seat. He had forgotten about the flares and thought they were the running lights of the plane ahead of us and that we were about to collide.

"I haven't been so scared in months," he said.

The leader kept shooting flares, which flashed for a few moments and then went out. But we really didn't need them. For we were right on his tail, just where we should have been, and everybody else was in place too. It was a beautiful piece of precision grouping in the dark.

As we caught up to within half a mile or so we could finally see the running lights of other planes, and then the dark shapes of grouped planes ahead silhouetted against a faintly lightening sky. Finally we were in position, flying almost wing to wing, there in the English night.

At twelve thousand feet up daylight comes before it does on the ground. While we could now see each other plainly, things were still darkly indistinct in England, far below us.

Now and then a light would flash on the ground—some kind of marker beacon for us. We passed over some airdromes with their runway lights still on. Far in the distance we could see one lone white light—probably a window some early-rising farmer had forgotten to black out.

Red Dog, the bombardier, was sitting in the copilot's seat, since we weren't carrying a copilot. The boys got me a tin box to sit on right behind him so I could get a better view. The sunrise was red and beautiful, and he kept pointing and remarking about it. Chief Collins, the pilot, got out some cigarettes and we all lit up except Red Dog, who didn't smoke.

We climbed higher, and at a certain place the whole group of B-26s made a turn and headed for the target. This wasn't a mission over enemy territory, and there was no danger to it.

As we neared the target Red Dog crawled forward through a little opening into the nose, where the bombardier usually sits. The entire nose of a B-26 is Plexiglas, and a man can see straight down, up and all around. Arnold motioned for me to come up with him.

I squeezed into the tiny compartment. There was barely room

for the two of us. The motors made less noise up there. By now day-light had come and everything below was clear and spectacular.

I stayed in the nose until we were well on the way home, and then crawled back and sat in the copilot's seat. The sun came out, the air was smooth, and it was wonderful flying over England so early in the morning.

Down below, the country was green, moist and enchanting in the warmth of the early dawn. Early-morning trains left rigidly straight trails of white smoke for a mile behind them. Now and then we would see a military convoy, but mostly the highways were empty and lonesome-looking. The average man wasn't out of bed yet.

Somehow a person always feels good being up early in the morning, feels a little ahead of the rest of the world and a little egotistical about it.

We lost altitude gradually, and kept clearing our ears by opening our mouths. Gradually it got warmer and warmer. Chief talked now and then on the interphone to the rest of the crew. Other times I would notice his mouth working, and I think he must have been singing to himself. Two or three times he leaned over and remarked on what an unusually nice formation they were flying that morning.

Once Red Dog turned and yelled back through the little door, "Did you see that supply dump we just passed? Biggest damn thing I ever saw in my life."

Suddenly I remembered I had seen only four men in our crew, when I knew there were supposed to be five. I asked one of the gunners about it. He said, "Oh, Pruitt, he's the tail gunner. He's back there. He's probably sound asleep."

We came back over our home airdrome, peeled off one by one, and landed. Red Dog stayed up in the nose during the landing, so I stayed in the copilot's seat. Landing is about the most dangerous part of flying, yet it's the one sensation I love most, especially when riding up front.

Chief put the big plane down so easily we hardly knew when the wheels touched. I was shocked to learn later that we landed at the frightening speed of more than a hundred miles an hour.

We sat in the plane for a couple of minutes while Chief filled out some reports, and then opened the hatch in the floor and dropped out. I was the first one to hit the ground. The second man out looked at me, startled-like, and said, "Good Lord, I didn't know you were with us. I'm the tail gunner. I recognize you from your picture, but I didn't know you were along. I've been asleep most of the trip."

That was Sergeant Pruitt.

A jeep carried us back to the locker room where we had left our gear. Then we headed for the mess hall.

"We'll have another breakfast now," Chief said.

It was just 7:30. So for the second time in five hours we ate breakfast. Had real eggs again, too.

"It's a tough war," one of the boys laughed. But nobody is qualified to joke like that who hasn't been scores of times across the Channel coast, in that other world of fighters and flak. And those boys all had. It was good to be with them.

The B-26 squadron lived exceedingly well for wartime. They realized it, and were full of appreciation. I almost never heard an airman griping about things around there.

It was an old station, and well-established. Our men were comfortably housed and wonderfully fed. The officers had a club of their own, with a bar and a lounge room, and the Red Cross provided a big club right on the station for the enlisted men.

There were all kinds of outdoor games, such as baseball, badminton, volleyball, tennis, and even golf at a nearby town. One of the pilots came back from golfing and said, "I don't know what they charged me a greens fee for, I was never anywhere near the greens."

At first I lived with the younger officers of the squadron, then I moved over with the enlisted gunners, radiomen, and flight engineers. They lived only a little differently. And the line between officers and enlisted men among the combat crews was so fine that I was barely aware of any difference after a few days acquaintance with them.

First I'll try to tell you how the officers lived. I stayed in the hut of my friends Lieutenants Lindsey Greene and Jack Arnold. There was usually a spare cot in any hut, for there was almost always one man away on leave. Their barracks was a curved steel Nissen hut, with doors and windows at each end but none along the sides. The floor was bare concrete. Eight men lived in the hut. Three were pilots, the others bombardiers and naviga-tors. One was a captain, the others were lieutenants.

The boys slept on black steel cots with cheap mattresses. They had rough white sheets and Army blankets. They were all wear-ing summer underwear then, and they slept in it. When the last one went to bed he turned out the light and opened one door for ventilation. Of course until the lights were out the hut had to be blacked out.

Each cot had a bed lamp rigged over it, with a shade made from an empty fruit-juice can. The boys had a few bureaus and tables they bought or dug up from somewhere. On the tables were pic-tures of their girls and parents, and on the corrugated steel walls they had pasted pin-up girls from *Yank* and other magazines.

In the center of the hut was a rectangular stove made of two steel boxes welded together. They burned wood or coal in it, and it threw out terrific heat. In front of the stove was a settee big enough for three people, and behind the stove was a deep chair. Both settee and chair were made by nailing small tree limbs together. The boys did it themselves.

In the top of the hut, when the lights went out, I could see two holes with moonlight streaming through. Somebody shot his .45 one night, just out of exuberance. Somebody else then bet he could put a bullet right through that hole. He lost his bet, which accounted for the other hole.

The latrines and washbasins were in a separate building about fifty yards from the hut. The boys and their mechanics had built a small shower room out of packing boxes and rigged up a tank for heating water. They were proud of it, and they took plenty of baths.

All around my hut were similar ones, connected by concrete or cinder paths. The one next door was about the fanciest. Its name was Piccadilly Palace, and it had a pretty sign over the door saying so. In that hut the boys had built a real brick fireplace, with a mantel and everything.

In there the biggest poker game was usually going. A sign on the front of the hut said, "Poker Seats by Reservation Only." On the other side of the door was another sign saying, "Robin Hood Slept Here." They put that up when they first arrived because somebody told them the station was in Sherwood Forest. They found out later they were a long way from Sherwood Forest but they left the sign up anyhow.

It was a good station. The boys were warm, clean, well fed; their life was dangerous and not very romantic to them, and between missions they got homesick and sometimes bored. But even so they had a pretty good time with their live young spirits and they were grateful that they could live as well and have as much pleasure as they did have. For they knew that anything good in wartime is just that much velvet.

"My crew" of two officers and three enlisted men had been flying together as a team since before leaving America more than a year before. Every one of them was then far beyond his allotted number of combat missions. Every one of them was perfectly willing to work through another complete tour of missions if he could just go home for a month. I believe the same thing was true of almost everybody at that station. And it was a new experience for me, because most of the combat men I had been with before wanted to feel finished forever when they went home.

Every one of the crew had the Distinguished Flying Cross and the Air Medal, with clusters. They had had flak through their plane numerous times, but none of them had ever been hit. They expected it to be rough when the invasion started, but they were anxious to get it over with.

They had usually flown one mission a day over France, with occasionally two as the tempo of the spring bombings increased. But during the invasion they knew they would probably be flying three and sometimes four missions a day. They would be in the air before daylight and would get home from their last mission after dark. They would go for days and maybe weeks in a frenzied routine, eating hurriedly between missions, snatching a few hours of weary sleep at night, and being up and at it again hours before daylight to shuttle back and forth across the Channel. They and thousands of others like them.

Fighting purely an air war—as they had been doing up to then—was in some ways so routine that it was like running a big business.

Usually a B-26 crew man "worked" only about two hours a day. He returned to a life that was pretty close to a normal one. There was no ground war to confuse him or disturb him or even inspire him with its horror. His war was highly technical, highly organized, and in a way somewhat academic.

Because of this it was easy to get bored. An air crew man had lots of spare time on his hands. Neither the officers nor the enlisted fliers had any duties whatever other than flying. When not flying they either loafed around their own huts, writing letters or playing poker or just sitting in front of the fire talking, or else they took leave for a few hours and went to the nearby villages. They could go to dances or sit in the local pubs and talk.

And every two weeks they got two days' leave. That again was something new to us who had been in the Mediterranean. Down there fliers did get leave to go to rest camps, and even to town once in a while if there was a town, but there was nothing regular or automatic about it. Those boys in England got their two days' leave twice a month just like clockwork. They could do anything they wanted with it.

Most of them went to London. Others went to nearby cities where they had made acquaintances. They went to dances and night clubs and shows. They painted the town and blew off steam as any active man who lives dangerously must do now and then. They made friends among the British people, and they looked up those same friends on the next trip to town.

They did a thousand and one things on their leave, and it did them good. Also, it gradually created an understanding between the two peoples, a conviction that the other fellow was all right in his own peculiar way.

After a certain number of missions a crew was usually given two weeks' leave. Most of them spent it traveling. Our fliers often toured Scotland on those leaves. It was amazing the number of men who had been to Edinburgh and loved the place. They had visited Wales and North Ireland and the rugged southwestern coast, and they knew the Midlands and the little towns of England.

Those two-week leaves didn't substitute in the fliers' minds for a trip back to America. That was all they lived for. That was what they talked about most of the time.

A goal is what anyone overseas needs—a definite time limit to shoot for. Naturally it wasn't possible at that time to send many people home, and the fliers appreciated and accepted that fact. But once the invasion was made and the first period of furious intensity had passed, our veteran fliers hoped to start going home in greater numbers.

Lieutenant Chief Collins was what is known as a "hot pilot." He used to be a fighter pilot, and he handled his Marauder bomber as though it were a fighter. He was daring, and everybody called him a "character," but his crew had a fanatical faith in him.

Chief was addicted to violent evasive action when they were in flak, and the boys liked that because it made them harder to hit. When they finished their allotted number of missions—which used to give them an automatic trip to America, but didn't any more—Chief buzzed the home field in celebration of their achievement.

He got that old B-26 wound up in a steep glide, came booming down at the runway, leveled off a foot above the ground and went screaming across the field at 250 miles an hour—only a foot above the ground all the way. And at the same time he shot out all the red flares he had in the plane. They said it looked like a Christmas tree flying down the runway.

Chief used to be a clerk with the Aetna Life Insurance Company, back in his home town of Hartford, Connecticut. He was twenty-five and didn't know whether he would go back to the insurance job or not after the war. He said it depended on how much they offered him.

Lieutenant Red Dog Arnold was only twenty-two, although he seemed much older to me. He had enlisted in the Army almost four years before, when he was just out of high school. He was an infantryman for a year and a half before he finally went to bombardier school and got wings for his chest and bars for his shoulders.

He figured that as a bombardier he had killed thousands of Germans, and he thought it was an excellent profession. He said his finest bombing experience was when they missed the target one day and quite accidentally hit a barracks full of German troops and killed hundreds of them.

Red Dog was friendly and gay and yet he was a fundamentally

serious man who took the war to heart. The enlisted men of the crew said that he wasn't afraid of anything, and that the same was true of Chief Collins. They were a cool pair, yet both as hospitable and friendly as you could imagine.

The plane's engineer-gunner was Sergeant Eugene Gaines of 2233 Cambrone Street, New Orleans. He married a British girl, and they had a little apartment in a town eight miles from the field. Every evening Gaines rode his bicycle home, stayed till about midnight, then rode back to the airdrome. For he never knew when he might be routed out at 2 a.m. on an early mission, and he had to be on hand. It took him about forty-five minutes to ride the eight miles, and he had made the round trip nightly all winter, in the blackout and through indescribable storms. Such is the course of love.

Gaines was a quiet and sincere young man of twenty-four. He was a carpenter before the war, and he figured that would be a pretty good trade to stick to after the war. But if a depression should come he had an ace in the hole. He owned a farm at Pearl River, Louisiana, and he figured that with a farm in the background he could always be safe and independent.

Gaines wore a plain wedding ring on his left hand. I noticed that a lot of the married soldiers wore wedding rings.

In flight it was Gaines's job to watch the engine temperatures and pressures and to help with the gadgets during landings and take-offs. As soon as they reached the other side of the Channel he went back and took over the top turret gun. He had shot at a few planes but never knocked one down.

The radioman-gunner was Sergeant John Siebert of 66 Chappie Street, Charlestown, Massachusetts. He had learned to fly before the war, although he was only twenty-three. He had about eight hundred hours in the air as pilot. Yet because of one defective eye he couldn't get into cadet school. He had had two years at Massachusetts Institute of Technology, and he hoped to go back and finish after the war.

Siebert too was quiet and sincere. His closest escape was when his waist gun was shot right out of his hand. The thing suddenly just wasn't there. Yet he didn't get a scratch.

Sergeant Kermit Pruitt, the tail gunner, was an old cowboy from Arizona—looked like one, acted like one, talked like one. But he was no hillbilly in the head.

Pruitt was the talking kind. He talked and sang on the slightest provocation. He liked old cowboy songs. They said that every once in a while he would start singing some cowboy song over the interphone while they were actually on the bomb run, and the pilot would have to yell at him to shut up.

He liked to tell stories about cowpokes in Arizona. He told one day about an old cowboy who went to the city and registered at a hotel for the first time in his life. The clerk asked if he wanted a room with running water, and the cowboy yelled, "Hell, no! What do you think I am, a trout?"

Pruitt drove the rest of the crew crazy by shooting his tail gun at the most unexpected times. In more than fifty missions he had never yet seen an enemy plane to shoot at, so he would break the monotony by shooting at gun emplacements and flak ships two miles below. Those sudden blasts scared the wits out of the rest of the crew, and Pruitt then would catch a little brimstone over the interphone from the pilot.

But that didn't faze him, or impair his affection for his pilot. Pruitt said he just shopped around in the Army till he found a pilot that suited him. Back in America he "missed" a couple of trains to avoid going overseas with an outfit he didn't like. He said his hunch proved right, for his entire old crew in that outfit were killed on their first mission.

Finally he got a chance to go with the B-26s. Pilot Chief Collins was a wild man then, and nearly everybody was afraid to ride with him. But when Pruitt saw him handle a plane he said to himself, "There's my man." So he got on Chief's crew, and he stayed on it. He said he wouldn't think of flying with anybody else.

Pruitt was thin, not much bigger than me, and he usually wore coveralls which made him look even thinner. He went around poking his head out from hunched-up shoulders with a quizzical half grin on his face. He sure did enjoy living.

Pleasant Valley, Arizona, was Pruitt's home diggings. He was thirty, and married to a beautiful girl who was part French and 1/32 Indian. On Christmas Day, 1943, they were blessed with an heir. Pruitt had a pocketbookful of pictures of his wife and offspring, and he showed them every few minutes. If I went out of the room and came back five minutes later, he showed me the pictures again.

I was sleeping near Pruitt one night when the crews were awakened at 2 a.m. for an early mission. It was funny to see them come out of bed. Not a soul moved a muscle for about five minutes, and then they all suddenly came out as though shot from a gun.

Pruitt always started talking as soon as he was awake. On this particular morning he said, "When the war's over I'm gonna get me an Apache Indian to work for me. I'm gonna tell him to get me up at two o'clock in the morning, and when he comes in I'm gonna take my .45 and kill the s.o.b."

The three sergeants in my crew sort of took me under their wing and we ran around together for two or three days. One night they slicked all up, put on their dress uniforms with all their sergeants' stripes and their silver wings and all their ribbons, and we went to a nearby town to a singing concert. Then we went into the back room of the local pub and sat around a big round table with two battered old British women—very cheerful and pleasant—who were drinking beer. They giggled when Pruitt told stories of his escapades as a cowboy and of his trips to London on leave.

There were about twenty flying sergeants in the same barracks with my pals. They lived about the same as the officers, except that they were more crowded and they didn't have settees around their stove or shelves for their stuff. But they had the same pin-up girls, the same flying talk, the same poker game, and the same guys in bed getting some daytime shut-eye while bedlam went on around them.

I got to know all those flying sergeants and I couldn't help being struck by what a swell bunch they were. All of them were sort of diffident at first, but they opened up when I had known them for a little while and treated me like a king. They told me their troubles and their fears and their ambitions, and they wanted so much for me to have a good time while I was with them.

With those boys, as with nearly all the specialized groups of soldiers I have been with, their deep sincerity and their concern about their future were apparent. They couldn't put into words what they were fighting for, but they knew it had to be done and almost invariably they considered themselves fortunate to be living well and fighting the enemy from the air instead of on the ground. But home, and what would be their fate in the postwar world, was always in the back of their minds, and every one of them had some kind of plan laid.

Sergeant Phil Scheier was a radio-gunner. That is, he operated the radio of his B-26 bomber when it needed operating, and when over enemy territory he switched to one of the plane's machine guns.

It was hard to think of Sergeant Scheier as a tough gunner. In fact it was hard to think of him as an enlisted man. He was what you would call the "officer type"—he would have seemed more natural with a major's leaves on his shoulders than a sergeant's stripes on his arms. But he didn't feel that way about it. "I'm the only satisfied soldier in the Army," he said. "I've found a home in the Army. I like what I'm doing, and I wouldn't trade my job for any other in the Army."

Not that he intended to stay in after the war. He was twenty-eight, but he intended to go to college as soon as he got out of uniform. He had been a radio script writer for several years but he wanted to go to Columbia School of Journalism and learn how to be a big fascinating newspaperman like me.

Sergeant Scheier's home was at 1039 Forest Avenue, Richmond, Staten Island. Like the others he had a DFC and an Air Medal with clusters.

"When I won a Boy Scout medal once they got out the band and had a big celebration," he said. "But when you get the DFC you just sign a paper and a guy hands it to you as though it was nothing."

Later, when I mentioned that I would like to put that remark in my column, Sergeant Scheier laughed and said, "Oh, I just made that up. I never was a Boy Scout."

Sergeant Kenneth Brown, of Ellwood City, Pennsylvania, was one of two men in my barracks who had the Purple Heart. He had been hit in the back and arm by flak several months before. He was a good-natured guy, and he had the next war figured out.

He wasn't planning to go hide in a cave or on a desert island, as so many threatened to do. He thought he had a better way. He said the minute the war started he was going to get a sand table and start making humps and valleys and drawing lines in the sand. He figured that would automatically make him a general and then he'd be all right.

Sergeant Kenneth Hackett used to work at the Martin plant near Baltimore, making B-26 bombers. He was thirty-four, and he had supposed that if he ever got into the Army he would be put in some backwash job far removed from combat. "I sure never figured when I was helping to build these planes that someday I'd be flying over France in one of them as a radio-gunner," he said. But there he was, with half his allotted missions already run off.

Sergeant Hackett's home was at 721 Northwest 121st Street, North Miami. In fact his father was chief of police in that section. But the sergeant's wife and daughter were in Baltimore.

Hackett showed me a snapshot of his daughter Theda sitting on the fender of their automobile. He said she was twelve, and I thought he was kidding. She seemed so grown-up that I thought she must be his sweetheart instead of his daughter. But I was convinced when the other boys chimed in and said, "Tell him about the lipstick."

It seems Theda wrote her daddy that all the other girls her age were using rouge and lipstick and was it all right if she did too.

Well, it wasn't all right. Sergeant Hackett said maybe he was old-fashioned but he sent word back to Theda that if she started using lipstick at her age he'd skin her alive when he got back, or words to that effect. And he didn't take time to write it in a letter. He sent it by full-rate cablegram.

Sergeant Howard Hanson was acting first sergeant of the squadron. He was the guy who ran the show and routed people out of bed and handed out demerits and bawled people out. Also, he was an engineer-gunner. He had long since flown past his allotted number of combat missions, and he was still flying.

Sergeant Hanson was thirty-seven and therefore automatically known in the Army as Pappy. Any soldier over thirty-five is almost always called Pop or Pappy. Sergeant Hanson didn't care. He liked his work and had a job to do and wanted to get it done. "I know what I'm fighting for," he said. "Here's what." And he handed me a snapshot of his family—wife, girl, and boy. The girl was almost grown and the boy was in the uniform of a military school. Hanson's home was at 610 West 10th Street, Topeka, Kansas.

Pappy used to be in the motor freight business before the war. I suppose in a way you could say he was still in the motor freight business. Kind of ticklish freight, though.

Sergeant Walter Hassinger was from Hutchinson, Kansas. He was twenty-nine, and in a way the most remarkable man at the station. In the first place, he was a radio-gunner who had more missions under his belt than any other crew member there. In the second place, they said he had contributed more to satisfied living and general morale than anybody else.

Hassinger spent $400 of his own money creating a little private radio station and hooking it by loud-speakers into barracks all over the place. Finally his station was heard by seventeen hundred men. Over this station he rebroadcast news bulletins, repeated orders and instructions that came from headquarters, played phonograph records, and carried on a spasmodic monologue razzing the officers and just gabbing about everything from the abominable weather to the latest guy who had wrecked a Jeep.

Lieutenant Jim Gray was from Wichita Falls, Texas, and he looked like a Texan—wind-burned and unsmooth. He was far over his allotted missions, and if it hadn't been for the nearing invasion he would probably have been on his way home by then.

Like every other Texan in the Air Forces—and it seemed to be half Texans—he had to take a lot of razzing about his state. But he was proud of it, and always in plain sight under the end of his cot was a beautifully scrolled pair of cowboy boots.

Lieutenant Gray was a firm believer in the flak vest. A flak vest is a sort of coat of mail, made up of little squares of steel plating. It hangs from the shoulders and covers the chest and back.

One day a hunk of hot metal about the size of a walnut struck him right in the chest. He said it felt as if some giant had hit him with his fist. It bent tile steel plating but didn't go through. Without it he would have been a dead duck.

Sergeant Hanson, who flew with him, had taken the bent plate out and was keeping it as a souvenir. Lieutenant Gray kept the hunk of shrapnel itself, with a little tag on it.

The lieutenant was anxious to get home. Not so much because he was homesick but because, as he said, "I'd just like to fly in a little Texas weather for a change."

The English weather was the fliers' biggest complaint. It's dark and cloudy and rainy most of the time, and it changes like lightning. They said that sometimes they would start to take off and the other end of the runway would close in before they got there. How those mighty air fleets ever operated at all is a modern miracle.

In that area I ran into an old friend, another Texan—Major Royal Roussel, who used to be managing editor of the Houston *Press*. He was about my age, and like me he was starting to feel decrepit. He was in the planning section of the bomber command, and he said it was worse than running a newspaper. The pressure of detail and the responsibility of mapping those complex missions for the whole command sometimes had him mentally swamped. At such times he just got up and walked out for half a day. Sometimes he went flying, sometimes he played golf. "I played golf yesterday," he said, "and I'm sure I'm the only man in England who ever succeeded in playing eighteen holes without even once, not one single time, being on the fairway."

Every pilot and enlisted combat crew man had an English bicycle, for the distances are long on a big airdrome. The boys in my hut had to go about a mile to the flying line and about a quarter of a mile to eat. Breakfast ended at eight, and like human beings the world over those not flying got up just in time to run fast and beat the breakfast deadline by five seconds.

They ate at long wooden tables, sitting on benches. But they had white tablecloths, and soldiers to serve them. At supper they had to wear neckties and their dress blouses. The officers' club bar opened half an hour before supper and some of the boys went and had a couple of drinks before eating. As everywhere else in England, the whisky and gin were all gone a few minutes after the bar opened.

The enlisted crew men ate in a big room adjoining the officers' mess. They ate exactly the same food, but they ate it a little differently. They lined up and passed through a chow line. White enamel plates were furnished them, but each man had to bring his own knife, fork, spoon and canteen cup.

Their tables were not covered. When they finished they carried out their own dishes and emptied anything left over into a garbage pail, but they didn't have to wash their dishes. The enlisted men didn't have to dress up, even for supper.

Everybody thought that the food was exceptionally good. While i was there we had real eggs for breakfast, and for other meals such things as pork chops, hamburger steak, chocolate cake and ice cream.

Of course both these messes were for combat crews only. Ground personnel ate at a different mess. They didn't have quite as fine a choice as the fliers, but I guess nobody begrudged the little extra.

In various clubrooms on the airdrome, and even in some of the huts, there were numerous paintings of beautiful girls, colored maps of Europe, and so on. One hut had been wonderfully decorated by one of the occupants—Lieutenant C. V. Cripe, a bombardier from Elkhart, Indiana. He also painted insignia on planes.

This same hut had a tiny little garden walk leading up to the door. On a high post flanking the walk there hung white wooden boards with the name of each flier in the hut painted in green letters, and under the name rows of little green bombs representing the number of missions he had been on.

All the names were of officers except for the bottom board, which read "Pfc. Gin Fizz," and under it were painted five little puppy dogs marching along in a row with their tails up.

Pfc. Gin Fizz was a small white dog with a face like a gargoyle, and altogether the most ratty and repulsive-looking animal I had ever seen. But she produced beautiful pups practically like an assembly line, and the station was covered with her offspring.

Dogs were rampant. There was everything from fat fuzzy little puppies with eyes barely open to a gigantic Great Dane. This one magnificent beast was owned by Lieutenant Richard Lightfine, of Garden City, Long Island, and went by the name of Tray.

The gunner sergeants in my barracks had a breedless but lovable cur named Omer. He came by his name in a peculiar fashion.

Some months before the squadron made a raid on a town in France named St. Omer. One plane got shot up over the target, and back in England had to make a forced landing at a strange field. While waiting for the crippled plane to be patched up the crew acquired the puppy. In celebration of their return from the dead they named him Omer. Omer slept impartially on anybody's cot, and the boys brought him scraps from the mess hall. He didn't even know he was at war. Life was very good.

The station had a glee club too, and a very good one. They gave a concert for the people of the nearest village and I went along to hear it. The club had twenty-nine men in it, mostly ground men but some fliers. The director was Corporal Frank Parisi of 23 Whiteacre Court, Bedford, Ohio. He had taught music in junior high school there.

The club had already given ten concerts, and they were so good they were booked for three concerts weekly for six weeks ahead, and slated to sing in London. So you see that lots of things besides shooting and dying can go along with a war.

TWENTY-FOUR

STAND BY

In London's West End there was a mess for American officers. They believed it to be the biggest Army officers' mess in the world. Sometimes they served six thousand meals a day. Transients in town on leave did eat at this mess, but the bulk of the diners were officers from our headquarters staffs in London—and not all our staffs were in London, by any means.

The vast dining room seated nearly a thousand people, and sometimes it was emptied and refilled three times in one continuous operation during one meal. The mass of humanity flowed through so smoothly that the mess was affectionately known as "Willow Run."

This mess was in Grosvenor House, one of London's biggest hotels. The dining room was just one vast space, two stories high, with no pillars in it. A balcony ran around the room and on one side of the balcony was a bar.

Willow Run was operated cafeteria style, but diners ate at tables seating four, with white linen and everything very civilized. Every meal cost the same—fifty cents. Everybody said it was the best food in London. A flossy hotel would have charged $3 for less.

The food was about what we had back home—pork chops, mashed potatoes, sometimes fried chicken, once in a while steak. Enlisted men told me the Army messes in London were better than in America. All the food, except fresh vegetables, came from America.

Willow Run believed it had the lowest wastage rate in the world. They made a fetish of every man eating every bit he took. They weren't joking about it, either. Three officers worked up and down the dining room constantly. If they caught somebody leaving something on his tray they took his name and turned it in. He got a warning letter.

If a man's name was turned in twice he had to explain formally why he left food on his tray. And if it should happen a third time, well, the lieutenant showing me around shook his head gravely and said, "I hate to think what they'd do to him." It hadn't happened three times to anybody.

The general who commanded all those Army messes really meant business on food wastage. He went around every day or so and inspected the throwaways. If there had been complaints from the diners that a certain item wasn't good the general would say, "The hell it isn't," and pick up something from the discard and eat it himself.

I seldom ate in Willow Run, because they had me scared to death. I'm a small eater and I never could get the girls behind the counter to put little enough on my tray. The result was that I ate till I was bulging and sick.

Willow Run was operated by three Army officers, a WAC dietitian, seven sergeants and about five hundred British employees, men and women. The boss was Major Walter Stansbury, who was vice-president of the Hotel Goldsboro, in Goldsboro, North Carolina. He was assisted by Captain Francis Madden, who was executive assistant at the Kenmore in Boston for twelve years, and Lieutenant Truett Gore, assistant manager of the Hilton Hotel in El Paso. The dietitian was Lieutenant Ethel Boelts of Archer, Nebraska.

I didn't get to meet all the sergeants, but was shown around by three of them. They were executives over their special departments and had dozens of people working under them.

Sergeant Carroll Chipps ran the bakeshop, where they baked around ten thousand rolls and cakes per meal. He owned Rand's Restaurant & Bakeshop in Morgantown, West Virginia, and his wife ran it while he was overseas baking his head off.

Another sergeant had charge of preparing all the food for cooking. That man was Sergeant Joseph Julian of Perth Amboy, New Jersey. He had run restaurants all over America, following fairs and expositions. He had made seven World's Fairs. He used to run the Taproom in Dallas and the Silver Rail on Market Street in San Francisco. In his department I saw twenty women peeling potatoes in one room, a roomful of butchers cutting up meat, and three women who did nothing all day long but roll butter into little round balls between two wooden paddles, for serving on individual bread plates.

Sergeant Milburn Palmer had charge of the kitchen. He had been in the Army seven years, but he too was a restaurant man. He had the Chicken Shack at Sabinal, Texas, his home town.

One day Lieutenant Gore saw two captains, rough and dirty-looking, being refused service by the girl in charge of the cafeteria counter. He went over to investigate and found they had just flown in from Italy. He ordered them served despite their unconventional (for London) appearance.

When Willow Run first opened it broadcast phonograph music, but the project was soon abandoned. The decision may have had some connection with the time the British boy who flipped off the records went to sleep or something, and "The Star-Spangled Banner" got on the machine. Everybody in the huge dining room stood up while it played. They had no sooner sat down than it started again, and everybody hopped up and stood at attention. This up-and-down business went on till the record had played four times. Finally somebody got the boy back on the job and something else on the machine.

In addition to the huge Willow Run mess, there were a number of smaller messes and clubs, all run by the Army. The smaller they were the more exclusive they became. Prices mounted in the advance to the higher echelons, although the food was about the same. The highest mess I was allowed in charged $1.20 for dinner.

There was a junior officers' mess which served about six hundred meals a day. The officers could bring guests, and the food was served by British waitresses. A person was supposed to eat everything on the plate here too, but they were not quite so strict about it as at Willow Run.

Then there was the senior officers' club. It was about the same size and it was run on the same principle as the junior officers' club, only a man had to be a major or above to get in. We called this the "Old Men's Club." One could take female guests there, and almost everybody did. The place was full of big stomachs and bald heads and service stripes from the last war.

Next up in the scale was the mess for full colonels and generals only, and no guests were allowed. Needless to say, I never dined in that mess.

But we haven't reached the top yet. The zenith was called the "Yankee Doodle Club," and it was open only to major generals and up, either American or British. It was a joke around town about the poor brigadier generals' being so low and common they couldn't even get into the generals' mess.

We correspondents and many of the other civilian workers over there, such as Red Cross people and aircraft technical men, were allowed membership in both Willow Run and the junior officers' club. In addition, a handful of old correspondents like me were allowed in the senior officers' club. So all this gave us a fine choice in eating. Just for diversity we sort of rotated among the three, and probably four times a week we ate at British restaurants, just because we happened to be in a different part of town or were invited out.

The only one of the many messes that served breakfast was Willow Run. But after I became a city man I couldn't get myself up in time to make Willow Run. So I was caught in the English custom of eating breakfast in my room. And what a concoction the hotel breakfast was! It consisted of porridge, toast, some coalblack mushrooms, and a small slice of ham—which the British for some reason call bacon.

Being an old Army scrounger, I found a way out of this. The floor waitress, although daily appalled by the suggestion, did bring me each morning one big beautiful American Shredded Wheat biscuit. From the Army I got enough extra sugar to make it palatable. I also got from the Army a can of condensed milk to add to my small hotel portion.

Best of all, I had eggs. This enviable acquisition came because of the big heart of Correspondent Gordon Gammack of the Des Moines *Register and Tribune*. "Gamm" returned from Ireland one day bearing five dozen duck eggs, and he gave me two dozen of them. A duck egg, my friends, is a big egg. One of them gives you all you can hold for breakfast.

So, all in all, we expatriates bleeding out the war in London did manage to suffer along and gain a little weight now and then.

Every one of the messes had a bar. At peak hours it was hard to get within yelling distance of the bar at Willow Run.

Liquor was very, very short in London. Each mess had a definite ration each day, and it wasn't much. Every person who went to the bar was on his honor not to drink more than two drinks. In addition to that, the bar had a rationing system of its own. It would sell whisky and gin for about fifteen minutes and then hang up the "all out" sign, leaving only beer and wine. The dense crowd at the bar gradually drifted away, and a new crowd formed. Then they started selling whisky and gin again for about fifteen minutes.

It seemed to work out to everybody's satisfaction. There was only one drawback. The shock of drinking good liquor after a winter of poisonous bootleg cognac was almost too much for soldiers up from Italy.

I went out one day with a tank-destroyer unit. They had been over there long enough to form an opinion of English weather, but no one could print it.

Not for ages had I been with a combat outfit which had not yet been in battle. There is less difference than you might think. The really noticeable difference was their eagerness to get a crack at the "Jerries." After they had a chance to crack at them for a few months, I knew they would be just as eager to let somebody else have a turn at it.

Aside from that, they talked and acted about the same as men who had been in combat. They cussed a lot, razzed each other about their home states, complained about the food, and talked about how they wished they were home, just as though they had been away for years.

This unit had been training together for nearly two years. They didn't yet realize what a terrific advantage that gave them, but they would as soon as they went into battle.

They were an impressive team of firepower composed of dozens of little teams, each one centering around one gun. They had trained so long that they functioned almost automatically. They all knew every man on the team; they knew his temperament and how he would react. They had faith in each other. Only those who have fought realize what confidence that produces.

A typical gun commander was Sergeant Dick Showalter, 53 South Gharker Street, Muncie, Indiana. While I was talking with a group of soldiers he came up and introduced himself and said, "I married a girl from your home town."

Now, things like that are always happening to me, except that nine times out of ten the people are mixed up. People will come up and say, "Don't you remember me? I used to deliver papers at your house." And it will turn out they lived in a town I had never heard of, and were thinking of two other fellows.

When Sergeant Showalter said he had married a girl from my home town I slightly arched my handsome eyebrows and said, "Yes?"

"Yes," he said. "I married Edna Kuhns."

"Why," I said, "I was raised with the Kuhns kids. They lived just across the fence from our farm. I've known them all my life."

"That's what I said," said Sergeant Showalter. And then we left the crowd and sat on the grass, leaning against a rock, and talked about Dana, Indiana, and Muncie and things.

Sergeant Showalter worked in factories before the war. He had been commander of his gun for more than a year and a half. He was a small fellow, quiet, serious, conscientious, and extremely proud of his crew and of the way they took their responsibility.

One of Showalter's best buddies in his crew was Pfc. Bob Cartwright, of Daytona Beach, Florida. He was a cannoneer—a small, reddish, good-natured fellow.

When we met I said, "What's that you've got in your mouth?"

He grinned and said, "Chawin' tobacco." Which was just what I had thought it was.

He managed to keep well-stocked by trading stuff with boys who didn't chew. Bob was very young. He didn't know much when he came into the Army, but Showalter said he had turned out to be one of the best.

Like all artillerymen, the boys were very proud of their guns. They had had fine training and lots of practice on moving targets. They said that on direct fire they could hit a moving tank at about a mile, and that they almost never missed. They were anxious to get at it and get it over with and go back home.

They knew it wouldn't be easy on the Continent. They were living rough then but they knew it would be lots rougher before long. As they said, the chow was bad compared to what it was in America, but they didn't complain too much because they knew it was going to get worse.

They knew they would be on C and K rations, and they had had experience with them on maneuvers. But when I spoke of our best ration—the 10-in-1 field ration—they had never heard of it.

They had been working hard since they hit England. They made long night trips, did a lot of practice firing and sometimes they had to work as late as ten o'clock at night.

When I saw them they were making preparations for the great day. It takes a lot of work to get equipment ready for an amphibious move. They had worked so hard they hadn't had time to get bored. There were some American outfits that had been in England for two years without action, and there were Canadians who had been marching up and down for four years. How men like that kept from going nuts is beyond me.

The commander of the tank-destroyer battalion was Lieutenant Colonel Joseph Deeley, of Sheboygan Falls, Wisconsin. He used to run a wool-carding mill there. I liked his attitude toward things.

When I first showed up he was perfectly courteous but he made plenty sure I had proper credentials and what not. As he said, they had had security preached into them back home, and the times were critical, and he wasn't taking any chances.

But once he had assured himself I was all right he called in his sergeants and told them to go around and tell their men they were perfectly free to show me any and all equipment they had and talk to me as freely as they liked.

As I told him later, he need not have bothered. For those boys, approaching war for the first time, pumped me so thoroughly on what war was like that I hardly got a chance to ask any questions of them.

One company commander, Captain Charles Harding, of Olmsted Falls, near Cleveland, had just had a letter from home telling him to keep an eye out for me. He figured that in a war this big our paths would never cross, but they did.

Another Ohioan came up and introduced himself. This was Pfc. James Francis McClory of 6711 Guthrie Street, Cleveland. McClory, who used to be a prize fighter, was what is aptly known in the battalion as a "character." He was crazy about apes. There was an almost-human ape at the zoo in a nearby city and McClory went to see the beast every time he could get a pass. He called him "Alfred the Ape," and said he sure wished he could take him back to Cleveland.

McClory used to work for the Cleveland Welding Company, which made bicycles. When I asked him what he did he said, "Oh, I was just a hod knocker."

He could take lots of kidding. When I went to write down his name I put "Sergeant" in front of it, and he said, "No, no. I'd never get to be a sergeant if the war lasted fifty years."

So I said, "Well, 'corporal' then." But he said, "No, I ain't even got sense enough to be a corporal."

So I said, "Well, we simply can't have you a private. What would the McClorys of the world think with you only a private?"

We compromised and made him a pfc.

McClory was one of those guys who are good for the morale of an outfit. He was always doing or saying something funny. And he was a good soldier, one of the fanatically loyal kind. He had a great affection for his company commander, Captain John Jay Kennedy of 15 Fawndale Road, Roslindale, Massachusetts. Once when some gasoline caught fire McClory threw himself on the captain and knocked him out of the way, saving him from serious injury. Another time, when Captain Kennedy's mother was very ill, McClory took the last money he had and telegraphed home to his own parish to have a Mass said for the captain's mother.

A number of men in the battalion told me later that McClory was the kind of man they would like to have with them when the going got tough.

There in England the battalion was living in pyramidal tents, sleeping on cots. But when they started across they would take only pup tents and two blankets apiece and they would be sleeping on the ground. Their barracks bags with extra clothes and stuff might catch up with them sometime in the dim future.

I had thought that all troops recently arrived from the States would be wearing the new infantry boot we had been issuing in Italy. I had heard that the old cumbersome and unsatisfactory legging was in limbo. But these boys all wore leggings and had never heard of the new boot.

English dogs had begun to attach themselves to the tank-destroyer boys, as dogs do to any and all camps of soldiers. The boys hadn't actually adopted any of them as individual pets, because they couldn't take them along to the Continent. They were, however, pet-minded. They said that back in the States they had a number of pigs for pets. In that case you could have your pet and eat it too.

One day at the hotel, there was a knock at my door and two young lieutenants with silver wings and bright medals on their chests walked in. They were in town on leave and had decided to pay a social call.

They were the pilot and navigator of a Flying Fortress. They came to see me because I had known the pilot's mother in San Francisco. She was Mrs. Mary White, and she used to manage the coffee shop at the Hotel Californian, which was my home whenever I was in San Francisco.

Her son, Lieutenant Bill White, was a likable young fellow whose blond hair stuck up high from his forehead and whose eyes crinkled when he smiled. His navigator was Lieutenant John D. Bowser of 19 Antonio Street, Johnstown, Pennsylvania. They had been overseas, whacking at the Germans, since February.

The boys were in the midst of an eight-day leave, given them as a sort of reward for having survived a ducking in the cold North Sea. They had had to "ditch," as the expression goes, and after a crew ditches it always gets a leave of absence.

They had a close call when they ditched. They had been to Berlin—their second mission over the big city. The flak was pretty bad. On the way back Bill White looked out and saw a big hole in the right wing. It didn't seem to be causing any trouble. Pretty soon he glanced in the other direction and saw a big hole in his left wing.

At first he thought he was crazy and had forgotten which wing he'd seen the hole in. His head went back and forth as though watching a tennis match. Actually, there were identical holes in the two wings.

But that wasn't what put them in the drink. Apparently the ignition system had been hit, for every now and then all four motors would stop for about five seconds at a time and then pick up again.

Finally the engines started going clear out, one by one. They saw that they couldn't make the coast of England. Lieutenant White had everybody get in "ditching position." The radioman sent his distress signal. They hit the water. The plane broke in two. And yet not a man was scratched or bruised.

When they hit, salt water rushed up over the windshield in gigantic waves. The plane stopped moving and Bill looked up. All he could see was water. He thought they had dived straight into the sea and were going on down head first.

"I thought this was it," he said. "I was so convinced I was going to drown that I almost just sat there and didn't even try to get out."

But actually they came piling out of that plane like rockets. They said that in training they had been taught that a man would be all right if he could get out in thirty seconds. They were all out in ten seconds.

The plane sank forty seconds after hitting the water. They were twenty-five miles from shore. The men clung to their rubber dinghies, and in less than an hour a rescue boat came alongside and took them aboard.

Ever since, they had had a wonderful time talking about their experience. They called themselves sailors. Before the ditching, the crew used to do a lot of joking about "White's little air force goes to war." Then they changed it to "White's little navy goes to sea."

Whenever a flier was fished out of the North Sea or the Channel, the RAF rescuers gave him a little felt insigne about an inch high, in the form of a half wing—showing a fish skipping over the water. This was a membership badge in the "Goldfish Club." It was sewn under the lapel, and displayed when occasion demanded. It wasn't worn outwardly because, I presume, we didn't want German agents to know how many guys had been fished out of the water.

The boys had another memento of their salt-water bath. They all had Short Snorter bills. But they had started a new series of signatures on bills which they called "Dinghy Snorters." Only fliers who had had to ditch were allowed to sign those bills. They flattered me by asking me to sign, and said mine would be the only non-Goldfish signature permitted on their bills.

All ten of the ditched crew had wrist watches. Two watches, apparently waterproof, were still running. The eight others were corroded by salt water and had stopped.

Lieutenant White still wore his, even though it didn't run. But while he ruined his watch he did save $40. He had ordered a $40 pair of fancy boots made, which he had expected to be ready the day before the fateful mission. They weren't. He was pretty sore about it at the time but later he was glad, for he would have had them on.

These two boys really enjoyed their jobs, I believe. They saw the funny side of life, and they were able to take things as they came. But still, of course, they wanted to go home.

England was certainly the crossroads of this warring world. Never a day passed that I didn't run onto half a dozen people I had known in Albuquerque, Washington, Tunisia, Ireland, the Belgian Congo or Cairo. A funny thing is that nine times out of ten these people had picked up weight since I last saw them. Time and time again I met officers and men who had been lean and thin and hard when they were in the thick of the Tunisia campaign. There in England their faces were filled out and they had gained anywhere from ten to forty pounds.

This was mainly because, I suppose, their lives hadn't been physically active, as in the field. For months they had been planning the invasion, working hard at desks, eating regularly and well, and getting little exercise. They all hated the physical inactivity of that long planning stage, and said they would be glad in a way when they could get outdoors again to hard living.

I knew that when our trails crossed again their paunches would be gone, their faces would be thin and brown and dirty, and they would look hard and alive and like the friends I used to know. They would look better. It's a silly world.

In roaming around the country one day I ran into Lieutenant Colonel William Profitt, whom I used to see occasionally in Africa and Sicily. His old outfit was the first hospital unit ashore in the African invasion, landing at dawn on D-day. They were so proud of that record that they would tear anyone's eyes out at the slightest intimation that they were being confused with the second unit to land.

This was the hospital where my friend Lieutenant Mary Ann Sullivan of Boston served. She finally wound up as chief nurse of the unit. But when I dropped in to say hello I discovered that Lieutenant Sullivan had gone back to America a couple of months before.

She well deserved to go, too. She had been overseas nearly three years, having shipped originally with the Harvard unit. She had a ship sunk under her at sea, and was shot at innumerable times. She lived like a beast of the field for nearly a year, and she bore the great burden of directing a staff of nurses and supplying both medical care and cheerful understanding to thousands of wounded men.

Colonel Profitt and I sat and chatted away in easy chairs in front of his cozy fireplace—sharp contrast to our other evenings on the windy plains of Tunisia. He told me about a storm they had just after I left them in Sicily. They were bivouacked on the edge of a cliff by the sea, and the wind blew so hard it blew all their tents over the cliff just at daylight one morning. Everybody turned to with such a mighty effort that in two hours and a quarter they had every one of their 450 patients dry and under cover again.

The unit was very sentimental about the number thirteen. They had been mixed up with thirteen so many times they wouldn't trade it for a dozen black cats or four-leafed clovers. They always sailed in convoys of thirteen ships. Colonel Profitt said he believed they would refuse to go if they were ever assigned to a convoy of fourteen ships.

Most of the original gang of nurses were still with the hospital after a solid year of war and nearly two years overseas.

Everywhere I went around our camps and marshaling areas, everything was being waterproofed for the invasion. That was perfectly natural, of course, since land vehicles won't run through water onto beaches unless all the vital mechanisms are covered up.

But the thing that surprised me was that so much of the equipment had been prepared in wooden boxes. It sort of gave me an idea. I stayed up for a couple of nights with a hammer and saw, preparing a large box for myself, with horseshoes tacked all over it.

FRANCE

JUNE–SEPTEMBER, 1944

TWENTY-FIVE

THE WHISTLE BLOWS

The Army occasionally got the correspondents together for instructions on preparing for the second front. Sometimes we had fun at these meetings.

For example, one day an officer got up and said the time had come for us to make our powers of attorney and prepare our wills, if we hadn't done so already. Everybody in the room laughed—you know, one of those cackly, mirthless laughs of a man who is a little sick at his stomach.

And then the officer explained that we could take with us only what we could carry on our backs; the rest of our stuff would be turned over to the Army and would probably catch up with us a couple of weeks after we reached the other side.

Whereupon one correspondent, newly arrived, asked, "Should we carry our steel helmets and gas masks or put them in the luggage to be forwarded later?"

The poor fellow was almost laughed out of the room. Does one send for the fire department two weeks after the house has burned down?

When we secretly left London a few days later, more than 450 American correspondents were gathered in Britain for that moment pending in history. But only 28 of those 450 were to take part in what was termed the assault phase. I was one of the 28. Some of the rest were to go over later, some would cover other angles, some would never go at all.

We assault correspondents had been under military jurisdiction for a month or more. We had had complete freedom in London, but occasionally the Army would suddenly order batches of us to take trips around England. Also, during those last few weeks we were called frequently for mass conferences and we were briefed by several commanding generals. We had completed all our field equipment, got our inoculations up to date, finished our official accrediting to Supreme Allied Headquarters, and even sent off our bedrolls ten days before the final call.

Of the twenty-eight correspondents in the Assault Group about two-thirds had already seen action in various war theaters. The old-timers sort of gravitated together, people such as Bill Stoneman, Don Whitehead, Jack Thompson, Clark Lee, Tex O'Reilly and myself.

We speculated on when we would get the final call, conjectured on what assignments we would draw, for few of us knew what unit we would go with. And in more pensive moments we also conjectured on our chances of coming through alive.

We felt our chances were not very good. And we were not happy about it. Men like Don Whitehead and Clark Lee, who had been through the mill so long and so boldly, began to get nerves. Frankly I was the worst of the lot, and continued to be.

I began having terrible periods of depression and often would dream hideous dreams. All the time fear lay blackly deep upon our consciousness. It bore down on our hearts like an all-consuming weight. People would talk to us and we wouldn't hear what they were saying.

The Army said they would try to give us twenty-four hours' notice of departure. Actually the call came at nine o'clock one morning and we were ordered to be at a certain place with full field kit at 10:30 a.m. We threw our stuff together. Some of us went away and left hotel rooms still running up bills. Many had dates that night but did not dare to telephone and call them off.

As we arrived one by one at the appointed place we looked both knowingly and sheepishly at each other. The Army continued to tell us that it was just another exercise, but we knew inside ourselves that this was it.

Bill Stoneman, who had been wounded once, never showed the slightest concern. Whether he felt any concern or not I could not tell. Bill had a humorous, sardonic manner. While we were waiting for the departure into the unknown, he took out a pencil and notebook as though starting to interview me. "Tell me, Mr. Pyle, how does it feel to be an assault correspondent?"

Being a man of few words, I said, "It feels awful."

When everybody was ready our luggage went into a truck and we went into jeeps. The first night we spent together at an assembly area, an Army tent camp. There we drew our final battle kit—such things as clothing impregnated against gas attack, a shovel to dig foxholes, seasickness capsules, a carton of cigarettes, a medical kit, and rations. We also drew three blankets just for the night, since our bedrolls had gone on ahead.

The weather was cold and three blankets were not enough. I hardly slept at all. When we awakened early the next morning, Jack Thompson said, "That's the coldest night I have ever spent."

Don Whitehead said, "It's just as miserable as it always was."

You see, we had all been living comfortably in hotels or apartments for the last few weeks. We had got a little soft, and there we were starting back to the old horrible life we had known for so long—sleeping on the ground, only cold water, rations, foxholes, and dirt. We were off to war again.

Shortly after breakfast the Army gave us assault correspondents a semifinal set of instructions and sent us off in jeeps in separate groups, each group to be divided up later until we were all separated.

We still weren't given any details of the coming invasion. We still didn't know where we were to go aboard ship, or what unit we would be with. As each batch left, the oldsters among us would shake hands. And because we weren't feeling very brilliant, almost our only words to each other were "Take it easy."

The following morning, at another camp, I was called at four o'clock. All around me officers were cussing and getting up. This was the headquarters of a certain outfit, and they were moving out in a motor convoy at dawn. For months those officers had been living a civilized existence, with good beds, good food, dress-up uniforms, polished desks, and a normal social life. But now once again they were in battle clothes. They wore steel helmets and combat boots, and many carried packs on their backs.

They joked in the sleepy predawn darkness. One said to another, "What are you dressed up for, a masquerade?"

Everybody was overloaded with gear. One officer said, "The Germans will have to come to us. We can never get to them with all this load."

The most-repeated question was: "Is your trip necessary?"

Those men had spent months helping to plan a gigantic invasion. They were relieved to finish the weary routine of paper work at last, and glad to start putting their plans into action. If they had any personal concern about themselves they didn't show it.

I rode with the convoy commander, who was an old friend. We were in an open jeep. It was just starting to get daylight when we pulled out. And just as we left rain began to fall—that dismal, cold, cruel rain of which England is so capable. It had rained like that a year and a half before when we left for Africa.

We drove all day. Motorcycles nursed each of our three sections along. We halted every two hours for a stretch. At noon we opened K rations. It was bitter cold.

Enlisted men had brought along a wire-haired terrier which belonged to one of the sergeants. It wouldn't have been an invasion without a few dogs along. At the rest halts the terrier would get out in the fields to play and chase stones, with never any worry. It seemed wonderful to be a dog.

The English roads had been almost wholly cleared of normal traffic. British civil and military police were at every crossing. As we neared the embarkation point people along the roads stood at their doors and windows and smiled bon voyage to us. Happy children gave us the American O.K. sign—thumb and forefinger in a circle. One boy smilingly pointed a stick at us like a gun, and one of the soldiers pointed his rifle back and asked us with a grin, "Shall I let him have it?"

One little girl, thinking the Lord knows what, made a nasty face at us.

Along toward evening we reached our ship. It was an LST, and it was already nearly loaded with trucks and armored cars and soldiers. Its ramp was down in the water, several yards from shore, and being an old campaigner I just waded aboard. But the officer behind me yelled up at the deck, "Hey, tell the captain to move the ship up closer."

So they waited a few minutes, and the ramp was eased up, onto dry ground, and our whole convoy walked aboard. I was the only one in the crowd to get his feet wet.

We had hardly got aboard when the lines were cast off and we pulled out. That evening the colonel commanding the troops on our ship gave me the whole invasion plan in detail—the secret the whole world had waited years to hear. Once a man had heard it he became permanently a part of it. Then he was committed. It was too late to back out, even if his heart failed him.

I asked a good many questions. I realized my voice was shaking when I spoke but I couldn't help it. Yes, it would be tough, the colonel admitted. Our own part would be precarious. He hoped to go in with as few casualties as possible, but there would be casualties.

From a vague anticipatory dread the invasion now turned into a horrible reality to me. In a matter of hours the holocaust of our own planning would swirl over us. No man could guarantee his own fate. It was almost too much for me. A feeling of utter desperation obsessed me throughout the night. It was nearly 4 a.m. before I got to sleep, and then it was a sleep harassed and torn by an awful knowledge.

We felt good about our position in the convoy, for we were about a third of the way back in the column. That meant we had ships on all sides of us and we wouldn't be on the outside in case of attack.

Our convoy, comprising what is known as a "force," was made up entirely of LSTs. Each of us towed a big steel pontoon section, these to be used as barges and docks in the shallow waters along the beach. And behind each pontoon we towed a smaller pontoon with two huge outboard motors on it—a thing called a "rhino."

Several ships broke cables and lost their pontoons during the journey. Special Coast Guard tugs were assigned to pick them up. We lost our own rhino on the last night out, and I don't know whether it was picked up or not.

We were told that if the ship sank our chances of being picked up would be slight. The water was so cold we would probably lose consciousness in fifteen minutes, and die within four hours. So we all conjectured about the possibility of clambering out onto the trailing pontoon if the ship went down. That brought up the question whether the pontoon would be cut loose if the ship sank, or be dragged under the water by its huge steel cable.

To show how rumors get around, one soldier said he had learned that the ship had a sailor standing aft with an ax for the sole purpose of hacking the cable off if the ship were torpedoed. Later I asked the captain, and he said there wasn't any such man at all.

Funny little things happen in a convoy. The steering gear on one ship broke in midafternoon and the ship came slowly careening around like a skidding automobile, until it was crosswise of the convoy and the ships behind had to veer around it.

We were lined up in straight columns, extending as far ahead and behind as we could see. On both sides of us ran destroyers and corvettes for escort, but as I've said before it never seems to the participants in a convoy that the escort is adequate.

Our only scare came late in the night before we hit the invasion area. I was in my bunk, and the colonel with whom I was rooming came down from the bridge.

"How are things going?" I asked.

"Terrible," he said. "Another convoy came along and pushed us out of the swept channel. One engine has broken clear down, and the other can only run at third speed. The wind and tide are drifting us toward the Belgian coast. We're steering straight west but barely holding our direction."

I thought how ironic it would be to wind up this war by drifting alone onto a hostile beach and spending the rest of the war in a prison camp—if we didn't hit a mine first. But unfortunately I was too sleepy to worry about it. When I awakened at dawn we had both engines going and were back in line again in the swept channel. Moral: Always be too sleepy to give a damn.

The night before sailing we were instructed to take two anti-seasickness capsules before breakfast the next day, and follow them up with one every four hours throughout the voyage. The capsules had been issued to us with our battle kits.

Well, we took the first two and they almost killed us. The capsules had a strong sleeping powder in them, and by noon all the Army personnel aboard was in a drugged stupor. Fortunately the Navy, being proud, didn't take any, so somebody was left to run the ship. The capsules not only put us to sleep but they constricted our throats, made our mouths bone-dry and dilated the pupils of our eyes until we could hardly see.

When we recovered from this insidious jag, along toward evening, we all threw our seasickness medicine away, and after that we felt fine. Although the Channel crossing was rough, I didn't hear of a single man aboard our ship who got sick.

My devastating sense of fear and depression disappeared when we approached the beachhead. There was the old familiar crack and roar of big guns all around us, and the shore was a great brown haze of smoke and dust, and we knew that bombers would be over us that night. Yet all the haunting premonition, the soul-consuming dread, was gone. The war was prosaic to me again. And I believe that was true of everyone aboard, even those who had never been in combat before.

All of us had dreaded the trip, for we had expected attacks from U-boats, E-boats, and at nighttime from aircraft. Yet nothing whatever happened.

We were at sea for a much longer time than it would ordinarily take to make a bee-line journey from England to France. As we came down, the English Channel was crammed with forces going both ways. Minesweepers had swept wide channels for us all the way. Each channel was miles wide, and marked with buoys.

Surely we saw there before us more ships than any human being had ever seen before at one glance. And going north were other vast convoys, some composed of fast liners speeding back to England for new loads of troops and equipment.

As far as you could see in every direction the ocean was infested with ships. There must have been every type of oceangoing vessel in the world. I even thought I saw a paddlewheel steamer in the distance, but that was probably an illusion.

There were battleships and all other kinds of warships clear down to patrol boats. There were great fleets of Liberty ships. There were fleets of luxury liners turned into troop transports, and fleets of big landing craft and tank carriers and tankers. And in and out through it all were nondescript ships—converted yachts, river boats, tugs, and barges.

The best way I can describe that vast armada and the frantic urgency of the traffic is to suggest that you visualize New York Harbor on its busiest day of the year and then just enlarge that scene until it takes in all the ocean the human eye can reach, clear around the horizon. And over the horizon, imagine dozens of times that many.

Everything was magnificently organized, and every ship, even the tiniest one, was always under exact orders timed to the minute. But at one time our convoy was so pushed along by the wind and the currents that we were five hours ahead of schedule, despite the fact that our engines had been stopped half the time. We adjusted that by circling.

Although we arrived just on time, they weren't ready for us on the beaches and we spent several hours weaving in and out among the multitude of ships just off the beachhead. Finally we just settled down to await our turn.

That was when the most incongruous—to us—part of the invasion came. There we were in a front-row seat at a great military epic. Shells from battleships were whamming over our heads, and occasionally a dead man floated face downward past us. Hundreds and hundreds of ships laden with death milled around us. We could stand at the rail and see both our shells and German shells exploding on the beaches, where struggling men were leaping ashore, desperately hauling guns and equipment through the water.

We were in the very vortex of the war—and yet, as we sat there waiting, Lieutenant Chuck Conick and I played gin rummy in the wardroom and Bing Crosby sang "Sweet Leilani" over the ship's phonograph.

Angry shells hitting near us would make heavy thuds as the concussion carried through the water and struck the hull of our ship. But in our wardroom men in gas-impregnated uniforms and wearing life belts sat reading *Life* and listening to the BBC telling us how the war before our eyes was going.

But it wasn't like that ashore. No, it wasn't like that ashore.

TWENTY-SIX

ON THE ROAD TO BERLIN

Owing to a last-minute alteration in the arrangements, I didn't arrive on the beachhead until the morning after D-day, after our first wave of assault troops had hit the shore.

By the time we got there the beaches had been taken and the fighting had moved a couple of miles inland. All that remained on the beach was some sniping and artillery fire, and the occasional startling blast of a mine geysering brown sand into the air. That plus a gigantic and pitiful litter of wreckage along miles of shore line.

Submerged tanks and overturned boats and burned trucks and shell-shattered jeeps and sad little personal belongings were strewn all over those bitter sands. That plus the bodies of soldiers lying in rows covered with blankets, the toes of their shoes sticking up in a line as though on drill. And other bodies, uncollected, still sprawling grotesquely in the sand or half hidden by the high grass beyond the beach. That plus an intense, grim determination of work-weary men to get that chaotic beach organized and get all the vital supplies and the reinforcements moving more rapidly over it from the stacked-up ships standing in droves out to sea.

After it was over it seemed to me a pure miracle that we ever took the beach at all. For some of our units it was easy, but in the special sector where I landed our troops faced such odds that our getting ashore was like my whipping Joe Louis down to a pulp. The men who did it on that beach were men of the First and Twenty-ninth Divisions.

I want to tell you what the opening of the second front in that one sector entailed, so that you can know and appreciate and forever be humbly grateful to those both dead and alive who did it for you.

Ashore, facing us, were more enemy troops than we had in our assault waves. The advantages were all theirs, the disadvantages all ours. The Germans were dug into positions they had been working on for months, although they were not entirely complete. A 100-foot bluff a couple of hundred yards back from the beach had great concrete gun emplacements built right into the hilltop. These opened to the sides instead of to the front, thus making it hard for naval fire from the sea to reach them. They could shoot parallel with the shore and cover every foot of it for miles with artillery fire.

Then they had hidden machine-gun nests on the forward slopes, with crossfire taking in every inch of the beach. These nests were connected by networks of trenches, so that the German gunners could move about without exposing themselves.

Throughout the length of the beach, running zigzag a couple of hundred yards back from the shore line, was an immense V-shaped ditch fifteen feet deep. Nothing could cross it, not even men on foot, until fills had been made. And in other places at the far end of the beach, where the ground was flatter, they had great concrete walls. These were blasted by our naval gunfire or by explosives set by hand after we got ashore.

Our only exits from the beach were several swales or valleys, each about a hundred yards wide. The Germans made the most of those funnellike traps, sowing them with buried mines. They also contained barbed-wire entanglements with mines attached, hidden ditches, and machine guns firing from the slopes.

All this was on the shore. But our men had to go through a maze nearly as deadly before they even got ashore. Underwater obstacles were terrific. Under the water the Germans had whole fields of evil devices to catch our boats. Several days after the landing we had cleared only channels through them and still could not approach the whole length of the beach with our ships. Even then some ship or boat would hit one of those mines and be knocked out of commission.

The Germans had masses of great six-pronged spiders—made of railroad iron and standing shoulder-high—just beneath the surface of the water, for our landing craft to run into. They had huge logs buried in the sand, pointing upward and outward, their tops just below the water. Attached to the logs were mines.

In addition to these obstacles they had floating mines offshore, land mines buried in the sand of the beach, and more mines in checkerboard rows in the tall grass beyond the sand. And the enemy had four men on shore for every three men we had approaching the shore.

And yet we got on.

Beach landings are always planned to a schedule that is set far ahead of time. They all have to be timed, in order for everything to mesh and for the following waves of troops to be standing off the beach and ready to land at the right moment. Some elements of the assault force are to break through quickly, push on inland, and attack the most obvious enemy strong points. It is usually the plan for units to be inland, attacking gun positions from behind, within a matter of minutes after the first men hit the beach.

I have always been amazed at the speed called for in these plans. Schedules will call for engineers to land at H-hour plus 2 minutes, and service troops at H-hour plus 30 minutes, and even for press censors to land at H-hour plus 75 minutes. But in the attack on my special portion of the beach—the toughest spot of all, incidentally—the schedule didn't hold.

Our men simply could not get past the beach. They were pinned down right on the water's edge by an inhuman wall of fire from the bluff. Our first waves were on that beach for hours, instead of a few minutes, before they could begin working inland.

The foxholes were still there—dug at the very edge of the water, in the sand and the small jumbled rocks that formed parts of the beach.

Medical corpsmen attended the wounded as best they could. Men were killed as they stepped out of landing craft. An officer whom I knew got a bullet through the head just as the door of his landing craft was let down. Some men were drowned.

The first crack in the beach defenses was finally accomplished by terrific and wonderful naval gunfire, which knocked out the big emplacements. Epic stories have been told of destroyers that ran right up into shallow water and had it out point-blank with the big guns in those concrete emplacements ashore.

When the heavy fire stopped, our men were organized by their officers and pushed on inland, circling machine-gun nests and taking them from the rear.

As one officer said, the only way to take a beach is to face it and keep going. It is costly at first, but it's the only way. If the men are pinned down on the beach, dug in and out of action, they might as well not be there at all. They hold up the waves behind them, and nothing is being gained.

Our men were pinned down for a while, but finally they stood up and went through, and so we took that beach and accomplished our landing. In the light of a couple of days of retrospection, we sat and talked and called it a miracle that our men ever got on at all or were able to stay on.

They suffered casualties. And yet considering the entire beach-head assault, including other units that had a much easier time, our total casualties in driving that wedge into the Continent of Europe were remarkably low—only a fraction, in fact, of what our commanders had been prepared to accept.

And those units that were so battered and went through such hell pushed on inland without rest, their spirits high, their egotism in victory almost reaching the smart-alecky stage.

Their tails were up. "We've done it again," they said. They figured that the rest of the Army wasn't needed at all. Which proves that, while their judgment in this respect was bad, they certainly had the spirit that wins battles, and eventually wars.

When I went ashore on the soil of France the first thing I wanted to do was hunt up the other correspondents I had said good-bye to a few days previously in England, and see how they had fared. Before the day of invasion we had accepted it as a fact that not everybody would come through alive.

Correspondents sort of gang together. They know the ins and outs of war, and they all work at it in much the same manner. So I knew about where to look, and I didn't have much trouble finding them.

It was early in the morning, before the boys had started out on their day's round of covering the war. I found them in foxholes dug into the rear slope of a grassy hill about a half mile from the beach. I picked them out from a distance, because I could spot Jack Thompson's beard. He was sitting on the edge of a foxhole lacing his paratrooper boots. About a dozen correspondents were there, among them three especially good friends of mine— Thompson, Don Whitehead and Tex O'Reilly.

First of all we checked with each other on what we had heard about other correspondents. Most of them were O.K. One had been killed, and one was supposed to have been lost on a sunken ship, but we didn't know who. One or two had been wounded. Three of our best friends had not been heard from at all, and it looked bad. They subsequently turned up safe.

The boys were unshaved, and their eyes were red. Their muscles were stiff and their bodies ached. They had carried ashore only their typewriters and some K rations. They had gone two days without sleep, and then had slept on the ground without blankets, in wet clothes.

But none of that mattered too much after what they had been through. They were in a sort of daze from the exhaustion and mental turmoil of battle. When anyone asked a question it would take them a few seconds to focus their thoughts and give an answer.

Two of them in particular had been through all the frightful nightmare that the assault troops had experienced—because they had gone ashore with them.

Don Whitehead hit the beach with one regiment just an hour after H-hour, Thompson at the same time with another regiment. They were on the beaches for more than four hours under that hideous cloudburst of shells and bullets.

Jack Thompson said, "You've never seen a beach like it before. Dead and wounded men were lying so thick you could hardly take a step. One officer was killed only two feet away from me."

Whitehead was still asleep when I went to his foxhole. I said, "Get up, you lazy so-and-so." He started grinning without even opening his eyes, for he knew who it was.

It was hard for him to wake up. He had been unable to sleep, from sheer exhaustion, and had taken a sleeping tablet.

Don had managed to steal one blanket on the beach and had

that wrapped around him. He had taken off his shoes. His feet were so sore from walking in wet shoes and socks that he had to give them some air.

Finally he began to get himself up. "I don't know why I'm alive at all," he said. "It was really awful. For hours there on the beach the shells were so close they were throwing mud and rocks all over you. It was so bad that after a while you didn't care whether you got hit or not."

Don fished in a cardboard ration box for some cigarettes. He pulled out an envelope and threw it into the bushes. "They ain't worth a damn," he said. The envelope contained his anti-seasickness tablets.

"I was sicker than hell while we were circling around in our landing craft waiting to come ashore," he said. "Everybody was sick. Soldiers were lying on the floor of the LCVP, sick as dogs."

Tex O'Reilly rode around in a boat for six hours waiting to get ashore. Everybody was wet and cold and seasick and scared. War is so romantic—if you're far away from it.

Whitehead had probably been in more amphibious landings than any other correspondent over there. I know of six he made, four of them murderously tough. And he said, "I think I have gone on one too many of these things. Not because of what might happen to me personally, but I've lost my perspective. It's like dreaming the same nightmare over and over again, and when you try to write you feel that you have written it all before. You can't think of any new or different words to say it with."

I knew only too well what he meant.

It is an ironic thing about correspondents who go in on the first few days of an invasion story. They are the only correspondents capable of telling the full and intimate drama and horror of the thing. And yet they are the ones who can't get their copy out to the world. By the time they do get it out, events have swirled on and the world doesn't care any more.

There that morning in their foxholes on the slope of the hill those correspondents were mainly worried about the communications situation. Although they had landed with the first wave, they felt sure that none of their copy had ever reached America. And even I, a day behind them, felt no assurance that my feeble reports would ever see the light of day. But in philosophical moments I can think of greater catastrophes than that.

I took a walk along the historic coast of Normandy in the country of France. It was a lovely day for strolling along the seashore. Men were sleeping on the sand, some of them sleeping forever. Men were floating in the water, but they didn't know they were in the water, for they were dead.

The water was full of squishy little jellyfish about the size of a man's hand. Millions of them. In the center of each of them was a green design exactly like a four-leafed clover. The good-luck emblem. Sure. Hell, yes.

I walked for a mile and a half along the water's edge of our many-miled invasion beach. I walked slowly, for the detail on that beach was infinite.

The wreckage was vast and startling. The awful waste and destruction of war, even aside from the loss of human life, has always been one of its outstanding features to those who are in it. Anything and everything is expendable. And we did expend on our beachhead in Normandy during those first few hours.

For a mile out from the beach there were scores of tanks and trucks and boats that were not visible, for they were at the bottom of the water—swamped by overloading, or hit by shells, or sunk by mines. Most of their crews were lost.

There were trucks tipped half over and swamped, partly sunken barges, and the angled-up corners of jeeps, and small landing craft half submerged. And at low tide you could still see those vicious six-pronged iron snares that helped snag and wreck them.

On the beach itself, high and dry, were all kinds of wrecked vehicles. There were tanks that had only just made the beach before being knocked out. There were jeeps that had burned to a dull gray. There were big derricks on caterpillar treads that didn't quite make it. There were half-tracks carrying office equipment that had been made into a shambles by a single shell hit, their interiors still holding the useless equipage of smashed typewriters, telephones, office files.

There were LCTs turned completely upside down, and lying on their backs, and how they got that way I don't know. There were boats stacked on top of each other, their sides caved in, their suspension doors knocked off.

In this shore-line museum of carnage there were abandoned rolls of barbed wire and smashed bulldozers and big stacks of thrown-away life belts and piles of shells still waiting to be moved. In the water floated empty life rafts and soldiers' packs and ration boxes, and mysterious oranges. On the beach lay snarled rolls of telephone wire and big rolls of steel matting and stacks of broken, rusting rifles.

On the beach lay, expended, sufficient men and mechanism for a small war. They were gone forever now. And yet we could afford it.

We could afford it because we were on, we had our toe hold, and behind us there were such enormous replacements for this wreckage on the beach that you could hardly conceive of the sum total. Men and equipment were flowing from England in such a gigantic stream that it made the waste on the beachhead seem like nothing at all, really nothing at all.

But there was another and more human litter. It extended in a thin little line, just like a high-water mark, for miles along the beach. This was the strewn personal gear, gear that would never be needed again by those who fought and died to give us our entrance into Europe.

There in a jumbled row for mile on mile were soldiers' packs. There were socks and shoe polish, sewing kits, diaries, Bibles, hand grenades. There were the latest letters from home, with the address on each one neatly razored out—one of the security precautions enforced before the boys embarked.

There were toothbrushes and razors, and snapshots of families back home staring up at you from the sand. There were pocketbooks, metal mirrors, extra trousers, and bloody, abandoned shoes. There were broken-handled shovels, and portable radios smashed almost beyond recognition, and mine detectors twisted and ruined.

There were torn pistol belts and canvas water buckets, first-aid kits, and jumbled heaps of life belts. I picked up a pocket Bible with a soldier's name in it, and put it in my jacket. I carried it half a mile or so and then put it back down on the beach. I don't know why I picked it up, or why I put it down again.

Soldiers carry strange things ashore with them. In every invasion there is at least one soldier hitting the beach at H-hour with a banjo slung over his shoulder. The most ironic piece of equipment marking our beach—this beach first of despair, then of victory—was a tennis racket that some soldier had brought along. It lay lonesomely on the sand, clamped in its press, not a string broken.

Two of the most dominant items in the beach refuse were cigarettes and writing paper. Each soldier was issued a carton of cigarettes just before he started. That day those cartons by the thousand, water-soaked and spilled out, marked the line of our first savage blow.

Writing paper and air-mail envelopes came second. The boys had intended to do a lot of writing in France. The letters—now forever incapable of being written—that might have filled those blank abandoned pages!

Always there are dogs in every invasion. There was a dog still on the beach, still pitifully looking for his masters.

He stayed at the water's edge, near a boat that lay twisted and half sunk at the waterline. He barked appealingly to every soldier who approached, trotted eagerly along with him for a few feet, and then, sensing himself unwanted in all the haste, he would run back to wait in vain for his own people at his own empty boat.

Over and around this long thin line of personal anguish, fresh men were rushing vast supplies to keep our armies pushing on into France. Other squads of men picked amidst the wreckage to salvage ammunition and equipment that was still usable.

Men worked and slept on the beach for days before the last D-day victim was taken away for burial.

I stepped over the form of one youngster whom I thought dead. But when I looked down I saw he was only sleeping. He was very young, and very tired. He lay on one elbow, his hand suspended in the air about six inches from the ground. And in the palm of his hand he held a large, smooth rock.

I stood and looked at him a long time. He seemed in his sleep to hold that rock lovingly, as though it were his last link with a vanishing world. I have no idea at all why he went to sleep with the rock in his hand, or what kept him from dropping it once he was asleep. It was just one of those little things without explanation that a person remembers for a long time.

The strong, swirling tides of the Normandy coast line shifted the contours of the sandy beach as they moved in and out. They carried soldiers' bodies out to sea, and later they returned them. They covered the corpses of heroes with sand, and then in their whims they uncovered them.

As I plowed out over the wet sand, I walked around what seemed to be a couple of pieces of driftwood sticking out of the sand. But they weren't driftwood. They were a soldier's two feet. He was completely covered except for his feet; the toes of his GI shoes pointed toward the land he had come so far to see, and which he saw so briefly.

A few hundred yards back on the beach was a high bluff. Up there we had a tent hospital, and a barbed-wire enclosure for prisoners of war. From up there you could see far up and down the beach, in a spectacular crow's-nest view, and far out to sea.

And standing out there on the water beyond all this wreckage was the greatest armada man has ever seen. You simply could not believe the gigantic collection of ships that lay out there waiting to unload. Looking from the bluff, it lay thick and clear to the far horizon of the sea and on beyond, and it spread out to the sides and was miles wide.

As I stood up there I noticed a group of freshly taken German prisoners standing nearby. They had not yet been put in the prison cage. They were just standing there, a couple of doughboys leisurely guarding them with tommy guns.

The prisoners too were looking out to sea—the same bit of sea that for months and years had been so safely empty before their gaze. Now they stood staring almost as if in a trance. They didn't say a word to each other. They didn't need to. The expression on their faces was something forever unforgettable. In it was the final, horrified acceptance of their doom.

TWENTY-SEVEN

VIVE LA FRANCE

When I landed on the beachhead I went ashore in a jeep with Private William Bates Wescott, of 4040 West Boulevard, Culver City, California. Wescott was a good-looking, intelligent man of twenty-six who used to be a salesman for the Edgemar Farms Dairy at Venice, California. His wife worked in downtown Los Angeles, making Pullman reservations for the Southern Pacific Railroad at Sixth and Main. Wescott was at war for the first time, and all the shooting and stuff were completely new to him, but he was doing all right.

That first evening Wescott and I drove out to our bivouac area. On the way we passed many bodies lying alongside the road—both German and American, but mostly German. Some of the French people along the roads smiled and waved, while others kept their heads down and wouldn't look up.

It was dark when we arrived at a grape and apple orchard on a hillside several miles from the beach. We pulled in and parked under a tree. First we posted sentries, and then Wescott dug into his big ration box in the jeep and got out some grapefruit juice, crackers and sardines. While we were eating, the first German planes of the night came over. One dropped its bombs not very far away—near enough to give us our first touch of nerves. There were antiaircraft guns all around and they made an awful racket. The night began to take on an ominous and spooky aspect. We felt lonely. There were still snipers around, and shell holes everywhere, and we could hear machine guns in the distance. By midnight we had finished eating and got a camouflage net over the jeep in preparation for the first light next morning. We decided to get what sleep we could. We didn't have our bedrolls, but we did have two blankets apiece. We just lay down on the ground.

Another jeep had pulled under the tree with us. Altogether our little group sleeping on the ground consisted of two colonels, three enlisted men and myself. We slept in all our clothes.

German planes came over one by one. Our guns kept up their booming and crackling all night long in fits and jerks. After an hour or so, one of our colonels said we'd better move our blankets so our heads would be under the jeeps, because pieces of flak were falling all over the orchard. He said the flak wouldn't kill us unless it hit us in the head. I said I guessed it would if it hit us in the stomach. He said it wouldn't. I still think it would. Anyhow, I moved my head under and left my stomach out in the open. My head was right behind the front wheel, under the fender. It was a good place, but the headroom was so scant that every time I turned over I got a mouthful of mud from the fender.

Then it turned cold. Our two blankets might as well have been handkerchiefs, for all the warmth there was in them. We lit cigarettes and smoked under our blankets. We couldn't sleep much anyhow, for the noise of the guns. Sometimes planes would come in low, and we would lie there scrunched up in knotty tenseness, waiting to be hit.

Finally daylight came. At dawn our planes always came over and the Germans left, so the days were safe and secure as far as the air was concerned. We all got up, welcoming a chance to move around and get warm. Private Wescott opened some K rations and we ate a scanty breakfast off the hood of the jeep. Then a colonel made a reconnaissance tour. When he came back he said that our little orchard, which looked so rural and pretty in the dawn, was full of dead Germans, killed the day before. We would have to help bury them pretty soon. That was our first night in France.

War constantly produces funny things as well as tragic ones. For example, that first night in France one of the colonels who slept with us under the apple tree was an Army observer from Washington. Usually we didn't care for observers from Washington, but this colonel was a very nice guy and a good field soldier too, and everybody liked him.

While we were eating our K rations next morning he said he had slept fine for the first hour, before we had moved in under our jeep for protection from the flak. He said that before we moved he had found a nice little mound of earth for a pillow. He said that all his life he had had to have a pillow of some kind. After moving under the jeep he couldn't find anything to put his head on. With that he walked over a few feet to show us the nice mound of earth. When he looked down he started laughing. His excellent pillow of the night before had turned out in the light of day to be a pile of horse manure.

Another story concerns a masterful piece of wartime understatement by one of our truck drivers, Private Carl Vonhorn, of RFD 2, Cooperstown, New York. He had pulled into an apple orchard adjoining ours the night before, parked his truck in the darkness, spread his blankets on the ground in front of the truck, and gone to sleep. When he woke up at daylight Vonhorn looked about him sleepily. And there on the ground right beside him, within arm's reach, was a dead German soldier. On the other side of him, equally close, were two potato mashers (hand grenades). Private Vonhorn got up very quickly. Later he was telling his officers about his startling experience, and he ended his description with this philosophical remark: "It was very distasteful." Everybody thought that was so funny it spread around the camp like fire, and the phrase "It's very distasteful" became practically a byword.

After breakfast the first morning we had to round up about fifty dead Germans and Americans in the series of orchards where we were camping, take them to a central spot in a pasture and bury them. I helped carry one corpse across a couple of fields. I did it partly because the group needed an extra man, and partly because I was forcing myself to get used to it, for you can't hide from death when you're in a war.

This German was just a kid, surely not over fifteen. His face had already turned black, but I could sense his youth through the death-distorted features. The boys spread a blanket on the ground beside him. Then we lifted him over onto it. One soldier and I each took hold of a foot, and two others took his arms. One of the two soldiers in front was hesitant about touching the corpse. Whereupon the other soldier said to him, "Go on, take hold of him, dammit. You might as well get used to it now, for you'll be carrying plenty of dead ones from now on. Hell, you may even be carrying me one of these days."

So we carried him across two fields, each of us holding a corner of the blanket. Our burden got pretty heavy, and we rested a couple of times. The boys made wisecracks along the way to cover up their distaste for the job. When we got to the field we weren't sure just where the lieutenant wanted the cemetery started. So we put our man down on the ground and went back for instructions. And as we walked away the funny guy of the group turned and shook a finger at the dead German and said, "Now don't you run away while we're gone."

The Germans left snipers behind when they retreated, so all American bivouac areas were heavily guarded by sentries at night. And the sentries really meant business. One night a pretty important general whom I knew was working late, as all our staff officers did those days. About midnight he left his tent to go to another general's tent and talk something over. He had gone only about twenty feet when a sentry challenged him. And just at that moment the general, groping around in the dark, fell headlong into a deep slit trench. It was funny, even to the general, but there was nothing humorous about it to the sentry. He suspected monkey business. He rushed up to the trench, pointed his gun at the general, and in a tone that was a mixture of terror and intent to kill he yelled, "Git out of there and git recognized, you!"

Sniping, as far as I know, is recognized as a legitimate means of warfare. And yet there is something sneaking about it that outrages the American sense of fairness. I had never sensed this before we landed in France and began pushing the Germans back. We had had snipers before—in Bizerte and Cassino and lots of other places, but always on a small scale. There in Normandy the Germans went in for sniping in a wholesale manner. There were snipers everywhere: in trees, in buildings, in piles of wreckage, in the grass. But mainly they were in the high, bushy hedgerows that form the fences of all the Norman fields and line every roadside and lane.

It was perfect sniping country. A man could hide himself in the thick fence-row shrubbery with several days' rations, and it was like hunting a needle in a haystack to find him. Every mile we advanced there were dozens of snipers left behind us. They picked off our soldiers one by one as they walked down the roads or across the fields. It wasn't safe to move into a new bivouac area until the snipers had been cleaned out. The first bivouac I moved into had shots ringing through it for a full day before all the hidden gunmen were rounded up. It gave me the same spooky feeling that I got on moving into a place I suspected of being sown with mines.

In past campaigns our soldiers would talk about the occasional snipers with contempt and disgust. But in France sniping became more important, and taking precautions against it was something we had to learn and learn fast. One officer friend of mine said, "Individual soldiers have become sniper-wise before, but now we're sniper-conscious as whole units."

Snipers killed as many Americans as they could, and then when their food and ammunition ran out they surrendered. Our men felt that wasn't quite ethical. The average American soldier had little feeling against the average German soldier who fought an open fight and lost. But his feelings about the sneaking snipers can't very well be put into print. He was learning how to kill the snipers before the time came for them to surrender.

As a matter of fact that part of France was difficult for any fighting except between small groups. It was a country of little fields, every one bordered by a thick hedge and a high fence of trees. There was hardly any place where a man could see beyond the field ahead of him. Most of the time a soldier didn't see more than a hundred yards in any direction. In other places the ground was flooded and swampy with a growth of high, jungle-like grass. In this kind of stuff it was almost man-to-man warfare. One officer who had served a long time in the Pacific said the fighting was the nearest thing to Guadalcanal that he had seen.

The day after troops of our Ninth Division pushed through and cut off the Cherbourg peninsula, I went touring in a jeep over the country they had just taken. The Norman country is truly lovely in many places. In the western part of the peninsula the ground becomes hilly and rolling. Everything was a vivid green, there were trees everywhere, and the view across the fields from a rise looked exactly like the rich, gentle land of eastern Pennsylvania. It was too wonderfully beautiful to be the scene of war, and yet so were parts of Tunisia and Sicily and Italy. Someday I would like to cover a war in a country that is as ugly as war itself.

Our ride was sort of eerie. The American troops had started north and were driving on Cherbourg. This was possible because the Germans in that section were thoroughly disorganized, and by that time capable of nothing more than trying to escape. There was no traffic whatever on the roads. We drove for miles without seeing a soul. We had been told that the country was still full of snipers, and we knew there were batches of Germans in the woods waiting to surrender. And yet we saw nothing. The beautiful, tree-bordered lanes were empty. Cattle grazed contentedly in the fields. It was as though life had taken a holiday and death was in hiding. It gave me the willies.

Finally we came to a stone schoolhouse that was being used as a prisoner-of-war collection point, so we stopped for a look. Groups of prisoners were constantly being brought in. And here individual American soldiers, cut off behind the lines for days, came wearily to rest for a while in the courtyard before going on back to hunt up their outfits.

Most of the prisoners coming in at the time were from a captured German hospital. German doctors had set up shop in a shed adjoining the school and were treating their prisoners, who had slight wounds. At the moment I walked up, one soldier had his pants down and a doctor was probing for a fragment in his hip. Two or three of the German officers spoke some English. They were in a very good humor. One of them, a doctor, said to me, "I've been in the army four years, and today is the best day I have spent in the service."

In this courtyard I ran onto two boys who had just walked back after losing their jeep and being surrounded for hours that morning by Germans. They were Pfc. Arthur MacDonald, of Portsmouth, New Hampshire, and Private T. C. McFarland, of Southern Pines, North Carolina. They were forward observers for the Ninth Division's artillery. They had bunked down the night before in a pasture. When they woke up they could hear voices all around, and they weren't American voices. They peeked out and saw a German at a latrine not thirty feet away. So they started crawling. They crawled for hours. Finally they got out of the danger zone, and they started walking. They met a French farmer along the road, and took him in tow.

"We sure captured that Frenchman," they said. "He was so scared he could hardly talk. We used high-school French and a dictionary and finally got it through his head that all we wanted was something to eat. So he took us to his house. He fried eggs and pork and made coffee for us. Our morale sure was low this morning, but that Frenchman we captured fixed it up."

The boys said they had taken a couple of snapshots of the Frenchman, and they were so grateful that I imagine they will carry those pictures the rest of their lives.

At this time the French in that vicinity had been "liberated" less than twelve hours, and they could hardly encompass it in their minds. They were relieved, but they scarcely knew what to do. As we left the prison enclosure and got into our jeep we noticed four or five French country people—young farmers in their twenties, I took them to be—leaning against a nearby house. We were sitting in the jeep getting our gear adjusted when one of the farmers walked toward us, rather hesitantly and timidly. Finally he came up and smilingly handed me a rose. I couldn't go around carrying a rose in my hand all afternoon, so I threw it away around the next bend. But little things like that do sort of make you feel good about the human race.

We stopped next at the picturesque little town of Barneville which looks down upon the western sea. In the center of Barneville is a sloping, paved court, a sort of public square except that it is rectangular instead of square. At one end of the square an Army truck was parked. Scattered around the square were half a dozen American soldiers standing in doorways with their rifles at the ready. There were a few French people on the streets. We went to the far end of the square, where three local French policemen were standing in front of the mayor's office. They couldn't speak any English, but they said there was one woman in town who did, and a little boy was sent running for her. Gradually a crowd of eager and curious people crushed in upon us until there must have been 200 of them, from babies to old women.

Finally the woman arrived—a little dark woman with graying

hair and spectacles, and a big smile. Her English was quite good, and we asked her if there were any Germans in the town. She turned and asked the policemen. Instantly everybody in the crowd started talking at once. The sound was like that of a machine that increases in speed until its noise drowns out all else. Finally the policemen had to shush the crowd so that the woman could answer us. She said there were Germans all around, in the woods, but none were left in the town. Just then a German stuck his head out of a nearby second-story window. Somebody saw him, and an American soldier was dispatched to get him.

Barneville is a fortunate place, because not a shell was fired into it by either side. The lieutenant with us told the woman we were glad nobody had been hurt. When she translated this for the crowd, there was much nodding in approval of our good wishes. We must have stood and talked for an hour and a half. It was a kind of holiday for the local people. They were relieved but not quite sure the Germans wouldn't be back. They were still under a restraint that wouldn't let them open up riotously. But we could sense from little things that they were glad to have us.

A little French shopkeeper came along with a spool of red, white and blue ribbon from his store. He cut off pieces about six inches long for all hands, both American and French. In a few minutes everybody was going around with a French tricolor in his buttonhole. Then a ruddy-faced man of middle age, who looked like a gentleman farmer, drove up in one of those one-horse, high-wheeled work carts that the French use. He had a German prisoner in uniform standing behind him, and another one, who was sick, lying on a stretcher. The farmer had captured these guys singlehanded, and he looked so pleased with himself that I expected him to take a bow at any moment.

French people kept coming up and asking us for instructions. A man who looked as if he might be the town banker asked what he was supposed to do with prisoners. We told him to bring them to the truck, and asked how many he had. To our astonishment he said he had 70 in the woods a couple of miles away, 120 in a nearby town, and 40 in another town. As far as I could figure it out he had captured them all himself. Another worried-looking Frenchman came up. He was a doctor. He said he had 26 badly wounded Germans down at the railroad station and desperately needed medical supplies. He wanted chloroform and sulfa drugs. We told him we would have some sent.

One character in the crowd looked as if he belonged in a novel of Bohemian life on the Left Bank in Paris. He couldn't possibly have been anything but a poet. He wore loose, floppy clothes that made him look like a woman. His glasses were thick, and hair about a foot long curled around his ears. I wish you could have seen the expressions of our tough, dirty soldiers when they looked at him.

When we finally started away from the crowd, a little old fellow in faded blue overalls ran up and asked us, in sign language, to come to his café for a drink. Since we didn't dare violate the spirit of hands-across-the-sea that was then wafting about the town, we had to sacrifice ourselves and accept. We sat on wooden benches at a long bare table while the little Frenchman puttered and sputtered around. He let two policemen and his own family in, and then took the handle out of the front door.

The Germans had drunk up all his stock except for some wine and some eau de vie. In case you don't know, eau de vie is a savage liquid made by boiling barbed wire, soapsuds, watch springs and old tent pegs together. The better brands have a touch of nitro-glycerine for flavor. So the little Frenchman filled our tiny glasses. We raised them, touched glasses all around, and vived la France all over the place, and good-will-towards-men rang out through the air and tears ran down our cheeks. In this case, however, the tears were largely induced by our violent efforts to refrain from clutching at our throats and crying out in anguish. This good-will business is a tough life, and I think every American who connected with a glass of eau de vie should have got a Purple Heart.

All our soldiers were impressed by the loveliness of the Normandy countryside. It differs from the English landscape chiefly in that rural England is fastidiously trimmed and cropped like a Venetian garden, while in Normandy the grass needs cutting and the hedgerows are wild, and everything has less of neatness and more of the way of nature. The main roads in Normandy are macadam and the side roads gravel. They are winding, narrow, and difficult for heavy military traffic. In many places we had to make roads one-way for miles at a stretch.

The average American found the climate of Normandy abom-
inable. We had about one nice day for three bad days. On nice days
the sky was clear blue and the sun was out and everything seemed
wonderful except that there was still a hidden chill in the air, and
in our tents or under a shade tree we were cold. On the bad days
the whole universe was dark and we needed lights in our tents at
noontime, and it drizzled or sprinkled, and often a cold wind blew,
and both our bones and our hearts were miserable.

Most everybody had on his long underwear. I wore four sweaters in addition to my regular uniform. Overcoats were taken away
from our troops before we left England, and there were a lot of
our boys not too warmly clad. At night we put our clothes under
our bedrolls or they would be wet in the morning, because of the
constant dampness in the air. All that dampness makes for ruddy
cheeks and green grass. But ruddy cheeks are for girls and green
grass for cows, and personally I find the ordinary American is
happiest when he's good and stinking hot.

It is the custom throughout our Army, as you doubtless know,
for soldiers to paint names on their vehicles. There are names on
airplanes, tanks, jeeps, trucks, guns and practically everything
that moves. Sometimes they are girls' names, and often they
are trick names such as "Sad Sack," "Invasion Blues," "Hitler's
Menace." Well, it wasn't long before the boys started painting
French names on their vehicles. I saw a jeep named "Bientot,"
which means "Soon," and a motorcycle named "Char de Mort,"
which means "Chariot of Death." The names of a lot of the French
towns were tongue twisters for our troops, so the towns quickly
became known by some unanimous application of Americanese.
For instance, Bricquebec was often called Bricabrac. And Isigny
was first known as Insignia but soon evolved into Easy Knee,
which is closer to the French pronunciation.

One day a friend and I were in a mid-peninsula town not many
miles from Cherbourg and we stopped to ask a couple of young
French policemen, wearing dark-blue uniforms and Sam Browne
belts, where to go to buy a certain article. Being quite hospitable,
they jumped in the car and went along to show us. After we had

finished our buying we all got back in the car. We tried to ask the policemen where they were going. They in turn asked us where we were going. Knowing it was hopeless in our limited French to explain that we were going to our camp up the road, we merely said Cherbourg, meaning our camp was in that direction. But the Frenchmen thought we meant to drive right into Cherbourg, which was still in German hands. Quick as a flash they jumped up, hit the driver on the shoulder to get the car stopped, shook hands rapidly all around, saluted, and scurried out with a terrified "Au revoir." None of that Cherbourg stuff for those boys.

Some of the German officers were pleased at being captured, but the dyed-in-the-wool Nazi was not. They brought in a young one who was furious. He considered it thoroughly unethical for us to fight so hard. The Americans had attacked all night, and the Germans don't like night attacks. When this special fellow was brought in he protested in rage, "*You* Americans! The way you fight! This is not war! This is madness!" The German was so outraged he never even got the irony of his own remarks—that madness though it were, it worked.

Another high-ranking officer was brought in and the first thing he asked was the whereabouts of his personal orderly. When told that his orderly was deader than a mackerel, he flew off the handle and accused us of depriving him of his personal comfort. "Who's going to dig my foxhole for me?" he demanded.

In the early days of the invasion a whole bevy of high-ranking Allied officers visited Normandy—Generals Marshall, Eisenhower and Arnold, Admirals King and Ramsay—there was so much brass we just bumped into two-star generals without even begging pardon. Now generals, it seems, like to be brave. Or I should say that, being generals, they know they must appear to be brave in order to set an example. Consequently, a high-ranking general never ducks or bats an eye when a shell hits near him. Well, the military police charged with conducting this glittering array of generals around our beachhead tried to get them to ride in armored cars, since the country was still full of snipers. But, being generals, they said no, certainly not, no armored cars for us, we'll just go in open command cars like anybody else. And that's the way they did go. But what the generals didn't know was this: Taking no chances on such a collection of talent, the MP's hid armored cars and tanks all along their route, behind hedges and under bushes, out of sight so that the generals couldn't see them, but there ready for action just in case anything did happen.

The most wrecked town I saw was Saint-Sauveur-le-Vicomte, known simply as San Sah-Vure. Its buildings were gutted and leaning, its streets were choked with rubble and vehicles drove over the top of it. Bombing and shellfire from both sides did it. The place looked exactly like World War I pictures of such places as Verdun. At the edge of the town the bomb craters were so immense that whole houses could have been put into them. A veteran of the last war pretty well summed up the two wars when he said, "This is just like the last war, only the holes are bigger."

So far as I know, we entered France without anybody making a historic remark about it. Last time, you know, it was "Lafayette, we are here." The nearest I heard to a historic remark was made by an ack-ack gunner, sitting on a mound of earth about two weeks after D-day, reading the *Stars and Stripes* from London. All of a sudden he said, "Say, where's this Normandy beachhead it talks about in here?"

I looked at him closely and saw that he was serious, so I said, "Why, you're sitting on it."

And he said, "Well, I'll be damned. I never knowed that."

TWENTY-EIGHT

AMERICAN ACK-ACK

One of the vital responsibilities during those opening weeks of our war on the Continent of Europe was the protection of our unloading beaches and ports. Over and through them, without interruption and in great masses, our buildup of men and material had to pass in sufficient masses to roll the Germans clear back out of France. Nothing could be allowed to interfere with that unloading. Everything we could lay our hands on was thrown into the guarding of those beaches and ports. Allied ground troops policed them from the land side. Our two navies protected them from sneak attacks by sea. Our great air supremacy made daytime air assaults rare and costly. It was only at night that the Germans had a chance. They did keep pecking away at us with night bombers, but their main success was in keeping us awake and making us dig our foxholes deeper.

The job of protecting the beaches at night was given over to the antiaircraft artillery, or ack-ack. I heard that we had there on the beachhead the greatest concentration of antiaircraft guns ever assembled in an equivalent space. After three solid weeks of being kept awake all night long by the guns, and having to snatch a little sleep at odd moments during the daytime, that was not hard for me to believe. The falling flak became a real menace— one of the few times I've known that to happen in this war. Every night for weeks, pieces of exploded shells came whizzing to earth within fifty yards of my tent. Once an unexploded ack-ack shell buried itself half a stone's throw from my tent. A good portion of our army on the beachhead slept all night in foxholes, and some of the troops swung over to the Anzio beachhead custom of building dugouts in order to be safe from falling flak.

Our ack-ack was commanded by a general officer, which indicates how important it was. His hundreds of gun batteries even intercepted planes before they neared the beaches. The gun positions were plotted on a big wall map in his command tent, just as the battle lines were plotted by infantry units. A daily score was kept of the planes shot down—confirmed ones and probables. Just as an example of the effectiveness of our ack-ack, one four-gun battery alone shot down fifteen planes in the first two weeks.

The Germans couldn't seem to make up their minds exactly what they were trying to do in the air. They wandered around all night long, usually in singles though sometimes in numbers, but they didn't do a great deal of bombing. Most of them turned away at the first near burst from one of our 90-millimeter guns. Our ack-ack men said they thought the German pilots were yellow, but I had seen the quality of German fighting for nearly two years and I could hardly believe that. Often the enemy dropped flares that lighted up the whole beach area, and then they would fail to follow through and bomb by the light of their flares. The ack-ack men said that not more than two out of ten planes that approached the beachhead ever made their bomb runs over our shipping. But we were liable to get a bomb anywhere along the coastal area, for many of the Germans apparently just jettisoned their bombs and hightailed home.

It was a spectacle to watch the antiaircraft fire when the Germans actually got over the beach area. All the machine guns on the ships lying off the beaches cut loose with their red tracer bullets, and those on shore did too. Their bullets arched in all directions and fused into a sky-filling pattern. The lines of tracers bent and waved and seemed like streams of red water from hoses. The whole thing became a gigantic, animated fountain of red in the black sky. And above all this were the split-second golden flashes of big-gun shells as they exploded high up toward the stars. The noise was terrific. Sometimes low clouds caught the crack of those many guns and scrambled them all into one gigantic roar which rolled and thundered like the blood-curdling approach of a hurricane. Our tent walls puffed from the concussion of the guns and bombs, and the earth trembled and shook. If we were sleeping in a foxhole, little clouds of dirt came rolling down on us. When the planes were really close and the guns were pounding out a mania of sound, we put on our steel helmets in bed and sometimes we would drop off to sleep and wake up with them on in the morning and feel very foolish.

American antiaircraft gunners began playing their important part in the Battle of Normandy right on D-day and shortly after H-hour. Ordinarily you wouldn't think of the antiaircraft coming ashore with the infantry, but a little bit of everything came ashore on that memorable day—from riflemen to press censors, from combat engineers to chaplains—and everybody had a hand in it.

The ack-ack was given a place in the very early waves because the general in command felt that the Germans would throw what air strength they had onto the beaches that day and he wanted his men there to repel it. As it turned out, the Germans didn't use their planes at all and the ack-ack wasn't needed to protect the landings from air attack. So, like many other units, they turned themselves into infantry or artillery and helped win the battle of the beaches. They took infantrylike casualties too. One unit lost half its men and guns. I ran onto the story of a crew of ack-ackers who had knocked out a German 88 deeply ensconced in a thick concrete emplacement—and did it with a tiny 37-millimeter gun, which is somewhat akin to David slaying Goliath.

I hunted up this crew to see how they did it. By that time they had moved several miles inland. I found them at the edge of a small open field far out in the country. Their gun had been dug into the ground. Two men sat constantly in their bucket seats behind the gun, keeping watch on the sky even in the daytime. The others slept in their pup tents under the bushes, or just loafed around and brewed an occasional cup of coffee. The commander of this gun was Sergeant Hyman Haas, of 1620 Ocean Avenue, Brooklyn. Sergeant Haas was an enthusiastic and flattering young man who was practically beside himself with delight when I showed up at their remote position, for he had read my column back in New York but hadn't supposed our trails would ever cross. When I told him I wanted to write a little about his crew he beamed and said, "Oh, boy! Wait till Flatbush Avenue hears about this!"

The outfit had landed behind the first wave of infantry. A narrow valley leading away from the beach at that point was blocked by the German 88, which stopped everything in front of it. So Driver Bill Hendrix, from Shreveport, Louisiana, turned their half-track around and drove the front end back into the water so the gun would be pointing in the right direction. Then the boys poured twenty-three rounds into the pillbox. Some of their shells hit the small gun slits and went inside. At the end of their firing, what Germans were left came out with their hands up. The boys were very proud of their achievement, but I was kind of amused at their modesty. One of them said, "The credit should go to Lieutenant Gibbs, because he gave us the order to fire."

The lieutenant was Wallace Gibbs, of RFD 2, Providence Road, Charlotte, North Carolina. The other members of the crew were Corporal John Jourdain, of 1466 North Claiborne, New Orleans; Private Frank Bartolomeo, of Ulevi, Pennsylvania; Private Joseph Sharpe, of Clover, South Carolina; Pfc. Frank Furey, of 710 Union Street, Brooklyn; Corporal Austin Laurent, Jr., of 1848 Gentilly Road, New Orleans; and Private Raymond Bullock, of Coello, Illinois. Their gun was named "BLIP," which represented the first letters of Brooklyn, Louisiana, Illinois and Pennsylvania, where most of the crew came from.

Our ack-ack can be divided into three categories. First there are the machine guns, both 50-caliber and 20-millimeter. Airplanes have to be fairly low for these to be effective. The ack-ack branch has thousands of such guns, and so does every other fighting unit. When a low-flying strafer comes in everybody who has anything bigger than a rifle shoots at him, whether he is an ack-ack man or not. In the second big category of ack-ack is the Bofors, a 40-millimeter long-barreled gun which can fire rapidly and with great accuracy at medium altitudes. Our ack-ack is equipped with thousands of these, and although they can't see their targets at night they put a lot of shells into the sky anyway. The big gun, and the elite, of our ack-ack is the 90-millimeter. This is for high-altitude shooting. It is the gun that keeps most of the planes away, and has such a high score of planes shot down.

I spent two days and nights with one of these 90-millimeter gun crews there on the Normandy beachhead. They were having their first taste of war, but already after three weeks or so of it they felt they were the best gun crew in the best battery of the best ack-ack battalion. It was close to impossible for a German bomber to pick out their position at night, yet the crew felt that the Germans had singled them out because they were so good. As far as I could learn, practically all the other gun crews felt the same way. That's what is known in military terms as good morale.

My crew consisted of thirteen men. Some of them operated the dials on the gun, others loaded and fired it, others lugged the big shells from a storage pit a few feet away. The big guns usually operate in batteries, and a battery consists of four guns and the family of technicians necessary to operate the many scientific devices that control the guns. The four guns of this particular battery were dug into the ground in a small open field, about fifty yards apart. The gunners slept in pup tents or under half-tracks hidden under trees and camouflage nets. The boys worked all night and slept in the daytime. They hadn't dug foxholes, for the only danger was at night and they were up all night firing.

The guns required a great deal of daytime work to keep them in shape, so half of the boys slept in the forenoon and half in the afternoon while the other half worked. Their life was rugged, but they didn't see the seamiest side of the war. They stayed quite a while in one place, which makes for comfort, and they were beyond enemy artillery range. Their only danger was from bombing or strafing, and that was not too great. They were so new at war that they still tried to keep themselves clean. They shaved and washed their clothes regularly. Their service section had not arrived yet from England, so they had to cook their own meals. They were pretty sick of that and said they would be glad when the service boys and the field kitchens caught up with them. They ate ten-in-one rations, heating them over a fire of wooden sticks in a shallow hole in the ground.

The sergeant in command of my gun was Sergeant Joseph Samuelson, a farm boy from Odebolt, Iowa. (None of the crew was past his middle twenties and only two of the thirteen were married.) "Sam" was a quiet fellow with a mellow voice. His mouth was very wide, and right then his lips were chapped and cracked from the cold climate. He was conscientious and the others liked him.

Two of the crew were from the same home town, Manchester, New Hampshire. They were Privates Armand Provencher and Jim Bresnahan. In fact there were six Manchester boys in the battery, and fifteen in the battalion. They all went into the Army on the same day at the same place, and they were firing within a few miles of each other in France. Private Provencher, of French-Canadian extraction, was the only one of our crew who spoke French, so he did all the foraging. His family spoke French in their home back in New Hampshire. I had always heard that the French-Canadian brand of French was unintelligible to real Frenchmen, but Provencher said he didn't have any trouble.

Three of the boys were from Massachusetts—Corporal Charles Malatesta, of Malden, Pfc. George Slaven, of Southbridge, and Private Walter Covel, of Roxbury. Covel had heavy black whiskers and it took two razor blades to shave him. With a two-day growth he looked like a hobo, and then when he cleaned up we could hardly recognize him. George Slaven was the entrepreneur of the battery. Back home he owned a drugstore, which his wife was running while he was away fighting. His wife kept sending him stuff from the store until he had built up a miniature drugstore. He had such things as aspirin, lip pomade, shampoo. He had had a stock of cigars but they were all gone. The boys said he got more packages from home than any fifteen other men in the battery. Slaven and Malatesta were the only married men in the crew.

Private Bill Millea, of Shelton, Connecticut, was the oracle. He told long and fascinating stories and thought about the world situation and had a great sense of fun. He was politically-minded, and said he was going to become an alderman in Shelton after the war. He called himself "Honest Bill" Millea. He was one of the ammunition carriers, and during lulls in the firing at night he curled up in an ammo dugout about twenty feet from the gun pit and slept on top of the shells. He slept so well we could hear him snoring clear over in the gun pit.

I didn't pick up much about the rest of the boys, but they were all pleasant lads who worked hard and got along together. They were Corporal Henry Omen, of Depew, New York; Pfc. Harold Dunlap, of Poplar Bluffs, Missouri; Private Norman Kimmey, of Hanover, Pennsylvania; Corporal Clyde Libbey, of Lincoln, Maine; Pfc. Jerry Fullington, of Fremont, Nebraska; and Corporal Bill Nelson, of Scotts Bluff, Nebraska. Corporal Libbey was from the potato-growing country in Maine, and I told him "That Girl" and I spent a night in Lincoln about seven years ago. But unfortunately all I could remember about Lincoln was that we'd stayed there, so our attempts to dig up some mutual acquaintance or even a building we both remembered fell kind of flat.

The battery commander was Captain Julius Reiver, of Wilmington, Delaware. He stayed up all night too, directing their firing from his dugout, where information was phoned in to him.

On my second day with the battery the boys asked their officers if it would be all right for them to write in their letters home that I was staying with them. The officers said yes, so the boys all got out paper, and since it had turned warm for a change we sat and lay around on the grass while they wrote short letters home, using ammunition and ration boxes for writing boards. When they got through all of them had me sign their letters.

The boys said they didn't choose ack-ack but were just automatically put into it. They did like it, however, as long as they had to be in the Army. They were all over being gun-shy, and since they had been through their opening weeks of war they weren't even especially afraid. They had been overseas more than six months, and like everybody else they were terribly anxious to go home. They liked to think in terms of anniversaries, and much of their conversation was given to remembering what they had been doing "a year ago today" when they were in camp back in America. They all hoped they wouldn't have to go to the Pacific when the European war was over.

My crew was a swell bunch of boys. There wasn't a smart aleck or gold-bricker in the crew. As in any group of men, some were talkative and some were quiet. Because he spoke French, Provencher had already made friends with the farmers nearby, and the crew got such stuff as eggs and butter occasionally. He had been promised some chicken, but it hadn't showed up yet. Although the noise and concussion of their gun was terrific, they had got used to it and no one wore cotton in his ears. They said the two best morale boosters were the *Stars and Stripes* and letters from home.

The boys were very proud of their first night on the soil of France. They began firing immediately from a field not far from the beach. The snipers were still thick in the surrounding hedges, and bullets were singing around them all night. The boys liked to tell over and over how the infantry all around them were crouching and crawling along while they had to stand straight up and dig their guns in. It takes about twelve hours of good hard work to dig in the guns when they move to a new position. They dug in one gun at a time while the three others were firing. My gun was dug into a circular pit about four feet deep and twenty feet across. This had been rimmed with a parapet of sandbags and dirt, so that when a man stood on the floor of the pit he could just see over the top. The boys were safe down there from anything but a direct hit.

The gun was covered in the daytime by a large camouflage net. My crew fired anywhere from 10 to 150 shells a night. In the early days on the beachhead they kept firing one night until they had only half a dozen shells left. But the supply had been built up, and there was no danger of their running short again. The first night I was with them was a slow night and they fired only nine shells. The boys were terribly disappointed. They said it would have to turn out to be the quietest and also the coldest night they had ever had. Just because of that, I stayed a second night with them.

The Germans were as methodical in their night air attacks on our positions in Normandy as they were in everything else. We began to hear the faint, faraway drone of the first bomber around 11:30 every night. Our own planes patrolled above us until darkness. It was dusk around eleven, and we were suddenly aware that the skies which had been roaring all day with our own fighters and bombers were now strangely silent. Nothing was in the air.

The ack-ack gunners, who had been loafing near their pup tents or sleeping or telling stories, now went to their guns. They brought blankets from the pup tents and piled them up against the wall of the gun pit, for the nights got very cold and the boys wrapped up during long lulls in the shooting. The gunners merely loafed in the gun pit as the dusk deepened into darkness, waiting for the first telephoned order to start shooting. They smoked a few last-minute cigarettes. Once it was dark they couldn't smoke except by draping blankets over themselves for blackout. They did smoke some that way during the night, but not much.

In four or five places in the wall of the circular pit, shelves had been dug and wooden shell boxes inserted to hold reserve shells. It was just like pigeonholes in a filing cabinet. When the firing started, two ammunition carriers brought new shells from a dump a few feet away up to the rim of the gun pit and handed them down to a carrier waiting below; he kept the pigeonholes filled. The gun was constantly turning in the pit and there was always a pigeonhole of fresh shells right behind it. The shells were as long as a man's arm and they weighed better than forty pounds. After each salvo the empty shell case kicked out onto the floor of the pit. They lay there until there was a lull in the firing, when the boys tossed them over the rim. Next morning they were gathered up and put in boxes for eventual shipment back to America, to be retooled for further use.

Each gun was connected by telephone to the battery command post in a dugout. At all times one member of each gun crew had a telephone to his ear. When a plane was picked up within range the battery commander gave a telephonic order, "Stand by!" Each gun commander shouted the order to his crew, and the boys all jumped to their positions. Everybody in the crew knew his job and did it. There was no necessity for harshness or short words on the part of the gun commander. When a plane either was shot down or went out of range, and there was nothing else in the vicinity, the command was given, "Rest!" and the crews relaxed and squatted or lay around on the floor of the pit. But they didn't leave the pit.

Sometimes the rest would be for only a few seconds. Other times it might last a couple of hours. In the long lulls the gunners wrapped up in blankets and slept on the floor of the pit—all except the man at the telephone. It was the usual German pattern to have a lull from about 2 to 4 a.m., and then get in another good batch of bombing attempts in the last hour before dawn. The nights were very short then—from 11 p.m. to 5 a.m.—for which everybody was grateful. Dawn actually started to break faintly just about 4:30, but the Germans kept roaming around the sky until real daylight came.

Our own patrol planes hit the sky at daylight and the Germans skedaddled. In the first few days, when our patrol planes had to come all the way from England, the boys told of mornings when they could see our planes approaching from one direction and the Germans heading for home at the opposite side of the sky.

As soon as it was broad daylight, the boys cranked down the barrel of their gun until it was horizontal, and then took a sight through it onto the stone turret of a nearby barn—to make sure the night's shooting hadn't moved the gun off its position. Then some of them gathered up the empty shells, others got wood fires started for heating breakfast, and others raised and tied the camouflage net. They were all through by seven o'clock, and half the shift crawled into their pup-tent beds while the other half went to work with oil, ramrod and waste cloth to clean up and readjust the gun.

It was 11:15 at night. The sky had darkened into an indistinct dusk, but it was not yet fully dark. I could make out the high hedgerow surrounding our field and the long barrels of the other ack-ack guns of our battery poking upward. We all leaned against the wall of our gun pit, just waiting for our night's work to start. We had plenty of time. The Germans wouldn't be coming for ten or fifteen minutes. But no. Suddenly the gun commander, who was at the phone, yelled, "Stand by!" The men jumped to their positions. The plane was invisible, but we could hear the distant motors throbbing in the sky. Somehow a man could always sense, just from the tempo in which things started, when it was going to be a heavy night. We felt that this would be one.

A gunner turned a switch on the side of the gun, and it went into remote control. From then on a mystic machine at the far end of the field handled the pointing of the gun, through electrical cables. It was all automatic. The long snout of the barrel began weaving in the air and the mechanism that directed it made a buzzing noise. The barrel went up and down, to the right and back to the left, grinding and whining and jerking. It was like a giant cobra, maddened and with its head raised, weaving back and forth before striking. Finally the gun settled rigidly in one spot and the gun commander called out, "On target! Three rounds! Commence firing!" The gun blasted forth with sickening force. A brief sheet of flame shot from the muzzle. Dense, sickening smoke boiled around in the gun pit. I heard the empty shell case clank to the ground. Darkly silhouetted figures moved silently, reloading. In a few seconds the gun blasted again. And once again. The smoke was stifling. I felt the blast sweep over me and set me back a little. The salvo was fired. The men stepped back. We took our fingers from our ears. The smoke gradually cleared. And then once more the gun was intently weaving about, grinding and whining and seeking for a new prey.

That's the way it was all night. We never saw a thing. We only heard the thrump, thrump of motors in the sky and saw the flash of guns and the streaking of red tracers far away. We never saw the plane we were shooting at, unless it went down in flames, and "flamers" were rare.

I found out one thing being with the ack-ack at night. A man is much less nervous when he's out in the open with a gun in front of him than when he's doubled up under blankets in a tent, coiled and intent for every little change of sound, doubtful and imagining and terrified.

We shot off and on, with rest periods of only a few minutes, for a couple of hours. The Germans were busy boys that night. Then suddenly a flare popped in the sky, out to sea, in front of us. Gradually the night brightened until the whole universe was alight and we could easily see each other in the gun pit and everything around us in the field. Everybody was tense and staring. We all dreaded flares. Planes were throbbing and droning all around in the sky above the light. Surely the Germans would go for the ships that were standing off the beach, or they might even pick out the gun batteries and come for us in the brightness. The red tracers of the machine guns began arching toward the flares but couldn't reach them. Then our own "Stand by!" order came, and the gun whined and swung and felt its way into the sky until it was dead on the high flare. Yes, we were shooting at the flare. And our showering bursts of flak hit it, too.

Flares are seldom completely shot out, but they can be broken into small pieces, and the light is dimmed, and the pieces come floating down more rapidly and the whole thing is over sooner. Flares in the sky were always frightening. They seemed to strip us naked and make us want to cower and hide and peek out from behind an elbow. We felt a great, welcome privacy when the last piece flickered to the ground and we could go back to shooting at the darkness from out of the dark.

The six hours of nighttime went swiftly for our ack-ack battery, which was a blessing. Time raced during the firing and in the long lulls between the waves of enemy planes we dozed and catnapped and the hours passed away. Once, during a lull long after midnight, half a dozen of the boys in our gun pit started singing softly. Their voices were excellent. Very low and sweetly they sang in perfect harmony such songs as "I've Been Workin' on the Railroad" and "Tipperary." There wasn't anything forced or dramatic about it. It was just some young fellows singing because they liked to sing—and the fact that they were in a gun pit in France shooting at people, trying to kill them, was just a circumstance.

The night grew bitterly chill. Between firings every man draped an army blanket around his shoulders, and sometimes up over his head. In the darkness they were just silhouettes, looking strange and foreign like Arabs. After 2 o'clock there was a long lull. Gradually the boys wrapped up in their blankets and lay down on the floor of the pit and fell asleep. Pretty soon I heard them snoring. I talked with the gun commander for a few minutes, in low tones. Then my eyes got heavy too. I wrapped a blanket around me and sat down on the floor of the pit, leaning against the wall. The night had become as silent as a grave. Not a shot, not a movement anywhere. My head slacked over to one side. But I couldn't relax enough to sleep in that position. And it was so cold. I was so sleepy I hurt, and I berated myself because I couldn't go to sleep like the others.

But I was asleep all the time, for, suddenly a voice shouted, "Stand by!"—and it was as shocking as a bucket of cold water in my face. I looked quickly at my watch and realized that an hour had passed. All the silent forms came frantically to life. Blankets flew, men bumped into each other. "Commence firing!" rang out above the confusion, and immediately the great gun was blasting away, and smoke again filled the gun pit. Sleep and rouse up. Catnap and fire. The night wore on. Sometimes a passing truck sounded exactly like a faraway plane. Frightened French dogs barked in distant barnyards.

Things are always confusing and mysterious in war. Just before dawn an airplane drew nearer and nearer, lower and lower, yet we got no order to shoot and we wondered why. But machine guns and Bofors guns for miles around went after it. The plane came booming on in, in a long dive. He seemed to be heading right at us. We felt like ducking low in the pit. He actually crossed the end of our field less than a hundred yards from us, and only two or three hundred feet up. Our hearts were pounding. We didn't know who he was or what he was doing. Our own planes were not supposed to be in the air. Yet if he was a German, why didn't he bomb or strafe us? We never did find out.

The first hint of dawn finally came. Most of us were asleep again when suddenly one of the boys called out, "Look! What's that?" We stared into the faint light, and there just above us went a great, silent, grotesque shape, floating slowly through the air. It was a ghostly sight. Then we recognized it, and we all felt a sense of relief. It was one of our barrage balloons which had broken loose and was drifting to earth. Something snagged it in the next field, and it hung there poised above the apple trees until somebody went and got it long after daylight.

As fuller light came we started lighting cigarettes in the open. Over the phone, the battery commander asked how many shells were fired, and told us that our tentative score for the night was seven planes shot down. The crew was proud and pleased. Dawn brought an imagined warmth and we threw off our blankets. Our eyes felt gravelly and our heads groggy. The blast of the gun had kicked up so much dirt that our faces were as grimy as though we had driven all night in a dust storm. The green Norman countryside was wet and glistening with dew.

Then we heard our own planes drumming in the distance.

Suddenly they popped out of a cloud bank and were over us. Security for another day had come, and we willingly surrendered the burden of protecting the beaches. The last "Rest!" was given and the gun was put away. There would be no more shooting until darkness came again.

TWENTY-NINE

STREET FIGHTING

One of the favorite generals among the war correspondents was Major General Manton S. Eddy, commander of the Ninth Division. We liked him because he was absolutely honest with us, because he was sort of old-shoe and easy to talk with, and because we thought he was a mighty good general. We had known him in Tunisia and Sicily, and then there in France.

Like his big chief, Lieutenant General Omar Bradley, General Eddy looked more like a schoolteacher than a soldier. He was a big, tall man but he wore glasses and his eyes had a sort of squint. Being a Midwesterner, he talked like one. He still claimed Chicago as home, although he had been an Army officer for twenty-eight years. He was wounded in the last war. He was not glib, but he talked well and laughed easily. In spite of being a professional soldier he despised war and, like any ordinary soul, was appalled by the waste and tragedy of it. He wanted to win it and get home just as badly as anybody else.

When the general was in the field he lived in a truck that used to be a machine shop. They had fixed it up nicely for him with a bed, a desk, cabinets, and rugs. His orderly was an obliging, dark-skinned sergeant who was a native of Ecuador. Some of his officers slept in foxholes, but the general slept in his truck. One night, however, while I was with his division, it got too hot even for him. Fragments from shells bursting nearby started hitting the top of the truck, so he got out.

As a rule he stayed at his desk during the morning and made a tour of regimental and battalion command posts (during the afternoon). Usually he went to the front in an unarmed jeep, with another jeep right behind him carrying a machine gunner and a rifleman on the alert for snipers. His drivers used to say when they started out, "Hold on, for the general doesn't spare the horses when he's traveling." He carried a portable telephone in his jeep, and if he suddenly wanted to talk with any of his units he just stopped along the road and plugged into one of the wires lying on the ground.

General Eddy especially liked to show up in places where his soldiers wouldn't expect to see him. He knew it helped the soldiers' spirits to see their commanding general right up at the front where it was hot. So he walked around the front with his long stride, never ducking or appearing to be concerned at all.

One day I rode around with him on one of his tours. We stopped at a command post and were sitting on the grass under a tree, looking at maps, with a group of officers around us. Our own artillery was banging nearby, but nothing was coming our way. Then, like a flash of lightning, there came a shell just over our heads, so low it went right through the treetops, it seemed. It didn't whine, it swished. Everybody, including full colonels, flopped over and began grabbing grass. The shell exploded in the next orchard. General Eddy didn't move. He just said, "Why, that was one of our shells."

And since I had known General Eddy for quite a while, I was bold enough to say, "General, if that was one of ours all I can say is that this is a hell of a way to run a war. We're fighting toward the north, and that shell was going due south."

The general just laughed.

The general also liked to get up at four o'clock in the morning once in a while and go poking around into message centers and mess halls, giving the boys a start. It was one of these night meanderings that produced his favorite war story. It was in Africa and they were in a new bivouac. It was raining cats and dogs, and the ground was knee-deep in mud. The tent pegs wouldn't stay in and the pup tents kept coming down. Everybody was wet and miserable. So, late at night, the general started out on foot around the area, just because he felt so sorry for all the kids out there. As he walked he passed a soldier trying to re-drive the stake that held down the front of his pup tent. The soldier was using his steel helmet as a hammer, and he was having a bad time of it. Every now and then he would miss the stake with the helmet and would squash mud all over himself. He was cussing and fuming. The general was using his flashlight, and when the soldier saw the light he called out, "Hey, bud, come and hold that light for me, will you?"

So General Eddy obediently squatted down and held the light while the soldier pounded and spattered mud, and they finally got the peg driven. Then, as they got up, the general said, "Soldier, what's your name?"

The startled soldier gasped, leaned forward and looked closely, then blurted out, "Jesus Christ!"

During the Cherbourg Peninsula Campaign I spent nine days with the Ninth Infantry Division—the division that cut the peninsula, and one of the three that overwhelmed the great port of Cherbourg. The Ninth is one of our best divisions. It landed in Africa and it fought through Tunisia and Sicily. Then it went to England in the fall of 1943, and trained all winter for the invasion of France. It was one of the American divisions in the invasion that had had previous battle experience.

An odd thing happened to the Ninth while we were in the Mediterranean. For some reason which we have never fathomed the Ninth wasn't released through censorship as early as it should have been, while other divisions were. As a result, the division got a complex that it was being slighted. They fought hard, took heavy casualties, and did a fine job generally, but nobody back home knew anything about it.

Lack of recognition definitely affects morale. Every commanding general is aware that publicity for his unit is a factor in morale. Not publicity in the manufactured sense, but a public report to the folks back home on what an outfit endures and what it accomplishes. The average doughfoot will go through his share of hell a lot more willingly if he knows that he is getting some credit for it and that the home folks know about it.

As a result of this neglect in the Mediterranean, the Ninth laid careful plans so that it wouldn't happen again. In the first place, a new censorship policy was arrived at, under which the identities of the divisions taking part in a campaign would be publicly released just as soon as it was definitely established that the Germans knew they were in combat. With that big hurdle accomplished, the Ninth made sure that the correspondents themselves would feel at home with them. They set up a small Public Relations section, with an officer in charge, and a squad of enlisted men to move the correspondents' gear, and a truck to haul it, and three tents with cots, electric lights and tables. Correspondents who came with the Ninth could get a meal, a place to write, a jeep for the front, or a courier to the rear—and at any time they asked.

Of course, in spite of all such facilities, a division has to be good in the first place if it is going to get good publicity. The Ninth was good. In the Cherbourg campaign, it performed like a beautiful machine. Its previous battle experience paid off. Not only in individual fighting but in the perfect way the whole organization clicked. As I have tried to explain before, war depends a great deal more on organization than most people would ever dream.

The Ninth did something in that campaign that we hadn't always done in the past. It kept tenaciously on the enemy's neck. When the Germans would withdraw a little the Ninth was right on top of them. It never gave them a chance to reassemble or get their balance. The Ninth moved so fast it got to be funny. I was based at the division command post, and we struck our tents and moved forward six times in seven days. That worked the daylights out of the boys who took down and put up the tents. I overheard one of the boys saying, "I'd rather be with Ringling Brothers."

Usually a division headquarters is a fairly safe place. But with the Ninth it was different. Something was always happening. They had a few bad shellings and lost some personnel. Every now and then snipers would pick off a man. In all the time I was with them we never had an uninterrupted night's sleep. Our own big guns were all around us and they fired all night. Usually German planes were over too, droning around in the darkness and making us tense and nervous. One night I was sitting in a tent with Captain Lindsey Nelson, of Knoxville, when there was a loud explosion, then a shrill whine through the treetops over our heads. But we didn't jump, or hit the dirt. Instead I said, "I know what that is. That's the rotating band off one of our shells. As an old artilleryman I've heard lots of rotating bands. Sometimes they sound like a dog howling. There's nothing to be afraid of."

"Sure," said Captain Nelson, "that's what it was, a rotating band." But our harmless rotating band, we found a few minutes later, was a jagged, red-hot, foot-square fragment of steel from a 240-millimeter German shell which had landed a hundred yards away from us. It's wonderful to be a wise guy.

War in the Normandy countryside was a war from hedgerow to hedgerow, and when we got into a town or city it was a war from street to street. One day I went along—quite accidentally, I assure you—with an infantry company that had been assigned to clean out a pocket in the suburbs of Cherbourg. Since the episode was typical of the way an infantry company advanced into a city held by the enemy, I would like to try to give you a picture of it.

As I say, I hadn't intended to do it. I started out in the normal fashion that afternoon to go up to a battalion command post and just look around. I was traveling with Correspondent Charles Wertenbaker and Photographer Bob Capa, both of *Time* and *Life* magazines.

Well, when we got to the CP we were practically at the front lines. The post was in a church that stood on a narrow street. In the courtyard across the street MP's were frisking freshly taken prisoners. I mingled with them for a while. They were still holding their hands high in the air, and it's pretty close to the front when prisoners do that. They were obviously frightened and eager to please their captors. A soldier standing beside me asked one German kid about the insigne on his cap, so the kid gave it to him. The prisoners had a rank odor about them, like silage. Some of them were Russians, and two of these had their wives with them. They had been living together right at the front. The women thought we were going to shoot their husbands and they were frantic. That's one way the Germans kept the conscripted Russians fighting—they had thoroughly sold them on the belief that we would shoot them as soon as they were captured.

Below us there were big fires in the city, and piles of black smoke. Explosions were going on all around us. Our own big shells would rustle over our heads and explode on beyond with a crash. German 20-millimeter shells would spray over our heads and hit somewhere in the town behind us. Single rifle shots and machine-pistol blurps were constant. The whole thing made me tense and jumpy. The nearest fighting Germans were only 200 yards away.

We were just hanging around absorbing all this stuff when a young lieutenant, in a trench coat and wearing sun glasses—although the day was miserably dark and chill—came over to us and said, "Our company is starting in a few minutes to go up this road and clean out a strong point. It's about half a mile from here. There are probably snipers in some of the houses along the way. Do you want to go with us?"

I certainly didn't. Going into battle with an infantry company is not the way to live to a ripe old age. But when I was invited, what could I do? So I said, "Sure." And so did Wertenbaker and Capa. Wert never seemed nervous, and Capa was notorious for his daring. Fine company for me to be keeping. We started walking. Soldiers of the company were already strung out on both sides of the road ahead of us, just lying and waiting till their officers came along and said go. We walked until we were at the head of the column. As we went the young officer introduced himself. He was Lieutenant Orion Shockley, of Jefferson City, Missouri. I asked him how he got the odd name Orion. He said he was named after Mark Twain's brother. Shockley was executive officer of the company. The company commander was Lieutenant Lawrence McLaughlin, from Boston. One of the company officers was a replacement who had arrived just three hours previously and had never been in battle before. I noticed that he ducked sometimes at our own shells, but he was trying his best to seem calm.

The soldiers around us had a two weeks' growth of beard. Their uniforms were worn slick and very dirty—the uncomfortable gas-impregnated clothes they had come ashore in. The boys were tired. They had been fighting and moving constantly forward on foot for nearly three weeks without rest—sleeping out on the ground, wet most of the time, always tense, eating cold rations, seeing their friends die. One of them came up to me and said, almost belligerently, "Why don't you tell the folks back home what this is like? All they hear about is victories and a lot of glory stuff. They don't know that for every hundred yards we advance somebody gets killed. Why don't you tell them how tough this life is?"

I told him that was what I tried to do all the time. This fellow was pretty fed up with it all. He said he didn't see why his outfit wasn't sent home; they had done all the fighting. That wasn't true at all, for there were other divisions that had fought more and taken heavier casualties. Exhaustion will make a man feel like that. A few days' rest usually has him smiling again.

As we waited to start our advance, the low black skies of Normandy let loose on us and we gradually became soaked to the skin. Lieutenant Shockley came over with a map and explained to us just what his company was going to do to wipe out the strong point of pillboxes and machine-gun nests. Our troops had made wedges into the city on both sides of us, but nobody had yet been up this street where we were heading. The street, they thought, was almost certainly under rifle fire.

"This is how we'll do it," the lieutenant said. "A rifle platoon goes first. Right behind them will go part of a heavy-weapons platoon, with machine guns to cover the first platoon. Then comes another rifle platoon. Then a small section with mortars, in case they run into something pretty heavy. Then another rifle platoon. And bringing up the rear, the rest of the heavy-weapons outfit to protect us from behind. We don't know what we'll run into, and I don't want to stick you right out in front, so why don't you come along with me? We'll go in the middle of the company."

I said, "Okay." By this time I wasn't scared. You seldom are once you're into something. Anticipation is the worst. Fortunately, this little foray came up so suddenly there wasn't time for much anticipation.

The rain kept coming down, and we could sense that it had set in for the afternoon. None of us had raincoats, and by evening there wasn't a dry thread on us. I could go back to a tent for the night, but the soldiers would have to sleep the way they were.

We were just ready to start when all of a sudden bullets came whipping savagely right above our heads. "It's those damn 20-millimeters again," the lieutenant said. "Better hold it up a minute." The soldiers all crouched lower behind the wall. The vicious little shells whanged into a grassy hillside just beyond us. A French suburban farmer was hitching up his horses in a barnyard on the hillside. He ran into the house. Shells struck all around it. Two dead Germans and a dead American still lay in his driveway. We could see them when we moved up a few feet.

The shells stopped, and finally the order to start was given. As we left the protection of the high wall we had to cross a little culvert right out in the open and then make a turn in the road.

The men went forward one at a time. They crouched and ran, ape-like, across this dangerous space. Then, beyond the culvert, they filtered to either side of the road, stopping and squatting down every now and then to wait a few moments. The lieutenant kept yelling at them as they started, "Spread it out now. Do you want to draw fire on yourselves? Don't bunch up like that. Keep five yards apart. Spread it out, dammit."

There is an almost irresistible pull to get close to somebody when you are in danger. In spite of themselves, the men would run up close to the fellow ahead for company. The other lieutenant now called out, "You on the right, watch the left side of the street for snipers; you on the left, watch the right side. Cover each other that way."

And a first sergeant said to a passing soldier, "Get that grenade out of its case. It won't do you no good in the case. Throw the case away. That's right."

Some of the men carried grenades already fixed in the ends of their rifles. All of them had hand grenades. Some had big Browning automatic rifles. One carried a bazooka. Interspersed in the thin line of men every now and then was a medic, with his bags of bandages and a Red Cross armband on his left arm. The men didn't talk among themselves. They just went. They weren't heroic figures as they moved forward one at a time, a few seconds apart. You think of attackers as being savage and bold. These men were hesitant and cautious. They were really the hunters, but they looked like the hunted. There was a confused excitement and a grim anxiety in their faces.

They seemed terribly pathetic to me. They weren't warriors. They were American boys who by mere chance of fate had wound up with guns in their hands, sneaking up a death-laden street in a strange and shattered city in a faraway country in a driving rain. They were afraid, but it was beyond their power to quit. They had no choice. They were good boys. I talked with them all afternoon as we sneaked slowly forward along the mysterious and rubbled street, and I know they were good boys. And even though they weren't warriors born to the kill, they won their battles. That's the point.

It came time for me to go—out alone into that empty expanse of fifteen feet—as we began our move into the street that led to what we did not know. One of the soldiers asked if I didn't have a rifle. Every time I was really in the battle lines they would ask me that. I said no, correspondents weren't allowed to; it was against international law. The soldiers thought that didn't seem right. Finally the sergeant motioned—it was my turn. I ran with bent knees, shoulders hunched, out across the culvert and across the open space. Lord, but I felt lonely out there. I had to stop right in the middle of the open space, to keep my distance behind the man ahead. I got down behind a little bush, as though that would have stopped anything.

Just before starting I had got into conversation with a group of soldiers who were to go right behind me. I was just starting to put down the boys' names when my turn came to go. So it wasn't till an hour or more later, during one of our long waits as we crouched against some buildings, that I worked my way back along the line and got their names. It was pouring rain, and as we squatted down for me to write on my knee each soldier would have to hold my helmet over my notebook to keep it from getting soaked.

Here are the names of just a few of my company mates in that little escapade that afternoon: Sergeant Joseph Palajsa, of 187 I Street, Pittsburgh. Pfc. Arthur Greene, of 618 Oxford Street, Auburn, Massachusetts; his New England accent was so broad I had to have him spell out "Arthur" and "Auburn" before I could catch what he said. Pfc. Dick Medici, of 5231 Lemy Avenue, Detroit. Lieutenant James Giles, a platoon leader, from Athens, Tennessee; he was so wet, so worn, so soldier-looking that I was startled when he said "lieutenant," for I thought he was a GI. Pfc. Arthur Slageter, of 3915 Taylor Avenue, Cincinnati; he was an old reader of my column back home, and therefore obviously a fine fellow. Pfc. Robert Edie, of New Philadelphia, Pennsylvania; Edie was thirty, he was married, and he used to work in a brewery back home; he was a bazooka man, but his bazooka was broken that day so he was just carrying a rifle. Pfc. Ben Rienzi, of 430 East 115 Street, New York. Sergeant Robert Hamilton, of 2940 Robbins Avenue, Philadelphia, who was wounded in Africa. Sergeant Joe Netscavge, of Shenandoah, Pennsylvania, who sported two souvenirs of the Normandy campaign—a deep dent in his helmet where a sniper's bullet glanced off, and a leather cigarette case he got from a German prisoner. These boys were Ninth Division veterans, most of whom had fought in Tunisia and in Sicily too.

Gradually we moved on, a few feet at a time. The soldiers hugged the walls on both sides of the street, crouching all the time. The city around us was still full of sound and fury. We couldn't tell where anything was coming from or going to. The houses had not been blown down. But now and then a wall would have a round hole through it, and the windows had all been knocked out by concussion, and shattered glass littered the pavements. Gnarled telephone wire was lying everywhere. Most of the people had left the city. Shots, incidentally, always sound louder and distorted in the vacuumlike emptiness of a nearly deserted city. Lonely doors and shutters banged noisily back and forth. All of a sudden a bunch of dogs came yowling down the street, chasing each other. Apparently their owners had left without them, and they were running wild. They made such a noise that we shooed them on in the erroneous fear that they would attract the Germans' attention.

The street was a winding one and we couldn't see as far ahead as our forward platoon. But soon we could hear rifle shots not far ahead, and the rat-tat-tat of our machine guns, and the quick blurp-blurp of German machine pistols. For a long time we didn't move at all. While we were waiting the lieutenant decided to go into the house just behind us. A middle-aged Frenchman and his wife were in the kitchen. They were poor people. The woman was holding a terrier dog in her arms, belly up, the way you cuddle a baby, and soothing it by rubbing her cheek against its head. The dog was trembling with fear from the noise.

Pretty soon the word was passed back down the line that the street had been cleared as far as a German hospital about a quarter of a mile ahead. There were lots of our own wounded in that hospital and they were now being liberated. So Lieutenant Shockley and Wertenbaker and Capa and I went on up the street, still keeping close to the walls. I lost the others before I had gone far. For as I passed doorways soldiers would call out to me and I would duck in and talk for a moment and put down a name or two.

By now the boys along the line were feeling cheerier, for no word of casualties had been passed back. And up there the city was built up enough so that the waiting riflemen had the protection of doorways. It took me half an hour to work my way up to the hospital—and then the excitement began. The hospital was in our hands, but just barely. There seemed to be fighting in the next block. I say seemed to be, because actually it was hard to tell. Street fighting is just as confusing as field fighting. One side would bang away for a while, then the other side. Between the sallies there were long lulls, with only stray and isolated shots. Just an occasional soldier was sneaking about, and I didn't see anything of the enemy at all. I couldn't tell half the time just what the situation was, and neither could the soldiers.

About a block beyond the hospital entrance two American tanks were sitting in the middle of the street, one about fifty yards ahead of the other. I walked toward them. Our infantrymen were in doorways along the street. I got within about fifty feet of our front tank when it let go its 75-millimeter gun. The blast was terrific there in the narrow street. Glass came tinkling down from nearby windows, smoke puffed around the tank, and the empty street was shaking and trembling with the concussion. As the tank continued to shoot I ducked into a doorway, because I figured the Germans would shoot back. Inside the doorway was a sort of street-level cellar, dirt-floored. Apparently there was a wine shop above, for the cellar was stacked with wire crates for holding wine bottles on their sides. There were lots of bottles, but they were all empty.

I went back to the doorway and stood peeking out at the tank. It started backing up. Then suddenly a yellow flame pierced the bottom of the tank and there was a crash of such intensity that I automatically blinked my eyes. The tank, hardly fifty feet from where I was standing, had been hit by an enemy shell. A second shot ripped the pavement at the side of the tank. There was smoke all around, but the tank didn't catch fire. In a moment the crew came boiling out of the turret. Grim as it was, I almost had to laugh as they ran toward me. I have never seen men run so violently. They ran all over, with arms and heads going up and down and with marathon-race grimaces. They plunged into my doorway.

I spent the next excited hour with them. We changed to another doorway and sat on boxes in the empty hallway. The floor and steps were thick with blood where a soldier had been treated within the hour. What had happened to the tank was this: They had been firing away at a pillbox ahead when their 75 backfired, filling the tank with smoke and blinding them. They decided to back up in order to get their bearings, but after backing a few yards the driver was so blinded that he stopped. Unfortunately, he stopped exactly at the foot of a side street. More unfortunately, there was another German pillbox up the side street. All the Germans had to do was take easy aim and let go at the sitting duck. The first shot hit a tread, so the tank couldn't move. That was when the boys got out. I don't know why the Germans didn't fire at them as they poured out.

The escaped tankers naturally were excited, but they were as jubilant as June bugs and ready for more. They had never been in combat before the invasion of Normandy, yet in three weeks their tank had been shot up three times. Each time it was repaired and put back into action. And it could be repaired again. The name of their tank, appropriately, was "Be Back Soon."

The main worry of these boys was the fact that they had left the engine running. We could hear it chugging away. It's bad for a tank motor to idle very long. But they were afraid to go back and turn the motor off, for the tank was still right in line with the hidden German gun. Also, they had come out wearing their leather crash helmets. Their steel helmets were still inside the tank, and so were their rifles. "We'll be a lot of good without helmets or rifles!" one of them said.

The crew consisted of Corporal Martin Kennelly, of 8040 Langley Street, Chicago, the tank commander; Sergeant L. Wortham, Leeds, Alabama, driver; Private Ralph Ogren, of 3551 32nd Avenue South, Minneapolis, assistant driver; Corporal Albin Stoops, Marshalltown, Delaware, gunner; and Private Charles Rains, of 1317 Madison Street, Kansas City, the loader. Private Rains was the oldest of the bunch, and the only married one. He used to work as a guard at the Sears, Roebuck plant in Kansas City. "I was MP to fifteen hundred women," he said with a grin, "and how I'd like to be back doing that!" The other tankers all expressed loud approval of this sentiment.

Commander Kennelly wanted to show me just where his tank had been hit. As a matter of fact he hadn't seen it for himself yet, for he came running up the street the moment he jumped out of the tank. So when the firing died down a little we sneaked up the Street until we were almost even with the disabled tank. But we were careful not to get our heads around the corner of the side street. The first shell had hit the heavy steel brace that the tread runs on, and then plunged on through the side of the tank, very low. "Say!" Kennelly said in amazement. "It went right through our lower ammunition storage box! I don't know what kept the ammunition from going off. We'd have been a mess if it had. Boy, it sure would have got hot in there in a hurry!"

The street was still empty. Beyond the tank about two blocks was a German truck, sitting all alone in the middle of the street. It had been blown up, and its tires had burned off. This truck was the only thing we could see. There wasn't a human being in sight anywhere. Then an American soldier came running up the street shouting for somebody to send a medic. He said a man was badly wounded just ahead. He was extremely excited, yelling, and getting madder because there was no medic in sight. Word was passed down the line, and pretty soon a medic came out of a doorway and started up the street. The excited soldier yelled at him and began cussing, and the medic broke into a run. They ran past the tanks together, and up the street a way they ducked into a doorway.

On the corner just across the street from where we were standing was a smashed pillbox. It was in a cut-away corner like the entrances to some of our corner drugstores at home, except that instead of there being a door there was a pillbox of reinforced concrete, with gun slits. The tank boys had shot it to pieces and then moved their tank up even with it to get the range of the next pillbox. That one was about a block ahead, set in a niche in the wall of a building. That's what the boys had been shooting at when their tank was hit. They had knocked it out, however, before being knocked out themselves.

For an hour there was a lull in the fighting. Nobody did anything about a third pillbox, around the corner. Our second tank pulled back a little and just waited. Infantrymen worked their way up to second-story windows and fired their rifles up the side street without actually seeing anything to shoot at. Now and then blasts from a 20-millimeter gun would splatter the buildings around us. Then our second tank would blast back in that general direction, over the low roofs, with its machine gun. There was a lot of dangerous-sounding noise, but I don't think anybody on either side got hit.

Then we saw coming up the street, past the wrecked German truck I spoke of, a group of German soldiers. An officer walked in front, carrying a Red Cross flag on a stick. Bob Capa braved the dangerous funnel at the end of the side street where the damaged tank stood, leapfrogging past it and on down the street to meet the Germans. First he snapped some pictures of them. Then, since he spoke German, he led them on back to our side of the invisible fence of battle. Eight of them were carrying two litters bearing two wounded German soldiers. The others walked behind with their hands up. They went on past us to the hospital. We assumed that they were from the second knocked-out pillbox. I didn't stay to see how the remaining pillbox was knocked out. But I suppose our second tank eventually pulled up to the corner, turned, and let the pillbox have it. After that the area would be clear of everything but snipers. The infantry, who up till then had been forced to keep in doorways, would then continue up the street and poke into the side streets and into the houses until everything was clear.

That's how a strong point in a city is taken. At least that's how ours was taken. There are not always tanks to help, and not always is it done with so little shedding of blood. But the city was already crumbling when we started in on this strong point, which was one of the last, and they didn't hold on too bitterly. But we didn't know that when we started.

THIRTY

RECONNOITERINGS

Came the day while we were up on the Cherbourg peninsula when I decided all of a sudden that I couldn't face C rations that evening. And Bob Capa said he never could face C rations in the first place. So we laid a plan. We got a friendly mess sergeant to drum us up some cans of Vienna sausage, some sugar, canned peas, and what not, and we put them in a pasteboard box. Then we walked around a couple of hedgerows to our motor pool and dug out Private Lawrence Wedley Cogan from the comfortable lair he had prepared for himself in an oatfield. Private Cogan drove a command car for the G-2 section of the Ninth Infantry Division. When we could catch him not driving for G-2, we could talk him into driving us somewhere.

So we piled in and directed Chauffeur Cogan to set out for the nearby village of Les Pieux. When we got there, Capa, who speaks eight languages—and, as his friends say, "none of them well"—went into a restaurant to make his investigations. Pretty soon he came to the door and motioned. So Cogan parked the car behind a building, we took our box of canned stuff, and in we went.

It was a typical French village restaurant, with low ceilings, and floors that sagged, and it consisted of four or five rooms. It was crammed with French people, for we had only just taken Les Pieux and not many Americans had found the place yet. The woman who ran the place took us to a long table. Private Cogan was dirty with the grease and dust of his job and went off to wash before eating in civilized fashion again. The cosmopolitan Capa made a deal and we traded our rations for the café's regular dinner, in order not to take anything away from the French. We had expected to pay the full price anyhow, but when the bill came they charged us only for the cooking, and wouldn't take a bit more.

The restaurant had no small tables, just one long one in each room; consequently, we were seated with French people. They seemed eager to be friendly, and pretty soon we were in the thick of conversation. That is, Capa and the French were in conversation, and occasionally he would relay the gist of it to Cogan and me, the hicks. The people told us about the German occupation, but they didn't have much bad to say about the Germans. Then we talked of the French underground, which had just been coming into the open during the previous few days.

Throughout our dinner Private Cogan, in his soiled coveralls, listened and beamed and ate and took in eagerly the words he couldn't understand and the scene which was so new and strange to him. One middle-aged Frenchwoman made a fuss over him because he looked so young. Cogan wasn't bashful, but he couldn't talk French so he just grinned. Private Cogan joined the Army at seventeen. He was overseas before he was eighteen, and he was only nineteen then. His home was at 128 East Walnut Street, Alexandria, Virginia. He was one of the nicest human beings I ever met. No matter what we asked him to do, or what time of night it was, or in what weather we dug him out, he did it good-naturedly and without the silent surliness of some drivers. Furthermore, he was an excellent driver, and he always had a box of rations in his car. When we left the restaurant he was all abubble and said over and over again that he'd had the best time that evening he had ever had in the Army. Imagine him, he said, as young as he was, seeing foreign stuff like that.

Captain John Jackson was an unusual fellow with an unusual job. It fell to his lot to be the guy who went in and brought out German generals who thought maybe they would like to surrender. This happened because he spoke German, and because he was on the staff of the Ninth Division which captured the German generals commanding the Cherbourg area.

Captain Jackson went by the nickname of "Brinck." He was a bachelor, thirty-two years old. It was quite a coincidence that he was born in the town of Dinard, about thirty miles from Cherbourg, but he was straight American, for generations back. His folks just happened to be traveling over there at the time he showed up. Captain Jackson's mother lived in New Canaan, Connecticut, but he liked to think of New Mexico as home. For several years he had been a rancher out there, and he loved it. His place was near Wagon Mound and Klines Corners, about forty miles east of Santa Fe. The war played hob with his business. Both he and his partner were overseas, and there was nobody left to look after it. They had lost money last year for the first time.

Captain Jackson was a short, dark man with a thin face. He wore a long trench coat with pack harness, and his helmet came down over his ears, giving him the appearance of a Russian soldier rather than an American. He spoke perfect French, but he said his German was only so-so. It was actually better in his job not to speak German too flawlessly, for then the captured officers might have thought he was a German turned American and been so contemptuous they wouldn't have talked to him.

When the now famous General Carl Wilhelm von Schlieben was captured I happened to be at the Ninth Division command post to which he was first brought. Major General Manton S. Eddy, division commander, had a long interview with him in his trailer. When he was about finished and ready to send the captured general on to higher headquarters, General Eddy sent word that the photographers could come and take pictures. So they stood in a group in an orchard while the photographers snapped away. Von Schlieben was obviously sourpuss about being captured, and even more sourpuss at having his picture taken. He made no effort to look other than sullenly displeased.

General Eddy was trying to be decent about it. He had an interpreter tell the prisoner that this was the price of being a general. Von Schlieben just snorted. And then General Eddy said to the interpreter, "Tell the general that our country is a democracy and therefore I haven't the authority to forbid these photographers to take pictures."

Von Schlieben snorted again. And we chuckled behind our beards at one of the slickest examples of working democracy we had ever seen. And General Eddy had the appearance of the traditional cat that swallowed something wonderful.

Another remarkable character was Pfc. Ivan Sanders. Sanders was the "Mr. Fixit" of the Ninth Division. His real job was that of electrician, but his knack for fixing things had given him a sort of haloed status that kept him working like a dog twenty-four hours a day, doing things for other people. Without previous experience he repaired fountain pens, radios, electric razors, typewriters, broken knives, stoves and watches. He had become an institution. Everybody from the commanding general on down depended on him and yelled for him whenever anything went wrong.

There was just one thing about Sanders. Nobody could get him to clean up. He was a sight to behold. Even the commanding general just threw up his hands and gave up. When distinguished visitors came, they tried to hide Sanders. But the funny part about Sanders's deplorable condition was that he was eager to be clean. They just never gave him time to wash. They kept him too busy fixing things.

In civil life Sanders was an automobile mechanic. He came from Vinton, Iowa. After the war he guessed he would set up another auto repair shop. He figured there would be enough veterans with cars to keep him busy. Another unusual thing about Sanders was that he didn't have to be over there at all. He was forty-three, and he had had three chances to go home. And do you know why he turned them down? Just because he was so conscientious he figured they couldn't get anybody else to do his work properly!

Small-world stuff: One evening I dropped past an ack-ack battery I knew, and a Red Cross man who served in the brigade came over and introduced himself. He did look vaguely familiar, but I couldn't have told you who he was. And no wonder—it had been twenty-one years since I'd seen him. His name was Byron Wallace. He was a freshman at Indiana University when I was a senior. He belonged to the Delta Upsilon fraternity, and had lived just across the alley from us. His home then was at Washington, Indiana. Ever since college he had been in recreational and physical education work—in New York's Bowery, in Los Angeles, in Pittsburgh. And then in Normandy. He went ashore on D + 1. He thought he was going to like it there all right.

Another small-world experience befell a couple of soldiers who came to our camp to tell me about the strange thing that had just happened to them. They were brothers, and the night before they had run onto each other for the first time in more than two years. They were Corporal John and Private Edward O'Donnell, of East Milton, Massachusetts. John was an artilleryman and had been overseas more than two years, all through Africa and Sicily. Edward had been overseas only a couple of months. John was twenty-two; Edward, nineteen. The first Edward knew his brother was in the vicinity was when he saw some soldiers, wearing the patch of John's division, getting ready to take a bath at an outdoor shower the Army had set up. He asked them where the division was and then began a several-hour hunt for his brother. John was attending an Army movie in a barn when Edward finally tracked him down. They sent in word for John to come out. When he got about halfway out and saw who was waiting he practically knocked everybody out of their chairs getting to the back. Their respective commanding officers gave John and Edward the next day off and they just roamed around with their tongues wagging—talking mostly about home.

Normandy is a land of rabbits. We saw them in the fields and around the farmyards. Most of them were semitame. Apparently the people eat a great deal of rabbit. When we first moved in and began capturing permanent German bivouac areas we found that nearly every little group of German soldiers had its own rabbit warren. They raised them for food.

One day my friend Private William Bates Wescott found a mother rabbit that had been killed in the shelling, and nearby, in a nest under a hedge, he found six baby rabbits, only a few days old. Wescott took them to his pup tent, got a ration box to put them in, and spent the afternoon feeding them condensed milk through an eye-dropper. They went for it like little babies. Next morning five of them were dead. The soldiers said the concussion of bombs falling during the night had killed them. I said undiluted condensed milk had killed them. At any rate, the sixth one thrived and became cute and gay. He followed Wescott around everywhere, and if the distance got too far he would go hopping back to the pup tent and snuggle up in Wescott's blankets. He was quite a little rabbit. Everybody was crazy about him. Then after about a week we found him dead out on the grass one morning. Which is a lousy way to end the story, but that's all there was to it.

The town of Montebourg on the Cherbourg peninsula was one of the worst-wrecked towns, shelled by both sides. We stopped at Montebourg the day after it was all over. On one side of the city square there was a large collection of rusting farm implements—all kinds of plows, planters, mowers and things. On one wrecked mowing machine was the familiar name "McCormick." And near the machine was stretched out in pathetic death a big white rabbit.

Mosquitoes were pretty bad in the swampy parts of Normandy. Especially along the hedgerows at night, they were ferocious. They had something there I'd never seen before even in Alaska, the mosquito capital of the world. Driving along a road just before dusk we would see dark columns extending two and three hundred feet straight up into the air above a treetop. Those were columns of mosquitoes swarming like bees, each column composed of millions. At first I thought they were gnats, but old mosquito people assured me they were genuine, all-wool mosquitoes. In a half-mile drive just before dusk we might see twenty of those columns. That's no cock and bull story; it's the truth. Our troops were not equipped with mosquito nets, so they just had to scratch and scratch. The mosquitoes, fortunately, didn't give us malaria, they merely drove us crazy.

One night I crawled down into an ack-ack battery command post, in a dugout. It was about 2 a.m. Only two people were there—a lieutenant, giving orders to the guns by telephone, and a sergeant, getting ready to fix some hot chocolate. He asked if I would have some, and following the old Army custom of never refusing anything I said sure. He was Sergeant Leopold Lamparty, first sergeant of the battery, from 916 Franklin Street, Youngstown, Ohio. He used to be a bartender, and in France he had already picked up several little antique whisky glasses of old and beautiful design. But the reason I'm writing about Lamparty was his electric iron. He made the hot chocolate on an electric iron turned upside down. Each ack-ack battery had a portable generator, so Lamparty just plugged in. His sister had sent him the iron two years back when he was in a camp near Chicago, and he had carried it ever since. Once upon a time he used to press his pants with it, but a guy with pressed pants in Normandy during the fighting would probably have been shot as a spy, so Lamparty was cooking with his iron.

One afternoon a soldier came by to say hello because his name was the same as mine. He was Private Stewart Pyle, of Orange, New Jersey. He was a driver, and now and then he got an assignment to drive some high officers. Private Pyle was married and had been overseas nine months. Try as we might, we couldn't establish any relationship. Perhaps it was due to the fact that my name isn't Pyle at all, but Count Sforza Chef DuPont D'Artagnan. Our family sprang from a long line of Norman milkmaids. We took the name Pyle after the Jones murder cases in 1739—January, I think it was. My great-grandfather built the Empire State Building. Why am I telling you all this?

Department of Wartime Distorted Values: A soldier offered to trade a French farmer three horses for three eggs. The soldier had captured the horses from the Germans. The trade didn't come off—the farmer already had three horses. And at one of our evacuation hospitals a wounded soldier turned over 90,000 francs, equivalent to $1,800. He'd picked up the money in a captured German headquarters. The Army was soon in the process of looking up regulations to see whether the soldier could keep the money.

When I was going into Cherbourg with an infantry company, one of the doughboys gave me two cans of French sardines they'd captured from the Germans. Right in the midst of battle is a funny place to be giving sardines to a man, but this is a funny war. At any rate, I was grateful and I put them in my musette bag when I got back to my tent that night. I forgot all about them. Several weeks later I got a hungry spell, and was rummaging around in the bag for candy or something and found these sardines. They tasted mighty good.

Everything seems old in Normandy. The hedgerows are thick

and ancient. The stone walls are sometimes so mounded over with earth that a person couldn't know there's a wall beneath. The trees in the apple orchards are mellow with moss so thick that it seems like a coat of green velvet. The towns and cities are just as old and worn-looking. I didn't see a building in Normandy that appeared to have been built within the last three generations. The tone is not one of decadence, but just of great and contented age. Even Cherbourg was a surprise. All of its buildings are old and worn.

It was a contrast to other war cities we passed through—Algiers and Palermo and even Naples—where much building and remodeling had been done in this century, and the new homes were shiny and modernistic, and the street fronts looked almost American.

A street scene in Cherbourg looks so much like the Hollywood sets of old European cities that the perspective is reversed and it seems that Cherbourg has just been copied from a movie set. It's the same way with the Norman architecture. The houses aren't so smooth and regular and nice as California homes of Norman design. When I looked at them I felt, before catching myself, that they had copied our California Norman homes and not done too good a job.

Everything is of stone. Even the barns and cowsheds are stone and in exactly the same design and usually the same size as the houses. They are grouped closely together around a square, so that a farmer's home makes a compact little settlement of buildings that from a distance resembles a country estate.

Normandy is dairy country. Right then the people had more butter on their hands than they knew what to do with. It was a stupid soldier indeed who couldn't get himself all the butter he wanted. But even though it was a glut on the market, the French still asked sixty cents a pound for it. When the Germans were there they bought all the Norman butter, and at fancy prices too. German soldiers would ship it home to their families. And although their New Order was strict and full of promises of an ordered world, the Germans themselves created and fostered the Paris black market, according to the local people. Much of the butter bought in Normandy by German officers went to Paris for resale at unheard-of prices.

To be honest about it, we couldn't sense that Normandy suffered too much under the German occupation. That was no doubt less because of German beneficence than because of the nature of the country. For in any throttled country the farm people always come out best. Normandy is rich agriculturally. The people can sustain themselves. It is in the cities that occupation hurts worst.

Normandy is certainly a land of children. I saw even more than in Italy. And I'll have to break down and admit that they were the most beautiful children I have ever seen. It was an exception to see a child who wasn't strikingly good-looking. But apparently they grow out of this, for on the whole the adults looked like people anywhere—both good and bad. One thing about the Normans is in contrast with the temperament we knew so long in the Mediterranean. The people are hard workers. Some of the American camps and city offices hired teenage French boys for kitchen and office work, and I noticed that they went to their work like the wind.

The story of the French underground, when the day comes for it to be written, will be one of the most fascinating stories in all history. On the Cherbourg peninsula the underground was made up of cells, five people to a cell. Those five knew each other, but none of them knew any other members of the underground anywhere. It was fun to see the Frenchmen on the day the underground began coming into the open. They identified themselves by special armbands which they had kept in hiding. One underground man would look at a neighbor wearing an armband and exclaim in amazement, "What! You too?"

In one village we asked some people who were not in the movement if they had ever known who the underground members in their town were. They said they could pretty well guess, just from the character of the people, but never knew for sure.

Eggs were not plentiful enough in Normandy to supply the whole army, but a good scrounger could dig up a few each day. We bought them from farmers' wives for six and eight cents apiece. We hoped someday to buy some from a farmer's daughter. Those Normandy eggs were fine, about every fourth one as big as a duck egg. The five men in our tent were all egg-conscious, so we made it a practice to shop for eggs as we went about the country.

We passed up regular breakfast in the mess and had our breakfast in our own tent every morning. By some inexplicable evolution of cruel fate I became the chef for this four-man crew of breakfast Gargantuas. Those four plutocrats lay in their cots and snored while I got out at the crack of dawn and slaved over two Coleman stoves, cooking their oeufs in real Normandy butter—fried, scrambled, boiled or poached, as suited the whims of their respective majesties. Except when I was away with troops, I was at this despicable occupation for all of two months. And although my clients were smart enough to keep me always graciously flattered about my culinary genius, I got damn sick of the job. I swore that someday I'd go on away and never come back again as long as I lived, never, not even if they put an ad in the paper. Then they would all wither away to nothing from lack of sustenance, and eventually they would starve plumb to death in that faraway and strangely beautiful land.

THIRTY-ONE

ORDNANCE

One of the things the layman doesn't hear much about is the Ordnance Department. In fact, it is one of the branches that even the average soldier is little aware of, except in a vague way. And yet the war couldn't keep going without it. For Ordnance repairs all the vehicles of an army and furnishes all the ammunition for its guns. There were more vehicles in the American sector of our beachhead than in the average-sized American city. And our big guns on an average heavy day were shooting up more than $10,000,000 worth of ammunition. So you see Ordnance had a man-sized job.

Ordnance personnel is usually about six or seven per cent of the total men of an army. That means we had many thousands of ordnancemen in Normandy. Their insigne is a flame coming out of a bomb—nicknamed in the Army the "Flaming Onion." Ordnance operated the ammunition dumps we had scattered about the beachhead. But much bigger than its ammunition mission was Ordnance's job of repair. Ordnance had millions of items in its catalogue of parts, and the catalogue itself covered a 20-foot shelf.

In a central headquarters there on the beachhead a modern filing system, housed in big tents, kept records on the number and condition of 500 major items in actual use on the beachhead—from tanks to pistols. We had scores and scores of separate ordnance companies at work there—each of them a complete firm within itself, able to repair anything the Army used. Ordnance could lift a 30-ton tank as easily as it could a bicycle. It could repair a blown-up jeep or the intricate breech of a mammoth gun.

Some of the highly specialized repair companies were made up largely of men who were craftsmen in the same line in civil life. In those companies the average age was much above the Army average. There were craftsmen in their late forties, men—wearing sergeants' stripes—who used to make $30,000 to $40,000 a year back home in their own established businesses. Their IQs were far above the average for the Army. It had to be that way or the work could not have been done. I found great soberness and sincerity among them, plus the normal satisfaction that comes from making things whole again instead of destroying them. Out under a tree I saw machines at work that would have been housed in a $50,000 shop back in America. Men worked sixteen hours a day, then slept on the ground—men who, because of their age, didn't have to be there at all.

Ordnance is one of the undramatic branches of the Army. These men are the mechanics and the craftsmen, the fixers and the suppliers. But their job is vital. Ordinarily they are not in a great deal of danger. There were times on newly won and congested beachheads when their casualty rate was high, but once the war settled down and there was room for movement and dispersal it was not necessary or desirable for them to do their basic work within gun range. Our ordnance branch in Normandy had had casualties. There were two small branches which continued to have casualties—disposal squads and retriever companies that went up to pull out crippled tanks under fire.

Ordnance is set up in a vast structure of organization the same as any other command. The farther back from the lines the bigger become the outfits and the more elaborately equipped and more capable of doing heavy, long-term work. Every infantry or armored division has an ordnance company with it all the time. This company does quick repair jobs. What it hasn't time or facilities for doing it hands on back to the next echelon in the rear.

The division ordnance companies hit the Normandy beach on D-day. The next echelon back began coming on D + 2. The heavy outfits arrived somewhat later. After seven weeks of war the wreckage was all in hand, and in one great depot after another it was worked out—repaired or rebuilt or sent back for salvage until everything possible was made available again to our men who did the fighting.

I visited what Ordnance calls a "mobile maintenance company." They repaired jeeps, light trucks, small arms and light artillery—

no tanks, heavy trucks or big guns. The company was bivouacked around the hedgerows of a large grassy L-shaped pasture. There were no trees in the pasture, and nothing in the center except some grazing horses. No men or vehicles walked or drove across the pasture. Always they stuck to the tree-high hedgerows. It was hard to believe that there in a thin, invisible line around the edges of the empty pasture there was a great machine shop with nearly 200 men working with wrenches and welding torches, that six teams of auto mechanics were busy. Actually there was little need for such perfect camouflage, for this company was perhaps ten miles behind the lines and German planes never appeared in the daytime. But it was good policy to keep in practice on camouflage.

This was a proud company. It was the first one to land in France—first, that is, behind the companies actually attached to divisions. It landed on D + 2 and lost three men killed and seven wounded when a shell hit their ship as they were unloading. For several days it and one other were the only ordnance companies of their type ashore. Its small complement, whose job in theory was to back up only one division in medium repair work, carried all repair work for four divisions until help arrived. The company had a proud record in the last war too, having been in nine major engagements. And it had a sentimental little coincidence in its history. In 1917 and in 1943 it left America for France on the same date, December 12.

In one corner of the pasture was the command post tent where two sergeants and two officers worked at folding tables and kept the records so necessary in Ordnance. A first lieutenant was in command of the company, assisted by five other lieutenants. Their stand-by was Warrant Officer Ernest Pike, of Savoy, Texas, who had been in the Army fifteen years, thirteen of them with this very company. What he didn't know about practical ordnance you could put in a dead German's eye.

In another corner of the pasture was a mess truck with its field kitchens under some trees. There the men of the company lined up for meals with mess kits, officers as well as men, and ate sitting on the grass. The officers lounged on the grass in a little group apart and when they finished eating they lit cigarettes and played awhile with some cute little French puppies they had found in

German strong points, or traded soap and cigarettes for. The officers knew the men intimately and if they were in a hurry and had left their mess kits behind they just borrowed from soldiers who had finished eating.

A company of this kind was highly mobile. It could pack up and be under way in probably less than an hour. Yet Ordnance figured, as a basic policy, that its companies should not move oftener than every six days if they were to work successfully. They figured one day for moving, one for settling down and four days of full-time work, then forward again. If at any time the fighting ahead of them got rolling faster than this rate, the ordnance companies began leapfrogging each other, one working while another of the same type moved around it and set up.

Their equipment was moved in trucks and trailers. Some trucks were machine shops, others were supply stores. Some plain trucks were for hauling miscellaneous stuff. Once set up, the men slept on the ground in pup tents along the hedges, with foxholes dug deep and handy.

The more skilled men worked at their benches and instruments inside the shop trucks. The bulk of the work outside was done under dark-green canvas canopies stretched outward from the hedgerows and held taut on upright poles, their walls formed of camouflage nets. Nothing but a vague blur was visible from a couple of hundred yards away. A person would have had to make a long tour clear around the big pasture, nosing in under the hedge and camouflage nets, in order to realize that anything was going on at all. In the far distance was a faint rumble of big guns, and overhead all day our own planes roared comfortingly. But outside those fringes of war it was as peaceful in that Normandy field as it would be in a pasture in Ohio. Even the three liberated horses grazed contentedly on the ankle-high grass, quite indifferent to the fact that the peaceful field was part of the great war machine that would destroy their recent masters.

Daily to the small-arms section of the company there came trucks with the picked-up, rusting rifles of men killed or wounded, and rifles broken in ordinary service. The outfit turned back around a hundred rifles a day to its division, all shiny and oiled and ready to shoot again. They operated on the simple salvage system of taking good parts off one gun and placing them on another. To do this they worked like a small assembly plant. The first few hours of the morning were devoted to taking broken rifles apart. They didn't try to keep the parts of each gun together. All parts were standard and transferable, hence they threw each type into a big steel pan full of similar parts. At the end of the job they had a dozen or so pans, each filled with the same kind of part. Then the whole gang shifted over and scrubbed the parts. They scrubbed in gasoline, using sandpaper for guns in bad condition after lying out in the rain and mud. When everything was clean they took the good parts and started putting them together and making guns out of them again. After all the pans were empty they had a stack of rifles—good rifles, ready to be taken to the front. Of the parts left over some were thrown away, quite beyond repair. But others were repairable and went into the section's shop truck for working on with lathes and welding torches. Thus the division got a hundred reclaimed rifles a day, in addition to the brand-new ones issued to it.

And, believe me, during the first few days of our invasion men at the front needed those rifles desperately. Repairmen told me how our paratroopers and infantrymen would straggle back, dirty and hazy-eyed with fatigue, and plead like children for a new rifle immediately so they could get back to the front and "get at them sonsabitches." One paratrooper brought in a German horse he had captured and offered to trade it for a new rifle, he needed it so badly. During those days the men in our little repair shop worked all hours trying to fill the need.

I sat around on the grass and chatted with the rifle repairmen most of one forenoon. They weren't working so frenziedly then, for the urgency was not so dire, but they kept steadily at it as we talked. The head of the section was Sergeant Edward Welch, of Watts, Oklahoma. He used to work in the oilfields. Shortly after the invasion he had invented a gadget that cleaned rust out of a rifle barrel in a few seconds whereas it used to take a man about twenty minutes. Sergeant Welch did it merely by rigging up a swivel shaft on the end of an electric drill and attaching a cylindrical wire brush to the end. He just stuck the brush into the gun barrel and pressed the button on the drill; away she would whirl and in a few seconds all the rust was ground out. The idea was turned over to other ordnance companies.

The soldiers did a lot of kidding as they sat around taking rusted guns apart. Like soldiers everywhere they razzed each other constantly about their home states. A couple were from Arkansas, and of course they took a lot of hillbilly razzing about not wearing shoes till they got in the Army, and so on. One of them was Corporal Herschel Grimsley, of Springdale, Arkansas. He jokingly asked if I'd put his name in my dispatch. So I took a chance and joked back. "Sure," I said, "except I didn't know anybody in Arkansas could read."

Everybody laughed loudly at this scintillating wit, most of all Corporal Grimsley, who can stand anything. Later he was talking about the paratroopers who used to come in and beg for another rifle. And he expressed the sincere feeling of the men throughout Ordnance, the balanced weighing of their own fairly safe job, when he said, "Them old boys at the front have sure got my sympathy. Least we can do is work our fingers off to give them the stuff."

In one small-arms repair section that I visited the only man who knew or cared anything about guns before the war was a professional gun collector. He was Sergeant Joseph Toth, of Mansfield, Ohio. He was stripped down to his undershirt as the day was warm for a change. He was washing the walnut stocks of damaged rifles in a tub of water with a sponge. Sergeant Toth used to work at the Westinghouse Electric plant in Mansfield and he spent all his extra money collecting guns. He belonged to the Ohio Gun Collectors Association. He said each one of the gun collectors back in Ohio had a different specialty. Some collected machine pistols. He had thirty-five in his collection, some of them very expensive ones. Ironically enough, he had not collected any guns at all in Normandy, even though he was in a world of machine pistols and many passed through his hands.

A stack of muddy, rusted rifles is a touching sight. As gun after gun came off the stack I looked to see what was the matter with it—rifle butt split by fragments; barrel dented by bullet; trigger knocked off; whole barrel splattered with shrapnel marks; guns gray from the slime of weeks in swamp mud; faint dark splotches of blood still showing. I wondered what had become of each owner. I pretty well knew.

Infantrymen, like soldiers everywhere, like to put names on their equipment. Just as a driver paints a name on his truck, so does a doughboy carve his name or initials on his rifle butt. I saw crude whittlings of initials in the hard walnut stocks and unbelievably craftsmanlike carvings of soldiers' names, and many, many names of girls. The boys said the most heartbreaking rifle they'd found was one belonging to a soldier who had carved a hole about silver-dollar size and put his wife's or girl's picture in it, and sealed it over with a crystal of Plexiglas. They didn't know who he was or what had happened to him. They only knew the rifle was repaired and somebody else was carrying it, picture and all.

I moved next to an ordnance evacuation company. These men handled the gigantic trucks, the long, low trailers, and the heavy wreckers that went out to haul back crippled tanks and wrecked antitank guns from the battlefield. Ordnance's policy on these wrecking companies was that if they didn't have a casualty now and then, or collect a few shrapnel marks on their vehicles, they weren't doing their job efficiently. Tanks had to be retrieved just as quickly as possible after they had been shot up. In the first place, we didn't want the Germans to get them; second, we wanted to get them repaired and back in action for ourselves.

An ordnance tank repair company gets some freakish jobs indeed. One day a tank destroyer rolled in. There was nothing whatever wrong with it except that the end of the gun barrel was corked tight with two and a half feet of wood. The vehicle had been running along a hedgerow and, as the turret operator swung his gun in a forward arc, the end of the barrel ran smack into a big tree. You would think the tank destroyer must have been going a hundred miles an hour to plug the end of the barrel for 2-1/2 feet simply by running into a tree. But it wasn't going over twenty miles an hour. It took the ordnance boys four hours to dig the wood out with chisels and reamers. The inside of the barrel wasn't hurt a bit and it went right back into action.

A three-inch antitank gun was brought in with a hole in the barrel about six inches back from the muzzle. The hole came from the inside! What happened was this: A German bazooka gunner fired a rocket at the antitank gun and made one of those freakish hole-in-one hits—right smack into the muzzle of the big gun. About six inches inside it went off and burned its way through the barrel. Nobody got hurt but the barrel was beyond repair and was sent back to England for salvage.

A tank was brought in that had been hit twice on the same side within a few seconds. The entrance holes were about two feet apart. But on the opposite side of the tank, where the shells came out, there was only one hole. The angle of fire had been such that the second shell went right through the hole made by the first one.

In another case an 88 shell struck the thick steel apron that shields the breech of one of a tank's guns. The shell didn't go through. It hit at an angle and just scooped out a big chunk of steel about a foot long and six inches wide. It was very improbable that in the whole war that same shield would get hit again in the same place. Yet they couldn't afford to take that chance, so the weakened armor had to be made strong again. With acetylene torches they cut out a plug with slanting sides around the weakened part, the same as you'd plug a watermelon. Then they fashioned a steel plate the same size and shape as the hole, and welded it in. As a result, the plug fitted into the hole like a wedge and it would have been impossible for a shell to drive it in. It was really stronger than it had been before.

The job of an ordnance evacuation company is often frightening, although this company's casualties had been amazingly low. In fact they had had only four and it was still a mystery what had happened to them. The four left one day in a jeep, just on a routine trip. They didn't come back. No trace could be found. Three weeks later two of them came in—just discharged from a hospital. On the same day a letter came from the third—from a hospital in England. Nothing had been heard from the fourth. And the strange part was that neither the two who returned nor the one who wrote from England could remember a thing about it. They were just riding along in their jeep and the next thing they woke up in a hospital. All three were wounded, but how they didn't know. Probably it was a shell hit.

A sergeant in charge of one section of the prime movers, known as M-19s, took me around to see some of his crew men. They all went by the name of the "Diesel Boys." Their vehicle was simply a gigantic truck with a long skeletonized trailer. Like all our Army over there they were strung out along the hedgerows of the field under camouflage nets, with the middle grassy fields completely empty. My friend was Sergeant Milton Radcliff, of 111 North 13th Street, Newark, Ohio. He used to be a furnace operator for the Owen Corning Fiberglas Co. there. He and all the other former employees still got a letter every two weeks from the company, assuring them that their jobs would still be there when they returned. And Radcliff, for one, was going to take his when he got back.

Sergeant Vann Jones, of 1712 Princeton Avenue, Birmingham, Alabama, crawled out of his tent and sat Indian fashion on the ground with us. On the other side of our pasture lay the silver remains of a transport plane that had come to a mangled end on the morning of D-day. It was a peaceful and sunny evening, in contrast to most of our days, and we sat on the grass and watched the sun go down in the east, which we all agreed was a hell of a place for the sun to be setting. Either we were turned around or France is a funny country. The other boys told me later that Sergeant Jones used to be the company cook, but he wanted to see more action so he transferred to the big wreckers and was then in command of one. His driver was a smiling, tall young fellow, with clipped hair—Dallas Hudgens, from Stonewall, Georgia. He was feeling stuffed as a pig, for he'd just got a big ham from home and had been having at it with a vengeance.

There were long lulls when the retriever boys didn't have anything to do besides work on their vehicles. They hated those periods and got restless. Some of them spent their time fixing up their tents homelike, even though they might have to move the next day. One driver even had a feather bed he had picked up from a French family. The average soldier couldn't carry a feather bed around with him, but the driver of an M-19 could carry ten thousand feather beds and never know the difference.

The boys were all pretty proud of their company. They said

they did such good work in the early days of the invasion that they were about to be put up for presidential citation. But one day, just for fun, they got into a bomb crater and started shooting captured German guns at the opposite bank. It was strictly against the rules, so the proposal was torn up. They just laughed about it—which was about all a fellow could do.

Corporal Grover Anderson, of Anniston, Alabama, was another one of the drivers. He swore by his colossal machine but cussed it too. The French roads are narrow for heavy two-way military traffic and an M-19 is big and awkward and slow. "You get so damn mad at it," Anderson said, "because convoys pile up behind you and can't get around and you know everybody's hating you and that makes you madder. They're aggravating, but if you let me leave the trailer off I can pull anything out of anywhere with it." Anderson had grown a red goatee which he was not going to shave off till the war was won. He used to be a taxi driver; that's another reason he found an M-19 so "aggravating."

"Because it hasn't got a meter on it?" I asked.

"Or maybe because you don't have any female passengers," another driver said.

To which Brother Anderson had a wholly satisfactory GI reply.

It was just beginning dusk when a soldier came running up the pasture and said there was an order for our ordnance evacuation company to pull out some crippled tanks. We jumped up and ran down the slope. Waiting at the gate stood an M-19 truck and behind it a big wrecker with a crane. The day had been warm but dusk was bringing a chill, as always. One of the soldiers lent me his mackinaw. Soldiers stood atop their big machine with a stance of impatience, like firemen waiting to start. We pulled out through the hedgerow gate onto the main macadam highway. It was about ten miles to the front lines. "We should make it before full darkness," one of the officers said.

We went through shattered Carentan and on beyond for a few miles. Then we turned off at an angle in the road. "This is Purple Heart Corner," the officer said. Beyond there the roadside soldiers thinned out. Traffic ceased altogether. With an increasing tempo, the big guns crashed around us. Hedges began to make weird shadows. We all peered closely at sentries in every open hedge gate, just out of nervous alertness. The smell of death washed past us in waves as we drove on. There is nothing worse in war than the foul odor of death. There is no last vestige of dignity in it.

We turned up a gravel lane, and drove slowly. The dusk was deepening. A gray stone farmhouse sat dimly off the road. A little yard and driveway semicircled in front of it. Against the front of the house stood five German soldiers, facing inward, their hands above their heads. An American doughboy stood in the driveway with a tommy gun pointed at them. We drove on for about fifty yards and stopped. The drivers shut off their diesel motors.

One officer went into an orchard to try to find where the tanks were. In wartime nobody ever knows where anything is. The rest of us waited along the road beside an old stone barn. Three jeeps were parked beside it. The dusk was deeper now. Out of the orchards around us roared and thundered our own artillery. An officer lit a cigarette. A sergeant with a rifle slung on his shoulder walked up and said, "You better put that out, sir. There's snipers all around and they'll shoot at a cigarette."

The officer crushed the cigarette in his fingers, not waiting to drop it to the ground, and said, "Thanks."

"It's for your own good," the sergeant said apologetically.

The only traffic was a slow stream of jeeps rigged up with a steel framework on top to carry two stretcher cases. Every few minutes a jeep would pass with wounded men, slowly as though it were feeling its way.

Somehow as darkness comes down in a land of great danger a man wants things hushed. People began to talk in low voices, and feet on jeep throttles trod less heavily. An early German plane droned overhead, passed, turned, dived—and his white tracers came slanting down out of the sky. We crouched behind a stone wall. He was half a mile away, but the night was big and bullets could go anywhere and we were nervous. An armored car drove around us, pulled into a ditch ahead and shut off its motor. They said it was there in case the German night patrols tried to filter through.

On ahead there were single rifle shots and the give-and-take of machine-gun rattles—one fast and one slow, one German and one American. I wondered after each blast if somebody who had been whole a moment before, some utter stranger, was then lying in sudden new anguish up there ahead in the illimitable darkness. A shell whined the old familiar wail and hit in the orchard ahead with a crash. I moved quickly around behind the barn.

"You don't like that?" inquired a soldier out of the dusk.

I said, "No, do you?"

And he replied as honestly, "I sure as hell don't."

A sergeant came up the road and said, "You can stay here if you want to, but they shell this barn every hour on the hour. They're zeroed in on it."

We looked at our watches. It was five minutes till midnight. Some of our soldiers stood boldly out in the middle of the road talking. But some of us, who were less composed, began easing close to the stone wall, even close to the motherhood of the big silent trucks. Then an officer came out of the orchard. He had the directions. We all gathered around and listened. We had to back up, cross two pastures, turn down another lane and go forward from there.

We were to drag back two German tanks for fear the enemy might retrieve them during the night. We backed ponderously up the road, our powerful exhaust blowing up dust as we moved. As we passed the gray-stone farmhouse we could see five silhouettes, faintly through the now almost complete night—five Germans still facing the gray farmhouse. We drove slowly across the two pastures in the big M-19 retriever truck. The wrecker truck followed us. It was just after midnight. We came to a lane at the far side of the pasture. Nobody was there to direct us. The officers had gone on ahead. We asked a sentry if he knew where the German tanks were. He had never heard of them. We shut off the motors and waited.

I think everybody was a little on edge. We certainly had American troops ahead of us, but we didn't know how far. When things are tense like that a person gets impatient of monkeying around. We wanted to get the job done and get the hell out of there. We waited about ten minutes, and finally a sergeant came back and said for us to drive on up the road about half a mile. It was very dark and we could only make out vague shapes. We could see dark walls of hedges and between them lighter strips of gravel road. Finally a huge black shape took form at one side of the road. It was the first of the German tanks. Just before we got to it we could make out two dark stripes on either side of the road on the ground. They were the size and shape of dead men, but they were only forms and we couldn't tell for sure.

Being tense and anxious to get finished, I hoped our truck would take the first tank. But no. We passed by, of course, and went backing on up the road. When a man's nervous he feels even twelve inches closer to the front is too much. And the noise of our motor sounded like all the clanging of hell, directing the Germans to us. Finally the dark shape of the second tank loomed up. Our officers and some men were standing in the road beside it. We backed to within about five feet of it, and the driver shut off his motor and we climbed down.

A layman would think all we had to do was hook a chain to the tank and pull it out of the ditch. But we were there half an hour. It seemed like all night to me. First it had to be gone over for booby traps. I couldn't help but admire our mechanics. They knew the foreign tanks as well as our own. One of them climbed down the hatch into the driver's seat and there in the dark, completely by feel, investigated the intricate gadgets of the cockpit and found just what shape it was in and told us the trouble. It seemed that on this tank two levers at the driver's seat had been left in gear and they were so bent there was not room to shift them into neutral. One man was sent back up the road to get a hacksaw from the wrecker truck so they could saw off the handles. After five minutes he came back and said there wasn't any hacksaw. Then they sent him back after a crowbar, and that finally did the trick.

During this time we stood in a group around the tank, about a dozen of us, just talking. Shells still roamed the dark sky, but they weren't coming as near as before. An officer asked if anybody had inspected the breech of the tank's 88 gun. Sometimes the Germans left a shell in the gun, rigged up to go off when the tank was towed. Another officer said the breech was empty. So we started. We'd planned to pull it a long way back. Actually we pulled it only about half a mile, then decided to put it in a field for the night. When we pulled into a likely pasture, the sentry at the hedgerow wanted to know what we were doing and we told him, "Leaving a German tank for the night."

And the sentry, in a horrified voice, said, "Good God, don't leave it here. They might come after it." But leave it there we did, and damn glad to get rid of it, I assure you. At last we came to our own hedgerow gate. As we drove in the sentry said, "Coffee's waiting at the mess tent." They feed twenty-four hours a day in outfits that work like firemen.

THIRTY-TWO

BREAK-THROUGH

Surely history will give a name to the battle that sent us boiling out of Normandy, some name comparable with Saint-Mihiel or Meuse-Argonne of the last war. But to us there on the spot at the time it was known simply as the "break-through." We correspondents could sense that a big drive was coming. There are many little ways you can tell without actually being told, if you are experienced in war. And then one evening Lieutenant General Omar Bradley, commanding all American troops in France, came to our camp and briefed us on the coming operation. It would start, he said, on the first day we had three hours of good flying weather in the forenoon.

We were all glad to hear the news. There wasn't a correspondent over there, or soldier, or officer I ever heard of who hadn't complete and utter faith in General Bradley. If he felt we were ready for the push, that was good enough for us. The general told us the attack would cover a segment of the German line west of Saint-Lo, about five miles wide. In that narrow segment we would have three infantry divisions, side by side. Right behind them would be another infantry and two armored divisions. Once a hole was broken, the armored divisions would slam through several miles beyond, then turn right toward the sea behind the Germans in that sector in the hope of cutting them off and trapping them. The remainder of our line on both sides of the attack would keep the pressure on to hold the Germans in front of them so they couldn't send reinforcements against our main push.

The attack was to open with a gigantic two-hour air bombardment by 1,800 planes—the biggest ever attempted by air in direct support of ground troops. It would start with dive bombers, then great four-motored heavies would come, and then mediums, then dive bombers again, and then the ground troops would kick off, with air fighters continuing to work ahead of them. It was a thrilling plan to listen to. General Bradley didn't tell us that it was the big thing, but other officers gave us the word. They said, "This is no limited objective drive. This is it. This is the big break-through."

In war everybody contributes something, no matter how small or how far removed he may be. But on the front line the break-through was accomplished by four fighting branches of the services and I don't see truly how one can be given credit above another. None of the four could have done the job without the other three. The way they worked together was beautiful and precisionlike, showering credit upon themselves and General Bradley's planning. The four branches were: Air Force, Tanks, Artillery and Infantry.

I went with the infantry because it is my old love, and because I suspected the tanks, being spectacular, might smother the credit due the infantry. I teamed up with the Fourth Infantry Division since it was in the middle of the forward three, and spearheading the attack. The first night behind the front lines I slept comfortably on a cot in a tent at the division command post, and met for the first time the Fourth's commander—Major General Raymond O. Barton, a fatherly, kindly, thoughtful, good soldier. The second night I spent on the dirty floor of a rickety French farmhouse, far up in the lines, with the nauseating odor of dead cows keeping me awake half the night. The third night I slept on the ground in an orchard even farther up, snugly dug in behind a hedgerow so the 88s couldn't get at me so easily. And on the next day the weather cleared, and the attack was on. It was July 25.

If you don't have July 25 pasted in your hat I would advise you to put it there immediately. At least paste it in your mind. For I have a hunch that July 25 of the year 1944 will be one of the great historic pinnacles of this war. It was the day we began a mighty surge out of our confined Normandy spaces, the day we stopped calling our area the beachhead and knew we were fighting a war across the whole expanse of France. From that day onward all dread possibilities and fears for disaster to our invasion were behind us. No longer was there any possibility of our getting kicked off. No longer would it be possible for fate, or weather, or enemy to wound us fatally; from that day onward the future could hold nothing for us but growing strength and eventual victory.

For five days and nights during that historic period I stayed at the front with our troops. The great attack began in the bright light of midday, not at the zero hour of a bleak and mysterious dawn as attacks are supposed to start in books. The attack had been delayed from day to day because of poor flying weather, and on the final day we hadn't known for sure till after breakfast whether it was on or off again. When the word came that it was on, the various battalion staffs of our regiment were called in from their command posts for a final review of the battle plan. Each one was given a mimeographed sketch of the front-line area, showing exactly where and when each type of bomber was to hammer the German lines ahead of them. Another mimeographed page was filled with specific orders for the grand attack to follow.

Officers stood or squatted in a circle in a little apple orchard behind a ramshackle stone farmhouse of a poor French family who had left before us. The stone wall in the front yard had been knocked down by shelling, and through the orchards there were shell craters and tree limbs knocked off and trunks sliced by bullets. Some enlisted men, sleeping the night before in the attic of the house, got the shock of their lives when the thin floor collapsed and they fell down into the cowshed below. Chickens and tame rabbits still scampered around the farmyard. Dead cows lay all around in the fields.

The regimental colonel stood in the center of the officers and went over the orders in detail. Battalion commanders took down notes in little books. The colonel said, "Ernie Pyle is with the regiment for this attack and will be with one of the battalions, so you'll be seeing him." The officers looked at me and smiled and I felt embarrassed.

Then General Barton arrived. The colonel called, "Attention!" and everybody stood rigid until the general gave them "Carry on." An enlisted man ran to the mess truck and got a folding canvas stool for the general to sit on. He sat listening intently while the colonel wound up his instructions. Then the general stepped into the center of the circle. He stood at a slouch on one foot with the other leg far out like a brace. He looked all around him as he talked. He didn't talk long. He said something like this: "This is one of the finest regiments in the American Army. It was the last regiment out of France in the last war. It was the first regiment into France in this war. It has spearheaded every one of the division's attacks in Normandy. It will spearhead this one. For many years this was my regiment and I feel very close to you, and very proud."

The general's lined face was a study in emotion. Sincerity and deep sentiment were in every contour and they shone from his eyes. General Barton was a man of deep affections. The tragedy of war, both personal and impersonal, hurt him. At the end his voice almost broke, and I for one had a lump in my throat. He ended: "That's all. God bless you and good luck."

Then we broke up and I went with one of the battalion commanders. By field telephone, radio, and liaison men, word was passed down to the very smallest unit of troops that the attack was on. There was still an hour before the bombers, and three hours before the infantry were to move. There was nothing for the infantry to do but dig a little deeper and wait. A cessation of motion seemed to come over the countryside and all its brown-clad inhabitants, a sense of last-minute sitting in silence before the holocaust.

The first planes of the mass onslaught came over a little before 10 a.m. They were the fighters and dive bombers. The main road, running crosswise in front of us, was their bomb line. They were to bomb only on the far side of that road. Our kickoff infantry had been pulled back a few hundred yards from the near side of the road. Everyone in the area had been given the strictest orders to be in foxholes, for high-level bombers can, and do quite excusably, make mistakes.

We were still in country so level and with hedgerows so tall there simply was no high spot—neither hill nor building—from which we could get a grandstand view of the bombing as we used to do in Sicily and Italy. So one place was as good as another unless we went right up and sat on the bomb line. Having been caught too close to these things before, I compromised and picked a farm-yard about 800 yards back of the kickoff line. And before the next two hours had passed I would have given every penny, every desire, every hope I ever had, to have been just another 800 yards farther back.

Our front lines were marked by long strips of colored cloth laid on the ground, and with colored smoke to guide our airmen during the mass bombing. Dive bombers hit it just right. We stood and watched them barrel nearly straight down out of the sky. They were bombing about half a mile ahead of where we stood. They came in groups, diving from every direction, perfectly timed, one right after another. Everywhere we looked separate groups of planes were on the way down, or on the way back up, or slanting over for a dive, or circling, circling, circling over our heads, waiting for their turn.

The air was full of sharp and distinct sounds of cracking bombs and the heavy rips of the planes' machine guns and the splitting screams of diving wings. It was all fast and furious, yet distinct. And then a new sound gradually droned into our ears, a sound deep and all-encompassing with no notes in it—just a gigantic faraway surge of doomlike sound. It was the heavies. They came from directly behind us. At first they were the merest dots in the sky. We could see clots of them against the far heavens, too tiny to count individually. They came on with a terrible slowness. They came in flights of twelve, three flights to a group and in groups stretched out across the sky. They came in "families" of about seventy planes each. Maybe those gigantic waves were two miles apart, maybe they were ten miles, I don't know. But I do know they came in a constant procession and I thought it would never end. What the Germans must have thought is beyond comprehension.

The flight across the sky was slow and studied. I've never known a storm, or a machine, or any resolve of man that had about it the aura of such a ghastly relentlessness. I had the feeling that even had God appeared beseechingly before them in the sky, with palms outstretched to persuade them back, they would not have had within them the power to turn from their irresistible course.

I stood with a little group of men, ranging from colonels to privates, back of the stone farmhouse. Slit trenches were all around the edges of the farmyard and a dugout with a tin roof was nearby. But we were so fascinated by the spectacle overhead that it never occurred to us that we might need the foxholes.

The first huge flight passed directly overhead and others followed. We spread our feet and leaned far back trying to look straight up, until our steel helmets fell off. We'd cup our fingers around our eyes, like field glasses, for a clearer view. And then the bombs came. They began like the crackle of popcorn and almost instantly swelled into a monstrous fury of noise that seemed surely to destroy all the world ahead of us. From then on for an hour and a half that had in it the agonies of centuries, the bombs came down. A wall of smoke and dust erected by them grew high in the sky. It filtered along the ground back through our orchards. It sifted around us and into our noses. The bright day grew slowly dark from it. By now everything was an indescribable caldron of sounds. Individual noises did not exist. The thundering of the motors in the sky and the roar of bombs ahead filled all the space for noise on earth. Our own heavy artillery was crashing all around us, yet we could hardly hear it.

The Germans began to shoot heavy, high ack-ack. Great black puffs of it by the score speckled the sky until it was hard to distinguish smoke puffs from planes. And then someone shouted that one of the planes was smoking. Yes, we could all see it. A faint line of black smoke stretched straight for a mile behind one of them. And as we watched there was a gigantic sweep of flame over the plane. From nose to tail it disappeared in flame, and it slanted slowly down and banked around the sky in great wide curves, this way and that way, as rhythmically and gracefully as in a slow-motion waltz. Then suddenly it seemed to change its mind and it swept upward, steeper and steeper and ever slower until finally it seemed poised motionless on its own black pillar of smoke. And then just as slowly it turned over and dived for the earth—a golden spearhead on the straight black shaft of its own creation—and disappeared behind the treetops. But before it was down there were more cries of, "There's another one smoking— and there's a third one now." Chutes came out of some of the planes. Out of some came no chutes at all. One of white silk caught on the tail of a plane. Men with binoculars could see him fighting to get loose until flames swept over him, and then a tiny black dot fell through space, all alone.

And all that time the great flat ceiling of the sky was roofed by all the other planes that didn't go down, plowing their way

forward as if there were no turmoil in the world. Nothing devi-
ated them by the slightest. They stalked on, slowly and with a
dreadful pall of sound, as though they were seeing only something at a great distance and nothing existed between. God,
how we admired those men up there and sickened for the ones
who fell.

It is possible to become so enthralled by some of the spectacles
of war that a man is momentarily captivated away from his own
danger. That's what happened to our little group of soldiers as
we stood watching the mighty bombing. But that benign state
didn't last long. As we watched, there crept into our consciousness a realization that the windrows of exploding bombs were
easing back toward us, flight by flight, instead of gradually forward, as the plan called for. Then we were horrified by the sus-
picion that those machines, high in the sky and completely
detached from us, were aiming their bombs at the smoke line on
the ground—and a gentle breeze was drifting the smoke line
back over us! An indescribable kind of panic came over us. We
stood tensed in muscle and frozen in intellect, watching each
flight approach and pass over, feeling trapped and completely
helpless. And then all of an instant the universe became filled
with a gigantic rattling as of huge ripe seeds in a mammoth dry
gourd. I doubt that any of us had ever heard that sound before,
but instinct told us what it was. It was bombs by the hundred,
hurtling down through the air above us.

Many times I've heard bombs whistle or swish or rustle, but
never before had I heard bombs rattle. I still don't know the explanation of it. But it is an awful sound. We dived. Some got
into a dugout. Others made foxholes and ditches and some got
behind a garden wall—although which side would be "behind"
was anybody's guess. I was too late for the dugout. The nearest
place was a wagon shed which formed one end of the stone house.
The rattle was right down upon us. I remember hitting the ground
flat, all spread out like the cartoons of people flattened by steam
rollers, and then squirming like an eel to get under one of the heavy
wagons in the shed.

An officer whom I didn't know was wriggling beside me. We
stopped at the same time, simultaneously feeling it was hopeless

to move farther. The bombs were already crashing around us. We lay with our heads slightly up—like two snakes—staring at each other. I know it was in both our minds and in our eyes, asking each other what to do. Neither of us knew. We said nothing. We just lay sprawled, gaping at each other in a futile appeal, our faces about a foot apart, until it was over.

There is no description of the sound and fury of those bombs except to say it was chaos, and a waiting for darkness. The feeling of the blast was sensational. The air struck us in hundreds of continuing flutters. Our ears drummed and rang. We could feel quick little waves of concussion on the chest and in the eyes.

At last the sound died down and we looked at each other in disbelief. Gradually we left the foxholes and sprawling places and came out to see what the sky had in store for us. As far as we could see other waves were approaching from behind. When a wave would pass a little to the side of us we were garrulously grateful, for most of them flew directly overhead. Time and again the rattle came down over us. Bombs struck in the orchard to our left. They struck in orchards ahead of us. They struck as far as half a mile behind us. Everything about us was shaken, but our group came through unhurt.

I can't record what any of us actually felt or thought during those horrible climaxes. I believe a person's feelings at such times are kaleidoscopic and indefinable. He just waits, that's all—with an inhuman tenseness of muscle and nerves. An hour or so later I began to get sore all over, and by midafternoon my back and shoulders ached as though I'd been beaten with a club. It was simply the result of muscles tensing themselves too tight for too long against anticipated shock. And I remember worrying about War Correspondent Ken Crawford, a friend from back in the old Washington days, who was several hundred yards ahead of me. As far as I knew, he and I were the only two correspondents with the Fourth Division. I didn't know who might be with the divisions on either side—which also were being hit, as we could see. It was not until three days later, back at camp, that I learned that Lieutenant General McNair and AP Photographer Bede Irvin had been killed in this same bombing and that Ken was safe.

When we came out of our ignominious sprawling and stood up again to watch, we knew that the error had been caught and checked. The bombs again were falling where they were intended, a mile or so ahead. Even at a mile away a thousand bombs hitting within a few seconds can shake the earth and shatter the air. There was still a dread in our hearts, but it gradually eased as the tumult and destruction moved slowly forward.

Two Mustang fighters, flying like a pair of doves, patrolled back and forth, back and forth, just in front of each oncoming wave of bombers, as if to shout to them by their mere presence that here was not the place to drop—wait a few seconds, wait a few more seconds. And then we could see a flare come out of the belly of one plane in each flight, just after they had passed over our heads. The flare shot forward, leaving smoke behind it in a vivid line, and then began a graceful, downward curve that was one of the most beautiful things I've ever seen. It was like an invisible crayon drawing a rapid line across the canvas of the sky, saying in a gesture for all to see: "Here! Here is where to drop. Follow me." And each succeeding flight of oncoming bombers obeyed, and in turn dropped its own hurtling marker to guide those behind.

Long before, the German ack-ack guns had gone out of existence. The ack-ack gunners either took to their holes or were annihilated. How many waves of heavy bombers we put over I have no idea. I had counted well above 400 planes when personal distraction obliterated any capacity or desire to count. I only know that 400 was just the beginning. There were supposed to be 1,800 planes that day, and I believe it was announced later that there were more than 3,000. It seems incredible to me that any German could have come out of that bombardment with his sanity. When it was over even I was grateful, in a chastened way that I had never experienced before, for just being alive.

I thought an attack by our troops was impossible then, for it is an unnerving thing to be bombed by your own planes. During the bad part a colonel I had known a long time was walking up and down behind the farmhouse, snapping his fingers and saying over and over to himself, "goddammit, goddammit!" As he passed me once he stopped and stared and said, "goddammit!"

And I said, "There can't be any attack now, can there?" And he said "No," and began walking again, snapping his fingers and tossing his arm as though he were throwing rocks at the ground.

The leading company of our battalion was to spearhead the attack forty minutes after our heavy bombing ceased. The company had been hit directly by our bombs. Their casualties, including casualties in shock, were heavy. Men went to pieces and had to be sent back. The company was shattered and shaken. And yet Company B attacked—and on time, to the minute! They attacked, and within an hour they sent word back that they had advanced 800 yards through German territory and were still going. Around our farmyard men with stars on their shoulders almost wept when the word came over the portable radio. The American soldier can be majestic when he needs to be.

I'm sure that back in England that night other men—bomber crews—almost wept, and maybe they did really, in the awful knowledge that they had killed our own American troops. But the chaos and the bitterness there in the orchards and between the hedgerows that afternoon soon passed. After the bitterness came the sober remembrance that the Air Force was the strong right arm in front of us. Not only at the beginning, but ceaselessly and everlastingly, every moment of the faintest daylight, the Air Force was up there banging away ahead of us.

Anybody makes mistakes. The enemy made them just the same as we did. The smoke and confusion of battle bewildered us on the ground as well as in the air. And in this case the percentage of error was really very small compared with the colossal storm of bombs that fell upon the enemy. The Air Force was wonderful throughout the invasion, and the men on the ground appreciated it.

THIRTY-THREE

HEDGEROW FIGHTING

I want to describe to you what the weird hedgerow fighting in north-western France was like. This type of fighting was always in small groups, so let's take as an example one company of men. Let's say they were working forward on both sides of a country lane, and the company was responsible for clearing the two fields on either side of the road as it advanced. That meant there was only about one platoon to a field, and with the company's under-strength from casualties, there might be no more than twenty-five or thirty men.

The fields were usually not more than fifty yards across and a couple of hundred yards long. They might have grain in them, or apple trees, but mostly they were just pastures of green grass, full of beautiful cows. The fields were surrounded on all sides by the immense hedgerows—ancient earthen banks, waist high, all matted with roots, and out of which grew weeds, bushes, and trees up to twenty feet high. The Germans used these barriers well. They put snipers in the trees. They dug deep trenches behind the hedgerows and covered them with timber, so that it was almost impossible for artillery to get at them. Sometimes they propped up machine guns with strings attached so that they could fire over the hedge without getting out of their holes. They even cut out a section of the hedgerow and hid a big gun or a tank in it, covering it with bush. Also they tunneled under the hedgerows from the back and made the opening on the forward side just large enough to stick a machine gun through. But mostly the hedge-row pattern was this: a heavy machine gun hidden at each end of the field and infantrymen hidden all along the hedgerow with rifles and machine pistols.

We had to dig them out. It was a slow and cautious business, and there was nothing dashing about it. Our men didn't go across the open fields in dramatic charges such as you see in the movies. They did at first, but they learned better. They went in tiny groups, a squad or less, moving yards apart and sticking close to the hedgerows on either end of the field. They crept a few yards, squatted, waited, then crept again.

If you could have been right up there between the Germans and the Americans you wouldn't have seen many men at any one time—just a few here and there, always trying to keep hidden. But you would have heard an awful lot of noise. Our men were taught in training not to fire until they saw something to fire at. But the principle didn't work in that country, because there was very little to see. So the alternative was to keep shooting constantly at the hedgerows. That pinned the Germans to their holes while we sneaked up on them. The attacking squads sneaked up the sides of the hedgerows while the rest of the platoon stayed back in their own hedgerow and kept the forward hedge saturated with bullets. They shot rifle grenades too, and a mortar squad a little farther back kept lobbing mortar shells over onto the Germans. The little advance groups worked their way up to the far ends of the hedgerows at the corners of the field. They first tried to knock out the machine guns at each corner. They did this with hand grenades, rifle grenades and machine guns.

Usually, when the pressure was on, the German defenders of the hedgerow started pulling back. They would take their heavier guns and most of the men back a couple of fields and start digging in for a new line. They left about two machine guns and a few riflemen scattered through the hedge to do a lot of shooting and hold up the Americans as long as they could. Our men would then sneak along the front side of the hedgerow, throwing grenades over onto the other side and spraying the hedges with their guns. The fighting was close—only a few yards apart—but it was seldom actual hand-to-hand stuff. Sometimes the remaining Germans came out of their holes with their hands up. Sometimes they tried to run for it and were mowed down. Sometimes they wouldn't come out at all, and a hand grenade, thrown into their hole, finished them off. And so another hedgerow was taken and we were ready to start on the one beyond.

This hedgerow business was a series of little skirmishes like that clear across the front, thousands and thousands of little skir-mishes. No single one of them was very big. Added up over the days and weeks, however, they made a man-sized war—with thou-sands on both sides getting killed. But that is only a general pattern of the hedgerow fighting. Actually each one was a little separate war, fought under different circumstances. For instance, the fight might be in a woods instead of an open field. The Germans would be dug in all over the woods, in little groups, and it was really tough to get them out. Often in cases like that we just went around the woods and kept going, and let later units take care of those surrounded and doomed fellows. Or we might go through a woods and clean it out, and another company, coming through a cou-ple of hours later, would find it full of Germans again. In a war like this everything was in such confusion that I never could see how either side ever got anywhere.

Sometimes we didn't know where the enemy was and didn't know where our own troops were. As somebody said one day, no battalion commander could have given you the exact location of his various units five minutes after they had jumped off. Grad-ually the front got all mixed up. There were Germans behind us and at the side. They would be shooting at us from behind and from our flank. Sometimes a unit got so far out ahead of those on either side that it had to swing around and fight to its rear. Sometimes we fired on our own troops, thinking we were in Ger-man territory. It was hard to see anything, or even tell from the sounds, for each side used some of the other's captured weapons.

The tanks and the infantry had to work in the closest coop-eration in breaking through the German ring that tried to pin us down in the beachhead area. Neither could have done it alone. The troops were of two minds about having tanks around them. If you're a foot soldier you hate to be near a tank, for it always draws fire. On the other hand, if the going gets tough you pray for a tank to come up and start blasting with its guns. In our break-through each infantry unit had tanks attached to it. It was the tanks and the infantry that broke through that ring and punched a hole for the armored divisions to follow after. The armored di-visions practically ran amuck, racing long distances and playing hob, once they got behind the German lines, but it was the in-fantry and their attached tanks that opened the gate for them.

Tanks shuttled back and forth, from one field to another, throughout our break-through battle, receiving their orders by radio. Bulldozers punched holes through the hedgerows for them, and then the tanks would come up and blast out the bad spots of the opposition.

It was necessary for us to wreck almost every farmhouse and little village in our path. The Germans used them for strong points or put artillery observers in them, and they just had to be blasted out. Most of the French farmers evacuated ahead of the fighting and filtered back after it had passed. It was pitiful to see them come back to their demolished homes and towns. Yet it was wonderful to see the grand way they took it.

In a long drive an infantry company often went for a couple of days without letting up. Ammunition was carried up to it by hand, and occasionally by jeep. The soldiers sometimes ate only one K ration a day. They sometimes ran out of water. Their strength was gradually whittled down by wounds, exhaustion cases and straggling. Finally they would get an order to sit where they were and dig in. Then another company would pass through, or around them, and go on with the fighting. The relieved company might get to rest as much as a day or two. But in a big push such as the one that broke us out of the beachhead, a few hours' respite was about all they could expect.

The company I was with got its orders to rest about five o'clock one afternoon. They dug foxholes along the hedgerows, or commandeered German ones already dug. Regardless of how tired a man might be, he always dug in the first thing. Then they sent some men looking for water. They got more K rations up by jeep, and sat on the ground eating them. They hoped they would stay there all night, but they weren't counting on it too much. Shortly after supper a lieutenant came out of a farmhouse and told the sergeants to pass the word to be ready to move in ten minutes. They bundled on their packs and started just before dark. Within half an hour they had run into a new fight that lasted all night. They had had less than four hours' rest in three solid days of fighting.

The afternoon was tense, and full of caution and dire little might-have-beens. I was wandering up a dirt lane where the infantrymen were squatting alongside in a ditch, waiting their turn to advance. They always squatted like that when they were close to the front. Suddenly German shells started banging around us. I jumped into a ditch between a couple of soldiers. Shells were clipping the hedgetops right over our heads and crashing into the next pasture. Then suddenly one exploded, not with a crash, but with a ring as though a high-toned bell had been struck. The debris of burned wadding and dirt came showering down over us. My head rang, and my right ear couldn't hear anything.

The shell had struck behind us, twenty feet away. We had been saved by the earthen bank of the hedgerow. It was the next day before my ear returned to normal. A minute later a soldier crouching next in line, a couple of feet away, turned to me and asked, "Are you a war correspondent?"

I said I was, and he said, "I want to shake your hand." And he reached around the bush and we shook hands. That's all either of us said. It didn't occur to me until later that it was a sort of unusual experience. And I was so addled by the close explosions that I forgot to put down his name.

A few minutes later a friend, Lieutenant Colonel Oma Bates, of Gloster, Mississippi, came past and said he was hunting our new battalion command post. It was supposed to be in a farmhouse about a hundred yards from us, so I got up and went with him. We couldn't find it at first. We lost about five minutes walking around in orchards looking for it. That was a blessed five minutes. For when we got within fifty yards of the house it got a direct shell hit which killed one officer and wounded several men.

The Germans started to rain shells around our little area. We couldn't walk ten feet without hitting the ground. They came past our heads so quickly we didn't take time to fall forward—I found the quickest way down was to flop back and sideways. In a little while the seat of my pants was plastered thick with wet red clay and my hands were scratched from hitting rocks and briers to break quick falls. Nobody ever fastened the chin strap on his helmet in the front lines, for the blasts from nearby bursts had been known to catch helmets and break people's necks. Consequently, when I squatted quickly I descended faster than my helmet and I left it in mid-air above me! Of course in a fraction of a second it followed me down and hit me on the head, and settled sideways over my ear and down over my eyes. It made me feel silly.

Once more shells drove us into a roadside ditch. I squatted there, just a bewildered guy in brown, part of a thin line of other bewildered guys as far up and down the ditch as the eye could see. It was really frightening. Our own shells were whanging overhead and hitting just beyond. The German shells tore through the orchards around us. There was machine-gunning all around, and bullets zipped through the trees above us. I could tell by their shoulder patches that the soldiers near me were from a division to our right, and I wondered what they were doing there. Then I heard one of them say, "This is a fine foul-up for you! I knew that lieutenant was getting lost. Hell, we're service troops, and here we are right in the front lines." Grim as the moment was, I had to laugh to myself at their pitiful plight.

Once I left a command post in a farmhouse and started to another about ten minutes away. When I got there, they said the one I had just left had been hit while I was on the way. A solid armor-piercing shell had gone right through a window and a man I knew had his leg cut off. That evening the other officers took the big steel slug over to the hospital so that he would have a souvenir.

When I got to another battalion command post, later in the day, they were just ready to move. A sergeant had been forwarded about half a mile in a jeep and picked out a farmhouse. He said it was the cleanest, nicest one he had been in for a long time. So we piled into several jeeps and drove up there. It had been only about twenty minutes since the sergeant had left. But when we got to the new house, it wasn't there. A shell had hit it in that twenty minutes and set it afire, and it had burned to the ground.

We drove up the road a little farther and picked out another one. We had been there about half an hour when a shell struck in an orchard fifty yards in front of us. In a few minutes our litter-bearers came past, carrying a captain. He was the surgeon of our adjoining battalion, and he had been looking in the orchard for a likely place to move his first-aid station. A shell hit right beside him.

That's the way war was on an afternoon that was tense and

full of might-have-beens for some of us, and awful realities for others. It just depended on what our number was. I don't believe in that number business at all, but in war a man sort of lets his belief hover around it, for it's about all he has left.

The commander of the regiment was one of my favorites. That was partly because he flattered me by calling me "General," partly because just looking at him made me chuckle to myself, and partly because I thought he was a very fine soldier. (Security forbids my giving his name.) He was a Regular Army colonel and he was overseas in the last war, too. His division commander said the only trouble with him was that he was too bold, and if he weren't careful he was liable to get clipped some fine day.

The colonel was rather unusual-looking. There was something almost Mongolian about his face. When cleaned up he could have passed for a Cossack. When tired and dirty he could have played a movie gangster. But either way, his eyes always twinkled. He had a faculty for direct thought that was outstanding. He was impatient of thinking that got off onto byways. He had a little habit of good-naturedly reprimanding people by cocking his head on one side, getting his face below the reprimandee and saying something sharp, and then looking up at him with a quizzical smirk like a laughing cat. One day I heard him ask a battalion commander what his position was. The battalion commander started telling in detail why his troops hadn't got as far as he had hoped. The colonel squinted up at the battalion commander and said: "I didn't ask you that. I asked you where you were."

The colonel went from one battalion to another during battle, from early light till darkness. He wore a new-type field jacket that fitted him like a sack, and he carried a long stick that Teddy Roosevelt had given him. He kept constantly prodding his commanders to push hard, not to let up, to keep driving and driving. He was impatient with commanders who lost the main point of the war by getting involved in details—the main point, of course, being to kill Germans. His philosophy of war was expressed in the simple formula of "shoot the sonsabitches." Once I was at a battalion command post when we got word that sixty Germans were coming down the road in a counterattack. Everybody got excited. They called the colonel on a field phone, gave him the details and asked him what to do. He had the solution in a nutshell. He just said, "Shoot the sonsabitches," and hung up.

Another of my favorites was a sergeant who ran the colonel's regimental mess. He cooked some himself, but mostly he bossed the cooking. His name was Charles J. Murphy and his home was at 225 East State Street, Trenton, New Jersey. Murphy was red-haired, but had his head nearly shaved like practically all the Western Front soldiers—officers as well as men. Murph was funny, but he seldom smiled. When I asked him what he did in civilian life, he thought a moment and then said: "Well, I was a shyster. Guess you'd call me a kind of promoter. I always had the sort of job where you made $50 a week salary and $1,500 on the side."

How's that for an honest man?

Murph and I got to talking about newspapermen one day. Murph said his grandfather was a newspaperman. He retired in old age and lived in Murph's house. "My grandfather went nuts reading newspapers," Murph said. "It was a phobia with him. Every day he'd buy $1.50 worth of three-cent newspapers and then read them all night. He wouldn't read the ads. He would just read the stories, looking for something to criticize. He'd get fuming mad. Lots of times when I was a kid he'd get me out of bed at two or three in the morning and point to some story in the paper and rave about reporters who didn't have sense enough to put a period at the end of a sentence."

Murph and I agreed that it was fortunate his grandfather passed on before he got to reading my stuff, or he would doubtless have run amuck.

Murph never smoked cigarettes until he landed in France on D-day, but after that he smoked one after another. He was about the tenth soldier who had told me that same thing. A guy in war has to have some outlet for his nerves, and I guess smoking is as good as anything.

All kinds of incongruous things happen during a battle. For instance, during one lull I got my portrait painted in water colors. The artist sat cross-legged on the grass and it took about an hour. The painter was Pfc. Leon Wall, from Wyoming, Pennsylvania. He went to the National Academy of Design in New York for six years, did research for the Metropolitan Museum and lectured on art at the New York World's Fair. Artist Wall was then, of all things, a cook and KP in an infantry regiment mess. He hadn't done any war paintings at all since the invasion. I asked him why not. He said: "Well, at first I was too scared, and since then I've been too busy."

Soldiers are made out of the strangest people. I made another friend—just a plain old Hoosier—who was so quiet and humble you would hardly know he was around. Yet in a few weeks of invasion he had learned war's wise little ways of destroying life while preserving one's own. He hadn't become the "killer" type that war makes of some soldiers; he had merely become adjusted to an obligatory new profession.

His name was George Thomas Clayton. Back home he was known as Tommy. In the Army he was sometimes called George, but usually just Clayton. He was from Evansville, Indiana, where he lived with his sister at 862 Covart Avenue. He was a front-line infantryman of a rifle company in the 29th Division. Out of combat for a brief rest, he spent a few days in an "Exhaustion Camp," then was assigned briefly to the camp where I worked from—a camp for correspondents. That's how we got acquainted. Clayton was a private first class. He operated a Browning automatic rifle. He had turned down two chances to become a buck sergeant and squad leader, simply because he preferred keeping his powerful B.A.R. to having stripes and less personal protection.

He landed in Normandy on D-day, on the toughest of the beaches, and was in the line for thirty-seven days without rest. He had innumerable narrow escapes. Twice, 88s hit within a couple of arm's lengths of him. But both times the funnel of the concussion was away from him and he didn't get a scratch, though the explosions covered him and his rifle with dirt. Then a third one hit about ten feet away, and made him deaf in his right ear. As a child, he had always had trouble with that ear anyway—earaches and things. Even in the Army back in America he had to beg the doctors to waive the ear defect in order to let him go overseas. He was still a little hard of hearing in that ear from the shellburst, but it was gradually coming back.

When Tommy finally left the lines he was pretty well done up and his sergeant wanted to send him to a hospital, but he begged not to go for fear he wouldn't get back to his old company, so they let him go to a rest camp instead. After a couple of weeks with us (provided the correspondents didn't drive him frantic), he was to return to the lines with his old outfit.

Clayton had worked at all kinds of things back in the other world of civilian life. He had been a farm hand, a cook and a bartender. Just before he joined the Army he was a gauge-honer in the Chrysler Ordnance Plant at Evansville. When the war was over he wanted to go into business for himself for the first time in his life. He thought he might set up a small restaurant in Evansville. He said his brother-in-law would back him.

Tommy was shipped overseas after only two months in the Army, and when I met him he had been out of America for eighteen months. He was medium-sized and dark-haired, and had a little mustache and the funniest-looking head of hair I ever saw this side of Buffalo Bill's show. While his division was killing time in the last few days before leaving England, he and three others decided to have their hair cut Indian-fashion. They had their heads clipped down to the skin, all except a two-inch ridge starting at the forehead and running clear to the back of the neck. It made them look more comical than ferocious, as they had intended. Two of the four had been wounded and evacuated to England.

I chatted off and on with Clayton for several days before he told me how old he was. I was amazed; so much so that I asked several other people to guess at his age and they all guessed about the same as I did—about twenty-six. Actually he was thirty-seven, and that's pretty well along in years to be a front-line infantryman. It's harder on a man at that age. As Clayton himself said, "When you pass that thirty mark you begin to slow up a little."

This Tommy Clayton, the mildest of men, had killed four of the enemy for sure, and probably dozens he couldn't account for. He wore an Expert Rifleman's badge and soon would have the proud badge of Combat Infantryman, worn only by those who had been through the mill. Three of his four victims he got in one long blast of his Browning automatic rifle. He was stationed in the bushes at a bend in a gravel road, covering a cross-road about eighty yards ahead of him. Suddenly three German soldiers came out a side road and foolishly stopped to talk right in the middle of the crossroads. The B.A.R. has twenty bullets in a clip. Clayton held her down for the whole clip. The three Germans went down, never to get up. His fourth one he thought was a Jap when he killed him. In the early days of the invasion lots of soldiers thought they were fighting Japs, scattered in with the German troops. They were actually Mongolian Russians, with strong Oriental features, who resembled Japs to the untraveled Americans. Clayton was covering an infantry squad as it worked forward along a hedgerow. There were snipers in the trees in front. Clayton spotted one, sprayed the tree with his automatic rifle, and out tumbled this man he thought was a Jap.

Do you want to know how Clayton located his sniper? Here's how! When a bullet passes smack overhead it doesn't zing; it pops the same as a rifle when it goes off. That's because the bullet's rapid passage creates a vacuum behind it, and the air rushes back with such force to fill this vacuum that it collides with itself, and makes a resounding "pop." Clayton didn't know what caused this, and I tried to explain. "You know what a vacuum is," I said. "We learned that in high school."

And Tommy said, "Ernie, I never went past third grade."

But Tommy was intelligent. A person doesn't have to know the reasons in war—he only has to know what things indicate when they happen. Well, Clayton had learned that the "pop" of a bullet over his head preceded the actual rifle report by a fraction of a second, because the sound of the rifle explosion had to travel some distance before hitting his ear. So the "pop" became his warning signal to listen for the crack of a sniper's rifle a moment later. Through much practice he had learned to gauge the direction of the sound almost exactly. And so out of this animal-like system of hunting, he had the wits to shoot into the right tree—and out tumbled his "Jap" sniper.

Clayton's weirdest experience would be funny if it weren't so filled with pathos. He was returning with a patrol one moonlit night when the enemy opened up on them. Tommy leaped right through a hedge and, spotting a foxhole, plunged into it. To his amazement and fright, there was a German in the foxhole, sitting pretty, holding a machine pistol in his hands. Clayton shot him three times in the chest before you could say scat. The German hardly moved. And then Tommy realized the man had been killed earlier. He had been shooting a corpse.

All his experiences seemed to have had no effect on this mild soldier from Indiana, except perhaps to make him even quieter than before. The worst experience of all is just the accumulated blur, and the hurting vagueness of being too long in the lines, the everlasting alertness, the noise and fear, the cell-by-cell exhaustion, the thinning of the surrounding ranks as day follows nameless day. And the constant march into eternity of one's own small quota of chances for survival. Those are the things that hurt and destroy. And soldiers like Tommy Clayton went back to them, because they were good soldiers and they had a duty they could not define.

In wandering around our far-flung front lines—the lines that in our rapid war were known as "fluid"—we could always tell how recently the battles had swept on ahead of us. We could sense it from the little things even more than the big things: From the scattered green leaves and the fresh branches of trees still lying in the middle of the road. From the wisps and coils of telephone wire, hanging brokenly from high poles and entwining across the roads. From the gray, burned-powder rims of the shell craters in the gravel roads, their edges not yet smoothed by the pounding of military traffic. From the little pools of blood on the roadside, blood that had only begun to congeal and turn black, and the punctured steel helmets lying nearby. From the square blocks of building stone still scattered in the village streets, and from the sharp-edged rocks in the roads, still uncrushed by traffic. From the burned-out tanks and broken carts still unremoved from the road. From the cows in the fields, lying grotesquely with their feet to the sky, so newly dead they had not begun to bloat or smell. From the scattered heaps of personal gear around a gun. I don't know why it was, but the Germans always seemed to take off their coats before they fled or died.

From all these things we could tell that the battle had been recent—from these and from the men so newly dead that they seemed to be merely asleep. And also from the inhuman quiet. Usually battles are noisy for miles around. But in the fast warfare after our break-through a battle sometimes left a complete vacuum behind it. The Germans would stand and fight it out until they saw there was no hope. Then some gave up, and the rest pulled out and ran for miles. Shooting stopped. Our fighters moved on after the enemy, and those who did not fight, but moved in the wake of the battles, would not catch up for hours. There was nothing left behind but the remains—the lifeless debris, the sunshine and the flowers, and utter silence. An amateur who wandered in this vacuum at the rear of a battle had a terrible sense of loneliness. Everything was dead—the men, the machines, the animals—and he alone was left alive.

One afternoon we drove in our jeep into a country like that. The little rural villages of gray stone were demolished—heartbreaking heaps of still-smoking rubble. We drove into the tiny town of Le Mesniltore, a sweet old stone village at the "T" of two gravel roads, a rural village in rolling country, a village of not more than fifty buildings. There was not a whole building left. Rubble and broken wires still littered the streets. Blackish-gray stone walls with no roofs still smoldered inside. Dead men still lay in the street, helmets and broken rifles askew around them. There was not a soul nor a sound in the village; it was lifeless.

We stopped and pondered our way, and with trepidation we drove on out of town for a quarter of a mile or so. The ditches were full of dead men. We drove around one without a head or arms or legs. We stared, and couldn't say anything about it to each other. We asked the driver to go very slowly, for there was an uncertainty in all the silence. There was no live human being, no sign of movement anywhere.

Seeing no one, hearing nothing, I became fearful of going on into the unknown. So we stopped. Just a few feet ahead of us was a brick-red American tank, still smoking, and with its turret knocked off. Near it was a German horse-drawn ammunition cart, upside down. In the road beside them was a shell crater. To our left lay two smashed airplanes in adjoining fields. Neither of them was more than thirty yards from the road. The hedge was low and we could see over. They were both British fighter planes. One lay right side up, the other on its back.

We were just ready to turn around and go back, when I spied a lone soldier at the far side of the field. He was standing there looking across the field at us like an Indian in a picture. I waved and he waved back. We walked toward each other. He turned out to be a second lieutenant—Ed Sasson, of Los Angeles. He was a graves registration officer for his armored division, and he was out scouring the field, locating the bodies of dead Americans. He was glad to see somebody, for it is a lonely job catering to the dead. As we stood there talking in the lonely field, a soldier in coveralls, with a rifle slung over his shoulder, ran up breathlessly and almost shouted: "Hey, there's a man alive in one of those planes across the road! He's been trapped there for days!"

We ran to the wrecked British plane, lying there upside down, and dropped on our hands and knees to peek through a tiny hole in the side. A man lay on his back in the small space of the upside-down cockpit. His feet disappeared somewhere in the jumble of dials and pedals above him. His shirt was open and his chest was bare to the waist. He was smoking a cigarette, the only immediate relief the two soldiers who had discovered him could offer. The pilot turned his eyes toward me when I peered in, and he said in a typical British manner of offhand friendliness, "Oh, hello."

"Are you all right?" I asked, stupidly.

He answered, "Yes, quite. Now that you chaps are here."

I asked him how long he had been trapped in the wrecked plane. He said he didn't know for sure as he had got mixed up about the passage of time. But he did know the date of the month he was shot down. He told me the date. And I said out loud, "Good God!" For, wounded and trapped, he had been lying there for eight days!

His left leg was broken and punctured by an ack-ack burst. His back was terribly burned by raw gasoline that had spilled. The foot of his injured leg was pinned rigidly under the rudder bar. The space was so small he couldn't squirm around to relieve his own weight from his paining back. He couldn't straighten out his legs, which were bent above him. He couldn't see out of his little prison. He had not had a bite to eat or a drop of water. All this for eight days and nights. Yet when we found him his physical condition was good, and his mind was calm and rational. He was in agony, yet in his correct Oxford accent he even apologized for taking up our time to get him out.

The American soldiers of our rescue party cussed as they worked, cussed with open admiration for this British flier's greatness of heart which had kept him alive and sane through his lonely and gradually hope-dimming ordeal. One of them said, "God, but these Limeys have got guts!"

It took us almost an hour to get him out. While we were ripping the plane open to make a hole, he talked to us. And here is what happened—in the best nutshell I can devise from the conversation of a brave man whom we didn't want to badger with trivial questions: He was an RAF flight lieutenant, piloting a night fighter. Over a certain area the Germans began letting him have it from the ground with machine-gun fire. The first hit knocked out his motor. He was too low to jump, so—foolishly, he said— he turned on his lights to try a crash landing. Then they really poured it on him. The second hit got him in the leg. And a third bullet cut right across his right-hand fingers, clipping every one of them to the bone.

He left his wheels up, and the plane's belly hit the ground going uphill on a slight slope. We could see the groove it had dug for about fifty yards. Then the plane flopped, tail over nose, onto its back. The pilot was absolutely sealed into the upside-down cockpit. "That's all I remember for a while," he told us. "When I came to, they were shelling all around me."

Thus began the eight days. He had crashed right between the Germans and Americans in a sort of pastoral no man's land. For days afterwards the field in which he lay passed back and forth between German hands and ours. The pasture was pocked with hundreds of shell craters. Many of them were only yards away. One was right at the end of his wing. The metal sides of the plane were speckled with hundreds of shrapnel holes.

He lay there, trapped in the midst of that inferno of explosions. The fields around him gradually became littered with dead. At last American strength pushed the Germans back, and silence came. But no help. Because, you see, he was in that vacuum behind the battle, and only a few people were left. The days passed. He thirsted terribly. He slept some; part of the time he was unconscious; part of the time he undoubtedly was delirious. But he never gave up hope.

After we had finally got him out, he said as he lay on the stretcher under a wing, "Is it possible that I've been out of this plane since I crashed?"

Everybody chuckled. The doctor who had arrived said, "Not the remotest possibility. You were sealed in there and it took men with tools half an hour to make an opening. And your leg was broken and your foot was pinned there. No, you haven't been out."

"I didn't think it was possible," the pilot said, "and yet it seems in my mind that I was out once and back in again."

That little suggestion of delirium was the only thing that re-markable man said, during the whole hour of his rescue, that wasn't as dispassionate and matter-of-fact as though he had been sitting comfortably at the end of the day in front of his own fireplace. We didn't know whether the flier would live or not, but the medic thought he had a chance. It was one of the really great demonstrations of courage in this war.

THIRTY-FOUR

PARIS

I had thought that for me there could never again be any elation in war. But I had reckoned without the liberation of Paris—I had reckoned without remembering that I might be a part of that richly historic day. We were in Paris on the first day—one of the great days of all time. Our approach to the city was hectic. We had waited for three days in a nearby town while hourly our reports on what was going on in Paris changed and contradicted themselves. Of a morning it would look as though we were about to break through the German ring around Paris and come to the aid of the brave French Forces of the Interior who were holding parts of the city. By afternoon it would seem the enemy had reinforced until another Stalingrad was developing. We could not bear to think of the destruction of Paris, and yet at times it seemed desperately inevitable.

That was the situation on the morning when we left Rambouillet and decided to feel our way timidly toward the very outskirts of Paris. And then, when we were within about eight miles, rumors began to circulate that the French Second Armored Division was in the city. We argued for half an hour at a crossroads with a French captain who was holding us up, and finally he freed us and waved us on. Then for fifteen minutes we drove through a flat, gardenlike country under a magnificent bright sun and amidst greenery, with distant banks of smoke pillaring the horizon ahead and to our left. Gradually we entered the suburbs, and soon into the midst of Paris itself and a pandemonium of surely the greatest mass joy that has ever happened.

The streets were lined as they are by Fourth of July parade crowds at home, only this crowd was almost hysterical. The streets of Paris are very wide, and they were packed on each side. The women were all brightly dressed in white or red blouses and colorful peasant skirts, with flowers in their hair and big, flashy earrings. Everybody was throwing flowers, and even serpentine.

As our jeep eased through the crowds, thousands of people crowded up, leaving only a narrow corridor, and frantic men, women and children grabbed us and kissed us and shook our hands and beat on our shoulders and slapped our backs and shouted their joy as we passed. I was in a jeep with Henry Gorrell of the United Press, Capt. Carl Pergler of Washington, DC, and Corp. Alexander Belon, of Amherst, Mass. We all got kissed until we were literally red in the face, and I must say we enjoyed it.

Once the jeep was simply swamped in human traffic and had to stop; instantly we were swarmed over and hugged and kissed and torn at. Everybody, even beautiful girls, insisted on kissing you on both cheeks. Somehow I got started kissing babies that were held up by their parents, and for a while I looked like a baby-kissing politician going down the street. The fact that I hadn't shaved for days, and was gray-bearded as well as bald-headed, made no difference. Finally some Frenchman told us there were still snipers shooting, so we put our steel helmets back on.

The people certainly looked well fed and well dressed. The streets were lined with green trees and modern buildings. All the stores were closed in holiday. Bicycles were so thick I have an idea there must have been plenty of accidents that day, with tanks and jeeps overrunning the populace.

A tall, thin, happy woman in a light brown dress who spoke perfect American came running over to our jeep. She was Mrs. Helen Cardon, who had lived in Paris for twenty-one years and had not been back to America since 1935. Her husband was an officer in French Army headquarters and back home after two and a half years as a German prisoner. He was with her, in civilian clothes.

Incidentally, Mrs. Cardon's two children, Edgar and Peter, were the only two American children, she said, who have been in Paris throughout the entire war.

We had entered Paris via Rue Aristide Briand and Rue d'Orleans. We were slightly apprehensive, but decided it was all right to keep going as long as there were crowds. But finally we were stymied by the people in the streets, and then above the din we heard some not-too-distant explosions—the Germans trying to destroy bridges across the Seine. And then the rattling of machine guns up the street, and that old battlefield whine of high-velocity shells just overhead. Some of us veterans ducked, but the Parisians just laughed and continued to carry on.

The farthest we got in our first hour in Paris was near the Senate building, where some Germans were holed up and firing desperately. So we took a hotel room nearby and decided to write while the others fought. The Germans were still battling in the heart of the city, along the Seine, but they were doomed. There was a full French armored division in the city, plus American troops entering constantly.

The other correspondents wrote thoroughly and well about the fantastic eruption of mass joy when Paris was liberated. I could not add much to what they reported in those first days. Actually the thing floored most of us. I felt totally incapable of reporting it. It was so big I felt inadequate to touch it. I didn't know where to start or what to say. The words you put down about it sounded feeble to the point of asininity. I was not alone in this feeling, for I heard a dozen other correspondents say the same thing. A good many of us feel we have failed to present adequately what was the loveliest, brightest story of our time. It may be that this was because we have been so unused, for so long, to anything bright.

At any rate, from two in the afternoon until darkness around ten, we few Americans in Paris on that first day were kissed and hauled and mauled by friendly mobs until we hardly knew where we were. Everybody kissed us—little children, old women, grown-up men, beautiful girls. They jumped and squealed and pushed in a literal frenzy. They pinned bright little flags and badges all over you. Amateur cameramen took pictures. They tossed flowers and friendly tomatoes into your jeep. One little girl even threw a bottle of cider into ours.

As we drove along, gigantic masses of waving and screaming humanity clapped their hands as though applauding a performance in a theater. We in the jeeps smiled back until we had set grins on our faces. We waved until our arms gave out, and then we just waggled our fingers. We shook hands until our hands were bruised and scratched. If the jeep stopped we were swamped instantly. Those who couldn't reach us threw kisses at us, and we threw kisses back.

They sang songs. They sang wonderful French songs we had never heard. And they sang "Tipperary" and "Madelon" and "Over There" and the "Marseillaise." French policemen saluted formally but smilingly as we passed. The French tanks that went in ahead of us pulled over to the sidewalks and were immediately swarmed over.

And then some weird cell in the inscrutable human makeup caused people to start wanting autographs. It began the first evening, and by the next day had grown to unbelievable proportions. Everybody wanted every soldier's autograph. They shoved notebooks and papers at us to sign. It was just like Hollywood. One woman, on the second day, had a stack of neat little white slips, at least three hundred of them, for people to sign.

The weather was marvelous for liberation day, and for the next day too. For two days previously it had been gloomy and raining. But on the big day the sky was pure blue, the sun was bright and warm—a perfect day for a perfect occasion.

That first afternoon only the main streets into the city were open and used, and they were packed with humanity. The side streets were roped off and deserted, because the Germans had feeble fortifications and some snipers there.

Paris seemed to have all the beautiful girls we always heard it had. The women have an art of getting themselves up fascinatingly. Their hair is done crazily, their clothes are worn imaginatively. They dress in riotous colors in this lovely warm season, and when the flag-draped holiday streets are packed with Parisians the color makes everything else in the world seem gray. As one soldier remarked, the biggest thrill in getting to Paris is to see people in bright summer clothes again.

Like any city, Paris has its quota of dirty and ugly people. But dirty and ugly people have emotions too, and Hank Gorrell got roundly kissed by one of the dirtiest and ugliest women I have ever seen. I must add that since he's a handsome creature he also got more than his share of embraces from the beautiful young things.

There was one funny little old woman, so short she couldn't

reach up to kiss men in military vehicles, who appeared on the second day carrying a stepladder. Whenever a car stopped she would climb her stepladder and let the boys have it with hugs, laughs and kisses.

The second day was a little different from the first. You could sense that during those first few hours of liberation the people were almost animal-like in their panic of joy and relief and gratitude. They were actually crying as they kissed you and screamed, "Thank you, oh, thank you, for coming!"

But on the second day it was a deliberate holiday. It was a festival prepared for and gone into on purpose. You could tell that the women had prettied up especially. The old men had on their old medals, and the children were scrubbed and Sunday-dressed until they hurt. And then everybody came downtown. By two in the afternoon the kissing and shouting and autographing and applauding were almost overwhelming. The pandemonium of a free and lovable Paris reigned again. It was wonderful to be there.

As we had driven toward Paris from the south we had seen hundreds of Parisians—refugees and returning vacationists—riding homeward on bicycles amidst the tanks and big guns.

Some Frenchmen have the faculty for making all of us Nervous Nellies look ridiculous. There should be a nonchalant Frenchman in every war movie. He would be a sort of French Charlie Chaplin. You would have tense soldiers crouching in ditches and firing from behind low walls. And in the middle of it you would have this Frenchman, in faded blue overalls and beret and with a nearly burned-up cigarette in his mouth, come striding down the middle of the road past the soldiers. I saw that very thing happen about four times after D-day, and I never could see it without laughing.

Well, the crowds were out in Paris like that while the shooting was still going on. People on bicycles would stop with one foot on the pavement to watch the firing that was going on right in that block.

As the French Second Armored Division rolled into the city at dangerous speed, I noticed one tank commander, with goggles, smoking a cigar, and another soldier in a truck playing a flute for his own amusement. There also were a good many pet dogs riding into the battle on top of tanks and trucks.

Amidst this fantastic Paris-ward battle traffic were people pushing baby carriages full of belongings, walking with suitcases, and riding bicycles so heavily loaded with gear that if they were to lay them down they had to have help to lift them upright.

And in the midst of it all was a tandem bicycle ridden by a man and a beautiful woman, both in bright blue shorts, just as though they were holidaying, which undoubtedly they were.

For twenty-four hours tanks were parked on the sidewalks all over downtown Paris. They were all manned by French soldiers, and each tank immediately became a sort of social center. Kids were all over the tanks like flies. Women in white dresses climbed up to kiss men with grimy faces. And early the second morning we saw a girl climbing sleepily out of a tank turret.

French soldiers of the armored division were all in American uniforms and they had American equipment. Consequently most people at first thought we few Americans were French. Then, puzzled, they would say, "English?" and we would say, "No, American." And then we would get a little scream and a couple more kisses.

Every place we stopped somebody in the crowd could speak English. They apologized for not inviting us to their homes for a drink, saying they didn't have any. Time and again they would say, "We've waited so long for you!" It almost got to be a refrain.

One elderly gentleman said that although we were long in reaching France we had come swiftly since then. He said the people hadn't expected us to be in Paris for six months after invasion day.

The armies still fighting in the field were practically deserted by the correspondents for a few days, as we all wanted to get in on the liberation of the city. There were so many correspondents it got to be a joke, even among us. I think at least two hundred must have entered the city that first day, both before and after the surrender. The Army had picked out a hotel for us ahead of time, and it was taken over as soon as the city surrendered. But though it was a big hotel it was full before dark the first day, so they took over another huge one across the street.

Hotel life seemed strange after so long in the field. My own room was a big corner one, with easy chairs, a soft bed, a bathroom, and maid and hall-porter service. There was no electricity in the daytime, no hot water anytime, and no restaurant or bar, but outside of that the hotel was just about the way it must have been in peacetime.

Sitting there writing within safe walls, and looking out the window occasionally at the street thronged with happy people, it was already hard to believe there ever had been a war; even harder to realize there still was a war.

Eating had been skimpy in Paris through the four years of German occupation, but reports that people were on the verge of starvation were apparently untrue. The country people of Normandy had all seemed so healthy and well fed that we said all along: "Well, country people always fare best, but just wait till we get to Paris. We'll see real suffering there."

Of course the people of Paris did suffer during these four years of darkness. But I don't believe they suffered physically as much as we had thought.

Certainly they did not look bedraggled and gaunt and pitiful, as the people of Italy did. In fact they looked to me just the way they must have looked in normal times.

However, the last three weeks before the liberation had been really rough. For the Germans, sensing that their withdrawal was inevitable, began taking everything for themselves. There was very little food in Paris right after the liberation. The restaurants either were closed entirely or served only the barest meals—coffee and sandwiches. And the "national coffee," as they called it, was made from bailey and was about the vilest stuff imaginable. France had had nothing else for four years. On the other hand, in little towns only ten miles from Paris you could get eggs and wonderful dinners of meat and noodles. Food did exist, but transportation was the temporary cause of the city's shortage.

Autos were almost nonexistent on the streets of Paris when we arrived. That first day we met an English girl who had been here throughout the war, and we drove her for some distance in our jeep. She was as excited as a child, and said that was her first ride in a motorcar in four years. We told her that it wasn't a motorcar, that it was a jeep, but she said it was a motorcar to her.

Outside of war vehicles, a few French civilian cars were running when we arrived but they were all in official use in the fighting. All of these had "FFI" (French Forces of the Interior) painted in rough white letters on the fenders, tops and sides.

Although it appears that the Germans did conduct themselves fairly properly up until the last few weeks, the French really detested them. One woman told me that for the first three weeks of the occupation the Germans were fine but that then they turned arrogant. The people of Paris simply tolerated them and nothing more.

The Germans did perpetrate medieval barbarities against leaders of the resistance movement as their plight became more and more desperate. But the bulk of the population of Paris—the average guy who just gets along no matter who is there—didn't really fare too badly from day to day. It was just the things he heard about, and the fact of being under a bullheaded and arrogant thumb, that created the smoldering hatred for the Germans in the average Parisian's heart.

You can get an idea how the people of the city felt from a little incident that occurred the first night we were there: We put up at a little family sort of hotel in Montparnasse. The landlady took us up to show us our rooms. A cute little French maid came along with her.

As we were looking around the room the landlady opened a wardrobe door, and there on a shelf lay a German soldier's cap that he had forgotten to take. The landlady picked it up with the tips of her fingers, held it out at arm's length, made a face, and dropped it on a chair.

Whereupon the little maid reached up with her pretty foot and gave it a huge kick that sent it sailing across the room.

We correspondents left Paris after a few days and went on again with the armies in the field. In Paris we had slept in beds and walked on carpeted floors for the first time in three months. It was a beautiful experience, and yet for some perverse reason a great inner feeling of calm and relief came over us when we once again set up our cots in a tent, with apple trees for our draperies and only the green grass for a rug.

Hank Gorrell of the United Press was with me, and he said:

"This is ironic, that we should have to go back with the armies to get some peace."

The gaiety and charm and big-cityness of Paris somehow had got a little on our nerves after so much of the opposite. I guess it indicates that all of us will have to make our return to normal life gradually and in small doses.

As usual, those Americans most deserving of seeing Paris will be the last ones to see it, if they ever do. By that I mean the fighting soldiers. Only one infantry regiment and one reconnaissance outfit of Americans actually came into Paris, and they passed on through the city quickly and went on with their war.

The first ones in the city to stay were such nonfighters as the psychological-warfare and civil-affairs people, public-relations men and correspondents. I heard more than one rear-echelon soldier say he felt a little ashamed to be getting all the grateful cheers and kisses for the liberation of Paris when the guys who broke the German army and opened the way for Paris to be free were still out there fighting without benefit of kisses or applause.

But that's the way things are in this world.

THIRTY-FIVE

A LAST WORD

This final chapter is being written in the latter part of August, 1944; it is being written under an apple tree in a lovely green orchard in the interior of France. It could well be that the European war will be over and done with by the time you read this book. Or it might not. But the end is inevitable, and it cannot be put off for long. The German is beaten and he knows it.

It will seem odd when, at some given hour, the shooting stops and everything suddenly changes again. It will be odd to drive down an unknown road without that little knot of fear in your stomach; odd not to listen with animal-like alertness for the meaning of every distant sound; odd to have your spirit released from the perpetual weight that is compounded of fear and death and dirt and noise and anguish.

The end of the war will be a gigantic relief, but it cannot be a matter of hilarity for most of us. Somehow it would seem sacrilegious to sing and dance when the great day comes—there are so many who can never sing and dance again. The war in France has not been easy by any manner of means. True, it has gone better than most of us had hoped. And our casualties have been fewer than our military leaders had been willing to accept. But do not let anyone lead you to believe that they have been low. Many, many thousands of Americans have come to join the ones who already have slept in France for a quarter of a century.

For some of us the war has already gone on too long. Our feelings have been wrung and drained; they cringe from the effort of coming alive again. Even the approach of the end seems to have brought little inner elation. It has brought only a tired sense of relief.

I do not pretend that my own feeling is the spirit of our armies. If it were, we probably would not have had the power to win. Most men are stronger. Our soldiers still can hate, or glorify, or be glad, with true emotion. For them death has a pang, and victory a sweet scent. But for me war has become a flat, black depression without highlights, a revulsion of the mind and an exhaustion of the spirit.

The war in France has been especially vicious because it was one of the last stands for the enemy. We have won because of many things. We have won partly because the enemy was weakened from our other battles. The war in France is our grand finale, but the victory here is the result of all the other victories that went before. It is the result of Russia, and the western desert, and the bombings, and the blocking of the sea. It is the result of Tunisia and Sicily and Italy; we must never forget or belittle those campaigns.

We have won because we have had magnificent top leadership, at home and in our Allies and with ourselves overseas. Surely America made its two perfect choices in General Eisenhower and General Bradley. They are great men—to me doubly great because they are direct and kind.

We won because we were audacious. One could not help but be moved by the colossus of our invasion. It was a bold and mighty thing, one of the epics of all history. In the emergency of war our nation's powers are unbelievable. The strength we have spread around the world is appalling even to those who make up the individual cells of that strength. I am sure that in the past two years I have heard soldiers say a thousand times, "If only we could have created all this energy for something good." But we rise above our normal powers only in times of destruction.

We have won this war because our men are brave, and because of many other things—because of Russia, and England, and the passage of time, and the gift of nature's materials. We did not win it because destiny created us better than all other peoples. I hope that in victory we are more grateful than we are proud. I hope we can rejoice in victory—but humbly. The dead men would not want us to gloat.

The end of one war is a great fetter broken from around our

lives. But there is still another to be broken. The Pacific war may yet be long and bloody. Nobody can foresee, but it would be disastrous to approach it with easy hopes. Our next few months at home will be torn between the new spiritual freedom of half peace and the old grinding blur of half war. It will be a confusing period for us.

Thousands of our men will soon be returning to you. They have been gone a long time and they have seen and done and felt things you cannot know. They will be changed. They will have to learn how to adjust themselves to peace. Last night we had a violent electrical storm around our countryside. The storm was half over before we realized that the flashes and the crashings around us were not artillery but plain old-fashioned thunder and lightning. It will be odd to hear only thunder again. You must remember that such little things as that are in our souls, and will take time.

And all of us together will have to learn how to reassemble our broken world into a pattern so firm and so fair that another great war cannot soon be possible. To tell the simple truth, most of us over in France don't pretend to know the right answer. Submersion in war does not necessarily qualify a man to be the master of the peace. All we can do is fumble and try once more— try out of the memory of our anguish—and be as tolerant with each other as we can.

Index of Persons and Places

STORM OF STEEL

A memoir of astonishing power, savagery, and ashen lyricism, *Storm of Steel* illuminates not only the horrors but also the fascination of total war, seen through the eyes of an ordinary German soldier. Young, tough, patriotic, but also disturbingly self-aware, Ernst Jünger exulted in the Great War, which he saw not just as a great national conflict but also—more importantly—as a unique personal struggle. He kept testing himself, braced for the death that will mark his failure.

THE CENTURIONS

When *The Centurions* was first published in 1960, readers were riveted by the thrilling account of soldiers fighting for survival in hostile environments. They were equally transfixed by the chilling moral question the novel posed: how to fight when the "age of heroics is over." As relevant today as it was then, *The Centurions* is a gripping military adventure, an extended symposium on waging war in a new global order, and an essential investigation of the ethics of counterinsurgency.

THE PRAETORIANS

The Praetorians is the unflinching sequel to *The Centurions*, based on the events of May 1958 in France and Algeria. After turning to tactics of guerilla warfare, a group of French para-troopers serving in the Algerian War is called to answer for actions they consider necessary, however immoral. With reso-nance to modern conflicts in Iraq, Afghanistan, and elsewhere, *The Praetorians* shows the ugly, morally conflicted nature of modern war.

MEMOIRS OF A FOX-HUNTING MAN

In the first novel of the semiautobiographical George Sherston trilogy, Siegfried Sassoon wonderfully captures the vanishing idylls of the Edwardian English countryside. His reminiscences about childhood and the beginning of World War I are channeled through young George Sherston, whose life of local cricket competitions and fox-hunts falls apart as war approaches and he joins up to fight.

MEMOIRS OF AN INFANTRY OFFICER

The second volume picks up in 1916, with the young Sherston deep in the trenches of World War I. After being wounded, he returns home to convalesce, where his questioning of the war and the British Military establishment leads him to write a public antiwar letter. Sassoon's stunning portrayal of a mind coming to terms with the brutal truths he has encountered in war is among the greatest books ever written about World War I, or war itself.

SHERSTON'S PROGRESS

Deemed mentally ill for his antiwar sentiments, after six months in the hospital, Sherston leaves to rejoin his regiment. He is dispatched to Ireland, then Palestine, and finally ends up at the Western Front in France. *Sherston's Progress* literally brings home the unforgettable journey of George Sherston from aristocratic childhood through war hero and antiwar martyr, all the way to wounded veteran trying to move on from the Great War.

🐧 PENGUIN CLASSICS

UNDER FIRE

For the group of ordinary men in the French Sixth Battalion, thrown together from all over France and longing for home, war is simply a matter of survival, lightened only by the arrival of their rations or a glimpse of a pretty girl or a brief reprieve in the hospital. Based on Henri Barbusse's own experience of the Great War, *Under Fire* vividly evokes life in the trenches: the mud, stench, and monotony of waiting while constantly fearing for one's life in an infernal and seemingly eternal battlefield.

BLOOD, TOIL, TEARS AND SWEAT
Winston Churchill's Famous Speeches

The most eloquent statesman of his time, Winston Churchill used language as his most powerful weapon. In this volume, David Cannadine selects thirty-three orations ranging over fifty years, demonstrating how Churchill hones his rhetoric until the day when, with spectacular effect, "he mobilized the English language, and sent it into battle" (Edward R. Murrow).